GLENN'S COMPLETE BICYCLE MANUAL

SELECTION · MAINTENANCE · REPAIR

GLENN'S COMPLETE BICYCLE MANUAL

SELECTION · MAINTENANCE · REPAIR

by CLARENCE W. COLES

and HAROLD T. GLENN

CROWN PUBLISHERS, INC., NEW YORK

NOTICE

Several of the illustrations used in this book have been borrowed from the Schwinn Bicycle Company. Notice is hereby given that these illustrations are copyrighted by the Company and, therefore, all rights pertaining thereto remain the property of the Company.

Inquiries should be addressed to Crown Publishers, Inc., One Park Avenue, New York, N.Y. 10016

Library of Congress Catalog Card Number: 70–185100
ISBN: 0-517-500922 (cloth)
ISBN: 0-517-500930 (paper)
Printed in the United States of America
Published simultaneously in Canada by
General Publishing Company Limited

20   19   18

TABLE OF CONTENTS

FOREWORD

This is a comprehensive repair and adjustment manual for virtually all makes of bicycles; American, Japanese, and European. The first three chapters provide invaluable information in the following areas: (1) making a sensible bicycle selection, (2) assembling a crated bike, (3) adjusting it to your physique so you will be able to obtain maximum efficiency, (4) riding comfortably and safely, (5) performing the necessary periodic maintenance tasks, and (6) troubleshooting when your machine does not function properly.

The eight overhaul chapters following are devoted to work on the principal parts of the bicycle. Detailed illustrated step-by-step instructions are provided to tell you exactly how to make complete repairs and adjustments using a minimum number of tools.

Procedures were written by actually performing the job and photographing each step as the work progressed. This method of developing and presenting the material gives the reader a sensitive "feeling" for what is to be done, how, and why. We suggest that you read through the complete section before starting any task to become familiar with the particular parts, or with the special techniques employed in making repairs, such as counting the number of loose ball bearings, placement of shims and spacers, the use of right- or left-hand threads, and how some parts are removed, overhauled, installed, and adjusted.

Procedural illustrations accompanying the text are identified by a circled number in the lower right-hand corner. These numbers are keyed and are correlated so closely with the steps, which are also sequenced with circled numbers, that legends are not required. Exploded views for many makes of each assembly are included together with specific directions advising you which parts are interchangeable with similar manufactured items.

Each section in each chapter is a complete unit, containing the steps for removing the assembly from the bicycle, overhauling, installing, and properly adjusting it. Therefore, cross-referencing, or "chapter hopping," has been avoided.

The illustrations supporting the text have been specially treated to drop out the backgrounds.

CLARENCE W. COLES and HAROLD T. GLENN

ACKNOWLEDGMENTS

The authors wish to express their grateful appreciation and indebtedness to the Schwinn Bicycle Company, and to Mr. Ray Burch, Vice-President, Marketing, and Mr. Peter Kaszonyi, Service Promotion Manager, Schwinn Bicycle Company, for their assistance and permission to use certain illustrations. The use of these illustrations in no way relieves the copyright privileges held by the Schwinn Company.

A very special thanks is extended to Mr. Mel Pavlisin of Circle Cycle in Torrance, California, for the use of his shop facilities to photograph the disassembly and assembly sequences used throughout the book. Without the assistance of Mr. Pat Hirz, bicycle mechanic at Circle Cycle, the detailed and special instructions included in the text would not have been possible.

A sincere expression of gratitude is due our wives, Clair Coles and Anna Glenn, for their patience and understanding of the many hours we spent in the various tasks of preparing the material. We also wish to express our appreciation for their assistance in proofreading the manuscript, and especially to Clair for the final typing.

To Mark Tsunawaki for his contribution with the artwork and to Brian Coles for his help during the paste-up, we are indeed grateful.

We would also like to express our appreciation to the League of American Wheelmen for their inspiration during the writing of this book.

1
THE BICYCLE AND YOU

Today more than eighty million cyclists are riding for health, recreation, and transportation. Conservative estimates indicate that, for the first time since 1897, more bicycles will be sold in the United States than pollution-belching automobiles.

American manufacturers are unable to keep pace with the increasing demand, and imports have more than doubled in the past decade to almost twelve million units. Still, the demand for the two-wheeled velocipede continues to overshadow production figures by five times. As late as 1962 more bicycles were sold to juveniles than to adults. Today the trend is reversed, with almost 55 percent of total sales being made to adults.

This unprecedented rise in cycling can be attributed in part to America's awakened interest in physical fitness. The most renowned advocate of cycling for maintaining or regaining proper health is Dr. Paul Dudley White, famous American cardiologist and personal physician to former president Dwight D Eisenhower. Dr. White insists that riding a bicycle is a sovereign preventive measure for heart disease and arteriosclerosis (hardening of the walls of the arteries). The late President John F. Kennedy and his physical fitness program for Americans probably had much to do with sowing the seeds for more active exercise, and the fermentation and results are now being felt in the cycling industry.

The ecologist, and his movement for a cleaner environment, has given cycling its greatest boost through young people, making it the acceptable "in thing" for them to do. Their position, which can have no argument, is that the bike is soundless, emits no noxious fumes, in no way pollutes the water, and does not stain the road with grease or oil.

Another group that has helped empty the racks of the bicycle shops is the commuter. He has become tired of fighting traffic: of "holding his own," making the green light at the next intersection, and racing against the clock to get to work on time. He has turned to "doing his own thing" and now rides to work on a bicycle. With a feeling of independence, the cyclist can move steadily along and, on surface roads over a distance under ten miles, is likely to do better time than his neighbor in his Detroit monster or impudent import.

The touring enthusiasm has burgeoned in the past five years, not only among these groups but also among those individuals who wish to "get back to nature"; to enjoy the quiet countryside at leisure: feel the wind and the rain on their faces and breathe the fragrance of spring flowers and freshly mowed fields. This elite band of cyclists has truly found the rebirth of the open road:

This young lady crossing the campus on her modern lightweight 10-speed bicycle exemplifies the unprecedented rise in cycling popularity, America's awakened interest in physical fitness, the ecology movement for a cleaner environment, and the desire to participate in an activity—"to do your own thing."

traveling through scenic, uncluttered, rural areas, along established bikeways or secondary roads with a minimum of automobile traffic.

The bicycle market has always existed, catering not only to youngsters but also to older practical users of the bicycle, including those engaged in making deliveries or factory rounds and students on sprawling campuses who have to beat the clock from class to class.

The growing popularity of bicycles among adults can be attributed largely to the change in design of the machines, the introduction of 10-speed gears, and the use of lightweight materials in its construction. These developments make even the steepest grade climbable for the average adult in reasonably good physical condition. The bicyclist's range of operation has been extended tenfold. He can now cover greater distances in shorter time. Trips from the Pacific to the Atlantic and from Maine to Florida are becoming commonplace. Today's bicycle is a far cry from the heavy, single-speed bike we first learned to ride and which we used for paper routes, delivery service, and for commuting to and from school.

In an effort to keep pace with the number of bikes being put to use, bikeways are being built or planned in almost every state. City, country, and state agencies have moved swiftly to obtain funds and construct bikeways, where the cyclist can pedal without having the auto pressing him and where the pedestrian will not be in danger of being struck down by a bike traveling at high speed. As more of these bike paths are completed, bike sales will undoubtedly continue to climb. (More on bikeways, legislation, and fund raising, including federal appropriations in the next chapter.)

Once the decision to purchase a bicycle has been made, the question that arises is where to obtain the equipment that will best fit your needs. Without hesitation, the answer should be a well-established bicycle shop that will service the product it sells.

In an effort to capture their share of the bicycle market, drug, department, discount, and chain stores now carry a variety of different styled bicycles. However, these outlets do not have the facilities or the staff to assemble and adjust a bike properly (an adult machine of acceptable quality probably represents an investment of over $100), nor do they have the necessary inventory to replace defective parts. Therefore, much time can be lost before a replacement part is ordered and arrives from a distant distributor or the factory. In the meantime your bike sets idly in the garage, your feet itch, and your heart demands that you get the pedals in motion. But imagine returning to a drugstore to complain of faulty bearings or poor workmanship—which leads us to the next point in favor of patronizing a specialty bicycle shop. Any mechanical piece of equipment is subject to wear, abuse, or damage, requiring service and possible replacement of parts. These parts constitute a standard inventory at recognized bicycle dealers. If you purchase a name-brand bicycle from an authorized franchise dealer, it is a safe bet you'll be able to obtain the manufacturer's specified part when it is needed. The fact is, however, that almost one out of every three bicycles sold is purchased in the crate from sources other than stores dealing solely in bicycles.

CHOOSING YOUR BICYCLE

Selecting a bicycle is no different than buying an automobile, camper-trailer, or boat. If you were shopping for a boat, the purchase for which it is to be used would be the primary consideration. Your choice would be narrowed considerably depending on whether you planned to water-ski, do some weekend sailing or class-type racing, or cruise to the South Seas.

In the simplest terms, the choice of a bicycle depends on who will ride the machine and for what purpose, and the amount of money he is willing to invest. The bicycle market can be classified into four basic groups; sidewalk bikes, medium-weight bikes, lightweight machines, and professional racer-types. The price of bicycles varies in each group: the narrowest gap is in the sidewalk class and the widest in the adult lightweight machine.

SIDEWALK BIKES

As the name implies, sidewalk bikes, many of which are classified as toys, are intended for use only on the sidewalk and are built for tiny tots aged three to five. The least expensive models (about $20) are rather dangerous because they do not have brakes. These bicycles should not be used, especially in hilly areas or where the auto traffic is heavy. These low-priced machines are not constructed to last or be handed down to a younger brother or sister. The pedals are made of plastic, rotating joints contain no bearings and, at best, they may last a couple of years.

The more expensive sidewalk bike (to $70) contains some solid material and better workmanship. A coaster-type brake is standard equipment, giving the child some control of stopping by applying pressure in

A well-built sidewalk-type bike for the youngster aged 3 to 5 is a Columbia, Model 9051, for boys, or the 9051 Convertible with detachable top tube for girls. The bicycle features 13-inch wheels, pneumatic tires, and rear coaster-brake mechanism.

a reverse direction. This procedure can be taught to and understood by a three-year-old. Bearings are used in the steering arrangement, which help control the bicycle. The pedals, saddle, and other components are designed to withstand the rigors of rough use, and the tires are pneumatic for a more comfortable ride. A bicycle of this type is a good investment because it can be passed on to a younger member of the family or sold. The horizontal bar on many of the better sidewalk bikes is removable, converting it to a boy's or girl's model.

Trainer wheels, which attach to the axle on both sides of the rear wheel, are available. However, considerable controversy exists as to whether they should be used or not. Many believe they contribute to a false sense of security and argue that the child will develop his balance and coordination more quickly if he is assisted by a parent or older brother when first learning to ride.

All hand-lever-operated braking systems should be avoided on sidewalk bikes because the fingers of a child are not long enough, and he does not have the strength to stop in an emergency. High-rise handlebars hamper the handling ability and, therefore, should not be considered when purchasing a sidewalk bike. Unfortunately, most of the better built bikes are equipped with this type of handlebar, but they can be easily removed and replaced with a conventional type. Most states have enacted legislation restricting the height of handlebars in an effort to reduce the rising accident rate among youngsters.

The "banana-type" saddle should also be avoided. The National Safety Council, in opposition to manufacturers, contends this type of seat encourages riding

The Schwinn Midget Sting-Ray bicycle is a quality-built machine for the age group 6 to 10 years. It is a scaled-down version of the Sting-Ray, with modified high-rise handlebars, banana seat, and short sissy bars. It is equipped with a rear coaster brake, which the National Safety Council feels is safer than the caliper-type mechanism for this age group.

double, thus making the bike more difficult to control and thereby causing accidents.

MIDDLEWEIGHT BICYCLES

The term "middleweight" is actually a misnomer and through usage will probably be changed to "heavyweight" in the coming years, because it is the heaviest of the present bicycles on the market with a total weight of sixty pounds. This classification can be split between juvenile (for boys and girls six to ten years old) and adult bikes.

The middleweight bike is designed to withstand the heavy punishment that youngsters may give it or anyone using it for constant delivery or patrol work. The frame is constructed of heavy gauge steel, the tires are heavy-duty balloon type, and the braking system is contained within the rear hub or possibly in the front hub, as with the internal-expanding brake shoe type. For the most part, they are single speed, requiring no external levers or cables. The standard version resembles the conventional bicycles commonly seen until the early '50s. However, those directed toward pre-teen customers are equipped with a wide assortment of gimmicks, gadgets, and accessories, which give the bike the appearance of a monstrosity; they certainly interfere with its efficient and safe operation.

The youngster makes an attempt to imitate his elders by directing his interests to what is available to him—his bicycle. Manufacturers, to meet the demands of these young customers, have flooded the market with gimmicky bikes equipped with high-rise handle bars, banana-type saddles, and sissy bars extending high above the rear of the seat—all in an effort to copy the "far-out" motorcycle fraternity. "Stick-Shift" controls on the horizontal top bar were added in an effort to give the rider a feeling of the sports car on-the-floor, four-and-five-speed stick shifts. All these items are hazardous. The National Safety Council, National Commission on Product Safety, Consumer Guide, and Bicycle Manufacturers' Association have made progress in restricting and controlling these components on juvenile bicycles. Most states now have laws governing their use and, beginning July 1, 1972, the maximum limit of high-rise handlebars was reduced to shoulder height when the rider is seated, and the rear support behind the seat was reduced to five inches.

Safety studies have revealed that the "stick-shift," mounted on the horizontal top bar, can and has caused serious injury to riders, especially boys, when the bicycle is involved in an accident.

Accident surveys indicate that the young rider (aged 6 to 10) is much safer on a bicycle equipped with a coaster brake than a caliper-type brake. Hand brakes take more coordination and, in an emergency situation, the rider may inadvertently apply the front brake harder than the rear, greatly increasing the possibility of the bike pitching over forward, especially if the rider is not seated. Another consideration is that the younger child does not react as quickly as does the teenager.

These are points that must be given careful consideration when purchasing a bicycle for your child.

The flashy hardware may be impressive, but mature adult cyclists do not use this type of equipment and, therefore, to ride as a professional is to have a machine that resembles theirs. As cycling becomes more widespread and we develop our own breed of national racing heroes, as has existed in Europe for years, perhaps the market will shift to the junior version of the racing machine, with medium narrow seat, drop handlebars, and rattrap pedals; a machine that is available for under $50, in a 22-inch size for the smaller (9-to-12-year-old) and in a 24-inch model for the larger boy or girl.

Middleweight bicycles for youngsters, costing over $50, are heavier built but tend to have more gadgets and be more complicated and confusing to the rider. However, they will hold up to protect your investment by meeting the requirements of a younger member of the family, possibly after getting a new paint job, adding handlebar grips and saddle.

Middleweight bicycles for adults consist of the conventional utility type; they are used for delivery service and for general transportation for very short distances. Recently, several metropolitan areas have resorted to using plainclothes policemen mounted on bicycles to patrol parks and college campuses. These bikes are the rugged, heavy-duty type in adult sizes, with coaster brakes and little or no accessories, except perhaps provision for special equipment, such as carrier racks or a two-way radio. The price range is usually very narrow, from $40 to $50.

LIGHTWEIGHT BICYCLES

The lightweight bicycle has the widest range in quality, weight, and price. This type comes in a variety of styles, from the so-called "English racer," equipped with a three-speed rear wheel hub arrangement, weighing approximately 40 pounds and costing approximately $80, to a true, lightweight stripped-down, track racing machine, weighing only 17 pounds and representing an investment of almost $400. In Europe, a professional

racer may spend the equivalent of 800 American dollars for a custom-made hand-crafted machine, built to his own requirements.

Aside from some very small lightweight models suitable only for the very experienced rider 10 to 12 years of age who is serious about racing, the lightweight models should be considered solely in the adult category. The one exception is available in 17- to 19-inch frame size, with 24-inch wheels and weighs 32 pounds. This bike is equipped with all the features of the full-size lightweight "big brother," including caliper brakes, with alternate brake lever, rattrap pedals, 10-speed gearing, three-piece cottered crank, and a narrow-racing-type saddle.

Every week, hundreds of potential U.S. Olympic contenders, 10 to 12 years of age, pedal on extended tours, preparing for the day they will race. They are able to make 20-mile cross-country races in slightly over an hour; 69.7 minutes in one case. During such a race, speeds in excess of 60 mph are common on downhill grades; an impressive record of speed, control, and coordination for a lad of 12 years riding a 32-pound piece of sophisticated equipment. For such an earnest enthusiast, the cost, ranging from $120 to $400, represents a worthwhile investment in a bona fide sport. It will help to shape the youngster's ambition, determination, and drive for success in later years.

All other lightweight bicycles should be considered as adult machines, since they are designed for the teenager and more mature rider. When you purchase a bicycle, the purpose for which it is to be used and the amount of money available for it are the primary considerations.

THREE-SPEED SHORT COMMUTING BIKES

If you plan to travel short distances or use your bike only occasionally, a three-speed, internally geared rear hub bicycle with caliper brakes, costing less than $100, may be the answer. People living in the Midwest, or any other hill-less area, will find that the three-speed bicycle meets their requirements. It can move along at a reasonable speed, with sufficient shift range for climbing moderate grades. Low gear is used for hill climbing or when moving against the wind. Middle gear is for pedaling on the level, and high gear for downhill or riding with the wind. Those who commute short distances may not need the more complicated equipment of the derailleur-type bike.

The three-speed English "tourist" bicycle with conventional handlebars is the one most frequently found at rent-a-bike establishments in metropolitan or resort areas. Incidentally, the number of places that rent bicycles now available has multiplied manyfold in the past few years—a testimony to the popularity of cycling. Although the ten-speed bike appears to be the "in" machine at present, it is not the "only" bicycle for everyone. If the ten-speed bike is in short supply in your area and the terrain or conditions do not warrant a wide range of gear changing, consider one of the many well-built three-speed bicycles available and save yourself some money.

The Raleigh Space Rider Model DL-54 for men or the DL-54-L for ladies is a standard middleweight bicycle with a 3-speed internal-geared hub, conventional handlebars, and spring-cushioned saddle, priced at under $100.

TEN-SPEED BICYCLES UNDER $100

The lower-priced derailleur-equipped bicycle is an efficient machine and capable of giving satisfactory service for a limited time. The frame is mass produced and the members are butt welded at the joints, as shown in the accompanying illustration. The moving components are less expensive and are not precision machined, lowering the cost considerably.

These bicycles are available in a wide range of frame sizes, are equipped with either side-pull or center-pull caliper brakes, and weigh about 30 pounds. They are rugged enough to take the rough treatment of city riding, but have the necessary equipment and are still light enough for general touring.

Long distances have been covered on the under-$100 machine, as well as on those costing three to four times as much. Whether such use should be continued over a period of time, however, is doubtful. As an example, three high-school graduates made a 600-mile trip from Billings, Montana, to Salt Lake City, Utah. One rode a bicycle purchased from a low-priced discount store in his area, another had a machine obtained with Blue Chip stamps, and the third bought his bike through a mail-order house. All three finished the trip without maintenance or repair problems, except for one flat tire. However, it is interesting and mystifying to note that after flying back to their home town in California, with their machines as luggage, six spokes failed on the right side of the rear wheel on one bike as the rider was pedaling home from the airport. The broken spokes could be attributed to metal fatigue or perhaps improper spoke tension. It is entirely possible that if another such trip were attempted on the same bicycles, without completely overhauling all major components, considerable trouble might be encountered.

When purchasing a ten-speed derailleur bicycle, your best insurance is to stick with well-known brands that offer widespread dealership organizations with adequate parts and properly trained servicemen, and then to buy the very best your pocketbook can afford. Spending a few extra dollars will give you considerably better-grade components: derailleurs, sprocket clusters, hubs, hanger sets, and other moving parts.

TEN-SPEED BICYCLES—$100 TO $500

Two bicycles, side by side on the showroom floor, with a couple of hundred dollars difference in price, might appear to have the same type of equipment at first glance and, therefore, present a puzzling question: Why such an apparent wide spread in price? The answer is in quality based on the construction, the finishing techniques, and the components attached to the frame. Close inspection and attention to workmanship, along with a knowledge of name-brand derailleurs, pedals, hanger sets, and brakes, is necessary to determine how closely the figure on the price tag reflects the true value of the bicycle. That's why it is so important to depend on a well-known name brand of merchandise. A quality manufacturer is not afraid to risk his reputation, and his name will be prominently displayed. The average customer may not have the expertise to judge values accurately, and this is why it is so important to depend on the reputation of the manufacturer when buying your first bicycle. For those with some experience, the following are guidelines to help you in judging values. One of the first items to catch your attention should be the frame, the type of tube material used, and the method employed in making the joints. Quality bicycles of over $100 use seamless chrome alloy steel tubing and the joints are fitted into lugs and then welded, as shown in the accompanying illustration. Machines priced over $250 use either Reynolds 531 or Columbus light, thin-walled manganese molybdenum alloy steel tubing, welded into lugs. Butted tubing means the ends of the tube inside the lugs have a double thickness for added strength. As the price of the bike increases, the number of double-butted joints in the frame increases; top-quality machines have double-butted joints in lugs throughout. A decal affixed to the frame will proudly show that the tubing is Reynolds 531 material, and the word "butted" will be superimposed over the numbers to signify this type of joint. In the lower-price range of top-quality bicycles, only the top tube, seat tube, and the down tube will be made from Reynolds 531 tubing, and it may be plain gauge. As the price rises, the chain and seat stays as well as the forks will be of the same material and still made of plain-gauge tubing. When the price tag goes over $250, the decal should clearly indicate butted joints; at the top of the line, it should clearly state that all tubes, stays, and forks are built with Reynolds 531 butted steel tubing. This is your "mark of quality" when shopping with an eye toward the better-built machines.

The joints of bicycles costing close to $500 are hand-brazed, and this results in the most precision alignment possible. These metals, and the method of construction in the top-quality line, make the bicycle more responsive to stress, make it extremely light in weight, and give it flexibility for a more comfortable ride.

In the price range above $100, there is probably the widest range from which to choose. This Atala Gran Prix Model 104 for men or 104L for ladies is made with seamless tubing and brazed joints in lugs, with Campagnolo derailleur units—all signs of quality components and workmanship.

Another feature of the over-$100 bike that should be apparent when inspecting the frame is the detailed finish work. The more expensive machines are hand painted, and time-consuming stripping is added for that "extra" touch to set the unit apart from all its lower-priced neighbors.

As your inspection of the higher-priced units continues, you will note the name of components that make the bicycle go. If ever there was a time when you needed to put your trust in a name-brand item, it is now. The manufacturers of quality items installed on the finest machines, both domestic and imported, have built their business and reputation on quality and performance. Winners of the Grand Prix races held throughout Europe and at the Olympic games have relied on those components which have given them the edge over competition. As bicycle racing in this country makes a comeback, riders follow in the footsteps of their Continental cousins and purchase those units which have been proved under grueling conditions in France, Italy, Belgium, and other countries with famous courses.

For the individual purchasing his first quality-built bike, here are names that indicate better component parts on bicycles in the price range indicated, but the list should not be considered all-inclusive.

At the derailleur units, the names of Simplex Prestige, Huret-Alvit, Campagnolo Gran Sport, and Campagnolo Gran Turismo are found on bikes in the $100-to-$250 bracket. The Italian firm of Campagnolo dominates the market of bikes costing over $250 with their Campagnolo Record and Campagnolo Nuovo Record units.

At the hanger set, Nervar steel cottered cranks or Stronglight 3-pin steel cranks are installed on the less expensive bikes of the top-quality line, whereas the names Campagnolo, T. A. Criterium, Stronglight, and Williams on cotterless cranks are the mark of quality. Each part in this last group is made from a strong aluminum alloy, machined to the closest tolerances possible, and then buffed and polished to reflect the fine craftsmanship involved.

Mafac and Weinmann center-pull caliper brakes are installed on a wide range of machines in the top-quality line, and the Campagnolo unit is found on those near the upper-price limit of this category. Until recently, the center-pull type caliper brake was believed to be superior to the side-pull type. However, Campagnolo recently introduced a new type of side-pull brake with performance equal to their center-pull line. Universal was quick to follow with their own slightly different design, which places two top-quality side-pull brake units on the market.

Wheel rims on the more expensive bikes are designed for the tubular (sewn-up) tires and are laced with double-butted spokes. This type of spoke can be identified easily because it is slightly thicker at the ends, where there is more strain. Steel rims are used

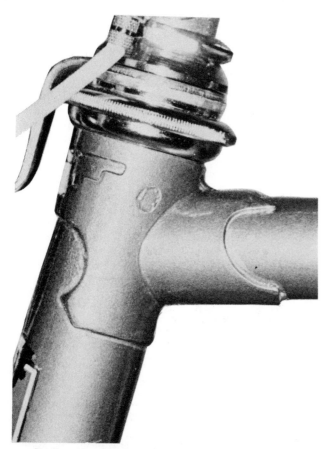

Quality bicycles over $100 use seamless chrome alloy tubing and the joints are fitted into lugs and then brazed.

The frames on bicycles under $100 are mass-produced, with the tube members butt-welded at the joints. They are heavier built to withstand the rough treatment of city riding.

on the lower-priced bikes in the top-quality line, whereas aluminum is used on the rims of machines listed above the $250 line.

Normandy, Simplex, and Cinelli hubs are found on the better-built bicycles, but Campagnolo hubs stand in a class of their own. They are considered the finest (and they are the most expensive) money can buy. A good-quality hub will have counter-sunk spoke holes to minimize strain at the bend of the spoke, where it leaves the hole. These hubs also have a hollow axle for the stud of a quick-release mechanism to pass through.

TEN-SPEED BICYCLES—$500 TO $800

A bicycle priced above $500 is a custom-tailored machine, built to the exacting specifications of a knowledgeable customer to fit his physical requirements and meet his special needs and taste. It is almost entirely handmade in small shops in England, France, and Italy. Production from each of these small firms is extremely limited, with probably no more than 600 units made each year. Orders from these shops must be filed at least a year in advance.

A cycling enthusiast interested in this class of bicycle finds his moment of glory in riding his machine, which will most likely be a one-of-a-kind in his area, and in realizing he is traveling on the finest piece of equipment money can buy. Surprisingly, the components on his bike may also be those found on the under-$500 production models, although they will be of the highest caliber of course, perhaps Campagnolo throughout.

TRACK BICYCLES

The track racing bicycle is designed for only one purpose, and its use is restricted to racing on a surface specially constructed for bike races. These machines are the ultimate in light weight. The rider sits on a saddle, conventionally secured to a frame suspended between two wheels, and he has a means of controlling its direction and of making it move forward but, beyond that, the similarity to a touring bike ends. The track bike does not have any braking system; the rider reaches over the handlebars and grasps the front wheel when he wishes to reduce speed or to stop. This maneuver requires considerable skill and practice to apply

Members of the University of Georgia Dancing Majorettes and the Georgettes of the U. of G. Redcoat band execute a colorful precision-riding performance during the half-time activities at the U. of G./Georgia Tech classic football contest on Thanksgiving Day, 1971. The girls went through their routine on Schwinn single-speed, middleweight bikes to the tune of "Daisy Bell" ("On a Bicycle Built for Two") without missing a stroke of the crank. This is an outstanding example of using the bicycle for an unusual form of entertainment. Courtesy University of Georgia Redcoat Band

the proper amount of friction without toppling the bike or burning a hole in your glove.

Track bikes have a direct-drive system from the chain wheel to the fixed rear sprocket, thereby eliminating the front and rear derailleurs, and their friction. This means that as long as the rear wheel is turning, the crank is also rotating; thus the rider's legs are always in motion. First-rate track bicycles use Campagnolo hubs, headset, and complete hanger set, including the chain wheel. The price for one of these energy-gulping machines begins at about $250.

GEARING ON THE 10-SPEED BICYCLE

The first time you look at a 10-speed bicycle and notice the rear sprocket cluster, with its set of five gears stacked one against the other, and then glance up to the hanger set to see the two large chain wheels, you have every reason to be mystified as to exactly how the two are matched to get you up a hill with a minimum of effort. The explanation is simple and can be explained by making a comparison to the gearing arrangement on a hand-operated egg beater. With every rotation of the handle, each of the beaters revolves approximately five times. This results from having five times as many teeth on the driving gear attached to the handle as there are on the gear connected to the beaters. The same principle applies to 10-speed bicycles, except that a chain is used to connect the two gears and you have a selection of gears from which to choose, depending on the demand of the terrain and weather conditions. With the chain on the largest chain wheel at the hanger set, and on the smallest sprocket of the rear cluster, the wheel will rotate faster than the crank; exactly the same as the egg beater. This arrangement is referred to as "high gear" because it gives you the greatest distance traveled for each revolution of the pedals.

Now, if the chain is shifted to a larger sprocket on the rear-wheel cluster, the wheel will rotate much slower, and this gives the rider his "low-gear" leverage for climbing hills. The sprockets between the smallest and the largest in the cluster, plus the two different size chain wheels, afford you the opportunity to move steadily from one grade to another without a large jump or strain on your leg muscles.

A great many cyclists have been pulling leg muscles while pumping uphill or against the wind on high-priced, 10-speed bicycles on which there is a narrow gap from one sprocket to the next, a feature familiar on most European machines. These imported bicycles are built and intended for use by athletes in top physical condition who are able to cope with the sudden change in energy required to keep moving after changing gears.

Americans are generally not in condition to handle the change in the amount of energy demanded by a narrow change in gear ratios. Therefore, until you have many miles under your saddle, and feel that your physical conditioning has improved to the point of handling a narrow gear ratio, it is best to buy the cluster-and-chain-wheel combination that will have

the wider gap (number of teeth) from one gear ratio to the next.

After you have become a seasoned touring rider, it is a simple matter to change the gear cluster at the rear wheel and/or the chain wheels at the hanger set to provide a gear range you feel capable of handling. Chapters 5 and 6 give step-by-step illustrated instructions for removing and installing a sprocket cluster. Chapter 9 provides detailed illustrated instructions for removing and installing chain wheels on the hanger set.

If a sprocket or chain wheel change is made, readjustment of the derailleur units is usually necessary, and this is covered in Chapter 7 for the rear derailleur and in Chapter 8 for the front derailleur.

PROPER SIZE

Two dimensions are used in reference to the size of a bicycle: the frame, measured as the length of the seat mast from the center of the hanger-set opening to the end of the mast as depicted in the accompanying illustration, and the diameter of the wheels. Purchasing the correct size bike and then fitting it properly for the individual rider cannot be overstressed. A recent study by the National Safety Council revealed that the possibility of having an accident, while riding a bicycle that is too large, is five times greater than if the machine were the correct size so that the cyclist was able to control it under all conditions. The highest number of violations of the commonsense rule of using a bicycle that matches your size is with the young person who attempts to ride a bicycle of an older member of the family.

To determine the correct size bike, regardless of your size or age, straddle the top tube with both feet flat on the floor, wearing the type of shoe you intend using while pedaling. There should be at least ½-inch clearance between the rider and the tube. In the accompanying illustration, note how the rider is able to straddle the top tube in comfort. If there is more than two inches, you should go to the next larger size. If the bar is too close, consider a smaller bike.

If you are contemplating making your purchase

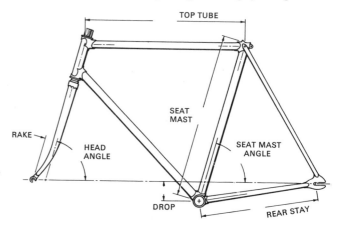

Terminology used in the language of the bicycle enthusiast. The size of the bike is the length of the seat mast.

To determine the correct size adult bike, the rider must be able to straddle the top tube comfortably with both feet firmly on the ground.

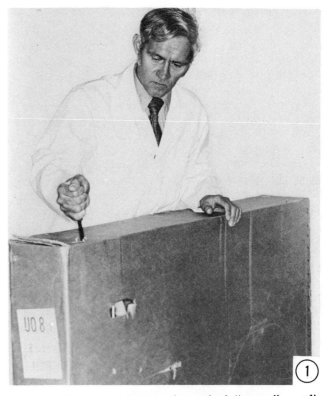

from a store other than a franchised dealer, the chances of them having your size assembled are remote. Therefore, you will be forced to make your selection as to type, color, and equipment, based on the models displayed. If this is the case, or if you are ordering from a mail-order catalog, measure your leg inseam, and then subtract 10 inches. The resultant figure is the correct size bike frame for you.

Many parents are prone to buy a machine that is too large, and then let the child "grow into it." This is poor reasoning, because the seat can be raised along with the handlebars on a smaller bike as the youngster grows, until he is ready for the next size bicycle. In the meantime, he will be comfortable and able to ride safely.

The wheel size is matched to the frame of juvenile bikes. All foreign and most American lightweight bicycles are equipped with standard 27-inch wheels.

ASSEMBLING YOUR CRATED BICYCLE

The following procedures provide complete step-by-step illustrated instructions for assembling and adjusting a 10-speed, derailleur-equipped bicycle out of a packing crate, to make it operate properly. The amount of work involved will depend on how thoroughly the manufacturer put the machine together prior to packaging. Bicycles purchased in drug, department, and chain stores will come in a wide range of assemblage. They may, or may not, have instructions included; therefore,

the following steps cover a theoretical "worse" condition. It may be possible to skip some of the steps if your bicycle has been partly assembled by the manufacturer.

REMOVING FROM THE CRATE

① Stand the crate in the upright position and open the top with a sharp knife by cutting around the edge. **CAUTION: Do not insert the blade too deep or you will damage the parts inside.**

② Carefully remove the contents from the crate. Many of the parts are secured to the main frame with wire tags. Small parts may be in a bag tied to the frame or lying loose in the crate. Remove the protective paper wrapping from the handlebars and the frame.

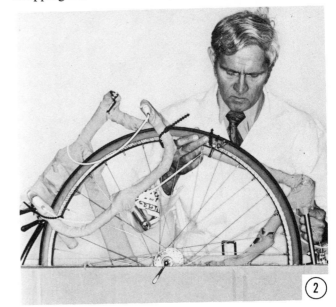

CHECKING THE CONDITION

③ Check the front-wheel bearing adjustment to see in just what condition the bike is. Reputable manufacturers will have the machine properly lubricated and the bearings adjusted. If your front-wheel bearings are properly adjusted, you can proceed with assembling the bike with assurance; otherwise you will be forewarned as to the need for essential servicing. To check the front-wheel bearing adjustment, hold each end of the axle with your fingers, and then slowly twist the axle with your thumbs and forefingers—the wheel must not turn. If it does turn, the cones are too tight. Loosen one of the locknuts, back off the cone approximately ⅛ turn, and then retighten the locknut. The cones are properly adjusted when the wheel rotates freely, comes to rest gradually with the valve stem at the lowest point of the wheel, and there is only the slightest trace of side play. On precision-built bicycles, it is possible, with patience, to adjust the cones so accurately that the wheel will turn freely without any indication of side play. **CAUTION: If the cones are adjusted too tight, it will cause binding and scoring of the hub. If the cones are adjusted too loose, it will cause fatigue, which can result in a damaged hub or broken axle.**

ASSEMBLING THE BIKE

④ Slide the wheel into place in the fork dropouts, and then turn the cam lever from the forward to the rearward position to lock the hub in place. You should

meet a little resistance in turning the lever to the closed (locked) position, if the adjustment is correct. To change the adjustment, turn the lever to the released position (facing forward), and then tighten the acorn adjusting nut on the opposite side of the hub approximately ½ turn. Now turn the lever back to the locked position. Repeat the procedure until you are satisfied with the tightness of the locking mechanism.

⑤ If the front-wheel bearings are out of adjustment, check the rear-wheel bearings in the same manner and make any corrective adjustment to the cones as you did for the front wheel. If you're satisfied that the rear-wheel bearings are adjusted properly, position the rear wheel between the frame members, and then engage the chain over the smallest sprocket. Pull the derailleur unit rearward and, simultaneously, move the wheel up and into the rear dropouts, with the axle washers on the outside of the frame and outside the derailleur fork-end bracket. Center the wheel in the frame, and then tighten both axle nuts.

⑥ If you are assembling a bicycle with a quick-release mechanism, turn the quick-release lever toward the frame to lock the wheel in place. If the lever does

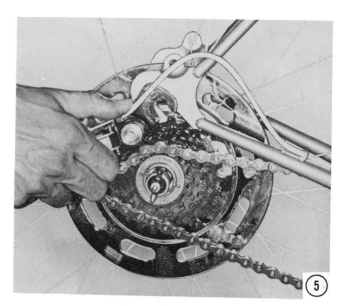

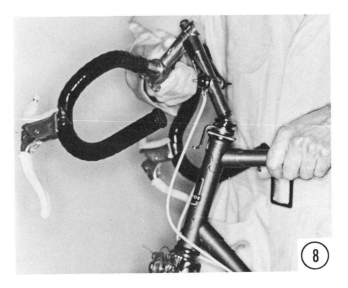

not turn with some effort, tighten the adjusting nut on the opposite side of the hub until resistance is experienced in turning the lever to the locked position.

⑦ The pedals are reversed on the cranks for shipping. Remove them, check each bearing adjustment and lubrication, and then thread the spindle of each pedal onto the outside of the cranks. The right-side pedal has right-hand threads and the left-side pedal has left-hand threads. Each pedal can be identified by the letters "L" and "R" stamped on the flat of the stationary cone or on the end of the spindle. Tighten the spindles in the crank securely.

⑧ Lubricate the stem bolt and wedge threads with high-quality cycle oil to prevent thread seizure

and to ensure proper tightening. Slide the handlebar stem into the fork stem until the handlebars are at the approximate desired height, and then hand-tighten the stem bolt. On some bicycles, the handlebar stem has a mark to indicate the maximum height to which the stem can be raised. **CAUTION: Do not raise the stem above this mark, because the grip of the contact surfaces between the two stems would be insufficient for safe cycling.** If the handlebar stem does not have a maximum-height mark, measure 2½ inches from the lower end of the stem, make your own mark, and then raise the stem to the desired height, but not high enough for the mark to show above the locknut.

⑨ Swing the handlebars right or left until the upper portion of the handlebar stem is aligned with the wheel. Hold the wheel between your legs for a firm grip, and then securely tighten the stem bolt. If the shift levers are attached to the handlebar stem, the control cables will have been installed in the levers.

⑩ Slide the shifting lever collar down the stem until it rests on top of the locknut, and then tighten the anchor nut securely. *NOTE: On some bicycles, the shifting lever hanger is installed on the stem under the locknut.*

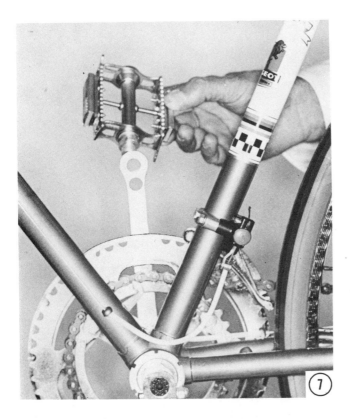

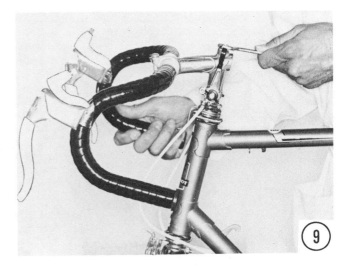

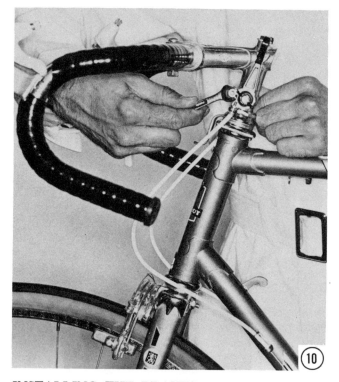

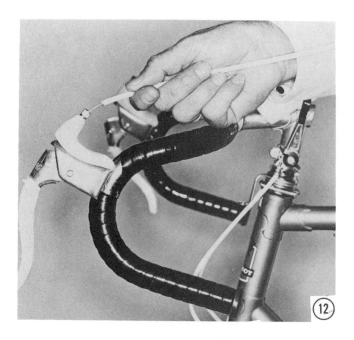

INSTALLING THE BRAKES

⑪   The rear caliper brakes are always installed on the frame. Install the front caliper brakes by first sliding a radius bushing against the brake arm and then inserting the pivot bolt through the mounting hole in the front fork. Slide another radius bushing onto the pivot bolt, with the flat side facing out. Slide a washer and then a lockwasher onto the mounting bolt. Tighten the locknut securely. Feed the short brake cable through the left-side lever retainer and housing. *NOTE: The left-side lever must always control the front-wheel brake and the right-side lever the rear-wheel brake.*

⑫   Pull the cable through until it is taut. On some brake levers, it is possible to feed the button end of the cable through from the back side of the lever, and then hook the button into the slot in the retainer. Apply a thin coating of multipurpose lubricant to the cable in the areas where it will be encased in the housing. Slide the long section of housing over the cable and seat it into the cable-adjusting ferrule.

⑬   Turn the cable-adjusting barrel at the front bracket down as far as it will go. Guide the cable through the barrel and front bracket, with the housing seated in the barrel. For center-pull brakes, insert the cable

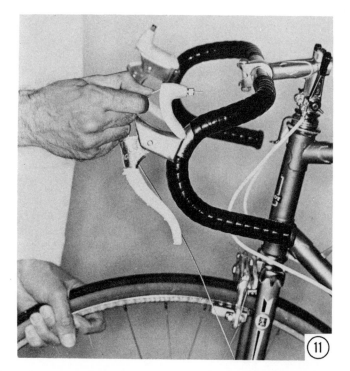

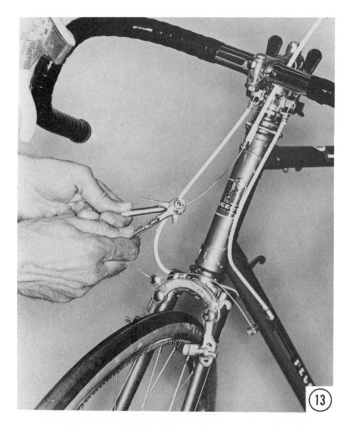

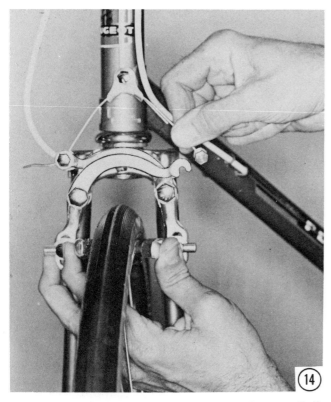

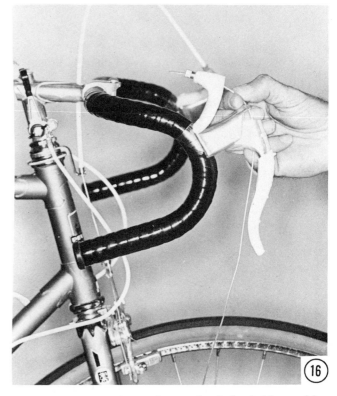

through the anchor bolt in the bridge. Make a preliminary measurement for the cable length by pulling up on the bridge cable and estimating how long the control cable should be. Tighten the anchor bolt securely. For side-pull caliper brakes, turn the adjusting barrel on the brake arm down as far as it will go, feed the cable through the barrel and anchor bolt, and then tighten the anchor bolt.

⑭ Lay the bridge cable in the groove of the bridge. Clamp the brake shoes firmly against the wheel rim, and then slide the free end of the cable into its recess at the end of the arm, as shown.

⑮ Loosen the anchor end of the bridge cable, pull the cable taut with a pair of pliers while you hold the brake shoes firmly against the wheel rim, and then tighten the anchor bolt. Clamp the brake shoes against the wheel rim with your hand, and then hook the other end of the bridge cable in the arm slot. For side-pull caliper brakes, pull the cable taut with a pair of pliers, and then tighten the cable anchor bolt.

⑯ Feed the long cable through the right-side brake lever in the same manner as you did for the left-side one. Pull the cable taut until the end-button is seated in the lever retainer.

⑰ Apply a thin coating of multipurpose lubricant to the cable in the areas where it will be encased in the

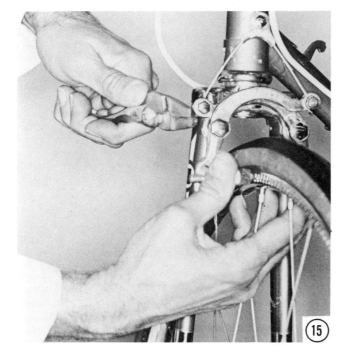

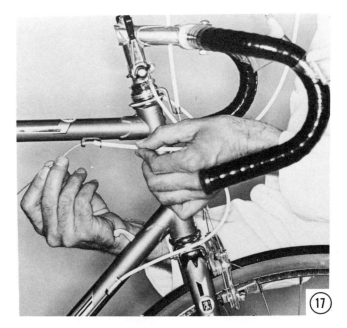

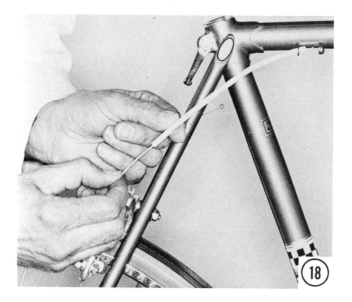

housing. Slide the long housing onto the cable and then through the cable guide until the end seats in the guide cup.

⑱ Slip the short housing onto the cable and through the cable guide until the end seats in the guide cup.

⑲ Guide the cable through the adjusting barrel on the seat post bracket, with the cable housing seated in the barrel. Insert the end of the cable through the anchor bolt of the bridge, estimate the length required, and then tighten the anchor bolt. Loop the bridge cable into the bridge groove.

⑳ Align the seat post bracket so the cable to the bridge is approximately parallel with the rear stays, and then tighten the retaining nut securely. On some bicycles, this rear guide bracket is welded to the stay and is not adjustable.

㉑ At the front and rear brakes, center the assembled brake unit over the wheel rim by loosening the

mounting locknut slightly and then turning the brake arms and pivot bolt until the brake shoes are approximately equally distant from the wheel rim. Tighten the pivot bolt locknut securely. Loosen the acorn nut of each brake shoe slightly, and then move the shoe assembly in the brake arm slot until the top edge of the shoe is approximately $\frac{1}{32}$ inch below the top of the wheel rim. Tilt the shoe to the approximate angle of the wheel rim, and then tighten the acorn nut securely. The brake shoes should release about $\frac{1}{8}$ inch from the rim. If they release more than $\frac{1}{8}$ inch or do not move clear of the rim, loosen the anchor nut, tighten or loosen the cable as required, and then retighten the anchor nut.

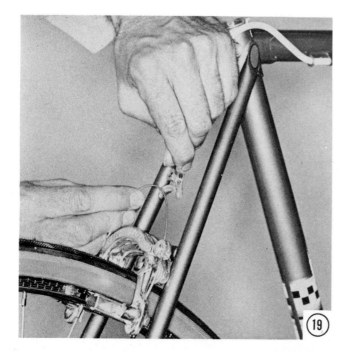

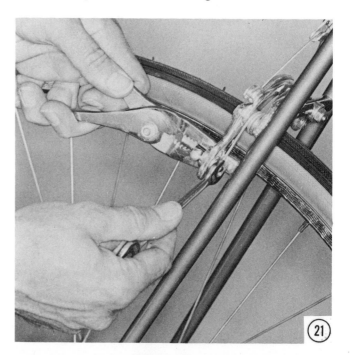

Check to be sure the front end of the brake shoe is just a bit closer to the wheel rim than the rear end. If it is not, grip the brake arm with a wrench directly below the brake shoe assembly, and then twist the arm slightly until the front end of the shoe contacts the wheel rim first when the brake lever is actuated. This position will keep the brake from squeaking. Slide a protective plastic cap over the ends of both brake cables.

㉒ Loosen the stem binder bolt, and then tilt the handle bars until the lower edge points directly toward the center of the rear axle, as depicted in the illustration.

㉓ Tighten the stem binder bolt securely. The bolt should be tight enough to hold the bar from moving downward when considerable pressure is applied at the ends of the handlebars. The position of the handlebars may be shifted to suit the individual preference of the rider after the bicycle has been used under varying conditions.

㉔ Loosen both clamp nuts on the under side of the saddle. Slide the saddle onto the seat post, align the center with the top tube of the bicycle (or directly toward the stem on a girl's bike), and then tilt the seat so the forward end is raised slightly. The saddle clamp is

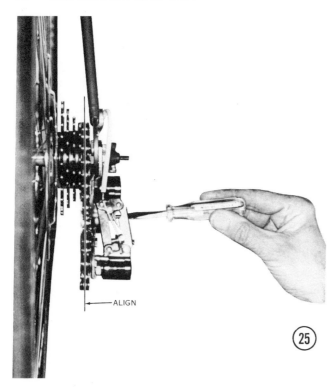

ALIGN

(25)

designed with serrations between the clamp and the saddle structure to hold it firmly in place without relying entirely on the friction of the clamp. Before tightening the nuts securely, check to be sure the serrations are meshed. The clamp should be tight enough to prevent the saddle from moving downward when struck at the forward end with a reasonably hard blow of your clenched fist.

ADJUSTING THE REAR DERAILLEUR

㉕ Lift the rear wheel clear of the floor, rotate the

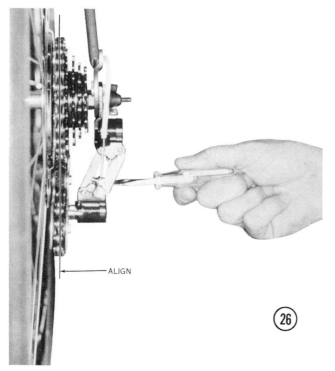

ALIGN

(26)

crank and simultaneously shift the chain from one sprocket to the next to check on the smoothness of shifting action. If the chain fails to shift smoothly to the smallest sprocket, proceed as follows: Place the chain on the smallest sprocket and the shift lever in the high-gear (full-forward) position. Rotate the high-gear adjusting screw clockwise or counterclockwise until the center line of the jockey pulley is aligned with the center line of the smallest sprocket, as shown.

㉖ To make an adjustment for the largest sprocket, move the chain to the largest (low-gear) sprocket either by hand or by using the shift lever. Set the shift lever to the low-gear (full-rearward) position. Adjust the low-gear screw until the center line of the jockey pulley is aligned with the center line of the largest sprocket as shown. *NOTE: For additional details on making major and minor adjustments to the rear derailleur, see Chapter 7.*

ADJUSTING THE FRONT DERAILLEUR

㉗ To adjust the low gear of the front derailleur, position the chain onto the low-gear (largest) rear sprocket and the low-gear (smaller) chain wheel. Place the control lever in the low-gear (full-forward) position. Turn the low-gear limit screw until the inner side of the chain guide clears the inner side of the chain by approximately $\frac{1}{32}$ inch. If the front derailleur does not have a low-gear limit screw, loosen the chain guide mounting bolt and position the chain guide until the inner side of the chain guide just clears the inner side of the chain and the guide follows the contour of the chain wheel. Tighten the mounting bolt.

㉘ To adjust the high gear of the front derailleur,

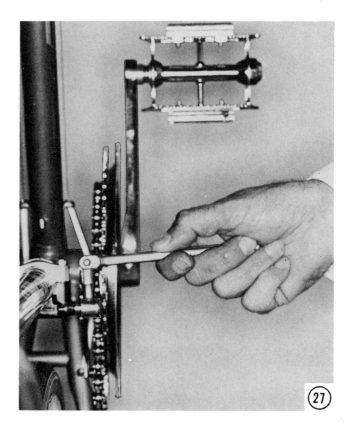

(27)

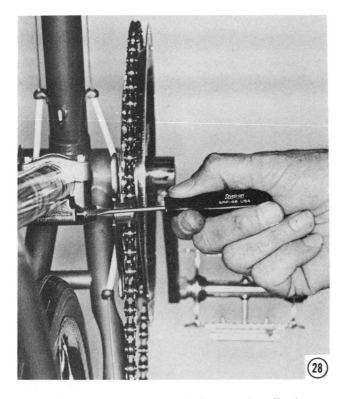

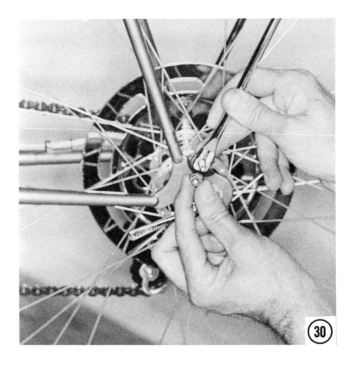

place the chain onto the high-gear (smallest) rear sprocket. *NOTE: The crank must be rotated in the forward direction while making this adjustment.* Turn out the high-gear limit screw until the derailleur shifts the chain onto the high gear (larger chain wheel). Move the front control lever very slightly until the outer side of the chain guide just clears the outer side of the chain. Leave the front derailleur in this position, and then turn in the high-gear limit screw until it just contacts the traversing arm. *NOTE: For additional details on making major and minor adjustments to the front derailleur, see Chapter 8.*

㉙ Inflate the tire to the recommended pressure as indicated on the sidewall or refer to the specification table in Chapter 3.

INSTALLING ACCESSORIES

㉚ *Rear carrier rack:* If the bicycle is equipped

with center-pull caliper brakes, clamp the brake shoes firmly against the rim and unhook the bridge cable from the groove in the bridge; or actuate the quick-release mechanism, and then unhook the cable. Secure the two support brackets finger-tight to the frame lugs on each side of the bicycle with bolts, lockwashers, and nuts.

㉛ Swing the carrier rack into position against the rear stays, and then secure it with the clamp, bolts, lockwashers, and nuts. Tighten the support bracket nuts securely.

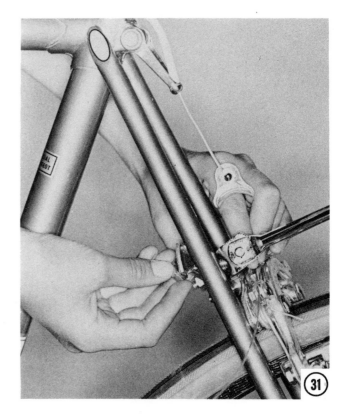

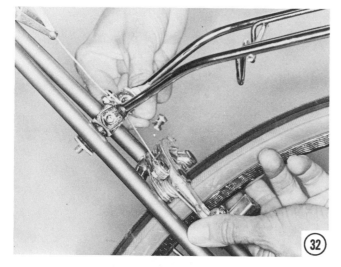

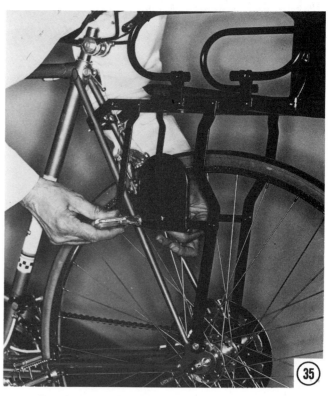

32 Bring the cable and bridge over the back side of the carrier bracket on bicycles equipped with center-pull caliper brakes, and then connect the bridge cable in the groove and brake arm, as shown.

33 *Rear baby seat:* On bicycles equipped with center-pull caliper brakes, actuate the quick-release mechanism or clamp the shoes against the rim, and then unhook the bridge cable from the bridge. Attach the two support brackets to the frame lugs finger-tight with bolts, lockwashers, and nuts.

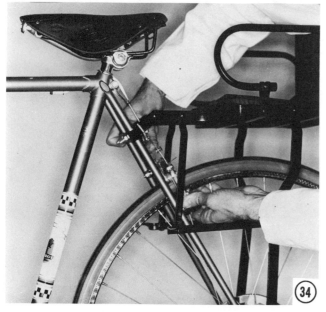

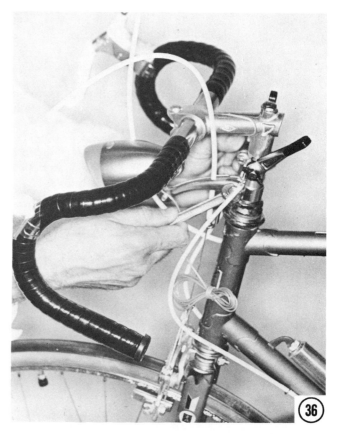

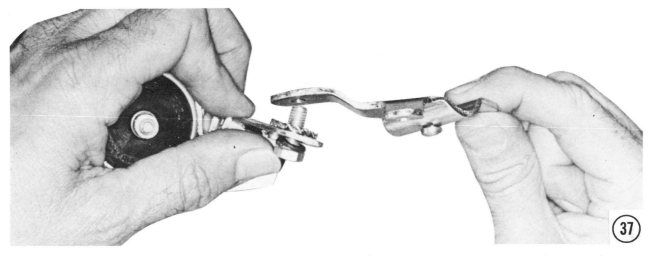

㉞ Swing the baby seat forward into position and secure it to the rear stays with the clamp, bolts, lockwashers, and nuts. On bicycles equipped with center-pull caliper brakes, bring the cable and bridge *over the back side* of the seat bracket, and then connect the bridge cable in the groove and brake arm.

㉟ Secure the footrests in place with the bolts, lockwashers, and nuts. Tighten the support bracket nuts firmly.

㊱ *Generator-light set:* Clamp the headlight-mounting bracket around the fork stem and secure it finger-tight with the long bolt and nut. Attach the headlight securely to the bracket with the short bolt and nut.

Adjust the headlight to shine on the ground at a convenient distance directly ahead of the bicycle, and then tighten the nut at the fork stem securely.

㊲ Combine the generator bracket and the mounting bracket with the lockwasher and bolt, as shown.

㊳ Attach the mounting brackets to the rear stays so that the generator will roll on the high portion of the tire; the terminals should point directly toward the center of the rear axle. Secure the mounting bolts in place so the generator will be approximately ¼ inch from the tire when it is in the retracted position. Insert a center punch through the ground screw hole and make an indentation in the rear stay for a good screw seat. Thread the ground screw into the hole and firmly against the frame to provide a satisfactory ground for the system.

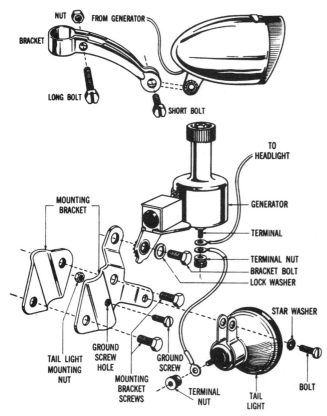

Exploded view of a typical generator-light system. The bicycle frame must be indented with a centerpunch through the screw hole to provide a proper ground for the system.

③⑨ Route the wiring from the front light along the frame members to the area of the generator-mounting bracket. Attach the rear light to the mounting bracket, as shown. Connect the wires from the front and rear lights to the terminal on the generator.

As a check for the correct saddle height, you should be able to place your heel on the pedal when it is at its lowest point, while sitting on the saddle.

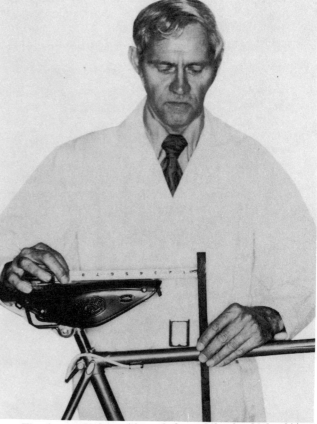

To obtain the maximum efficiency from your bicycle, raise the saddle until the distance from the saddle to the center of the pedal spindle is between 9 and 10 per cent greater than your inseam, as measured from your crotch to the floor while you are standing in the shoes you intend to wear while cycling.

The fore-and-aft position of the saddle should be 2½ to 3 inches toward the rear of the bicycle, measured from a vertical line at the center of the hanger set, with the nose of the saddle tilted very slightly upward.

FITTING THE BICYCLE TO YOU

After the bicycle is assembled, it must be fitted to your body measurements in order to obtain maximum results from the energy you use in moving it forward. Do this by adjusting the saddle height as measured in a straight line down the seat mast and crank to the center of the pedal spindle.

Laboratories in Europe have conducted scientific studies under the most controlled conditions to determine the most efficient seat position. Bear in mind that bicycle racing has long been a national sport in most European countries, with the winners of the Grand Prix races having streets, babies, and products named in their honor. When Eddy Merckx of Belgium won the 2,400-mile Tour de France for the fourth time in 1972, many people proposed changing the name of their town as a lasting tribute to his remarkable feat.

Merckx feels the saddle height to be such a critical measurement that he checks and makes an adjustment to the nearest millimeter, prior to starting each race. He has been known to pull a wrench from his kit, and actually make a saddle-height change while pedaling during a race.

The measurement for the greatest efficiency, as determined by the European laboratories, is 109 percent of the rider's inseam, measured from the floor to his crotch, while standing in the shoes he will wear while cycling. Therefore, if your inseam is 36 inches, for example, loosen the seat post clamp nut, raise the saddle until the top is 39¼ inches from the center of the pedal spindle, and then tighten the nut.

This position will assure that your leg and thigh muscles reach maximum extension on each pedal stroke. To check the adjustment, you should be able to sit on the saddle and place your heel on the pedal with the

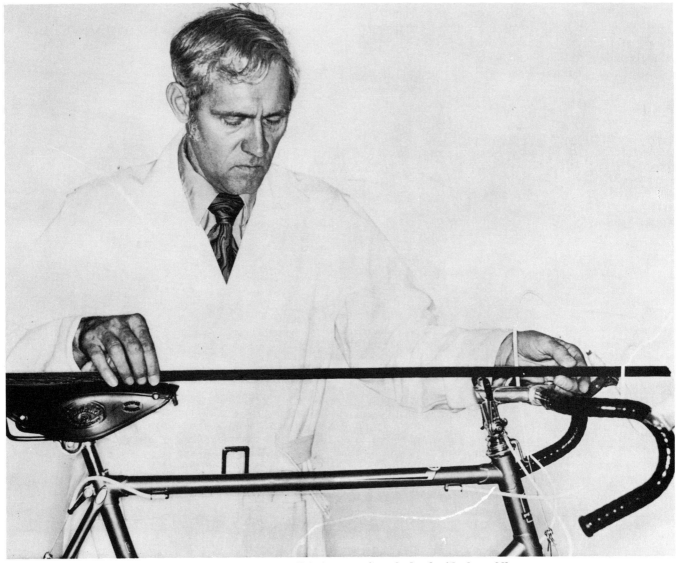

Raise the handlebar stem until it is approximately level with the saddle.

crank at its lowest point. This does not mean you should pedal with your heel, but it is done here only as a test.

The fore-and-aft position of the saddle should be 2½ to 3 inches toward the rear of the bicycle, measured from a vertical line at the center of the hanger set (as illustrated), with the nose of the saddle tilted very slightly upward.

For maximum efficiency, the handlebar stem should be level with the nose of the saddle. To raise the stem, loosen the stem bolt about 1½ turns, rap the head of the bolt with a mallet to loosen the wedge, pull up on the handlebars until the desired height is reached, and then tighten the stem bolt securely.

The handlebar position can be checked for best efficiency by first measuring the length of your lower arm and hand, from elbow to fingertips. This should be the distance from the forward tip of the saddle to the rear edge of the center portion of the handlebar. Various sizes of stems for shifting the handlebars forward or backward are available at a modest cost, and would be well worth the investment if extended touring or racing is anticipated.

The described saddle and handlebar positions may seem strange at first, but bear in mind that they are based on scientific calculations and are used by professionals under the most demanding circumstances.

If these positions seem strange or awkward, give them a fair chance of at least 100 miles, and then make minor changes for the most comfortable ride. Remember, anything new or different should be tested honestly before passing judgment.

"Ankling" is the technique of using your foot and the muscles of your ankle to maintain constant force on the pedal for the full revolution of the crank. The ball of your foot should be directly over the pedal spindle. The use of toe straps forces your foot into this position. The ankle then serves as a fulcrum as your foot shifts position to keep constant pressure on the pedal, as indicated in the four accompanying illustrations.

At the twelve o'clock position, the heel should be slightly down, with the toes pointing upward. At the six o'clock position, the heel should be up at approximately a 45-degree angle (as shown).

The movement should be smooth, and with a little practice in a parking lot on an early Sunday morning, you could watch your foot movement, without worrying about traffic or obstacles, and soon master the technique.

There are five basic positions for your hands on the drop-style handlebars, as shown in the accompanying illustrations. Each will put new muscles to work and relax others during a long tour or race.

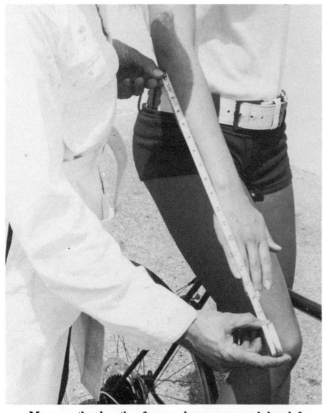

Measure the length of your lower arm and hand from elbow to fingertips. This total length should be the distance from the tip of the saddle to the back edge of the handlebar cross arm.

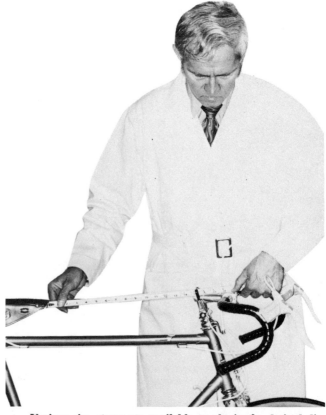

Various size stems are available to obtain the desired distance of the handlebars from the saddle. The modest investment in a new stem is well worth the money, if you intend to participate in extended tours or to race.

At the twelve o'clock position of the crank, the heel should be pointing slightly down and the toes up for proper "ankling" and maximum efficiency.

When the crank reaches the six o'clock position, the heel of the foot is now pointing upward at approximately a 45-degree angle. The ball of the foot is still over the pedal spindle.

As the crank rotates to the nine o'clock position, the toe points downward. Notice how the ball of the foot is directly over the pedal spindle.

The heel remains upward at the 45-degree angle through the three o'clock position, when it begins to move downward.

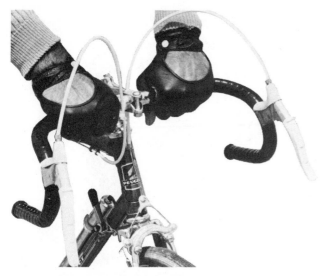

The first of five basic positions for your hands on the handlebars is on the crossover portion of the bar just outward of the stem, at the edge of the tape. This is an easy riding position for level terrain with no wind.

Hands at the turn of the bar is a very comfortable position and is used by many touring riders. This position places the hands within easier reach of the brake levers than when they are on the crossbar.

The third position is with the hand against the brake lever body, a particularly restful position on a downhill run, because the weight of your body is absorbed by the brake body and your hands are ready to use the levers when necessary.

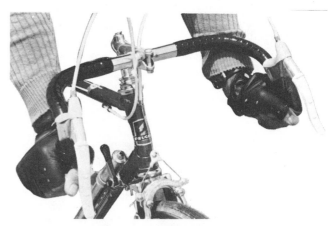

When the rider shifts his hands below the brake lever body at the turn of the bar, it means the going is getting just a little bit harder, for this is one of two "work" positions.

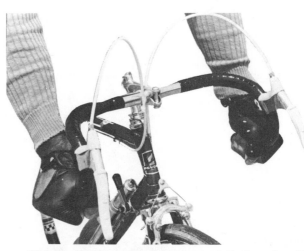

With the hands on the lower part of the bar, the rider's body is bent forward, offering the least wind resistance. This is the hard working position for uphill climbs or when bucking a strong head wind.

2

SAFE AND SERIOUS CYCLING

With the invention and marketing of each new mechanical means of transportation, someone has tried to break a record or be the first to accomplish an unusual feat, thus bringing fame to himself and the machine. Barney Oldfield drove his old No. 999 to a new speed record to become the first man to travel "a-mile-a-minute." Charles A. Lindbergh gained worldwide recognition following his successful solo flight across the Atlantic in a single-engine monoplane, the *Spirit of St. Louis*. The list of achievements, including almost any sport or activity, is long and impressive.

THOMAS STEVENS

For the bicycle, the name Thomas Stevens will be emblazoned on historical record plaques. He was the first man to "pedal" from coast to coast. In the year 1884 this 29-year-old rode, pushed, pulled, shoved, hauled, floated, and slid an "ordinary" high-wheeled bicycle from Oakland, California, to Boston, Massachusetts.

In preceding years, several stout and certainly more athletic-type men had made the attempt, only to be turned back by the elements, terrain, and the lack of suitable surfaces on which to ride. Stevens, slight of build, and hardly taller than his machine, succeeded through dogged determination to do one thing with a bicycle that no other person had done before.

Before he started he spent hours practicing taking "headers" (toppling over forward) from his five-foot perch atop the huge front wheel. Maps were unknown, so he had only a fair idea of the route he would have to follow. When you consider the condition or the non-existence of the roads in his day, it is little wonder many thought him odd to contemplate such a venture.

The first of many obstacles he had to overcome was crossing the Sacramento River at flood stage via a long railroad trestle. A train approached when he was almost at the midpoint and Stevens quickly scampered to a girder below the tracks. Somehow he managed to keep himself and his bicycle in this precarious position while the train thundered overhead and the swollen river rushed under him.

As he entered the ascending foothills of the Sierra Nevada, Stevens found it to his advantage to follow the access paths paralleling the railroad tracks instead of struggling along the muddy wagon roads. In the high mountains, he found temporary relief from the elements by using the many snowsheds built to protect the railroad tracks. In one section, he pushed his ponderous machine through some 40 miles of snowshed, with few openings. He sought shelter from passing trains by scurrying into tiny niches in the mountain walls; the triple-coupled steam locomotives belched their acrid,

High-wheeled "ordinaries" were the vehicle of the 1880s. One of the authors, Clarence Coles, wearing an authentic outfit of that era, rides an 1878 machine he restored. This bicycle is almost identical to the one used by Thomas Stevens in his epic ride across the United States in 1884. Notice the straight handlebar, the spokes radiating directly out from the hub (no crossovers), and the step above the rear wheel used for mounting.

choking smoke over him as they pulled a long line of freight cars up the steep grade.

Stevens was forced to carry his 50-pound bike through miles of loose sand in Nevada, but was able to ride across some of the alkali flats. Following the tracks of the early covered wagons, he moved steadily eastward, until the trail disappeared and then moved out across the open country, at times carrying the bike over his head in order to make his way through sagebrush.

More than once he used his machine to "vault" streams by placing one hand on the headset, the other on the saddle, and then leaping over, retaining his hold and pulling the bicycle after him. When the rushing waters were too wide for this maneuver, he built rafts of driftwood and floated the bike to the other side, often swimming in icy waters to prevent being separated from his equipment.

With pluck and determination, this unusual man crossed the Rocky Mountains, and then pedaled through the grass prairie lands of Nebraska. At Omaha, he crossed the Missouri River and entered the farmlands of Iowa. One "header" followed another as his front wheel continually stuck in the ooze of muddy roads. The two-thirds mark in his journey was passed when he reached the Mississippi River. On he struggled to the Windy City, Chicago, and then into Ohio. The roads improved in northeastern Pennsylvania and western New York. Riding the towpath along the Erie Canal and between the tracks of the New York Central Railroad provided Stevens the opportunity to stay mounted much of the time; the remainder of this herculean journey to Boston was made without incident.

The following year, 1885, Stevens undertook a more ambitious venture to continue around the world on his two-wheeled machine. This undertaking moved smoothly through France and Germany, up the Danube River, and on through Asia Minor. When the Russian government canceled earlier permission to cross Siberia, he was forced to alter his plans and follow a roundabout course of over 6,000 miles. Nevertheless he did complete his globe-circling odyssey by traveling through India, China, Japan, and then by ship across the Pacific, arriving at San Francisco in January 1887.

Thus, Thomas Stevens, one of the first truly serious wheelmen, gained international recognition. He was heralded a modern Sinbad and declared the cycling hero of the decade.

MARGARET VALENTINE LE LONG

Twelve years after Stevens's successful trip across the United States, a pert young woman in her early twenties pedaled one of the first dropped-frame safety bicycles equipped with pneumatic tires, from Chicago westward to San Francisco. Margaret Valentine Le Long, declaring her feminine independence, and against the advice of friends, relatives, and even those she did not know, struck out alone in 1896, along roads that had changed very little since Stevens had passed by in 1884.

From the start, she bucked adverse head winds, which slowed her progress, but she doggedly moved ahead, wearing attire proper for a lady of her day, ankle-length dress, multiple petticoats, and bonnet. A clean handkerchief was wrapped around the handlebars and a borrowed pistol was stowed in her tool bag, certainly difficult to reach if needed.

By the end of the third day, the adventurous woman reached Homestead, Iowa, and two months later pedaled into San Francisco. Her adventures left her with no broken bones. She was not attacked by marauding Indians or assaulted by roving cowboys and had escaped death from starvation and thirst. She had to fire her pistol on only one occasion, when a herd of cattle blocked her way and failed to disperse even though she shouted and waved at them.

The most serious incident of the trip occurred between Cheyenne and Laramie, Wyoming, as she was descending a steep grade on a road with rocks and boulders, potholes, and hairpin turns. Suddenly, she encountered a barbed-wire fence stretched across the road. Only through the immediate and almost instinctive reaction of throwing herself to one side of the road was she able to avoid a frontal contact with the fence. After a careful and fruitless examination for broken bones, she painfully plucked the gravel from her legs and knees with a hairpin, straightened the handlebars,

After the bicycle has been adjusted to fit your body, the energy you exert will be giving you the maximum benefit. You're now ready for daily workouts to keep slim and trim, commute to work or school, or tour with a group for a weekend or longer.

and then remounted to cover the eight miles to the nearest ranch before nightfall.

Miss Le Long was heralded as the social phenomenon of the 1890s. She had opened the door to women's liberation by abandoning the sheltered life and striking out to accomplish an unparalleled feat in a man's world.

MODERN CYCLING

With the introduction of mass-produced automobiles, cycling in this country declined among adults. Motorized vehicles offered young people a chance to travel in comfort and extended their horizons manyfold, compared with the limited opportunities of bicycling. In Europe, however, the reverse was true. Because of the economies involved, cycling continued to grow in popularity, both as a means of recreation, transportation, and as a sport through short- and long-distance racing.

Since the '30s cycling and the growth of the hostel system on the Continent has steadily increased. Today it is not unusual to find many common-interest tour groups and families covering hundreds of miles on their cycles. Many, however, go it alone; pedaling through scenic areas with the comfort-providing hostels.

DERVLA MURPHY

In 1963, a 32-year-old Irish girl rode her bicycle alone from Dunkirk, France, 3,000 miles to New Delhi, India. Her bike was a 3-speed machine, converted to single-speed hub, because she felt the multispeed unit would not withstand the rigorous road conditions of the anticipated route. Her machine weighed 37 pounds and she carried 28 pounds of gear in a saddlebag and panniers on both sides of the rear wheel. Another 6 pounds of personal effects were carried in a knapsack. Miss Murphy sent three tires ahead to British embassies along the way, because the tires she used were an odd size. The possibility of finding suitable replacements in the Middle East, Pakistan, and India were indeed remote. She passed through some regions of Pakistan and Afghanistan, where the bicycle was such an oddity that the natives were fascinated by her demonstration rides.

Leaving the English Channel coast during the coldest winter in eighty years, Miss Murphy fought her way south through rain, snow, ice, and gale winds. She crossed the Alps from Grenoble to Turin by train and found the roads there clear of snow, enabling her to make good time.

As she entered the Middle East, she had her hair cut short, boyish fashion, and wore a man's shirt to make her appearance less conspicuous. Unfortunately, she discovered she could not trust her bike repairs to people in these foreign lands, because they knew less about its operation, maintenance, and repair than she did.

On one occasion in Afghanistan, she had a tire puncture. Hardly had she made this repair when the chain broke, and this time it took an hour and three-quarters of intense concentration to figure out the repair.

In the high mountains of Pakistan, the snow-covered roads forced her to carry her bike, mile after mile, on her shoulders. During one encounter with the snowfields, she came upon a place where an avalanche completely blocked the road. To complicate the problem, a rushing river, swollen to flood stage by the melting snow, crossed at the base of the slide. As she pondered the difficult situation, a small caravan with pack animals appeared moving slowly upstream along the riverbank. She conveyed her predicament, using international sign language. The porters unloaded the animals, and placed their packs in position so her bike could be slid along the snow without continuing into the river. After watching the bicycle slide to safety, she followed in the same way, in a very unladylike manner, sliding along on her posterior.

Her biggest problem was obtaining proper meals. She was often invited to eat with the natives, but their food was so strange that many times she did not eat and went to sleep hungry. As a result of the diet and the intense heat of Central India she lost sixteen pounds in a matter of days.

It is interesting to note that, where women have not been liberated, still wear veils over their faces, and are not allowed to enter into the post-meal conversations in the Middle East, Miss Murphy was unquestionably accepted and permitted to join the men in their discussions on a wide range of subjects.

Today, hundreds of cyclists crisscross Western Europe each year traveling individually, in pairs, as a family, in groups large and small, safely and comfortably. Some join organized groups, such as the International Youth Hostel Federation, founded in Germany by Richard Schirrmann. From the single hostel he established in 1909, the number in the network has increased to 4,241. Their facilities are located in 47 countries in Europe, North and South America, Asia and Africa. Total membership of all participating segments of the federation has now passed the two-million mark.

AMERICAN YOUTH HOSTELS, INC. (AYH)

AYH is an American organization that offers people "young in spirit" a wide range of activities, including cycling in the United States, Canada, and many countries abroad: Europe, Australia, and New Zealand.

The purpose of AYH, in their own words, is "to spice up your life with a touch of adventure." Their tours take you off the beaten track and give you an opportunity to escape "the trappings of civilization" for a day or week.

AYH serves individuals and organizations, such as scouts, churches, colleges, high schools, recreation departments, Ys, and outing clubs. It's a unique world of travel, taking advantage of low-cost hostels, camps, lodges, huts, and camping areas. It can provide for a weekend outing or a long vacation.

In the U.S.A. and Canada, a hostel may be a

school, camp, church, student house, mountain lodge, community center, farmhouse, or a specially built facility for overnight accommodations. Some overseas hostels are found in picturesque old castles, villas, or even retired sailing ships.

Some hostels are sponsored by local organizations or committees of townspeople. They are chartered by the National Headquarters of AYH. They meet standards set by AYH and are inspected by field staff members. At these hostels, "house parents," usually retired couples, receive the traveler when he arrives. They have separate dorms and washrooms for boys and girls, a common kitchen where hostelers may cook their meals and, usually, a recreation room. Bunks, blankets, cooking utensils, and cleaning equipment are provided, but all services are on a do-it-yourself basis.

There are hostels in the New England, Middle Atlantic, Great Lakes, and West Coast states, usually in scenic, historic, and recreational areas, with some located in cities. Often they are within a day's bike ride from each other. Smoking is not permitted in bunkrooms; alcoholic beverages and illegal drugs are not permitted. Participating members must be at least 14 years old, with no maximum age.

If your budget requires careful accounting of dimes and dollars, then the hosteling program may be for you. It is nonprofit, nonsectarian, nonpolitical—a corporation organized "exclusively for charitable and educational purposes." For further information, contact the AYH national headquarters at 20 West 17th Street, New York, N.Y. 10011, or a local AYH office in your area.

LEAGUE OF AMERICAN WHEELMEN (L.A.W.)

During the infancy years of the bicycle, riders of the high-wheeled "ordinaries" were dubbed "wheelmen." It was only natural, therefore, that when a small band of about 120 hardy wheelmen gathered at Newport, Rhode Island, in the spring of 1880 to unite as an effective working organization, they would simply call themselves The League of American Wheelmen.

The chosen name identified their membership as bicycle riders and gave an indication of their purpose. Webster defines "league" to mean "an association of

Happiness is riding in the rain with someone who cares.   Courtesy AYH, Inc.

persons, parties, or countries formed to help one another" and that was exactly why the L.A.W. formed and was able to function continuously to the present. This fact enables them to now claim the distinction of being the oldest cycling club in America.

In their own words, the original purpose of the League was to "Promote the general interests of bicycling; ascertain, defend and protect the rights of wheelmen; and encourage and facilitate touring." These objectives have been diligently pursued for almost 100 years.

In the early 1880s, the League established a touring bureau to furnish information relative to routes, maps, accommodations, etc. Each state division gathered information and many divisions published road books covering conditions in their area. Hotels granting reduced rates to League members were listed, in addition to railroads which permitted bicycles to be carried as luggage.

The Wheelmen's growth kept abreast of the expanding bicycle boom and by 1889 they boasted a phenomenal membership of 102,636 cyclists. A host of famous Americans whose names have become a part of our nation's history were members of the League, including Orville and Wilbur Wright, Commodore Vanderbilt, and Diamond Jim Brady.

Following the introduction of the mass-produced "horseless carriage," the roster of the Wheelmen dwindled to about 9,000 in 1902 and to less than 1,000 members after World War II. Still this stalwart organization continued to function. In 1955, what was thought to be their last convention was held in St. Charles, Illinois, and during the following nine years the L.A.W. struggled on, almost in name only.

A new birth through reorganization in October, 1964, caused the League of American Wheelmen to spring back to life with renewed vigor and determination. Monthly, their numbers increased and by early 1973 more than 10,000 modern cyclists had rallied to the call of the League. Their members now hail from all 50 states and tours (rallies) are held somewhere in the United States or abroad every month of the year. Special patches are often awarded for century (100-mile) rides or for participation in selected rallies. Annual conventions, now called "roundups," are again held and have summoned their ranks to Illinois, Indiana, Massachusetts, California, Oregon, and Tennessee.

In the early days, the case of the individual cyclist or affiliated club was defended by the League in court and at law making sessions. Today, as then, the L.A.W. continues to champion the cause of the cyclist by encouraging favorable legislation at all levels of government; acquainting bicyclists with their neighbors who share similar interests in the joys of cycling; distributing information of interest to individuals and organizations; assisting in planning and conducting cycling programs; informing the cyclist in correct riding techniques to enhance his riding enjoyment; and aiding in establishing modern bicycle facilities.

The League provides its members with an excellent illustrated monthly publication, a directory of members and clubs throughout the United States, detailed information on cycling events and activities, and special decals and patches.

A permanent national headquarters is being established in the Midwest and will soon be open for business. Until this location is announced, inquiries from interested individuals or clubs desiring to affiliate with the L.A.W. should be addressed to League of American Wheelmen, 356 Robert Avenue, Wheeling, Illinois 60090.

INTERNATIONAL BICYCLE TOURING SOCIETY (IBTS)

In the fall of 1964, Clifford Graves, a La Jolla, California, surgeon, invited his friends and fellow cyclists to join him on a tour of New England. Writers, artists, executives, professional people, both under and over 40 years of age, women as well as men, all vigorous not only physically but mentally, answered the call. They came from all parts of this country and Europe to ride with Graves. Before the group disbanded after the trip, they formed the International Bicycle Touring Society, affectionately referred to as the "huff-and-puffers." From this modest beginning, their numbers increased to over 300 active members. Their ranks are open to adults over 21, the membership rang-

Doubling up on a tandem doubles the fun, at least for these "huff-and-puffers" on tour in New England. This group of adults, officially known as the International Bicycle Touring Society, welcomes new members over 21 who wish to join them on tour in this country and abroad. Courtesy The International Bicycle Touring Society

ing from 24 to 72, with the majority between 30 and 60 years of age. A colorful shoulder patch identifies them as members.

Since 1964 they have made successful tours through New England, the Blue Ridge Mountains, the Mississippi Valley, Ohio, California, England, and France. The routes are carefully planned and scouted in advance to utilize secondary roads over rolling country with little traffic; the emphasis is placed on atmosphere, historic culture, or scenic interest.

A huff-and-puffer is permitted to set his own pace, follow his own whims, and indulge in his own tastes. His only commitment is to reach the scheduled overnight stop for a gathering of the clan, because reservations are made in advance. The huff-and-puffers never camp out. Lodging is always in a comfortable (but not fancy) inn or motel. Tours usually last two weeks. Some groups have included as many as 50 riders, but 20 is the ideal size. For further information about this organization, write: International Bicycle Touring Society, 846 Prospect Street, La Jolla, California, 92037.

WANDERING WHEELS

Aside from the American Youth Hostels, probably the best-known cyclist organization today is the Wandering Wheels, a name given to a group of young men (and later women) led by Bob Davenport. In 1963, Davenport, head football coach at Taylor University, Upland, Indiana, conceived the idea of extended bicycle tours. The following summer he led his first group of young cyclists on a thousand-mile trip down the Mississippi River Valley.

During the next two summers he led several groups on extended tours through Indiana, Michigan, Ohio, Pennsylvania, West Virginia, and Kentucky. In July of '66 Davenport made his first transcontinental bicycle trip with 35 teenagers from San Francisco to Washington, D.C.

By 1970 the Wandering Wheels had crisscrossed the United States more than a half-dozen times: from San Diego, California, to Savannah, Georgia; Long Beach, California, to Rehoboth Beach, Delaware; San Francisco to New York City; Miami, Florida, to Seattle, Washington; and Seattle to Washington, D.C. By the summer's end of '70 more than 350 young people were proud to be counted as Wandering Wheels alumni; the distance traveled exceeded 30,000 miles.

In the early years most of the riders consisted of young men from Taylor University but, as their fame spread, applications were accepted from college students across the country, and then the age requirements were lowered in order to accept senior high school students.

The required gear is carried in a truck equipped with lockers, accessible from the outside, one for each rider. The riders do not carry packs or any gear. A custom-built kitchen is mounted in the rear of the truck, and a professional cook prepares nourishing meals to satisfy the ravenous appetites created by the strenuous exercise.

Davenport purchased 24 French-built Louison Bobet sports bikes for the initial trip. Each machine featured a three-piece crank; frame assembled by lugs and brazing at the joints; center-pull caliper-type alloy brakes; high-flange, quick-release alloy hubs; 15-speed derailleur; and 27-inch wheels, but no kickstand. He tried to teach the boys how to stack their bikes one against another as the European touring groups do, in much the same fashion as stacking rifles in the military. The knack was never mastered so he had a kickstand installed on each bike, in spite of the added weight.

Bobet bicycles were used for the first cross-country trip, but the Schwinn Bicycle Company loaned the Wandering Wheels one Schwinn Super Sport to test. Davenport was impressed with its performance, quality of components, and heavier construction, although it weighed 29 pounds compared with the 27-pound Bobet. He discovered that many of the parts on the Schwinn Super Sport were built in Europe, but they were sturdier than similar parts on the European machines. He also learned that the 10-speed gearing on the Schwinn Super Sport had a range equal to that on the 15-speed Bobet bikes, which proved an advantage on long tours and in training new cyclists in shifting gears properly.

In 1967, Davenport made the change to the Schwinn Super Sport, and it is now their official bike.

The rider of this bike leaves little doubt as to his purpose in cycling to work. Workers and students by the thousands are following his example in doing their part for a cleaner environment.

With their safety pennants waving and their spirits high with prospects for a good day's ride, members of the Wandering Wheels move out in the early morning hours on one of their many cross-country trips. Soon they will re-form into groups of less than ten and ride single file, with their gear and kitchen truck bringing up the rear. *Wandering Wheels,* by Jack Houston, Baker Book House, Grand Rapids, Mich., 1970

Davenport says: "The Schwinn has proved itself to be the bike for the Wandering Wheels. It has the guts to withstand the abuse of the typical American youth."

During their 1972 trek from the Pacific to the Atlantic, the number of riders swelled to 120, and many who eagerly sought to join this unusual group had to be turned away.

Davenport proved that girls are "pound for pound" as tough as the guys. In January of '69 he led a group of 20 girls and 15 boys on a 900-mile trip from Savannah, Georgia, to Jacksonville, Florida, then on to Miami, back to Tallahassee, and again south to Tampa. The complete circuit took eighteen days for an average of 50 miles a day.

Since the Florida trip, coed rides have become a standard part of the Wandering Wheels program. Several such trips have been made and the girls are clamoring for an all-girl cross-country trip. The Wandering Wheels can be reached by contacting them at Taylor University, Upland, Indiana.

CYCLEMATES

During the summer of 1971, fifteen ninth-graders from North Mercer JHS (near Seattle, Washington) pedaled their bicycles 3,700 miles to Washington, D.C. Their leader was a young teacher, Miss Frances Call.

The Cyclemates, aged 14 and 15, may well be one of the youngest groups to complete such a marathon ride. The trip was completed without mishap, a credit to Miss Call's leadership and the discipline of today's young teenagers when properly directed.

Highlight of the trip was an invitation to cycle to the White House and meet President Nixon. During their visit the President commended them for their safe journey and accepted one of their bright red windbreakers, with reflectorized safety strips, thus becoming an honorary member of their elite fraternity. The reflective striping on the jackets and the reflectors on the bike make the rider more visible when lighting is poor.

Fifteen members of the Cyclemates of Mercer Island, Washington, watch as President Nixon shakes hands with their leader, Miss Frances Call, at the White House following the Cyclemates 3,700-mile pedaling junket to Washington, D.C. Each rider carefully maintained his bike with regular lubrication and adjustment to obtain maximum efficiency for every ounce of energy expended in crossing the continent.

During their trip, they began each day at sunrise. By sunset, they had biked between 80 and 95 miles. The weather conditions varied from blistering hot days and drenching downpours to stiff head winds. They found lodgings for the night in churches and motels, or bedded in sleeping bags under the stars.

In the 59 pedaling days, they suffered 50 flat tires, many caused by cactus thorns, but regular maintenance and lubrication prevented serious mechanical failures.

BAUER AND FAMILY

Organized groups are not the only cyclists making extended tours on bicycles. One such group—Fred Bauer, 35, his wife Shirley, 32, and their three children, Laraine, 13, Steve, 11, and 3-year-old Christopher who rode on a child's seat on his dad's bike—left Battery Park, near the Statue of Liberty in New York City on June 7, 1968: destination, Disneyland, California. They pedaled two-thirds of the entire distance, to Springer, New Mexico, and then rode the train for the rest of the trip to the famous amusement park.

The Bauers were plagued by head winds—one disadvantage of riding from east to west. Still they managed to average 45 miles a day on their Schwinn 5-speed machines. Fred Bauer used a bike with a 23-inch frame, his wife Shirley and daughter Laraine, 21-inchers, and young son Steve, a 19-incher, the latter being specially ordered; little Christopher rode securely strapped in a child's seat installed on Mr. Bauer's bicycle.

The second day, 25 pounds of gear was jettisoned, a wise move on their part. Touring veterans advise: "Take the least you think you can get by with, and then divide it in half." One of the Bauer's greatest problems was in reaching daily destinations offering them adequate meals and a suitable place to camp.

Little Chris was perfectly happy on his seat behind dad. He whiled away the hours running matchbox cars over his dad's back, until the middle of the afternoon when Fred would feel the thump of Chris's head between his shoulders, indicating the youngster had fallen asleep. It was time to stop, find some shade, and allow the little fellow his nap.

The Bauers missed a tornado by less than a half hour and felt this piece of good fortune to be the most exciting episode of their trip. Their greatest hazard, as with most touring cyclists, is the magnetic attraction of turning wheels for dogs. Most farms have dogs and the animals seem to feel it their duty to harass two-wheeled riders. One dog at a time can be handled, but when three attack, as they did the Bauers in Missouri, the situation calls for speed and skillful gymnastics to keep both feet out of reach of the dogs' snapping jaws. To maintain or increase speed with your feet high in the air part of the time is no small task. All agreed the venture brought them closer together as a family, because each member had to contribute his share.

CYCLING ABROAD

The U.S. State Department has published a pamphlet of suggestions for young Americans planning to travel abroad. The publication contains practical information on passports, visas, vaccination requirements, and a pretravel checklist. How to obtain help from U.S. embassies and consulates and advice on how to avoid being jailed or stranded are also included. The pamphlet

Two young cyclists pause in Yellowstone National Park, while a third takes their picture during a 600-mile ride from Billings, Montana, to Salt Lake City, Utah. One of the bikes was purchased from a discount store, another from a mail-order house, and the third was obtained with Blue Chip stamps. Dennis Stoutsenberger Photo

The summit of McKenzie Pass, Oregon, elevation 5,325 feet, proved a good place to rest for these five hardy young men as they biked their way across Oregon during the summer of 1971. Lauren Burch Photo, Courtesy *Oregon Outdoors*

is available at the Superintendent of Documents, U.S. Government Printing Office, Washington, D.C. 20402, for 20 cents. Specify "Youth Travel Abroad: What to Know Before You Go," Catalogue No. S 1.71:263.

COMMUTING

As the cry for a cleaner environment echoes across the nation, literally thousands of workers and students are answering the call by riding bicycles to jobs or to schools. With college students, it's a clear case of economics. They can save $7 to $10 a month in parking fees alone, not counting the cost of gas, oil, and the rising expense of maintenance and repairs on an automobile. At the same time, they send their red corpuscles chasing each other a little faster, which, in turn, stimulates the brain and prepares them for the day's activities.

Women have found that they can save time and money as well as keep fit and slim by bicycling. Young mothers have discovered a threefold advantage to cycling. First, it gives them the chance to "get out of the house" for a bona fide reason; second, it helps keep them in shape, and third, if they take their tots along on the special seats available, they will "get an airing," reviving an old custom that has almost ended. In addition, reports one mother, "you meet the nicest people while pedaling."

Stores and businesses woo the cyclist by permitting him to park his machine inside the store as a deterrent to theft while shopping. One banking firm has installed "pedal-in" teller windows to accommodate customers who ride their bikes. The system allows them to conduct financial transactions without entering the bank, or leaving their bicycles.

New shopping centers across the country are having theft-protection-type bike racks designed as an integral part of the development. Bicycle rental facilities have increased at an unbelievable rate in the past few years, and at least one major car-rental agency has turned to leasing bicycles, some on an extended year-round basis.

At Central Park in New York City automobiles are banned on certain weekends and holidays, giving the cyclist free reign of the roadways while leaving the paths to pedestrians.

Corporations, large and small, are making their contribution by providing special areas with racks for the employee riding his bike to work. For convenience, protection of the bikes, and as an incentive, these areas are located close to entrances of the plant, saving the rider walking time.

One California company instituted a program of subsidizing employees who wish to ride a bicycle to work by donating the down-payment for a new lightweight 10-speed machine. The company made arrangements with the cycle shop for monthly payroll deductions over a 90-day period. Within a few months, over half the 260 employees had taken advantage of the program. As the company president exclaims: "It looks like the start of a Grand Prix race at quitting time. The half-empty auto parking lot gives them plenty of room to move out and get going."

In an effort to meet the safety demand of this influx of commuters, city, county, and state agencies have begun to plan, design, and construct paths, lanes, and routes specifically for the cyclist. The Department of Transportation has informed the states that money from the National Highway Trust Fund can be utilized for the construction of bike trails in conjunction with federally aided highway projects. In almost every state, particularly in the large metropolitan areas, thousands of cyclists have banded together in "mass rides," clamoring for more trails and safety lanes.

The wheels of legal machinery move slowly, but political figures have responded and legislation has been passed or is pending in the following states: Alabama, Alaska, California, Connecticut, Delaware, Florida, Georgia, Hawaii, Oklahoma, Rhode Island, South Dakota, Massachusetts, Michigan, Nebraska, New Hampshire, New Jersey, New York, Kansas, Kentucky, Maryland, Vermont, Virginia, Washington, West Vir-

Six Sunday riders (Can you find the sixth?) emerge from one of three tunnels of the Wisconsin cross-state bikeway. A 32-mile stretch utilizes an abandoned railroad bed, where bikers can ride unhampered by motorists or pedestrians. Photo by Wisconsin Natural Resources Department, Madison, Wisconsin

ginia, and Wisconsin. Others are bound to follow as the movement gains momentum.

Oregon probably ranks as one of the leaders, since its governing body voted to spend $1.3 million a year from highway funds to build new bike trails. Matching federal funds could possibly increase this figure three-fold and, in the case of bikeways alongside interstate highways, the state's commitment would be only 10 percent, with the remainder available from the National Highway Trust Fund.

At present, Wisconsin has the longest continuous bikeway, extending from La Crosse, on the Mississippi River, 320 miles across the state to Kenosha, on the shores of Lake Michigan. A 32-mile stretch of the bikeway utilizes an abandoned railroad bed, and the cyclist riding this section finds the grade never exceeds three percent. He passes through three tunnels, one almost a half-mile long, and crosses no less than 33 trestles. The trestles have planks over the ties for easy riding,

and the ties have been removed on other sections of the roadbed. In 1972 more than 33,000 tourists are expected to use some portion of the Wisconsin Bikeway.

Today more people are engaged in cycling in this country than in any other participant sport; it is not only fun but healthy, too. Newspapers, political leaders, and the general public are helping make the case for more bike routes stronger each day. The *Christian Science Monitor,* an international daily newspaper, points out that "bicycle riders need to make themselves more clearly heard before public planning agencies. If they organize properly and speak with one voice, we can expect more consideration for the modest vehicle that emits no fumes, asks little highway space, and provides outdoor fun for millions."

The Bicycle Institute of America has produced many tools that will help you get a bikeway started in your community. The material includes a bikeway folder; a 20-minute bikeways filmstrip; a "how-to-do-it"

A bike route sign authorized by the Bureau of Public Roads, Department of Commerce, clearly indicates this old railroad trestle to be one of 33 on the Wisconsin Bikeway. To date, Wisconsin has the longest continuous bikeway, extending 320 miles across the state from the Mississippi River to Lake Michigan. Photo by Wisconsin Natural Resources Department, Madison, Wisconsin

brochure titled "What's all this jazz about bikeways?"; a newsletter; a bike film catalogue describing audio-visual materials available on the subject of cycling, plus a sample presentation to city officials written by various interested individuals and groups. For further information on how to obtain this free material, contact Bicycle Institute of America, 122 East 42 St., New York, N.Y. 10017.

CYCLING FOR PHYSICAL AND MENTAL THERAPY

Dr. Paul Dudley White, the eminent heart specialist, is probably one of the greatest advocates for using the bicycle for health and fitness today. Dr. White maintains that cycling is one of the best aids to good muscle tone available to the American people. At the age of 90, he rides daily and tells us not to worry about our heart—some other muscle will give out first.

By riding a bicycle regularly, your leg muscles are strengthened without adding strain to other parts of the body. Dr. White explains that "when leg muscles contract, they squeeze the veins and actually pump

The city of Denver, Colorado, is one of many progressive cities that have discovered they have land available, which, for a modest cost, can be put to use for the cyclists, such as the area between the eight-lane freeway and the lake shown in this aerial photograph. Courtesy Denver Police Department

blood up toward the heart. This allows the heart to receive more blood with which to supply the brain." This is the reason riding is so relaxing and an excellent therapy for releasing the keyed-up emotions generated during a hectic work session.

Speaking out on the advantages of cycling, Dr. White firmly states that "it aids the lungs through good tone of the diaphragm and makes it easier to bring oxygen into the body and pump out carbon dioxide. By aiding circulation, blood clots can be prevented." Dr. White points out that "such clots can go from our legs to our lungs and kill us."

He also notes that cycling aids our digestion and it may even protect us against peptic ulcers "provided we don't try to establish a new speed record."

To Dr. White's advice, the former director of the Bureau of Health Education of the American Medical Association, Dr. W. W. Bauer, adds: "The bicycle is one of the great unappreciated vehicles for good, wholesome exercise that can be continued to an advanced age."

Dr. Elizabeth Rose, 65-year-old assistant professor of preventive medicine at the University of Pennsylvania Medical School, is another who cycles for fun and fitness. "Bicycling keeps you mentally fit, makes good use of leisure time, helps release tensions, and is a boon in busy traffic." Dr. Rose urges cycling for Americans of all ages.

Enter any health spa and you will find a row of special cycle machines that are used for conditioning, muscle building, and weight trimming. Talk to any athletic coach or director of a program requiring strenuous physical exertion and he'll confirm the fact that riding a bicycle on a regular basis is one of the best tools for keeping fit.

RACING

Bicycle racing is only one of the many activities available to the cycling enthusiast. The machines are a "special breed" of bikes as explained earlier in this chapter, and the contestants must be in the best of physical condition. Racing, traditionally a European sport, has been gaining in popularity in the United States through the efforts of the Amateur Bicycle League of America, the governing body of amateur cycling in this country. Each year, the ABL sanctions and supervises hundreds of races. It is through this system, and the points accumulated by individual riders, that the U.S. Olympic team is selected.

Shortly after the conclusion of the 1968 Olympic games in Mexico City, the United States Olympic Committee reframed its policy so that the United States effort in the so-called minor sports would receive greater emphasis and assistance. Since cycling had long been neglected as a potential Olympic medal source, the committee directed some of their attention to this traditional European sport. In the 1971 Pan American Games, held in Cali, Colombia, a gold medal and five bronze medals were awarded the United States cycling team, an achievement that exceeded all previous efforts.

Watching a bicycle race is an exciting experience. Racing is competitive and fast moving; riders tend to stay in a pack, riding one another's tail and waiting for the right moment to break loose. Even a many-hundred kilometer race can be won in the last hundred yards, with the lead changing several times and half the field still bunched together. Bicycle racing is thrilling for both the contestant and the spectator. It represents months of training for the competitor and months of planning by the cycling committee. It is this combination of effort in a common endeavor that makes cycle racing successful and a major sport throughout the world.

The various types of races are as follows:

Road races—from 10 to over 120 miles, held on open roads with traffic.
Criteriums—run on city streets closed to traffic.
Time trials—individual or teams race against the clock.
Track races—held on an oval, banked cement or wooden-decked track.

Scratch races—all riders start from a scratch mark. The fastest man wins on his merits.
Point races—sprints for points are held on certain laps or miles as may be designated on the entry blank by the promoter of the meet. Points are scored in these sprints, with the rider scoring the highest point score designated as the winner, provided he has completed the full distance. In order to score points, riders must be even in mileage with other riders. Riders who are lapped do not score in sprints.

National B.A.R. (Best All-around Rider)—On a national basis, each state is allotted a number of races in which to score overall points, so that the first five senior and junior riders receive trophies at season's end, to be designated as best all-around riders. Points are scored 20–18–16 (on down to 2 points) to the first ten placers in a race, both in the senior and junior divisions. In addition to scoring points, the B.A.R. winner also receives a wall plaque from the Amateur Bicycle League for his victory. The points are sent to the B.A.R. head-

More than one thousand Long Beach, California, bicycle enthusiasts line up to begin a demonstration ride favoring bike lanes, paths, and facilities for safely parking their machines in the downtown area. As bicycle riders from coast to coast arise and make themselves heard, legislators are taking action to meet the need for routes restricted for cycling.

quarters in Chicago, where the points are tabulated. After the B.A.R. competition is closed, the high-point scorers receive their awards.

Several types of track races are held as follows:

Match races—consists of 2 or 3 riders racing a mile or less. The first rider across the finish line wins. This type of race requires considerable finesse and tactical wit. Each rider attempts to capitalize on his opponent's mistakes, therefore he rides comparatively slowly, and continues to change position until the last lap, when he tries to jump the others and sprint to the finish line.

Open races—races open to any rider.

Miss and out—consists of a large field of riders. The last rider across the finish line in each lap is out of the race. When four riders remain, they sprint for two laps to the finish line.

Pursuits—can be run either as an individual or team event. One rider or team starts on one side of the track and the other rider or team starts on the opposite side. The race continues until one rider or team laps the other, or until they have completed a predetermined distance.

Point races—a definite distance is determined and the riders are required to sprint every time a certain number of laps have been completed. Points are awarded for places in each sprint. The rider with the most points is declared the winner.

Team races—two riders comprise a team. The teams are identified by their jerseys and the numbers on their backs. One member from each team must be on the track at all times. Once the race starts, only one member of each team is actually racing. He is considered to be in the field, riding low on the track. His partner or "relief" rides slowly around the track and must stay above the center red line. When the racer in the field reaches his relief, he pushes him into the field and he moves up on the track to become the relief rider. A "jam" results from the attempt of one or more teams to gain a lap on the field. Before a lap is awarded by the referee, the team or teams must ride into the largest group of the field.

CYCLING SAFETY

Any sport or activity can be enjoyed only as long as those participating can do so safely without fear of injury. Cycling can be a most rewarding experience for any age group, but it also has its hazards. The tragic statistics reveal that 800 people were killed in bicycle accidents last year and another 34,000 were injured.

Keeping the bicycle in good mechanical condition, obeying traffic laws and being constantly alert, as well as using your common sense, are your best defenses against accidents. In the case of youngsters, proper training and discipline must be added.

All states now consider the bicycle a "vehicle" and, therefore, subject to the laws and conditions governing automobiles. This means that the cyclist, mounted on his 25-to-40-pound bike is actually "driving" and is competing with the motorist behind the wheel of a several-ton machine with hundreds of horsepower. This comparison is a difficult point to impress on juveniles. Many large cities have instructed their officers to issue citations for flagrant or hazardous violations of the traffic code, especially if an accident or near-accident is involved. Surprisingly, the reaction of the public has not always been appreciative, with some mothers taking the attitude that the police department "should be out chasing criminals instead of picking on poor little Johnny."

Progressive-minded cities are providing training sessions for boys and girls at the elementary school level in an effort to familiarize them with the vehicular laws and the seriousness and importance of safe riding. With the competitive nature of children in mind, many police departments conduct bicycle safety inspection periods, obstacle courses, rides, and written examinations to test the knowledge and skills of the young rider. These programs are to be commended for their earnestness and success as indicated by research reports conducted by the National Safety Council. One such report revealed that bicycle riders in the 15-to-34 age group were to blame in the majority of accidents, undoubtedly never exposed to such safety training. Riding on the wrong side of the road against oncoming traffic heads the list of accident causes. Making an improper turn,

A beginning bicycle rider fills out her application to enter a safe riding contest to prove her skills and knowledge of the law. Such programs are being held in major cities throughout the United States and are becoming increasingly popular with young people anxious to prove their ability with the two-wheeled machine. The safety lessons they learn at this early age will become a part of their cycling habits and may help save their lives someday. Courtesy Long Beach, California, Police Department

violating an automobile driver's right-of-way, and riding at night without proper lights follow in that order.

When youngsters in the lower age groups are involved, safety studies report that riding a bicycle too large for the child to handle properly is the dominant cause. High-rise handlebars, banana-type seats allowing more than one person to ride, and sissy bars behind the seat are also factors that prevent the child from handling his bike safely.

Manufacturers have made an attempt to discourage riding two on a seat and from performing hazardous acrobatics by modifying seats so they flare upward at the rear to make it harder to carry a passenger or to move back into the position favored for stunting. The height of the high-rise handlebars and the maximum height of the support behind the seat have been reduced on all new bicycles.

For safe riding on city streets, the following rules can add to your hours of skillful and enjoyable cycling. Always keep your bicycle in good mechanical condition by making the inspections suggested in Chapter 3. Be sure your bicycle is equipped with a light, front and rear. All state laws require that the light shall be visible from a distance of 300 feet in front of the bicycle and that a red reflector on the rear of the bike must be in-

stalled which "shall be visible from a distance of 300 feet to the rear when directly in front of the upper beams of a motor vehicle headlamp." Many states add to their code, advising that "a lamp emitting a red light visible from 300 feet to the rear should be used in addition to the red reflector."

Observe all traffic regulations, including riding on the right side of the street with the flow of traffic and obeying regulating lights and signs. Many accidents are caused by cyclists traveling at high speed on the new lightweight machines and then failing to stop at a red light, or making an attempt to beat the light. Motorists are not yet accustomed to the speed of these multispeed bikes and, therefore, fail to judge their closing collision rate accurately. Unfortunately, some adult riders are irked if they have to come to a complete stop at a red light, not realizing the danger from cross-traffic if they attempt to ride on through the intersection.

Be constantly on the alert for an opening car door by watching parked cars ahead for movement that might indicate that a driver is coming out of the car. It may be impossible to veer enough to avoid an opening door while riding in heavy traffic.

Broken glass and debris can be hazardous because they are difficult to avoid on busy streets. Try to

An opening car door presents one of the most hazardous conditions to the cyclist traveling in heavy traffic because it forces the cyclist into the path of a moving auto. Be alert for movement in parked cars ahead that might indicate a driver is about to open a door. Courtesy Long Beach, California, Police Department

A left turn from a clearly indicated left turn lane is a legal maneuver, provided you do not cut in front of motorists to reach that lane, give a proper signal and yield the right-of-way to oncoming traffic. Courtesy Long Beach, California, Police Department

develop a sense of feeling for vehicles that may be behind you, thus giving you an opportunity to ride around the obstacle without coming into conflict with a motor car.

Storm drains are another hazard that must be avoided. If you are traveling at a rapid speed and the front wheel should suddenly drop between the grating (as shown in an accompanying illustration), the sudden stop would catapult you over the handlebars with serious consequences.

When riding in a large group on city streets, always maintain single file. Do not hesitate to call out a dangerous condition to the rider behind. Use your right hand to point out holes in the pavement, glass, grating, or other potential dangers. If you use your right hand, it will avoid confusion with a signal maneuver.

Use your left hand when making a turn or changing position. Let the riders ahead know you are attempting to pass by calling out "on your right" or "on your left," etc. Develop the habit of riding in a straight line. Weaving and wandering confuses everyone behind you (including auto drivers), makes them nervous as to what your intentions might be, and it burns up unnecessary energy that should be saved for the next hill.

Always give the pedestrians the right-of-way. If you are forced to use sidewalks, dismount and walk your bike.

Cars pulling out from narrow alleyways or normal side streets present a definite hazard. Again, drivers may fail to realize your speed. Many judge from their days on the heavy, balloon-tired bicycle they rode as a child and may, therefore, feel they have time to pull out in front of you.

Carry books, packages, and other objects in baskets or carrier racks, properly mounted on the bike instead of carrying them in one hand, where they can hamper your movements and control of the bike. The bicycle was engineered and constructed for a single

President Nixon accepts a bright red jacket from a cycling group, dubbed the "Cyclemates," making him an honorary member. The jackets, worn by these 14- and 15-year-old students, during their 3,700-mile trip from Seattle, Washington, had reflectorized stripes to make the riders more visible to motorists. All organized clubs encourage their members to wear bright colored clothes, because it might save their lives during inclement weather or periods of poor visibility.

Storm drains are another serious hazard for the bicycle rider. The front wheel dropping between the grating could catapult you over the handlebars with serious consequences. The two drains shown in this picture were installed in early 1972 and emphasize the fact that city engineers are still not fully cognizant of the fact that they build traps for cyclists into their street system.

rider, and you'll ride longer and much safer if you are its only occupant.

Be especially alert at intersections, even if you are traveling on a thoroughfare, because you can never tell when a motorist may cut you off. A left turn from a clearly indicated left-turn lane is a legal maneuver, provided a proper hand signal is given and you do not cut in front of a moving vehicle.

Touring presents some special hazards but, if these are recognized and identified in advance, they should help make the ride enjoyable. Most organized clubs require their members to wear bright colored clothes so they can be seen during the early morning hours, at sunset, or while riding in the fog. During their trip from Seattle, Washington, to Washington, D.C., the Cyclemates wore bright red jackets, with reflectorized stripes to make them visible to motorists.

Each rider of the Wandering Wheels has an iridescent orange pennant at the end of a five-foot fiberglass pole, attached to the left handlebar. These pennants, swaying as the group moves down the road, are visible for several miles. They also give warning when traveling over a rise, when the cyclists might be hidden from view.

Railroad tracks present a definite hazard to the tourist, as do the muddy ridges left from a farm vehicle crossing the road. Oil slicks, loose gravel, potholes, and breaks in the pavement can easily throw a bike out of control. Caution and complete control of the bike is necessary at all times when approaching these conditions. To be forewarned is to be forearmed.

When traveling with very large groups, the safety experiences of the Wandering Wheels, with their many thousands of miles of accident-free riding, should become part of your safety practices. They move out at the start in small groups of less than ten riders, at five-minute intervals, depending on the weather and terrain. A veteran leads the pack and one of his jobs is to note road hazards and to warn those who follow. As a further safety measure, their luggage and kitchen truck follows the pack, with a large sign indicating the number of cyclists ahead.

Many touring groups have found that when they are passing through large cities, it is best to schedule their eating or rest periods during the peak rush hour traffic. Touring organizations rarely ride at night, except in a dire necessity, and safety-minded riders also avoid riding directly into the sun. It is very difficult for them to see and enjoy the trip; motorists likewise are sometimes blinded by the sun and may not see the cyclists.

Common sense, prudence, and alertness, as well as a desire to ride because it is fun, healthy, and gives you the chance "to do your own thing," are the keynotes to safe cycling.

3
MAINTENANCE AND TROUBLESHOOTING

This chapter outlines a systematic program for routine maintenance of your bicycle. Troubleshooting tables are provided to assist you in locating malfunctions. Possible causes and suggestive corrective action are included in the tables. Repair of clincher-type and tubular tires; chain maintenance and replacement of defective links; cable and lever repair, and replacement of spokes, including wheel building, trueing, and centering, are covered with detailed procedures in this chapter. Complete step-by-step illustrated instructions for overhauling all major bicycle components are given in the following chapters and are referenced in the maintenance listing whenever they apply.

If an owner performs the maintenance tasks himself, he can be assured his machine is in good condition to give him the performance he expects and deserves. For the cyclist active in racing, touring, or merely riding for pleasure or health, the results of his maintenance work are immediately evident in less effort for the distance traveled, or in more speed for the amount of energy expended, not to mention the dollar savings in parts and labor because they have received proper attention.

The girl or boy in his early teens in maintaining his bicycle will have his first association with mechanical devices and will develop an accurate appreciation for their care.

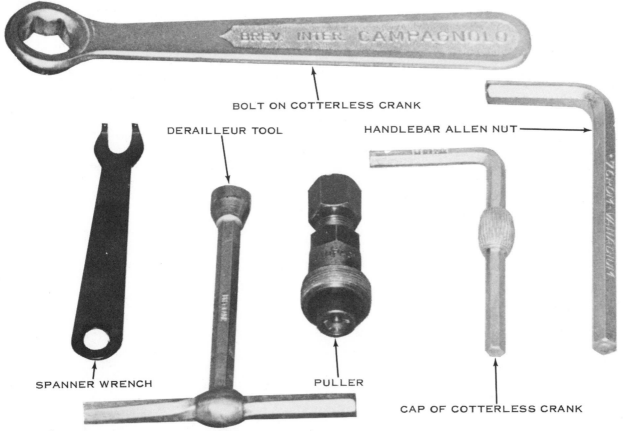

BOLT ON COTTERLESS CRANK

DERAILLEUR TOOL

HANDLEBAR ALLEN NUT

SPANNER WRENCH

PULLER

CAP OF COTTERLESS CRANK

These tools are included with the purchase of better-built bicycles, such as the Schwinn Paramount series, to enable you to perform routine maintenance and overhaul tasks.

PERIODIC MAINTENANCE

The accompanying illustration and listings point out specific areas requiring periodic attention and the type of lubrication to be used. The tasks are keyed to the illustration.

MONTHLY MAINTENANCE TASKS

M1 Lubricate front hub. Use a few drops of light oil if an oil fitting is provided. Use grease if equipped with a fitting.

M2 Lubricate the rear hub. Use a few drops of light oil or grease depending on the type of fitting.

M3 Remove the chain. Clean it in solvent, soak it in lightweight oil, drain it, remove the excess, and then reinstall it.

M4 Apply a few drops of lightweight oil to the brake and shift cables.

M5 Apply lightweight oil to all pivot points of the caliper brakes.

M6 Apply lightweight oil to the moving parts and pivot points of the rear derailleur.

M7 Apply lightweight oil to the pivot points of the front derailleur.

M8 American-type pedals—apply mediumweight oil to each end. European rattrap pedals require no lubrication.

M9 Apply lightweight oil to the freewheel mechanism.

M10 Clean the saddle with warm soap and water.

SEMIANNUAL MAINTENANCE TASKS

S1 Overhaul the front wheel hub. See Chapter 4.

S2 Overhaul the pedals. See Chapter 9.

S3 Overhaul the headset. See Chapter 12.

S4 Overhaul the rear derailleur. See Chapter 7.

S5 Overhaul the front derailleur. See Chapter 8.

ANNUAL MAINTENANCE TASKS

A1 Overhaul the rear hub. This task applies to single and multispeed rear hubs. See Chapter 5.

A2 Overhaul the hanger set. See Chapter 9.

A3 Overhaul the freewheel cluster body. See Chapter 6.

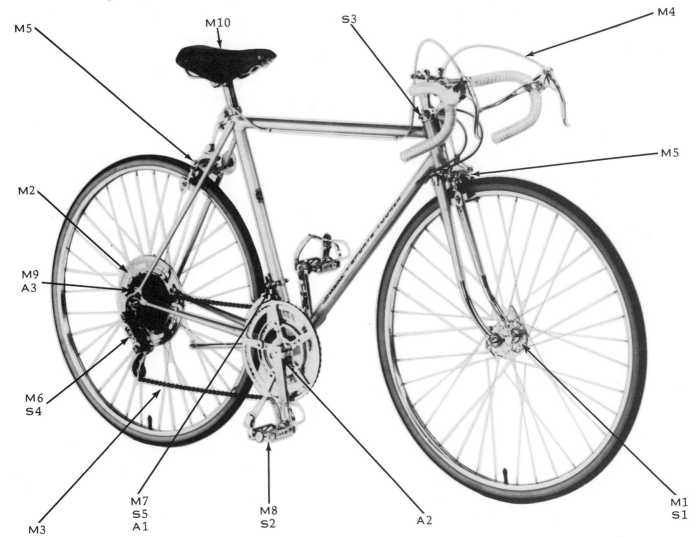

Periodic maintenance points on a typical derailleur-equipped bicycle. The letter prefix indicates M for monthly, S for semi-annually, and A for annual tasks, as outlined in the text.

their care. He will develop a sensitivity for making adjustments. His pride of ownership will be enhanced, and the manner of his riding will surely become safe, more sensible, and less demanding on the bike. As he continues to gain knowledge of his machine and confidence in handling tools and following written instructions from doing his own work, or helping dad, the overhaul tasks will develop his mechanical aptitude. He will be able to observe firsthand how machined parts are fitted together, how friction is reduced, and the important role of bearings and their need for periodic lubrication and adjustment. These lessons will provide excellent training experience and prepare a solid foundation on which to build for work in later years on more complex mechanical devices: the automobile, motor bike, or outboard motor.

Because of the relatively small size and weight of a bicycle, maintenance and most overhaul work can be performed anywhere there is adequate light and room for movement. Whether you live in a house, condominium, apartment, or flat, a covering on the kitchen floor and a place to clamp a vise are all that is required. However, cleaning parts with solvent should be done outdoors or with adequate ventilation to minimize the inhalation of poisonous fumes. **CAUTION: Never use gasoline for cleaning purposes, because it is highly volatile and the possibility of ignition is extreme. Besides, in most communities, the practice is illegal.**

Take care to keep oil and other lubricants from coming into contact with the tires, caliper brake pads, wheel rims, and other rubber, plastic, or leather parts. If partial disassembly is necessary for maintenance, keep the parts on clean paper towels and cover to avoid contamination. Note the arrangement of spacers, shims, and washers when disassembling as an aid to making proper replacement, adjustments, and alignment during assembling.

Very few tools are required. When purchasing a more expensive bicycle, a tool kit is usually included. It contains most of the items required for routine maintenance and partial overhaul.

TIRE MAINTENANCE

Modern bicycle tires are classified into two broad groups: conventional clincher "wired-on" tires and tubular tires.

The *clincher tires* are similar to automobile tires used prior to the introduction of modern tubeless tires. The tire is open on the inside next to the rim and two wire "beads," one on each side, are embedded in the rubber lip; they bear against the wheel rim to hold (clinch) the tire in place after the inner tube is inflated.

Clincher tires are used on children's bicycles and less-expensive adult machines for almost all purposes except track and road racing. The clincher tire is easy to repair and has a strong defensive against punctures and other hazards found on city streets, because of the heavy construction of the tire and tube.

Tubular tires are sewn together on the inside next to the rim, completely encasing the inner tube within the tire. The tire is mounted to the wheel with a special cement to prevent it from "creeping" over the edge of the rim under the pressure of a high-speed turn. This type of tire and its tube is much lighter than the clincher type with weights for the complete unit ranging from a low of only 4 ounces to a high of 14 ounces. Therefore, they are used on all track and road racing bikes. In recent years the tubulars are gaining favor for extended touring, and trips of several thousand miles have been made by careful riders.

Tubulars are not practical for average riding on city streets, because the tire and tube are almost paper-thin, which means they are much more vulnerable to punctures and other road hazard damages.

In addition to its light weight, another advantage of the tubular tire is the fact that it can be folded and

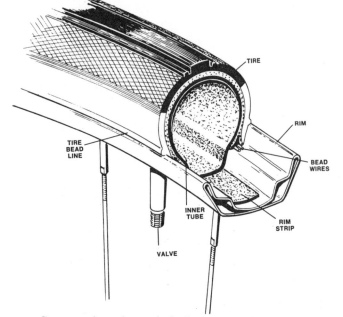

Cutaway view of a typical clincher-type tire, showing the principal parts of the tire and rim.

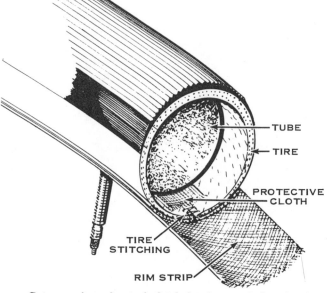

Cutaway view of a typical tubular (sewn-up) tire, showing the principal parts of the tire and tube.

carried under the seat as a spare. However, because it is difficult to repair but can be quickly changed, the spare is usually mounted and the patching work performed at a later, more convenient time. The repaired tire is then carried as a spare.

Clincher-type and tubular tires cannot be interchanged on the same rim. Each must be used only on a wheel designed for its specific use. For this reason, many serious cyclists have two sets of wheels and tires, one set for the clincher tires used for normal riding and the other with tubular tires mounted for racing or extended touring.

The type and design of tire treads for bicycles is as varied as for the automobile. A wide range of patterns is available to meet the preference of the individual rider and the purpose for which he intends to use his bike.

Thorn-resistant tubes are available for riding through areas that abound in cactus vegetation. These plants lose their thorns which are blown onto the roadway, where they lie in wait for the cyclist, ready to do their dirty work. One defense against such an attack is to install a device commonly called a "thorn puller" in the Southwestern United States or a "nail puller" in other areas. This is a very lightweight device (approximately ½ ounce) attached to the pivot bolt of the caliper brake assembly on the side opposite the brakes.

The puller actually rides on the tire and, if a thorn or nail is picked up, it will scrape it off during the next revolution of the wheel to prevent puncture of the tire.

INFLATION

One of the most common causes of tire failure, and the one that the rider can control, is maintaining the correct pressure for varying conditions. Riding a bicycle with the tire pressure too low will cause the tire to buckle under the load, putting an added strain on the sidewalls. If the situation is not corrected, a star-shaped wound or rim cut in the sidewall will result, and the tire will have to be replaced along with the tube. An underinflated tire will also force the casing inward until it pinches the tube against the wheel rim or causes the inner tube to shift and tear the valve stem, ruining the tube. Riding a bicycle with underinflated tires or overloading it can cause a blowout.

Overinflation is one of the most common causes of blowouts and usually occurs at the neighborhood service station. If the tire pressure is low and the rider feels he can make it to the station, he may then attach an air hose with 200 psi (pounds per square inch) pressure. If he squeezes the trigger, the tire will be blown apart. For this reason, service station air supplies should be avoided whenever possible, and the tire pumped up with a hand pump. If service station air

Maximum strain is placed on a tire and wheel when cornering during a criterium race on city streets. Seconds after this picture was taken, a rear tubular tire rolled off the rim as a rider crossed the railroad tracks, resulting in nasty skin burns to his arms and legs. Proper inflation and careful attention to maintenance, especially cementing of tubulars to the rim, cannot be overemphasized.

supplies must be used, attach and inflate the tire for only a second at a time, and then check the firmness of the tire with your thumb and forefinger. If a selector valve is available on the hose, the problem is minimized because the desired pressure can be preselected and the possibility of a blowout is greatly reduced, provided the valve is functioning properly.

The best guarantee of maintaining the correct tire pressure is to have your own pocket gauge and tire pump available. Due to the porosity of tubular tires, the air will seep through the walls of the tube and tire. Tubulars must be brought up to the proper pressure at regular intervals.

Bear in mind that heated air expands. If you are touring and you have checked your tires in the cool of the morning, it may be necessary to relieve about 5 to 10 psi during the course of the day's riding to prevent overinflating and possible damage. Constant vigilance on a long trip will reward you with an easier ride and less time spent on tire and tube repair.

If you plan to ship your bicycle by air as freight or baggage, be sure to deflate the tires to half-pressure to prevent possible blowout, because the bike is usually carried in an unpressurized compartment.

Tubular tires and some clincher-type foreign tires are equipped with a Presta or Woods Continental-type valve. In order to use a service station air supply, an adapter is required that screws onto the valve stem. The Presta valve is not a spring-loaded type, such as used on American-type tires, but it must be rotated counterclockwise to open it prior to inflating, and then rotated clockwise to close it after the desired pressure is reached. If you use a press-on-type bicycle pump, you do not need an adapter, but you must push it on quickly and remove it fast, using a quick rap with a clinched fist to prevent leakage.

Most tires have the recommended inflation pressure embossed on the side wall. If the tire is not so marked or it is illegible, the following chart can be used

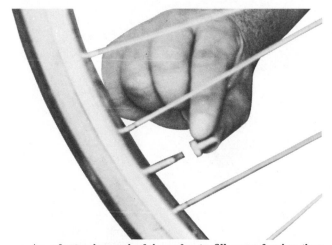

An adapter is required in order to fill some foreign tires with American air pumps. Open the valve stem of the tire, thread the adapter onto the stem, inflate the tire, remove the adapter, and then close the valve stem. The adapter may be threaded onto the mounting stud of the front derailleur, where it can be safely carried and ready for instant use.

INFLATION CHART

Tire Size	Pressure (Psi)
Clincher tires	
12 x 1⅜	30–40
16 x 1⅜	35–45
16 x 1¾	40–45
18 x 1⅜	35–45
20 x 1⅜	55–60
20 x 1¾	40–45
20 x 2.125	30–35
24 x 1¾	40–45
26 x 1¼	45–50
26 x 1⅜	55–60
26 x 1¾	40–45
26 x 2.125	35–45
27 x 1⅛	90–100
27 x 1¼	70–75
Tubular tires	
27 x 1	
Track—smooth surface	
Front tire	80–110
Rear tire	90–120
Road–uneven to rough surface	
Front tire	70–90
Rear tire	75–100
Touring	
Front tire	85–100
Rear tire	75–90

as a guide for minimum pressures to be used for the tire sizes indicated. If the tire bulges noticeably, due to an above-average load, its life can be extended by adding approximately 5 psi to the amount listed.

If you plan to do extended touring or to ride in remote areas, it is a good idea to carry tube repair materials with you. For bicycles equipped with clincher-type tires, a repair kit or a spare tube can be carried with very little additional weight. A spare tubular tire can be folded and carried under the seat for quick and easy access. If you carry a spare tubular tire, be sure to refold it every few days to prevent a set from developing at the fold. Fold the tire with the tread on the outside and the valve stem positioned at one end of a fold so it does not chafe against the tire.

TYPES OF TIRE DAMAGE

Blowouts are most often caused by overinflation. Many times this happens at a service station when attempting to bring the tire up to pressure. Blowouts can also be caused by the tire not being evenly seated on the rim. As the tire is inflated the bead is forced over the rim, causing part of the tube to escape and to blow out. Overloading a bicycle with underinflated tires may also result in a blowout.

Ruptures are usually caused by running over sharp

objects, jumping curbs, or riding over a rough hole in pavement or concrete.

Star breaks result from running over pointed objects, such as rocks or pieces of metal and are difficult to detect from the outside of the tire. Therefore, if the cause of the flat is not readily determined, inspect the inside carefully for this type of damage.

Rim cuts are identified by an actual cut in the rim of the tire and may result from overloading the bicycle, a rusty rim, or underinflating the tire.

Broken beads can almost always be traced to the use of improper tools when mounting the tire. To prevent breaking a bead, use only your hands or a smooth, rounded tool when working the tire onto the rim. Never use a screwdriver or other pointed tool.

Rim bruises may be the result of running into a curb; jumping over a curb; running into rocks, holes, or other objects with the tire underinflated.

Chafing on the side of the tire may be caused by a crooked wheel, misalignment of the wheel in the frame, or a generator roller that is not properly positioned.

Uneven tread wear may be the result of a crooked wheel, brakes that grab or lock when applied, or by the rider making skidding stops.

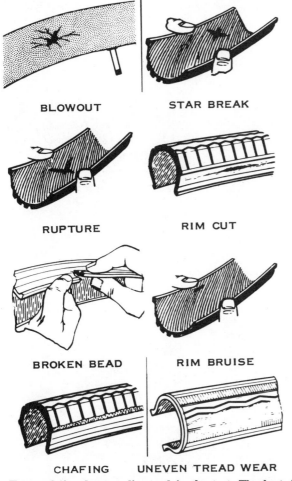

BLOWOUT   STAR BREAK

RUPTURE   RIM CUT

BROKEN BEAD   RIM BRUISE

CHAFING   UNEVEN TREAD WEAR

Types of tire damage discussed in the text. The best defense against tire injury is careful riding with a sharp eye for road hazards.

CLINCHER TIRE REPAIR

If the cause of the flat is easily recognized, such as a nail, thorn, or piece of broken glass, the tube can be repaired without removing the wheel from the bicycle. Mark the damaged area of the tire with a piece of chalk or crayon, and then work one side of the tire off the wheel using a pair of tire levers (as shown in the accompanying illustration). Do not use a screwdriver or pointed tool. Tire levers cost less than 50 cents and you need only two. One lever can be hooked on an adjacent spoke while the other lever is being used to pry the head off the rim. Pull the tube from the tire in the area of your chalk mark on the tire, and the puncture can usually be located. Mark the spot and you are ready to make a repair.

If the cause of the flat cannot be determined from an inspection of the exterior of the tire, the wheel will have to be removed from the bicycle and then the tube completely removed from the tire. Work one side of the tire from the rim using the tire levers. Start on the opposite side of the wheel from the valve. After one side of the tire is off the rim, pull the tube out of the tire. **CAUTION: Be careful when removing the tire from the rim not to break the bead or to pinch the tube, causing further damage.** Remove the other side of the tire from the rim, and then pull off the rim strip. Check the spoke heads and file smooth any protrusion that might damage the tube.

Inflate the tube slightly, and then immerse it in a container of water. Move the tube slowly through the water and watch for bubbles, indicating the leak. When the source of the escaping air is discovered, dry the tube and mark the hole with a piece of chalk or crayon.

An inexpensive hot-patch kit (about $1.00 for the clamp and three patches) will make a more uniform repair job, because the patch rubber will be vulcanized with the rubber of the tube and the edges blended smoothly. The kit is more bulky and heavier than the cold-type kit, but it can be used for repair work at home.

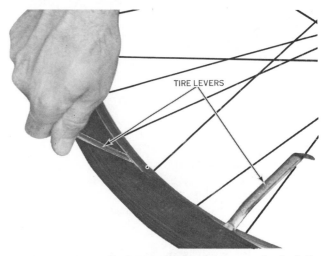

TIRE LEVERS

To remove a clincher-type tire, always use standard tire levers. They cost less than 50 cents and you need only two. CAUTION: Never use sharp tools such as a screwdriver, to prevent damaging the tire or tube. Notice how one tool is hooked onto a spoke while the other tire lever is being worked.

MAKING A HOT-PATCH REPAIR

① Roughen an area around the injury slightly larger than the size of the patch, using a pocket knife or similar tool. If the damage to the tube is a large hole or tear, fill in the opening with a piece of rubber cut from one of the patches. Carefully remove the cloth backing from the rubber. **CAUTION: Do not touch the rubber with your fingers.** Center the patch over the injury. Place the plate of the clamp under the tube and turn the handle clockwise until the holder is firm on the heat container.

② Pry up a corner of the fuel, light it, and allow all of it to burn. Leave the clamp in position for five minutes until the fuel container is cold. **CAUTION: The container is hot, so don't touch it.**

③ Remove the clamp and carefully peel the tube away from the container.

MAKING A COLD-PATCH REPAIR

④ Roughen the area around the puncture using the cap of the repair kit. Work an area slightly larger than the size of the patch you intend to use.

⑤ Apply an even coating of cement onto the tube and allow it to dry until it is tacky.

⑥ Separate the backing from the patch and place the center over the hole, with the adhesive side facing down. Hold the patch firmly in place for a short time to allow the cement to set, and then sprinkle some talcum powder over the patch to prevent it from sticking to the tire.

INSTALLING A CLINCHER TIRE AND TUBE

⑦ Stretch the rim strip around the rim, starting at the valve stem hole. Be sure the strip is the correct width. It must not be wide enough to cover any portion of the bead part of the rim.

⑧ Inflate the tube just enough to hold its shape, and then insert it into the tire. Feed the valve through the hole in the rim strip and wheel rim. Position both sides of the tire bead into the wheel rim in the area of the valve.

⑨ Use your hands and thumbs to work both beads of the tire onto the rim in both directions, working evenly away from the valve. If you have difficulty working both sides of the tire onto the wheel at the same time, do one side and then work the other

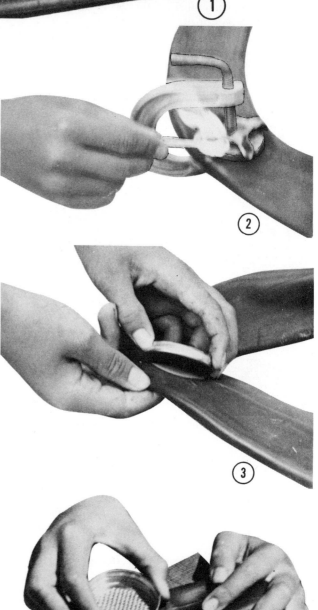

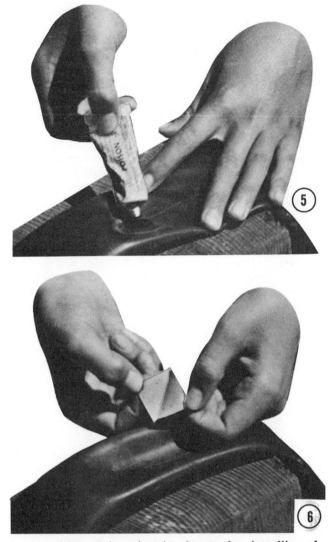

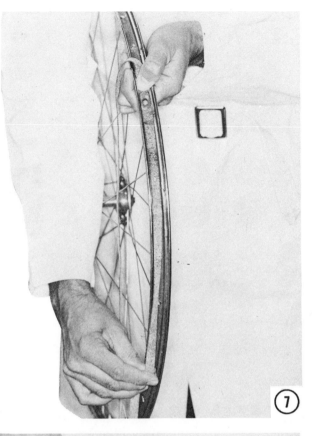

into position, using the tire levers for installing the final portion. **CAUTION: Be careful not to pinch the tube.** Inflate the tire partly and check to be sure the bead is properly positioned in the rim and that the valve stem is straight. Install the valve stem nut to hold the stem in place. Inflate the tire to the specified pressure and install the wheel on the bicycle.

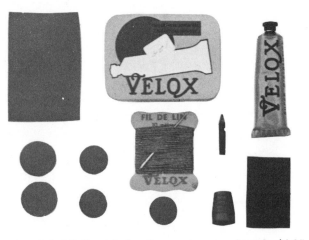

A repair kit for tubular tires costs approximately $1.25 and contains all the items needed to make about a dozen repairs, as explained in the text.

MAKING A TUBULAR TIRE REPAIR

Special materials are needed to repair a tubular tire and they can be purchased in kit form for about $1.25. The kit includes very thin patches, plus a large piece to enable you to cut one to your own size, waxed linen thread, a needle, a thimble, some fine sandpaper, a tube of rubber cement, and a small colored marking pencil. The quantity of items is enough to make about a dozen repairs. In addition to the kit, you will need a sharp knife or single-edged razor blade and some talcum powder. **CAUTION: Do not attempt to repair a tubular tire with a regular bicycle patch, because the patch material is too thick and will cause a lump inside the tire, which will thump each time the tire rotates.**

Remove the wheel and damaged tire from the bicycle. If the tire is not mounted, install it on an old rim if you have one handy. If not, you will have to work with just the tire. Inflate the tire to approximately 60 psi, and then slowly rotate it in a container of water; watch for air bubbles. You may notice air seeping from around the valve stem for a short time. This is normal, because the tire has a rubber strip cemented over the sewing in the area of the valve and this is the only place trapped air can escape except from an injury. When you locate the puncture, mark the spot with the colored pencil from the kit or a piece of chalk. Remove the valve nut and deflate the tire. Remove the tire from the rim by working it off with your hands and thumbs, starting on the side of the wheel opposite the valve. **CAUTION: Do not use any type of tool in order to prevent possible damage to the tire or the tube.**

If tape is used on the rim, be careful not to wrinkle or pull it loose from the rim unless you intend to remove it for inspection or work on the spoke heads.

① Carefully peel back five inches of the rim strip from the tire on both sides of the puncture. Make a couple of marks across the stitching with the pencil. This will ensure that the original holes are used during the restitching so the tire will retain its proper shape. Fold the tire at the stitching, and then carefully cut about 2 inches of the stitching on both sides of the injury, using a single-edged razor blade or sharp knife. Work cautiously to prevent cutting the tire cords or the tube. Remove the old thread.

② Push back the protective cloth and pull out about 6 to 8 inches of the tube. Inflate the tube slightly

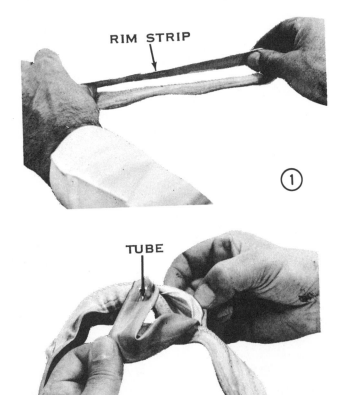

RIM STRIP

①

TUBE

②

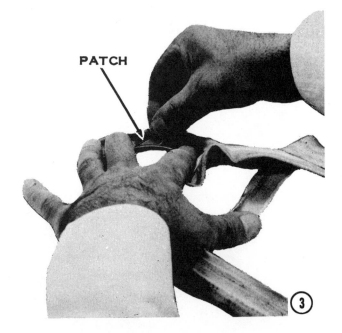

PATCH

③

with a hand pump and locate the puncture by holding the tube close to your face and feeling for escaping air. Or wet the area with soapy water, and then watch for bubbles. Dry the tube thoroughly and mark the hole plainly with a colored pencil or piece of chalk.

③ Deflate the tube and stretch it out on a flat surface until it is free of wrinkles. Roughen the area around the injury with a piece of sandpaper. Be careful not to let any dust or dirt enter the tire casing. Work an area slightly larger than the size of the patch you intend to use. Cover the buffed area with a smooth coating of cement and allow it to dry until it has a hard glaze. Remove the backing from the patch, and then place the center of the patch over the hole, with the adhesive side facing down. Hold the patch firmly in place for a short time to allow the cement to set. Sprinkle some talcum powder over the patch to prevent it from sticking to the tire. *NOTE: If the tire casing has a small fracture, apply a canvas or regular patch on the inside of the tire following the same procedure used for patching the tube. However, if you do patch the casing, the tire should only be used for a spare, because it has lost considerable strength.*

④ Place the protective cloth over the tube and smooth it free of wrinkles. Fold the tire at the stitching and align the pencil marks you made before cutting the tire open. This will ensure that the old holes are aligned and that the tire will retain its proper shape. Thread the needle with the waxed linen thread from the kit and begin stitching the tire, starting a few stitches back from the cut. Make the first few stitches over the end of the thread to prevent having to make a knot for the thread to hold. **CAUTION: Be extremely careful during the sewing operation to ensure tha the holes on both sides of the tire are aligned, and that the tube is not punctured with the needle. Pull the thread up snug, but not so tight that the thread cuts into the casing.** Place the end of the thread under the last few stitches, and then pull the stitches taut. This is a sailmaker's method and eliminates the necessity of knotting the thread at the end of the job.

⑤ Apply a thin coating of rubber cement to the rim strip and to the tire over the repaired area; and let it dry for a few minutes. Position the rim strip onto the tire evenly and without wrinkles.

INSTALLING A TUBULAR TIRE

⑥ Check all the spoke heads to be sure they do not protrude to cause tire damage. If any of the heads do extend above the rim, file them smooth. Remove any old tape that is wrinkled, dirty, or if you suspect it will not hold the tire properly. If cement is used instead of tape and it is dirty, flaky, or does not appear to be in good condition, clean the rim thoroughly with solvent. It is not good practice to apply new cement over the old because a buildup will result in bulged areas on the rim. Apply new rim tape by starting about eight inches from the valve hole and setting it evenly in the rim channel. The tape is a double-coated type, with adhesive material on both sides. Pull the tape firmly around the rim and overlap the starting end by approxi-

mately two inches. Press the tape firmly into the rim channel, with the handle of a wrench or other rounded object. If cement is used instead of the rim tape, apply several even coats and allow each to dry for thirty minutes, or until it is just tacky before applying the next.

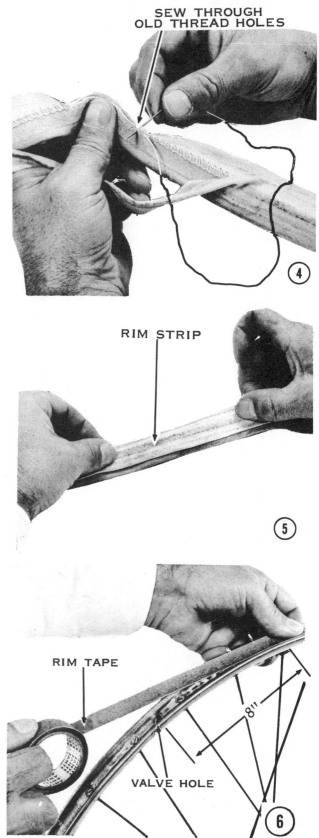

SEW THROUGH OLD THREAD HOLES

④

RIM STRIP

⑤

RIM TAPE

8"

VALVE HOLE

⑥

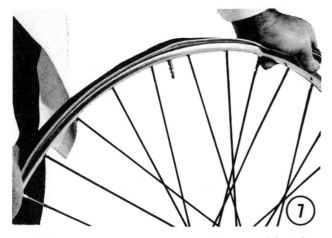

⑦ Cut a valve stem hole in the tape with a sharp knife or single-edged razor blade. As an aid to removing the tire to repair the next puncture, apply a thin strip of paper, the width of the tape and about two inches long, on the tape or cement opposite the valve hole. Moisten the tape or cement with just a trace of water on your finger. The dampness will allow the tire to be shifted more easily into position. Deflate the tire completely or until there is just enough air to give it a little shape. Place the valve stem through the hole in the rim, with the wheel in an upright position, as shown. Position the tire in place on the rim by working it on with your hands and moving it in both directions from the valve.

⑧ As you reach the opposite side of the rim from the valve, lift the wheel clear of the ground and work the last section on with your thumbs. Use a roll-on motion, but do not use a tool when mounting tubular tires. Inflate the tire slightly and work it around to lay properly on the rim. Inflate the tire to the recommended pressure and tighten the valve nut. Spin the wheel and check to be sure the tire is aligned properly on the rim and running true. If it is not turning true, deflate the tire, smooth out the high and low spots with your hands, inflate the tire, and then recheck it for running true. Clean any excess cement from the rim and tire with alcohol. If cement was used instead of the rim tape, allow the wheel to set for several hours, preferably overnight, before riding on it.

CHAIN MAINTENANCE AND REPAIR

Bicycle chains are classified as wide, for use on single-speed or multispeed internally geared rear hubs, and narrow for use on derailleur and single-speed track racing bicycles. The wide type is available in various lengths to meet all requirements. Narrow-type chains are sold in limited lengths, but links can be added or removed to obtain the desired length. The wide-type with the master link cannot be used on a derailleur bicycle, because the extra width plus the master link will not pass through the cage of the derailleur, and the distance between the sprockets of the cluster is not sufficient to permit the chain to make a complete rotation without binding.

Two terms are used when referring to the chain: the pitch, which is the distance between the centers of the rivets; and the width, which is the length of the rollers (not the rivets). Wide chains usually have a ½-inch pitch and the roller length is ⅛ inch. The narrow chains also have ½-inch pitch, but are ³⁄₃₂-inch. wide and carry a metric measurement instead of the inch unit, such as 12.7 mm pitch by 2.38 mm length.

CHAIN REMOVAL AND INSTALLATION— DERAILLEUR TYPE BICYCLES

To remove the chain from a derailleur-equipped bicycle, a riveter extractor is required. This handy little tool can be purchased at any bike shop for less than $3 complete with an extra punch.

Back out the punch by turning the tool handle counterclockwise, and then lay any one of the links of the chain over the flanges, with the rivet aligned with the punch. Push the rivet almost all the way out by turning the handle clockwise, but leave approximately ¹⁄₃₂ inch of the rivet holding the chain roller. One method of gauging how far to push the rivet out is to count six complete turns of the handle once the punch is firmly against the rivet. Back out the punch, and then remove the tool.

Hold the chain on both sides of the extended rivet, and then bend the chain slightly to unhook it from the rivet, as shown in the accompanying illustration. Remove the chain from the chain wheel and rear derailleur unit.

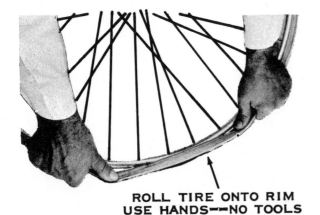

**ROLL TIRE ONTO RIM
USE HANDS—NO TOOLS**

⑧

A rivet-extractor tool, complete with an extra punch, can be purchased at any bike shop for under $3.

To install the chain, feed the end with the extended rivet around the chain wheel, with the rivet facing out (away from the bicycle) to make the extractor tool easier to use. Feed the other end of the chain around the rear sprocket cluster and through the derailleur cage. Bring the two ends together in the tool, and then push the rivet through by turning the handle clockwise.

If the rivet was accidentally pushed out of the side plate during removal, place the roller link of the chain between the side plates, with the chain lying on its side on a flat surface. Hold the rivet in position with a pair of needle-nosed pliers and, at the same time, tap the rivet into the side plate until it extends approximately $\frac{1}{32}$ inch past the inside of the plate. Continue to install the chain in the normal manner as described above.

CHAIN REMOVAL AND INSTALLATION— NON-DERAILLEUR-TYPE BICYCLES

To remove the chain from a single-speed or multi-speed, internally geared, rear-hub bicycle, first loosen the axle nuts at the rear wheel and then move the wheel forward slightly to obtain slack in the chain.

Locate the master link of the chain. This link can be identified by a wide link plate or by a U-shaped plate that fits between the roller. Move the U-shaped link to one side or pry the plate off using a screwdriver. Remove the chain from the chain wheel and rear sprocket.

To install the chain, place it over the chain wheel and then turn the crank to allow the chain to drop between the sprocket and the chain guard. Feed the other end of the chain around the rear sprocket.

Place the master link into the chain rollers on each end of the chain. Position the side plate onto the master link rivet. Hold the chain on each side of the master link, and then bend the chain toward the side plate until the side plate snaps onto the other rivet.

Lay a straightedge on the upper portion of the chain, between the chain wheel and the rear sprocket, and then measure the amount of sag at the midway point. Shift the rear wheel in the dropouts until the chain has about $\frac{3}{8}$ to $\frac{1}{2}$ inch of slack, center the wheel between the frame members, and then tighten the axle nuts securely.

CLEANING AND LUBRICATING

A dirty and/or slightly rusted chain can be restored by first removing it from the bicycle, soaking it in solvent, and then working on the rusted area with a stiff wire brush. Hang the chain to dry thoroughly, and then check each and every link for free movement. A link that is stiff due to a bent side plate should be replaced. If the side plates are not bent, but the link is too stiff, apply a liberal amount of penetrating oil or liquid wrench, and then work the link back and forth to loosen it. Another method to free up a stiff link is to place it in the extractor tool, and then rotate the handle about $\frac{1}{3}$ turn to free the rivet. Shift the extractor to the other side and move the rivet back until it is equidistant from the plates on both sides. The chain should be replaced if the links are rusted so badly that they cannot be made

A rivet-extractor tool is used to disconnect the chain on derailleur-equipped bicycles. Count six complete turns of the handle to push the rivet to within 1/32 inch of being completely free of the link.

to flex properly as the chain moves around the sprocket and chain wheel.

After the chain has been cleaned and dried, soak it in a pan of mediumweight oil, and then hang it up to drip dry, preferably overnight.

Following a trip in the rain or through water, wipe the chain dry and apply a coating of penetrating oil; work it into the joints of the chain to force out the

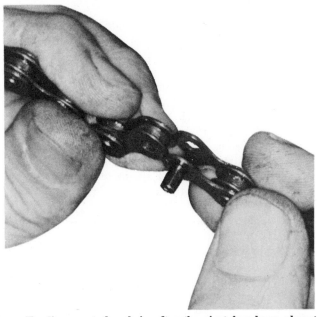

To disconnect the chain after the rivet has been almost pushed out, bend the chain slightly and unhook it from the rivet.

moisture. Wipe the chain again and apply a coating of mediumweight oil or dry lube. Several brands of lube are available in spray can form. Each contains a liquid that carries the lubricating agent to the inner bearing surfaces of the chain and then evaporates, leaving only the dry lubricant.

New chains are lubricated at the time of manufacture, and the package is sealed to protect the chain prior to installation. Too much lubrication on the chain is harmful because foreign material is quickly picked up; it sticks to the chain causing added wear. Therefore, always wipe off excess lubricant from the surface of a new chain before you install it.

REPLACING A LINK

A defective link can easily be replaced by pushing out the rivet at both ends of the link using the extractor tool. Be careful and do not push the rivet completely out of the side plate. Count six complete turns of the extractor handle after the punch has made contact with the rivet. Bend the chain, and then remove the link from both rivets.

Place one end of the chain in the extractor with the extended rivet facing toward the punch. Insert a new link in position and push one of the rivets through by turning the handle clockwise. Install the chain onto the bicycle, and then connect the other half of the link with the extractor tool in the normal manner.

ADJUSTING THE CHAIN LENGTH

Proper chain length is essential to the efficient operation of your bicycle. If the chain is too long and cannot be adjusted to remove excess slack, it may jump a tooth on the chain wheel or rear sprocket, causing unnecessary wear. If the condition is not corrected, the added wear may require replacing one of these expensive units. A chain that is too tight even when adjusted to the full-slack position causes excessive wear on the chain, chain wheel, and rear sprockets. This makes it difficult to shift on derailleur bicycles, not to mention the added effort required for pedaling.

If you are installing a new chain on a non-derailleur-type bicycle, measure the old one, and then purchase the same size chain. For derailleur-type bicycles, buy and make the new chain the same length as the old one by removing links using the extractor tool. *NOTE: Be sure to cut the chain so that a roller link is on each end of the chain.*

The correct chain length for non-derailleur-type bicycles is to have between ⅜ to ½ inch slack at a point midway between the chain wheel and the rear sprocket, when the rear axle is positioned about midway in the rear dropouts.

The proper chain length for derailleur-type bicycles can be determined as follows: Place the chain on the largest chain wheel at the hanger set and on the largest sprocket of the rear cluster. Rotate the derailleur cage assembly until it is approximately horizontal, and then pull up on the chain at the chain wheel. There should be about ½ to 1 full link of extra chain, when the chain is pulled taut.

ADJUSTING THE CHAIN TENSION

On derailleur-equipped bicycles, it is best to have the least amount of tension on the chain as possible to reduce friction and wear. However, there should be some chain tension when the chain is on the smallest chain wheel and the smallest sprocket of the cluster. The method of adjusting chain tension depends on the type of derailleur used. (See Chapter 7 for detailed instructions on rear derailleurs.)

For Sprint, Huret-Alvit, Huret Svelto, Schwinn-Approved, Shimano 3.3.3, Shimano Lark, and Sun Tour.

The outside face of the pulley cage of the derailleur unit has cast lips for the tension spring hook. Shift the spring hook to the lip counterclockwise to increase tension on the chain and clockwise to decrease tension.

For Campagnolo Record, Campagnolo Gran Sport, Campagnolo Nuovo Record, and Simplex Prestige.

Remove the tension pulley spindle nut, spindle, pulley, and chain from the derailleur. Rotate the cage assembly slightly to relieve pressure on the stop stud, and then remove the stud. Allow the cage to unwind until all tension on the pulley cage spring is released.

Next, remove the pulley cage spindle, using the correct size Allen wrench. Disengage the pulley cage assembly from the spring and note which hole of the cage was used. Engage the spring leg in the next hole counterclockwise, and then reinstall the pulley cage spindle. *NOTE: Prior to installing the spindle, it will be necessary to shift the shim between the spring cap and the cage so that the hole in the shim will align with the next hole in the cage to be used.*

Insert the pulley spindle through the traversing arm body, and then thread it into the cage assembly. Tighten the spindle securely, using an Allen wrench. The shoulder on the spindle will "bottom out" and thus prevent you from tightening it too much or from stripping the threads.

Rotate the pulley cage assembly one full turn counterclockwise. Hold the pulley cage with tension on the spring to keep the hole for the stop stud clear of the traversing arm body. Thread the stop stud into place securely, and then let the cage spring back until the stop stud bears against the body.

Place the chain in position, and then install the tension pulley, spindle, and spindle nut. Lift the chain clear of the tension pulley and check the pulley for freedom of rotation without side play. If an adjustment is required, loosen the spindle slightly, tighten or loosen the cone of the pulley, and then retighten the spindle.

For Shimano Sun Tour GT

Loosen the spindle nut of the tension pulley slightly, and then rotate the inner arm of the cage assembly; remove the chain. Rotate the derailleur cage assembly slightly to relieve pressure on the stop stud, and then remove the stud. Allow the cage assembly to unwind until all tension on the spring is released.

Remove the pulley cage spindle cap, using the correct size Allen wrench. Partly withdraw the pulley cage and spindle assembly from the traversing arm body, rotate the cage clockwise to increase tension and counterclockwise to release tension, and then insert the spindle back into the body, with the spring leg indexed in one of the slots of the spindle.

Thread the pulley cage spindle cap into the spindle with an Allen wrench, until the outer surface is flush with the edge of the traversing arm body. If you cannot tighten the cap until it is flush, back it out, and then position the short leg of the spring into the nearest slot in the end of the spindle. *NOTE: The cap will not seat*

properly unless the spring leg is correctly seated in one of the spindle slots.

Rotate the pulley cage assembly one-half turn counterclockwise. Hold the cage in this position, and then thread the stop stud into the cage until the shoulder of the stud "bottoms out" against the inside face of the cage. Allow the cage to move back until the stop stud contacts the shoulder on the traversing arm body.

Place the chain in position on the tension pulley, rotate the inner arm of the cage assembly until the hook end is in position under the tension pulley nut, and then tighten the nut securely.

The escort of a modern miss explains the importance of proper chain tension to the efficient operation of the front and rear derailleur units. He will probably advise her that having the handlebars in the turned-up position invalidates the warranty of most manufacturers, places added strain on the brake cables and levers, and is not considered safe practice. However, the young set (almost always the girls) seem to prefer the bars up rather than down, even though they have to pedal harder and use much more energy because of poor riding posture. Don Sweetman Photo

CABLE AND LEVER MAINTENANCE

Brake and shifting cable lubrication and replacement should be given careful attention in order to maintain your bicycle in a safe and operable condition. As soon as a cable shows evidence of damage or fraying, it should be replaced, particularly the brake cables, to ensure your ability to stop in an emergency.

BRAKE CABLES

The procedures that follow for cables of all types of tourist and hooded lever-type brakes are essentially the same.

REMOVING BRAKE CABLES

To remove a brake cable on either side-pull or center-pull caliper brakes, front or rear, first loosen the cable anchor bolt nut, and then pull the cable out of the anchor bolt and the lower housing. Next, squeeze the brake lever, pull the housing and ferrule back on the cable, push the cable-end button free of the retainer slot, and then pull the cable out of the upper housing-and-lever assembly.

Take your old cable along when purchasing a new one to ensure obtaining the same diameter, and that it will be long enough. If the only one available is too long, you can cut off the excess after the cable is installed and properly adjusted.

INSTALLING BRAKE CABLES

Before installing the new cable, apply a small coating of multipurpose lubricant in the areas of the cable where it is enclosed in the housing. Place a drop or two of high-quality cycle oil on the cable-end button. *NOTE: The front-wheel caliper brake cable should always be installed to the left-hand brake lever, and the rear-wheel cable to the right lever.*

Push the lubricated cable through the ferrule and the upper housing. Leave approximately six inches of the cable, with the button on it, exposed from the end of the housing. Insert the cable-end button through the ferrule hole in the bracket, and then place the button in the retainer slot at the inner side of the brake lever. Pull the cable taut, and then seat the ferrule in the bracket. Slide the cable housing up against the ferrule.

Feed the free end of the cable through the lower housing and cable anchor bolt. Squeeze the brake shoes against the wheel rim, using a "third hand" tool, or tighten a piece of cord around both arms and through the wheel. Pull the cable taut with a pair of pliers and simultaneously tighten the anchor nut. Remove the "third hand" tool or piece of cord. The brake shoes should release to about ⅛ inch from the rim.

If the brake shoes release more than ⅛ inch or do not move clear of the rim, make a final adjustment by turning the adjusting barrel. *NOTE: A new cable will*

To remove the brake cable on either side-pull or center-pull caliper brakes, first loosen the anchor bolt nut, and then pull the cable free of the anchor bolt.

At the brake-control lever, insert the cable-end button through the ferrule hole in the bracket, and then place the button in the retainer slot at the inner side of the brake lever.

stretch after it has been in use, therefore be sure to check the distance of the shoes from the rim periodically and make an adjustment, if necessary.

Cut off any excess cable, leaving about an inch beyond the anchor bolt, and then slide a plastic cap over the end of the cable to prevent your being cut by the sharp end.

SHIFT-CONTROL CABLES

The following instructions are for removing, installing, and adjusting a new cable to frame- or stem-mounted shift controls. The procedures for these two types of controls are almost identical as can be seen in the two accompanying exploded views. The main difference is that the lever assembly does not have to be disassembled on the stem-mounted unit in order to replace the cable. Instead, the adjusting wing nut can be loosened.

Separate procedures are included for the fingertip controls installed in the end of the handlebars.

On bicycles equipped with front and rear derailleur units, the right-side lever must always control the rear derailleur and the left-side lever the front derailleur.

Several methods are used to mount the control cables on the frame. A solid cable housing may be used, extending from the control to the derailleur unit, held in place by one or more cable clips. Another method is to have a split housing and the fittings either welded

to the frame or clamped with mounting screws.

Be sure to take your old cable with you when purchasing a new one to ensure your getting the same diameter and that the new cable will be long enough.

REMOVING A FRAME = OR STEM-MOUNTED LEVER CONTROL CABLE

Rear derailleur control cable. Turn the pedals and shift the chain onto the smallest sprocket of the rear cluster and the smallest chain wheel. Move the control lever to the full-forward position. Next, remove the plastic end cap, loosen the cable anchor bolt nut at the rear derailleur, and then pull the cable and housing out of the anchor bolt and adjusting barrel. Slide the cable housing off the cable and the cable out of the fulcrum on the frame. Pull the cable out of the housing and the clips at the hanger set.

For frame-mounted control units, remove the adjusting wing screw at the control lever, and then remove the pressure plate, dished tension cup, cable stop, and lever from the lever stud, as shown in the accompanying exploded drawing. Remove the cable-end button from the lever.

For stem-mounted control units, loosen the adjusting wing screw, and then pull the cable out through the back side of the lever.

After feeding the cable through the housings and anchor bolt, clamp the brake shoes with a "third-hand" tool, pull the cable taut with a pair of pliers, and then tighten the anchor bolt nut.

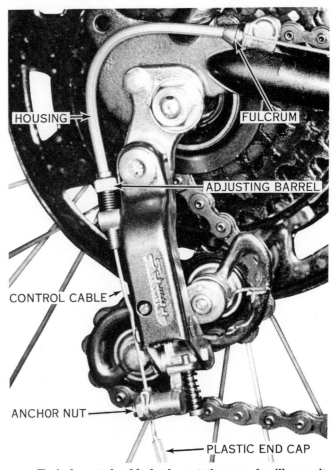

Typical control cable hookup at the rear derailleur unit, showing principal attaching points, as discussed in the text.

Front derailleur control cable. Loosen the cable anchor bolt nut, and then pull the cable out of the bolt and cable guide. Slide the cable housing off the cable and the cable out of the frame clip.

Remove the adjusting wing screw at the control lever, and then remove the pressure plate, dished tension cup, cable stop, and lever from the lever stud. Remove the cable-end button from the lever.

INSTALLING A FRAME- OR STEM-MOUNTED LEVER CONTROL CABLE

Before installing a new cable, apply a light coating of multipurpose lubricant in the areas where it is enclosed in the cable housing. Place a drop or two of high-quality cycle oil on the cable-end button.

For frame-mounted control levers, guide the cable-end button into the button hole in the control lever. Assemble the cable stop, tension cup, pressure plate, and wing screw in the order shown in the accompanying exploded drawing.

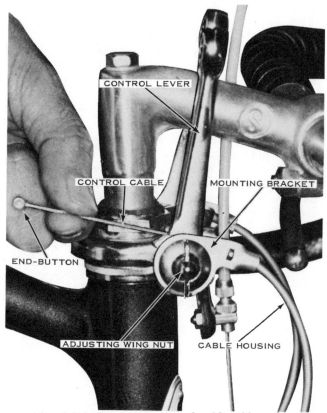

After lubricating a new control cable with multipurpose lubricant, feed the cable through the back side of the lever and through the mounting bracket hole. Seat the cable-end button in the lever hole.

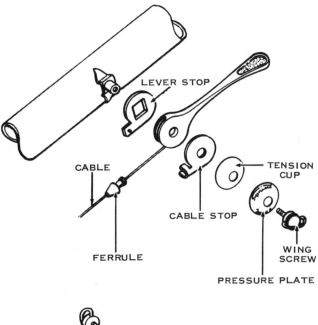

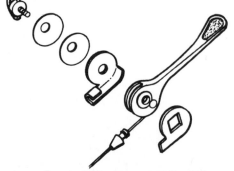

Exploded view of a typical stem-mounted, shift-control lever assembly. The control levers differ, left from right, and can be identified by holding the lever horizontally, with the cable slot facing you and the flat side of the lever facing left. For a right-side lever, the buttonhole should be at the bottom of the lever.

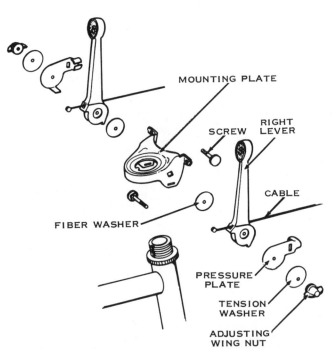

Exploded view of a typical stem-mounted, shift control lever assembly. The controls levers are interchangeable, right and left sides, but the hole for the control cable must always face to the rear.

At the rear derailleur, slide the cable through the adjusting barrel and anchor bolt, and then pull it taut with a pair of pliers. The housing should be fully seated in the fulcrum and adjusting barrel. Tighten the anchor bolt nut and cut off all cable that extends one inch beyond the anchor nut.

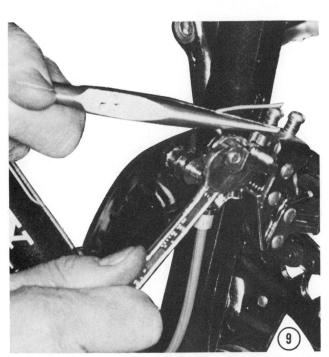

At the front derailleur, guide the cable into the cable guide and anchor bolt. Draw the cable taut and be sure the cable housing is seated properly. Tighten the anchor bolt nut securely and cut off all excess cable, leaving about one inch beyond the anchor nut.

For stem-mounted control levers, feed the lubricated cable through the back side of the lever and through the mounting bracket hole. Seat the cable-end button in the lever hole. Slide the cable through the housing and clips to the derailleur.

At the rear derailleur, position the chain onto the smallest sprocket at the rear cluster and the control lever in the full-forward position. Turn the cable-adjusting barrel down as far as it will go. Slide the cable through the barrel and the cable anchor bolt. Pull the cable taut with a pair of pliers. Check to be sure the housing is properly seated in the fulcrum and adjusting barrel. Tighten the anchor bolt nut. Cut off any excess cable, leaving approximately one inch beyond the anchor bolt. Slip a plastic cap over the end of the cable to cover the sharp exposed end.

At the front derailleur, position the chain onto the smallest chain wheel and the control lever as far forward as possible. Guide the cable into the cable guide and anchor bolt. Draw the cable taut and be sure the cable housing is seated properly. Tighten the anchor bolt nut securely. Cut off any excess cable leaving approximately one inch beyond the anchor bolt, and then slide a plastic cap over the end of the cable to cover the sharp end.

Check the tension adjustment on the control lever; tighten the wing nut just enough to prevent the chain

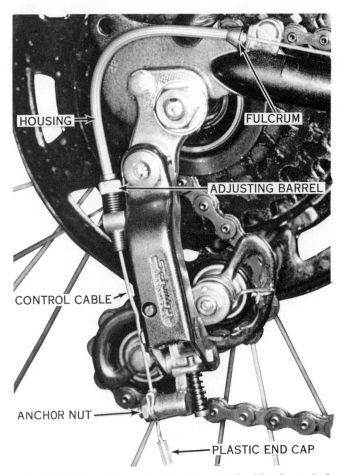

Principal attaching points for the control cable of a typical rear derailleur unit.

from shifting off the large sprockets while the pedals are being turned but are still loose enough to allow easy shifting. *NOTE: A new cable will stretch after it has been in use; therefore, as it lengthens, take up the slack by backing out the adjusting barrel.*

REMOVING FINGERTIP LEVER CONTROL CABLES

Procedures for replacing a control cable for the front or rear derailleur are essentially the same, except for the work at the derailleur unit and the adjustment. The rear derailleur control must always be connected to the right-hand lever and the front derailleur control to the left-hand lever.

For the rear derailleur control cable, place the control lever in the full-forward position, and then turn the pedals to allow the chain to shift onto the smallest sprocket of the cluster. Remove the cable from the cable anchor bolt and adjusting barrel. Slide the cable housing off the cable, and then remove the cable from the fulcrums or clips.

For the front derailleur control cable, loosen the cable anchor bolt, and then pull the cable out of the bolt and cable guide or housing.

NOTE: The remainder of the procedures apply to both front and rear derailleur control cables.

Remove the locknut from the handlebar control lever, using the correct size metric wrench, and then take out the lever screw. Push the lever bushing out of the mounting body, and then remove the lever and washers (on both sides of the lever) from the mounting body. Pull the cable out of the cable housing and the lever holes.

Typical front derailleur control-cable routing.

If the mounting body is to be removed in order to install new tape on the handlebars, insert the correct size Allen wrench in the hexagonal hole of the mounting body. Turn it clockwise until the body is loose, and then pull the body out of the handlebar, as indicated in the accompanying exploded view. Remove the handlebar tape and cable housing, if it needs to be replaced.

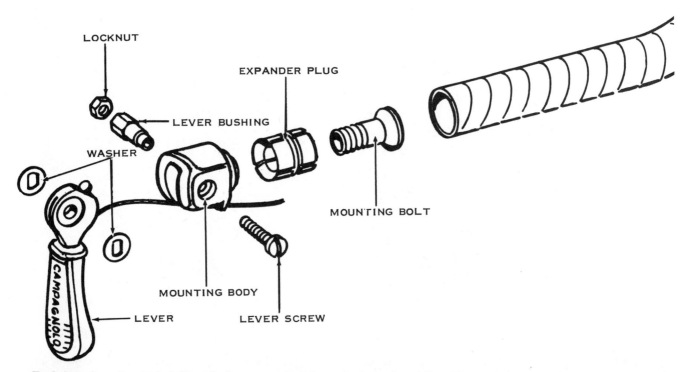

Exploded view of a typical fingertip lever control at the end of the handlebar. The parts are interchangeabie between the right-side rear derailleur control and the left-side front derailleur control.

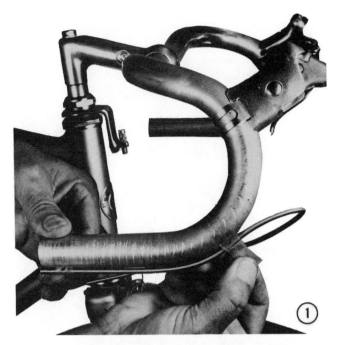

INSTALLING FINGERTIP CONTROL CABLES

① Position the end of the cable housing at the bottom of the handlebar and let it extend approximately ⅛ inch past the end of the bar. Secure the housing in place with a piece of tape.

② Tape the handlebar, beginning about two inches from the stem and overlapping each turn about ⅓ the width of the tape. Leave a couple of inches of tape beyond the end of the handlebar, cut off the excess, and then tuck the end of the tape inside the handlebar.

③ Insert the control body into the handlebar, with the slotted portion of the body facing down and the cable hole aligned with the cable housing. Secure the body in the handlebar by turning the mounting screw inside the body counterclockwise with the correct size Allen wrench.

④ Place a washer on each side of the lever, and then guide the lever into the mounting body, with the

lever key indexed with the keyway in the body. Install the mounting bushing into the mounting body, with the flats of the bushing aligned with the flats of the washers and the head fully seated in the hexagon hole in the body.

⑤ Thread the mounting screw into the body until the lever is snug, and then install and tighten the locknut.

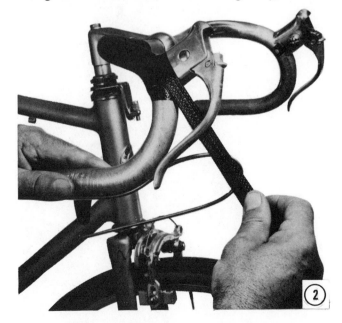

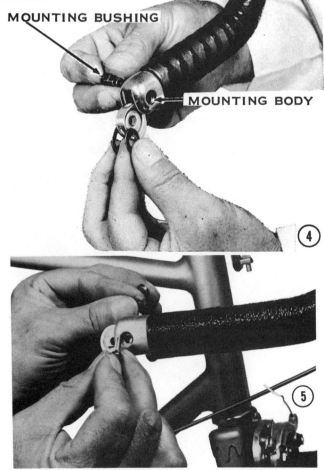

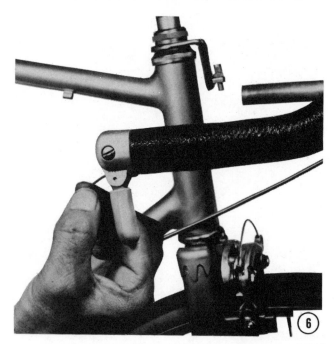

⑥ Apply a light coating of multipurpose lubricant to a new cable in the areas where it is enclosed within the cable housing. Place a couple of drops of high-quality cycle oil on the cable-end button. Place the lever in the down position, and then guide the cable through the lever hole, cable housings, clips, and/or fulcrums to the derailleur.

⑦ At the rear derailleur, position the chain onto the smallest sprocket of the cluster and the control lever in the full-down position. Turn the cable-adjusting barrel down as far as it will go. Slide the cable through the barrel and the cable anchor bolt. Pull the cable taut with a pair of pliers. Check to be sure the housing is properly seated in the fulcrum and the adjusting barrel. Tighten the anchor bolt nut. Cut off any excess cable, leaving about one inch beyond the anchor bolt. Slip a plastic cap over the end of the cable to cover the sharp exposed end.

⑧ Check the tension on the control lever as follows: Shift the chain onto the largest sprocket at the rear cluster, and then release the lever while continuing to pedal. If the chain shifts onto one of the smaller sprockets, loosen the locknut, tighten the pivot screw until the lever action is stiff enough to prevent the chain from moving off the largest sprocket, and then retighten the locknut.

⑨ At the front derailleur, position the chain onto the smallest chain wheel and the control lever in the down position. Draw the cable taut with the housing properly seated. Tighten the anchor nut securely. Cut off excess cable leaving approximately one inch beyond the anchor bolt, and then slide a plastic cap over the end of the cable to cover the sharp end.

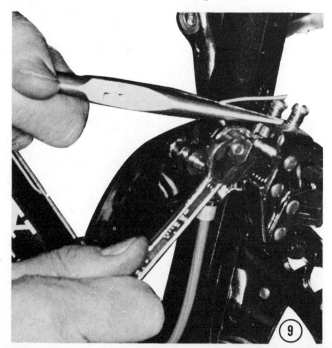

Check the tension adjustment on the control lever by shifting the chain onto the large chain wheel and continuing to turn the pedals. If the chain shifts onto the smaller sprocket when the lever is released, loosen the locknut and tighten the pivot screw until the lever is stiff enough to prevent the chain from moving off the largest chain wheel. Then retighten the locknut.

WHEEL MAINTENANCE

Each spoke of a bicycle wheel has an important role to perform toward the successful operation of the machine. It must carry an equal share of the load placed on the wheel by the rider and his gear in addition to doing its part in keeping the wheel true by preventing wobble or flat spots in the rim.

Spoke failure is commonly caused by a collision with another bicycle or the bike falling on an object in such a way as to bend or break some spokes. Rusted spokes will also fail at their weakest point, generally at the bend where it enters the hole in the hub. Foreign particles thrown into a moving wheel can quickly break one or several spokes. Jumping curbs, hitting a jagged hole in the pavement, or bad riding habits can place an added and sudden strain on the spokes, causing them to break.

On occasion, rear wheel spokes on the sprocket side will fail from metal fatigue because there is a constant force applied to that side while the bicycle is in motion. For whatever reason, it is vitally important to replace broken spokes as soon as possible to prevent further injury to the wheel. Always take the old spoke and nipple with you to the bicycle shop to ensure your obtaining exactly the same size and type as a replacement. If this is not possible, remove the spoke next to the missing one and take it with you as a sample.

REPLACING A SINGLE SPOKE

A single spoke on bicycles equipped with tubular (sewn-up) tires can be replaced by an experienced cyclist in a matter of minutes, without removing the tire or the wheel. Deflate the tire and roll it off the rim in the area of the spoke to be replaced. Lift the rim tape and pull the nipple from the rim. Push the spoke out of the hub flange.

If the broken spoke is on a wheel equipped with a conventional clincher tire or on the sprocket side of a wheel with a tubular tire, the wheel must be removed from the bicycle. Work the tire off the rim and remove the nipple. Push the spoke out of the hub flange. If the broken spoke is on the sprocket side of the wheel, the sprocket or sprocket cluster must be removed before

Members of the United States Olympic team line up in the first rank, prior to the start of a race for national points and a trophy. Each rider is confident his machine is properly serviced and adjusted to give him optimum performance and the best possible chance to win, because he takes care of it himself. Racing places the greatest demand on the rider and every part of his bike.

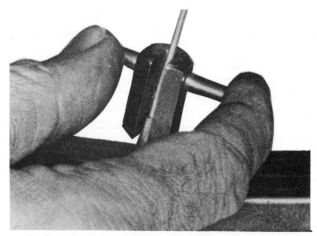

An inexpensive spoke-tightening tool can be used to draw the spoke up to the proper tension, as explained in the text.

the spoke can be pushed clear of the hub flange. Refer to Chapter 6 for detailed illustrated procedures for removing splined- or notched-body sprocket clusters.

Push the new spoke through the hole in the hub flange. Observe that the heads of the spokes alternate between the outside and inside of the flange and that the head is on the side of the flange opposite the countersunk hole.

The purpose of the countersink is to give the spoke a chance to make the bend toward the rim, not for the head to fit into. If you install the spoke in the wrong direction, it will fail in a few miles due to the added strain at the curve in the spoke caused by the sharp edge of the hole.

If you install more than one spoke at the same time, pay particular attention to the pattern of adjacent spokes and the number of cross-overs to be made by the new spokes.

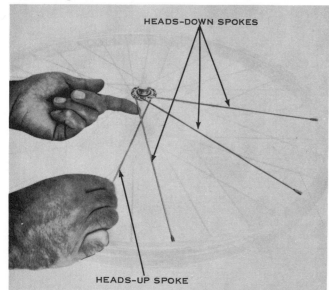

HEADS-DOWN SPOKES

HEADS-UP SPOKE

Before lacing a wheel, observe a built-up wheel and notice the pattern of heads-up and heads-down spokes. Also note how each heads-up spoke crosses over a specific number of heads-down spokes. In this illustration, the heads-up spoke with the hand on it crosses three heads-down spokes. The finger points to one of the heads-down spokes.

Insert the nipple through the hole in the rim and attach the spoke fingertight. Tighten the spoke, using a spoke wrench (about 35¢) until the spoke gives off a tone similar to the others when it is snapped with the back of your finger and your fingernail strikes the spoke. An alternate method is to draw it up until the same number of threads are exposed below the nipple as on the others. As a double check, you might test the adjacent spokes with the wrench to determine how tight they are, and then tighten the new one until approximately the same amount of force is required to turn it. If you use this system, be sure to return the other spokes to their original tension.

Check to be sure the end of the new spoke does not extend beyond the nipple on the inside of the rim, which would cause damage to the tube or tire in a short time. If it does protrude, file it smooth.

Replace the tire on the rim, and then install the wheel. Inflate the tire to the recommended pressure.

FILLING THE HUB AND LACING THE WHEEL

If you plan on serious cycling, either touring or racing, you should know the principles involved in re-spoking (lacing) a wheel. The job is not difficult if each step is taken in turn and the step-by-step illustrated instructions are followed closely. The circumstance may arise when you wish to change a hub or rim, keeping one but replacing the other. If the old spokes are to be discarded, which is the usual practice, the quickest method is to cut them out with a pair of wire cutters.

The most practical method of lacing a wheel is to fill the hub with spokes first, and then lace them to the rim as outlined in the following step-by-step illustrated procedures.

FILLING A HUB

Observe a built-up wheel and note that every other

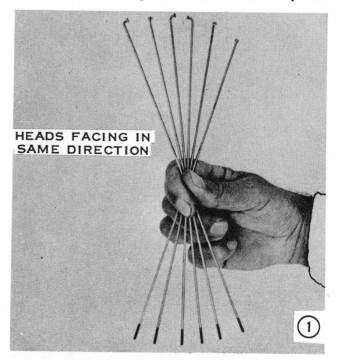

HEADS FACING IN SAME DIRECTION

①

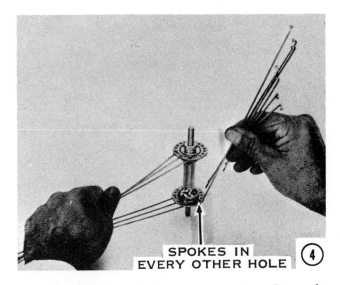

spoke has the head on the outside of the flange and the other spoke has its head on the inside. Also note how the hole on one side of a better-built hub is countersunk. The countersink is to permit the spoke to make the bend from the hole toward the rim without the sharp edge of the hole placing a strain on the spoke. This is an important factor when racing and cornering at high speeds or extended touring under varying road conditions.

Another factor to consider before lacing a wheel is the number of crosses by first locating a heads-up spoke, and then counting the number of heads-down spokes that cross over the heads-up ones.

① Line up approximately six spokes, with the

head of each facing in the same direction. Grasp the center of the group with your thumb and index finger, and then twist to fan them out, as shown. As you insert the spokes, start with the one nearest the outside edge of your thumb.

② Hold the hub in a vertical position, and then insert three spokes downward into three alternating holes in the bottom hub flange, with the countersink of the hole on the outside of the flange. If the hub flange does not have countersunk holes, disregard this detail.

③ Insert three spokes downward into three alternate holes in the top hub flange, with the top flange holes slightly to the right of the filled spoke hole in the bottom flange.

④ Hold the hub in a horizontal position, with the six spokes hanging down. Grasp the ends of the spokes and turn the hub to the vertical position, with the spoke heads facing up. Hold the hub in this position and continue inserting spokes into every other hole in the bottom flange. When the bottom flange is filled, insert spokes downward into every other hole in the top flange.

⑤ Rotate the downward hub to a horizontal position with the spokes hanging down to prevent them from falling out.

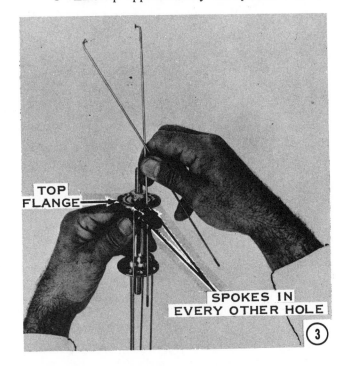

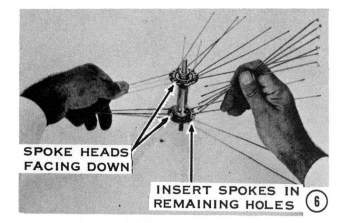

SPOKE HEADS FACING DOWN

INSERT SPOKES IN REMAINING HOLES ⑥

⑥ Turn the hub to a vertical position with the spoke heads facing down. Install spokes downward into the remaining holes in the bottom flange. After the bottom flange is filled, insert spokes downward into the remaining holes in the top flange.

⑦ When the hub is completely filled with spokes, turn it to a horizontal position, and then hold the axle or the hub, shaking it slightly so the spokes drop into place. Divide the spokes into two equal bunches, and then insert the axle into a hole in the workbench.

LACING A RIM

Look closely at the rim and note how the holes are consecutively punched off-center toward the top (one side) and off-center toward the bottom (the other side). Most American rims have the first hole to the right of the valve hole as a bottom hole. Imported rims and some American rims have the first hole to the right of the valve hole as a top hole. Wheel lacing begins with the first top hole to the right of the valve hole so the valve will lie between parallel spokes.

⑧ Place the rim on the workbench over the hub and spokes, with the valve hole facing toward you. Pick a heads-up spoke that is facing you on the top of the hub flange and insert it into the first top hole to the right of the valve hole. Thread a nipple onto the spoke approximately four turns. *NOTE: In the remainder of these procedures, the term "lace the spoke to the rim" means inserting the spoke through the designated hole, and then threading a nipple four turns onto the spoke.*

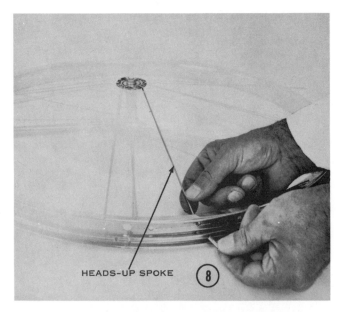

HEADS-UP SPOKE ⑧

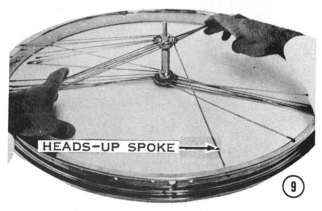

HEADS-UP SPOKE ⑨

⑨ Sort out the spokes on the top flange to the left and right of the installed spoke.

⑩ Working clockwise around the hub flange from the head of the spoke laced to the rim, count off the number of heads-down spokes corresponding to the

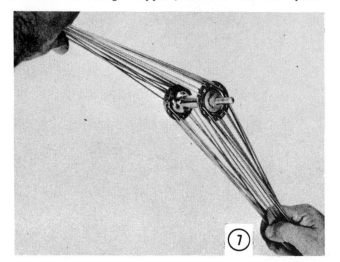

⑦

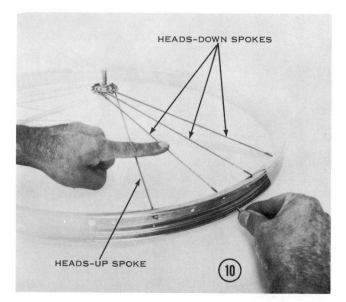

HEADS-DOWN SPOKES

HEADS-UP SPOKE ⑩

number of crosses you intend to use for the wheel (two heads-down spokes for two crosses, three heads-down spokes for three crosses, etc.). Lay these spokes over the spoke laced to the rim. Take the last of these heads-down spokes and lace it into the next top hole to the right of the first laced spoke. You have just made the first crossover of the wheel. Check the number of heads-down spokes crossing the first heads-up spoke to be sure the number corresponds to the number of crosses you selected for the wheel. *NOTE: On derailleur-equipped bicycles and some others, the spokes are "interlaced," in which case take the last heads-down spoke, place it under the first laced spoke, and lace it to the rim. Repeat this pattern while lacing the remainder of the spokes.*

⑪ Find the spoke that is on the extreme left of the rim. Locate the head of this spoke in the hub flange. Go clockwise from this head along the hub flange and find the heads-down spoke directly to the left of the last heads-down spoke already laced to the rim. Lace this spoke into the next top hole on the left of the rim.

⑫ Locate the spoke that is on the left side of the rim. Find the head of this spoke in the hub flange. Go counterclockwise from this head along the hub flange and find the heads-up spoke directly to the left of a heads-up spoke already installed in the rim. Lace this heads-up spoke in the next top hole on the left of the rim.

⑬ Locate the spoke that is on the left side of the rim and its head in the hub flange. Go clockwise from this spoke head along the flange and find the heads-down spoke directly to the left of the last heads-down spoke already laced to the rim. Lace this spoke in the next top hole on the left side of the rim.

⑭ Find the spoke that is in the extreme left side of the rim. Locate the head of this spoke in the hub flange, and then go counterclockwise from this head along the hub flange and find the heads-up spoke

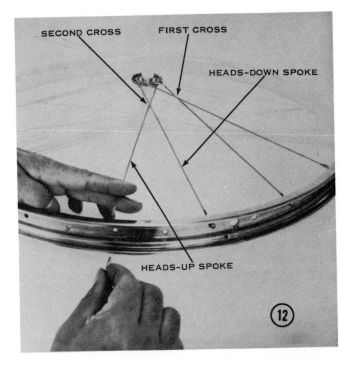

directly to the left of a heads-up spoke already laced to the rim. Lace this heads-up spoke in the next top hole on the left of the rim. Repeat the procedures in Steps ⑪ through ⑭ until all the spokes in the top flange have been laced to the rim. Pay particular attention to the following details as you proceed with the lacing: (a) Always use the already laced spoke on the extreme left of the rim as a guide for finding the next spoke. (b) If the spoke on the left of the rim is a heads-up spoke, the next spoke to be laced to the rim will be a heads-down spoke and vice versa. (c) If the spoke on the left side of the rim is a heads-up spoke, find the head of this spoke in the hub flange and go clockwise from this spoke and find the heads-down

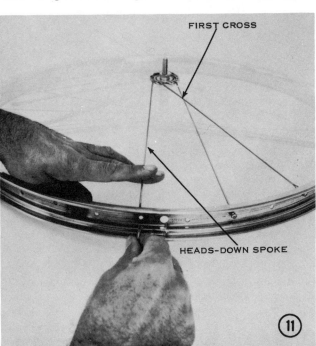

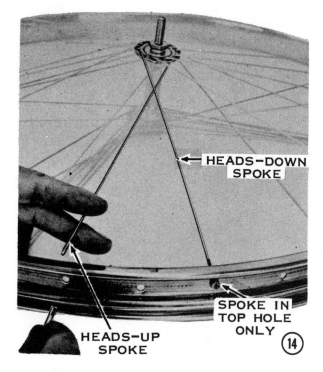

HEADS-DOWN SPOKE

HEADS-UP SPOKE

SPOKE IN TOP HOLE ONLY ⑭

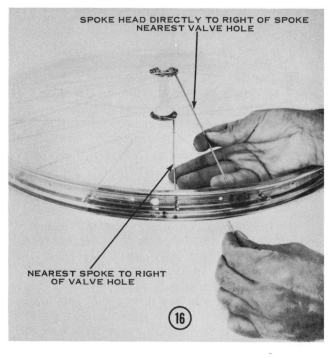

SPOKE HEAD DIRECTLY TO RIGHT OF SPOKE NEAREST VALVE HOLE

NEAREST SPOKE TO RIGHT OF VALVE HOLE

⑯

spoke directly to the left of a heads-down spoke already laced to the rim. (d) If the spoke on the left of the rim is a heads-down spoke, find the head of this spoke in the hub flange and go counterclockwise from this head along the hub flange and find the heads-up spoke directly to the left of a heads-up spoke already laced to the rim. (e) Insert spokes only in the top holes of the rim.

⑮ Turn the rim and hub counterclockwise as you continue lacing the rim to keep the next top hole to be filled in front of you. After you have finished lacing the spokes from one hub flange, reach under the rim with both hands, grasp half the loose spokes in each hand, and carefully turn the wheel over so the valve hole faces you.

⑯ If the spoke laced nearest the valve hole is to the right of the valve hole, locate the spoke that is directly to the right (counterclockwise) of this bottom flange spoke. Lace this spoke to the rim hole just to the right (counterclockwise) of the spoke nearest the valve hole. The spoke selected in this step must be a

heads-up spoke. If the spoke laced nearest the valve hole is to the left of the valve hole, locate the top flange spoke which is directly to the left (clockwise) of this bottom flange spoke and lace this spoke to the rim hole just to the left (clockwise) from the spoke nearest the valve hole.

⑰ If the top flange spoke already laced to the rim goes from the right side of the flange toward the left side of the rim, go clockwise along the hub flange and count off the number of heads-down spokes corresponding to the number of crosses. Lay these spokes over the laced spoke, and then insert the last of these spokes into the rim hole directly to the left of the beginning spoke. If the wheel is being "interlaced," place the last heads-down spoke under the beginning spoke and then into the rim. Repeat this pattern while lacing the remainder of the spokes.

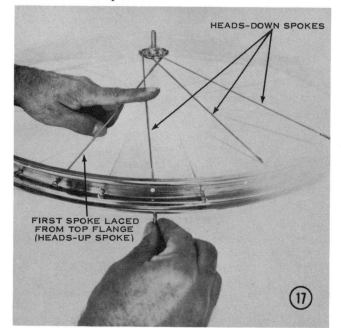

HEADS-DOWN SPOKES

FIRST SPOKE LACED FROM TOP FLANGE (HEADS-UP SPOKE)

⑰

VALVE HOLE ⑮

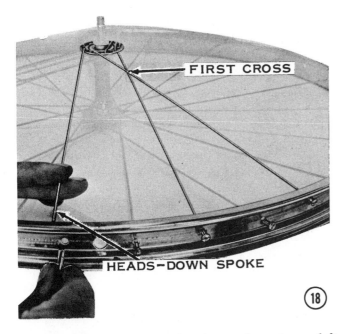

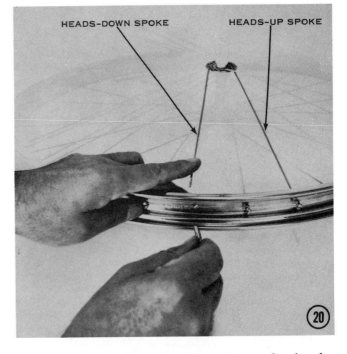

⑱ Find the spoke that is on the extreme left of the rim. Locate the head of this spoke in the hub flange, and then go clockwise from this head along the hub flange and find the heads-down spoke directly to the left of the last heads-down spoke already laced to the rim. Lace this spoke into the next top hole on the left of the rim.

⑲ Locate the spoke that is on the left side of the rim and its head in the hub flange. Go counterclockwise from this spoke head along the hub flange and find the heads-up spoke directly to the left of the heads-up spoke already laced to the rim. Lace this heads-up spoke into the next top hole on the left of the rim.

⑳ Locate the spoke that is on the left side of the rim and its head in the hub flange. Go clockwise from this head along the flange and find the heads-down spoke directly to the left of the last heads-down spoke

already laced to the rim. Lace this spoke in the next top hole on the left side of the rim.

㉑ Locate the spoke which is on the left side of the rim and its head in the hub flange. Go counterclockwise from this head along the hub flange and find the heads-up spoke directly to the left of a heads-up spoke already laced to the rim. Lace this heads-up spoke in the next top hole on the left of the rim. Repeat the procedures in Steps ⑱ through ㉑ until all the spokes in the top flange have been laced. Pay special attention to the following details as you proceed with the lacing: (a) Always use the already laced spoke on the extreme left of the rim as a guide for finding the next spoke. (b) If the spoke on the left of the rim is a heads-up spoke, the next spoke to be laced to the rim will be

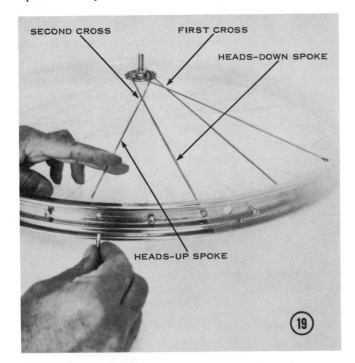

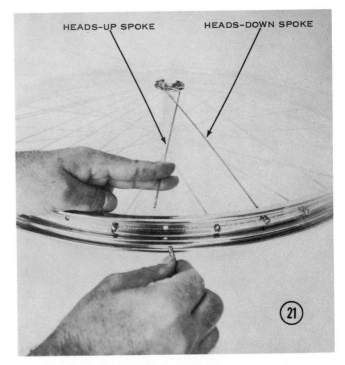

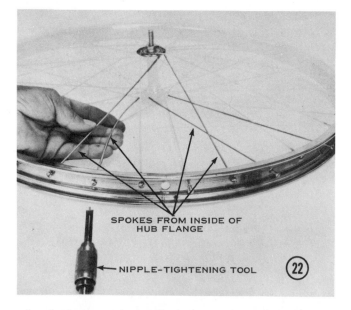

SPOKES FROM INSIDE OF
HUB FLANGE

← NIPPLE-TIGHTENING TOOL ㉒

a heads-down spoke, and vice versa. (c) If the spoke on the left side of the rim is a heads-up spoke, locate the head of this spoke in the hub flange, and then go clockwise from this heads-up spoke and find the heads-down spoke directly to the left of a heads-down spoke already laced to the rim. (d) If the spoke on the left of the rim is a heads-down spoke, find the head of this spoke in the hub flange, and then go counterclockwise from this spoke head along the hub flange and find the heads-up spoke directly to the left of a heads-up spoke already laced to the rim. (e) Insert spokes only in the top holes of the rim. (f) Turn the rim and hub counterclockwise as you continue lacing the rim to keep the next top hole to be filled in front of you.

TENSIONING SPOKES

㉒   Tighten the spokes first that come from the inside of the hub flanges, starting near the valve hole.

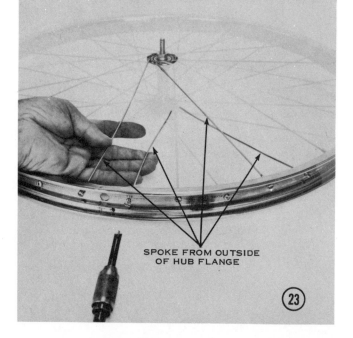

SPOKE FROM OUTSIDE
OF HUB FLANGE

㉓

Turn the nipples down evenly with a screwdriver, using the amount of visible spoke threads as a gauge.

㉓   Tighten the spokes next that come from the outside of the hub flange, starting near the valve hole. Turn the nipples down evenly with a screwdriver, using the amount of visible spoke threads as a gauge.

㉔   Make a final tension adjustment of one or two turns, using a nipple wrench and working consecutively around the rim. Pluck the spokes and adjust to obtain the same tone from each spoke. Loose spokes will have a dull sound and a properly tensioned one a higher pitch.

TRUEING A WHEEL

㉕   Check to be sure all the spokes are tight and that the cones are properly adjusted with no side play. Place the wheel in a trueing stand. An effective jig can be purchased for under $7. A front fork will serve for trueing a front wheel if a stand or jig is not available. Use a piece of chalk against the jig or the caliper arms of the trueing stand and spin the wheel, moving the chalk or arms closer to the rim until it marks only the high spots on that side. To pull the rim in on the left side, for example, tighten the spokes that come from the right-side flange approximately one full turn in the area of the chalk mark. Loosen the spokes coming from the left-side flange about one full turn. To pull the rim to the right, tighten the spokes coming from the left-side flange and loosen the ones coming from the right-side flange. Work both sides of the rim evenly, adjusting the spokes just a little at a time.

㉖   Set the trueing stand calipers or piece of chalk *under* the rim to test for high spots or hop. When you find a section that has a high spot, loosen the spokes on the outside of the high spot and tighten the spoke in the center of it. Tighten and loosen the nipples only a turn at a time until the wheel is free of high spots.

㉗   On front wheels, and rear wheels except those equipped with a sprocket cluster, the rim should be centered over the cones or locknuts.

㉘   On rear wheels equipped with a sprocket cluster, the rim is not centered over the mounting points, but pulled to the cluster side in order for it to turn

NIPPLE WRENCH   ㉔

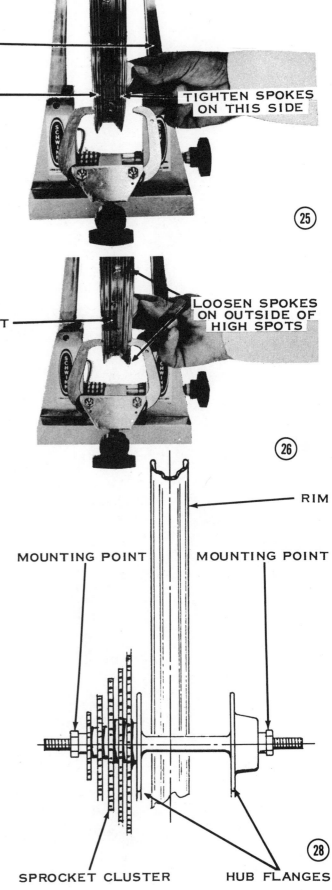

TO SHIFT THE RIM TO THE RIGHT

LOOSEN SPOKES ON THIS SIDE

TIGHTEN SPOKES ON THIS SIDE

midway between the rear frame members. This shifting of the rim with respect to the hub flanges is accomplished by first loosening nipples of the spokes coming from the hub flange on the side opposite the cluster about 1½ turns and then tightening the nipples of the spokes coming from the flange on the sprocket side 1½ turns. Check for trueness after shifting the rim.

㉙ To check the centering of the wheel, first make sure that all washers and locknuts are installed on the axle in the same order they will be when the wheel is mounted on the bicycle, including the sprocket

TIGHTEN SPOKES IN CENTER OF HIGH SPOT

LOOSEN SPOKES ON OUTSIDE OF HIGH SPOTS

cluster for a rear wheel so equipped. Place the ends of a wheel-aligning tool (about $8) against the sides of the rim. Position the pointer against the outermost point that will be mounted in the frame. Secure the pointer, and then turn the wheel over and check the other side. The pointer should just touch the mounting item on that side, as shown.

㉕

㉖

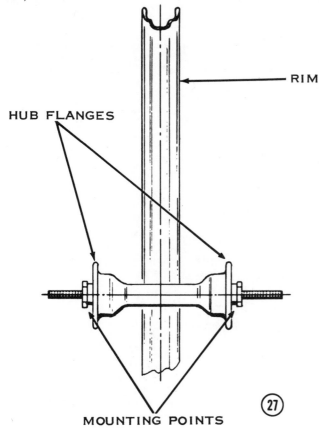

RIM

HUB FLANGES

MOUNTING POINTS

㉗

MOUNTING POINT

MOUNTING POINT

RIM

SPROCKET CLUSTER

HUB FLANGES

㉘

MOUNTING POINT   WHEEL ALIGNING TOOL

Hours of enjoyable riding are available to this cyclist, who keeps his machine properly adjusted and lubricated through a regular scheduled maintenance program.

TROUBLESHOOTING

The following tables are designed to assist you in isolating problem areas when your bicycle is not functioning properly. The common problems are listed first, followed by likely causes and corrective action to be taken. Detailed procedures for making adjustments are not given in this table. However, the introductory paragraph for each section makes reference to the chapter where step-by-step illustrated instructions can be found.

INTERNALLY GEARED REAR HUBS

Most problems associated with internally geared rear hubs require a complete overhaul of the unit as outlined in Chapter 5. The illustrated table of contents for that chapter will assist you in identifying and finding the section for the particular hub on which you are working. The following table provides adjustments that can be made to restore a malfunctioning unit to proper working order. If the suggested corrective action does not remedy the problem, then the hub must be overhauled and defective parts replaced.

Problem: Hub binds and drags while driving.

Possible Cause:	Corrective Action:
1. Cone is adjusted too tight.	Adjust the cone.
2. Drive chain is too tight.	Adjust drive chain tension until the chain has approximately ⅜-in slack midway between the chain wheel and the rear sprocket.

Problem: Hub makes grinding or cracking noises while driving.

Possible Cause:	Corrective Action:
1. Drive chain is too tight, dirty, or rusted.	Adjust the chain tension. Clean or replace the chain.

Problem: Hub binds, drags, or makes noise while coasting.

Possible Cause:	Corrective Action:
1. Cone adjusted too tight.	Adjust the cone.
2. Drive chain is too tight.	Adjust the chain.

Problem: Gears slip or fail to remain in selected position.

Possible Cause:	Corrective Action:
1. Indicator rod not adjusted properly.	Sturmey-Archer hubs: adjust cable until end of rod aligns with end of axle. Shimano hubs: place control lever in N position and adjust cable until line through the N at the bell crank aligns with the slot.

Problem: Gear change is sluggish or will not shift at all.

Possible Cause:	Corrective Action:
1. Control cable bent, kinked, or requires lubrication.	Lubricate or replace control cable. Use high quality cycle oil for indicator rod or shift lever and multi-purpose lubricant for cable.
2. Control cable not adjusted properly.	Adjust control cable until end of indicator rod is even with end of axle.
3. Internal parts worn or corroded.	Overhaul the hub and replace defective parts.

Problem: Chain rubs on chain stays or binds at rear sprocket.

Possible Cause:	Corrective Action:
1. Rear sprocket out of alignment with chain wheel.	Remove rear wheel, sprocket lock ring, and then the sprocket. Turn sprocket over with concave side facing in opposite direction, or reposition spacers to move sprocket in desired direction on the axle. Reinstall parts and wheel.

COASTER BRAKES

Problems associated with coaster-type brakes usually result from excessive wear or failure of internal parts and require overhauling and replacing of the damaged parts. Refer to the table of contents for Chapter 5 to find the section for the specific hub on which you are working. The following table will pinpoint the parts that may be causing the problem and alert you to pay special attention to these areas while overhauling the hub.

Problem: Hub brakes poorly.

Possible Cause:	Corrective Action:
1. Lack of lubrication.	Overhaul hub and use proper lubrication.
2. Internal parts dirty, gummed up, or damaged.	Overhaul hub, clean, replace damaged parts, and lubricate.
3. Hub shell braking surface glazed.	Roughen braking surface of hub shell using coarse emery cloth or a small grinding wheel.
4. Brake shoes or brake cylinder glazed.	Replace brake shoes or brake cylinder.
5. Drive-side expander and brake-arm side expander brake surface rough.	Remove burrs from drive-side expander or replace the expander.

Problem: Brake squeaks.

Possible Cause:	Corrective Action:
1. Lack of lubrication.	Overhaul hub and use proper lubrication.
2. Hub shell brake surface glazed.	Roughen braking surface of hub shell with coarse emery cloth or a small grinding wheel.
3. Brake shoes or brake cylinder glazed.	Replace the brake shoes or brake cylinder.
4. On hubs with brake disks, the disks are highly polished.	Replace the complete brake disk set.

Problem: Pedals travel excessively between driving and braking.

Possible Cause:	Corrective Action:
1. Brake shoes or brake cylinders worn.	Replace brake shoes or brake cylinder.
2. Adjusting cone too loose.	Adjust the cone.
3. Brake disks worn or missing.	Replace the complete brake disk set.

Problem: Pedals rotate backwards without applying brake.

Possible Cause:	Corrective Action:
1. Retarder spring(s) weak or damaged.	Replace retarder spring for drive-side expander.
2. Yellow and blue band hubs: dentils on low-speed drive clutch and drive-side expander dirty or worn.	Clean or replace drive clutch and drive-end expander as a set.
3. Sturmey-Archer hubs: right-side cone not adjusted properly.	Rotate adjusting nut so there is just the slightest trace of side play at the wheel rim.

Problem: Brake does not release readily.

Possible Cause:	Corrective Action:
1. Improper lubrication.	Overhaul hub and use proper lubrication.
2. Cone adjusted too tight.	Adjust the cones.
3. Axle bent.	Replace axle.
4. Internal parts dirty, corroded, or gummed up.	Overhaul, clean, and lubricate complete hub.

EXPANDER BRAKES

Complete overhaul procedures for this type of brake are covered in Chapter 4.

Problem: Hub brakes poorly.

Possible Cause:	Corrective Action:
1. Control cable loose, kinked, or corroded.	Adjust or replace the brake cable.
2. Brake shoes or hub shell dirty, worn, or highly polished.	Replace worn or highly polished brake shoes. Roughen polished brake surface with coarse emery cloth.

Problem: Cones cannot be adjusted properly.

Possible Cause:	Corrective Action:
1. Axle bent.	Replace the axle.
2. Bearing cups worn and not concentric.	Install new bearing cups.
3. Bearing surfaces, cones, ball retainers, loose ball bearings, or cups pitted or worn.	Overhaul hub and replace defective parts.

Problem: Hub binds and drags.

Possible Cause:	Corrective Action:
1. Cones adjusted too tight.	Adjust the cones.
2. Weak brake shoe springs.	Replace the brake shoe springs.
3. Brake cable adjusted too tight.	Adjust cable at cable adjusting barrel.
4. Internal parts dirty, gummed up, or worn.	Overhaul, replace defective parts, and lubricate.
5. Brake plate not centered in brake drum.	Loosen wheel nut on brake side of hub and loosen nut holding brake plate to hub. Apply brake and tighten nut holding brake plate assembly.

Problem: Hub makes cracking or grinding noises.

Possible Cause:	Corrective Action:
1. Internal parts dirty, or worn.	Overhaul hub and replace defective parts.
2. Dust caps bent or damaged.	Replace defective dust caps.

CALIPER BRAKES

Step-by-step illustrated instructions for complete overhaul of side-pull and center-pull caliper brakes are given in Chapter 10.

Problem: One or both brake shoes fail to release from surface of wheel rim.

Possible Cause:	Corrective Action:
1. Caliper moving parts require lubrication.	Lubricate pivot points of side-pull type or main pivot bolt of center-pull type.
2. Caliper assembly is not centered properly.	Adjust pivot bolt or mounting bolt.
3. Arms are bent or are rubbing against one another.	Disassemble and straighten arms to eliminate friction, or use emery cloth or a file until arms do not contact each other.

Possible Cause:	Corrective Action:
4. Wheel rim is not true.	Adjust spokes to true wheel.
5. Wheel is not centered properly.	Loosen axle nuts and center wheel by adjusting cones.
6. Control cable adjusted too tight.	Loosen cable by turning cable adjusting barrel or obtain slack through cable anchor bolt until both brake shoes are approximately ⅛ inch from wheel rim.

Problem: Brakes squeak.

Possible Cause:	Corrective Action:
1. Brake shoe arms out of adjustment.	Twist the brake arm carefully and very slightly by gripping the arm with a wrench directly below the brake shoe assembly and then twisting the arm until the front end of the shoe contacts the wheel rim first.
2. Brake shoes or wheel rim glazed or gummed up.	Clean rim with solvent and/or replace the brake shoes.

Problem: Poor braking.

Possible Cause:	Corrective Action:
1. Brake shoes or wheel rim glazed or oily.	Clean rim with solvent and replace brake shoes.
2. Brake shoes worn.	Replace brake shoes.
3. Brake-shoe holders out of adjustment.	Loosen mounting nut, move holder up or down in arm slot until top of shoe contacts wheel rim just below edge of rim and the angle of the shoes align with the angle of the rim.
4. Wheel rim badly damaged.	Replace wheel rim or install a new wheel.

Problem: Brake lever travels excessively when brake is applied.

Possible Cause:	Corrective Action:
1. Brake shoes worn.	Replace brake shoes.
2. Cable not adjusted properly.	Loosen cable anchor nut, remove slack from cable, and then retighten anchor nut.

Problem: Brakes chatter or jerk when brake is applied.

Possible Cause:	Corrective Action:
1. Adjusting nut on pivot bolt is too loose.	Loosen locknut on main pivot bolt, adjust until arms pivot freely without side play, and then retighten locknut.

Possible Cause:	Corrective Action:
2. Rim is dented.	Replace rim or install a new wheel.

Problem: Brake lever difficult to operate and does not release.

Possible Cause:	Corrective Action:
1. Caliper pivot bolt requires lubrication.	Lubricate brake arms at pivot bolt. Lubricate cable.
2. Cable or cable housing frayed or damaged.	Replace cable or cable housing.
3. Pivot bolt nut adjusted too tight.	Loosen locknut, adjust main pivot bolt until arms rotate freely but without side play, and then retighten locknut.
4. Brake lever defective or requires lubrication.	Lubricate brake lever pivot point or replace defective lever.

FRONT DERAILLEURS

Detailed instructions for overhauling and adjusting front derailleurs are given in Chapter 8.

Problem: Chain shifts beyond small (low-gear) sprocket.

Possible Cause:	Corrective Action:
1. Low-gear limit screw not set properly.	Adjust low-gear limit screw.

Problem: Chain shifts sluggishly or does not shift at all onto small sprocket.

Possible Cause:	Corrective Action:
1. Low-gear limit screw not set properly.	Adjust low-gear limit screw.
2. Control cable adjusted too tight.	Position chain onto small sprocket. Place control lever as far forward as possible. Pull cable through cable anchor bolt until taut, and then tighten the anchor bolt.
3. Derailleur linkage dirty or adjusted too tight.	Overhaul, lubricate, and adjust linkage.

Problem: Chain shifts beyond large (high-gear) sprocket.

Possible Cause:	Corrective Action:
1. High-gear limit screw not set properly.	Adjust high-gear limit screw.

Problem: Chain shifts sluggishly or does not shift at all onto large sprocket.

Possible Cause:	Corrective Action:
1. High-gear limit screw not set properly.	Adjust high-gear limit screw.
2. Chain guide out of alignment.	Carefully bend inner side of chain guide toward chain.

3. Derailleur not positioned properly on bicycle frame.	Position derailleur until chain guide is not more than ⅛ inch above tip of teeth on largest chain wheel.
4. Control cable adjusted too loose.	Position chain on small chain wheel and control lever as far forward as possible. Draw cable taut, and then tighten cable anchor bolt.
5. Teeth on chain wheel not tapered properly.	File chain wheel teeth until they have a slight taper on each side.

REAR DERAILLEURS

Complete illustrated procedures for overhauling and adjusting rear derailleurs are covered in Chapter 7. Because of its exposed position with no protection, the rear derailleur is subject to abuse and shock, which can result in knocking it out of adjustment. The jockey and tension wheels must be properly aligned with the cluster for the derailleur to function through the complete range of sprockets. Therefore, care and patience must be exercised when making adjustments.

Problem: Chain shifts beyond small (high-gear) sprocket.

Possible Cause:	*Corrective Action:*
1. High-gear limit screw not set properly.	Adjust high-gear limit screw.
2. Derailleur bent or out of alignment.	Realign derailleur until jockey wheel is in vertical alignment with small sprocket.

Problem: Chain does not remain on small sprockets.

Possible Cause:	*Corrective Action:*
1. Tension adjustment on control lever too loose.	Tighten control tension nut or screw.
2. Washers not properly placed on control lever.	Remove nut, washers, pressure plate, and any additional washers installed on control lever stud. Replace parts as indicated in accompanying illustration.

Problem: Chain shifts beyond largest (low-gear) sprocket.

Possible Cause:	*Corrective Action:*
1. Low-gear limit screw not set properly.	Adjust low-gear limit screw.
2. Derailleur bent or out of alignment.	Realign derailleur until jockey wheel is in vertical alignment with largest sprocket.

Problem: Chain shifts sluggishly or does not shift onto smallest sprocket properly.

Possible Cause:	*Corrective Action:*
1. High-gear limit screw not set properly.	Adjust high-gear limit screw.
2. Control cable adjusted too tight.	Shift chain onto smallest sprocket and control lever as far forward as possible. Pull cable through cable anchor bolt until taut, and then tighten anchor bolt.
3. Derailleur linkage dirty or adjusted too tight.	Clean, lubricate, and adjust derailleur linkage.
4. Derailleur bent or out of alignment.	Realign derailleur until jockey wheel is in vertical alignment with smallest sprocket.

Problem: Chain shifts sluggishly or does not shift onto largest sprocket properly.

Possible Cause:	*Corrective Action:*
1. Low-gear limit screw not properly adjusted.	Adjust low-gear limit screw.
2. Derailleur bent or out of alignment.	Realign derailleur until jockey wheel is in vertical alignment with largest sprocket.

Problem: Control bottoms out against stop before chain shifts to largest sprocket.

Possible Cause:	*Corrective Action:*
1. Control cable too loose.	Shift chain onto smallest sprocket and control lever as far forward as possible. Pull cable through cable anchor bolt until taut, and then tighten anchor bolt.
2. Rear hub spacer nut not completely tightened.	Loosen right-hand axle nut and fully tighten rear hub spacer nut.
3. Derailleur bent or out of alignment.	Realign derailleur until jockey wheel is in vertical alignment with largest sprocket.

Problem: Chain slips in high gear under pressure.

Possible Cause:	*Corrective Action:*
1. Derailleur is not free to pivot.	Readjust and reposition derailleur arm.
2. Sprocket teeth worn.	Replace sprocket or freewheel cluster.
3. Defective freewheel cluster.	Replace freewheel cluster.
4. Freewheel sprocket threads stripped.	Replace sprocket or sprocket cluster.
5. Freewheel cluster body mounting threads or hub threads stripped.	Replace damaged hub or install new wheel or new freewheel cluster body.

Problem: Chain too loose when positioned on smallest sprocket.

Possible Cause:	Corrective Action:
1. Chain too long.	Shorten chain to proper length. Position chain on largest rear sprocket and largest chain wheel. Pull chain tight, allowing the derailleur cage to pivot. There should be ½ to one full link of excess chain.
2. Spring tension on cage assembly too loose.	Adjust tension on cage assembly until tension on chain is reasonably snug when chain is on smallest rear sprocket and smallest chain wheel.

Problem: Chain shifts with difficulty onto largest sprocket and derailleur bends while shifting.

Possible Cause:	Corrective Action:
1. Chain too short.	Position chain onto largest rear sprocket and largest chain wheel. Pull chain up tight allowing derailleur cage to rotate. Correct length of chain will provide ½ to one full link of excess chain. Add links as required.

Problem: Chain slips in all gears.

Possible Cause:	Corrective Action:
1. Rear hub cluster mounting threads stripped.	Replace hub or install a new rear wheel.
2. Defective freewheel cluster.	Replace freewheel cluster.

HEADSETS

Procedures for complete overhaul of American and European-type headsets are covered in Chapter 11.

Problem: Front fork binds or turns stiffly.

Possible Cause:	Corrective Action:
1. Adjusting cup too tight.	Loosen locknut, back off the adjusting cup approximately ¼ turn, and then retighten the locknut.

Problem: Excessive vertical or side play.

Possible Cause:	Corrective Action:
1. Adjusting cup too loose.	Loosen locknut, tighten adjusting cup approximately ¼ turn, and then retighten the locknut.
2. Upper or lower set of ball bearings worn.	Overhaul headset and replace complete set of worn bearings.

HANGER SETS

Detailed instructions for overhauling and adjusting hanger sets (including one-piece, cottered, and cotterless cranks) and American and European-type pedals are listed in Chapter 9.

Problem: Chain wheel does not turn freely with chain disengaged.

Possible Cause:	Corrective Action:
1. Adjustable ball cup set too tight.	Loosen lock ring on side opposite chain wheel by turning it counterclockwise or loosen the locknut by turning it clockwise. Back off the ball cup until the crank rotates freely with just a discernible amount of end play.
2. Right or left side bearing set damaged.	Overhaul hanger set and replace defective bearing set.

Problem: Crank has excessive end play.

Possible Cause:	Corrective Action:
1. Adjustable ball cup set too loose.	Remove chain from chain wheel. On side opposite chain wheel, loosen lock ring by turning it counterclockwise or locknut by turning it clockwise. Tighten ball cup until crank rotates freely with just a discernible amount of end play.
2. Right- or left-side bearing set worn.	Overhaul hanger set and replace complete set of bearings.

Problem: Cottered cranks: Crank seems to "give" on the spindle.

Possible Cause:	Corrective Action:
1. Cotter is not secured tightly in the spindle.	Support underside of crank with block of wood with hole in it to receive nut of cotter. Strike head end of cotter a solid blow to drive it home, and then tighten cotter nut.

Problem: Pedals do not rotate freely or have excessive end play.

Possible Cause:	Corrective Action:
1. Cone not adjusted properly.	American-type pedals: Remove pedal, partly disassemble, and adjust cone as described in Chapter 9. European-type pedals: Remove dust cap, loosen locknut, adjust cone, and then reassemble parts.

4
OVERHAULING
FRONT-WHEEL HUBS

This chapter contains complete overhaul procedures for the three basic types of front hubs using step-by-step fully illustrated instructions. In addition, a detailed exploded drawing, showing every part of the hub, follows the Cleaning and Inspecting portion for each hub. The keyed photographs, coupled with the exploded view, support the written text to tell you verbally and visually exactly what to do and why. The overhauled hub is then installed in the front fork. In all cases you will have to make a final cone check after the wheel is installed, because tightening the axle nuts may disturb the adjustment.

TYPES OF FRONT-WHEEL HUBS

Three basic types of front hubs are in common use: a conventional front hub, one with a quick-release mechanism, and another with an expander-type brake.

CONVENTIONAL FRONT-WHEEL HUBS

All types of hubs without an expander brake or quick-release mechanism can be considered in this category. They have the least number of parts and have been commonly used for many years. Differences between various makes of conventional hubs include: the weight and strength of materials used in its manufacture; the size and shape of the hub flanges; and the type of bearings and bearing cups.

Heavy-duty conventional front-wheel hubs on traditional, middleweight heavy-frame (50 to 60 pounds), balloon-tired bicycles have thick-walled shells with small flanges and are designed to take daily abuse from youngsters or from rugged work such as delivery routes or patrol duty with large plant protection agencies.

Lightweight conventional hubs made of machined one-piece aluminum alloy material are used on most recreational, touring, and racing bicycles. Some hubs are secured in the front fork dropouts with axle nuts and others are held in place with large wing nuts. The flanges of these hubs are much larger than the heavy-duty type to give them strength, but have a pattern of cutout holes for weight reduction.

The conventional hub consists of an axle passing through the hub shell (to which the spokes are attached), a set of ball bearings at each end of the hub shell, a cone at each end of the axle for adjustment, and locknuts or large wing nuts to hold it all in place. The cones act as the inner ball bearing races and, as they are shifted together on the threaded axle, become

This is a typical conventional front-wheel hub. Overhaul procedures for this type of hub start on page 79.

the means of adjusting the ball bearing play. On most American-manufactured front hubs, the bearings are held in place with a retainer; on most imported hubs, the bearings are loose in a bearing cup formed in the end of the hub shell. Some imported lightweight front-wheel hubs have removable bearing cups.

QUICK-RELEASE HUBS

The quick-release hub can be considered a lightweight conventional hub fitted with a mechanism that allows it to be removed quickly from the bicycle without the use of tools. The axle of the quick-release hub is hollow, allowing a full-length stud to hold the entire arrangement together; it also provides a means of mounting it onto the bicycle front fork. This is accomplished by one end of the stud having a cam-action type body and spring secured to it with a cam lever and nut. The other end of the stud is fitted with an

This is a typical quick-release front-wheel hub. The service procedures begin on page 86.

adjusting nut and tension spring. To remove the front wheel, it is a simple matter to turn the cam lever 180°, releasing the hub from the dropouts in the fork. To install the wheel, the hub is slid into the dropouts and the cam lever is rotated toward the rear of the bicycle, locking it in place.

INTERNAL-EXPANDING-TYPE BRAKE HUBS

This type of front hub contains an internal-expanding, double-shoe, drum-type brake arrangement. The two brake shoes act against a brake drum, which is an integral part of one end of the hub shell. The brake is operated by an external lever, which is connected to a cable controlled by another lever on the handle bar. The principle of the axle, ball bearings, adjustable cones, and attachment to the front fork is the same as with the conventional hub.

OVERHAULING A CONVENTIONAL FRONT-WHEEL HUB

The following step-by-step illustrated procedures provide complete instructions for disassembling, assembling, and adjusting a conventional front-wheel hub. Three detailed exploded drawings, showing all internal parts of a typical heavy-duty and two lightweight conventional front-wheel hubs, follow the Cleaning and Inspecting portion of this section.

For photographic clarity, the illustrations were made of a hub without the tire, rim, or spokes.

This is an Atom internal-expanding type brake hub. Overhaul procedures for the hub and service instructions for the brake mechanism start on page 95.

REMOVING THE WHEEL

If the bicycle you are going to work on has no levers mounted on the handlebars, you can turn the bicycle upside down, resting it on the seat and handlebars. A better method, and a must for bicycles with caliper brakes or a shifting lever mounted on the handlebars, is to support the bicycle in an upright position from a set of hooks, a bracket, or a rope attached to the garage ceiling. Or secure it in an automobile carrier rack attached to the car.

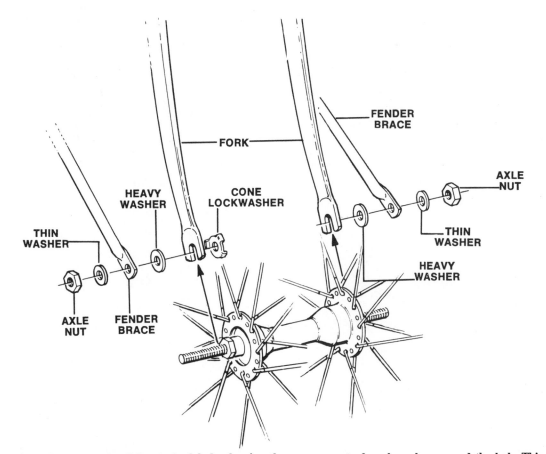

Exploded view of a conventional front-wheel hub, showing the arrangement of washers, braces, and the hub. This illustration should be used for removing and installing the parts in the proper order.

Remove the front wheel by loosening the two axle or wing nuts, and then sliding the axle out of the front-fork dropouts. If basket or fender supports are attached to the axle, remove the axle nuts, and then slide the supports off the axle prior to removing the wheel.

If you are working on a bicycle with front-wheel caliper brakes, sight down over the tire to see if there is enough room for the tire to clear the brake shoes. If there is not sufficient clearance, it will be necessary to release the brake shoes farther than normal in order for the tire to clear. This is accomplished by squeezing the front brake handle slightly, pushing in on the quick-release button, and then releasing the brake handle. This retracts the caliper arms farther than normal, allowing the tire to clear the brake shoes. The only function of this button is to facilitate easy removal of the wheel for a tire change, an overhaul, or an adjustment.

If you are working on a bicycle without the quick-release button, there may be a quick-release lever just above the brake on the cable hanger. Turning this lever will release the brake shoes farther than normal. If neither of these quick-release mechanisms is installed, a quick way to gain the necessary clearance is to remove the mounting nut from one of the brake-shoe holders, and then remove the complete brake shoe assembly. Still another method, provided you have a pump or air supply handy, is to deflate the tire, which will usually clear the shoes, and you need not disturb the brake shoes or the brake adjustment.

DISASSEMBLING

① After the wheel has been removed, remove the two axle nuts, and then clamp one end of the axle in a vise. **CAUTION: Use soft vise jaws to protect the axle threads.** Hold the cone with a thin wrench or pair of cone pliers while you loosen the locknut.

② Take off the locknut, and then unscrew and remove the cone.

③ Remove the ball bearing retainer assembly from the bearing cup of the hub, and then lift off the hub. If you are working on a lightweight hub with a

dust cap and loose ball bearings, remove the dust cap by prying it up with a screwdriver. Work around the cap edge and it will pop out. Be careful not to crimp or distort the cap. Remove and count the ball bearings.

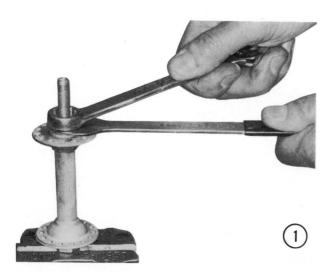

Removing the dust cap on a lightweight hub. Be sure to count the number of loose ball bearings in each end to assist you in assembly.

④ Lift off the other ball bearing assembly. Remove the dust cap and loose ball bearings from the other end of the lightweight hub. Turn the axle end for end in the vise; unscrew the locknut, and then the bearing cone.

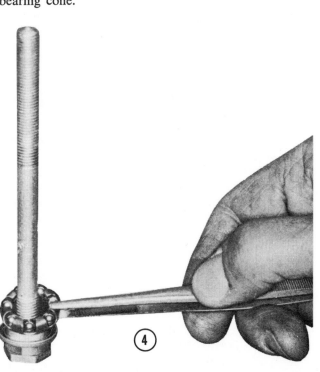

④

CLEANING AND INSPECTING

Clean all parts in solvent and blow dry with compressed air, or wipe them dry with a lintless cloth. Keep all cleaned parts on paper towels to avoid contamination. Cover them with a clean towel to keep grit from entering the internal parts and bearings. A tiny piece of grit can do a tremendous amount of damage if allowed to work on a part over an extended period of time or while the wheel is turning at high speed.

Inspect the *ball bearings and retainer.* If any of the ball bearings come out of the retainer, are pitted, cracked, or show other signs of damage, the complete assembly must be replaced. Check the retainer for cracks or pits and replace the complete bearing assembly if this type of damage is visible. *NOTE: If working on a hub with loose ball bearings, check each bearing carefully for signs of excessive wear (dull spots, pits, or cracks) and replace the complete set even if one is damaged.* Replacing the complete set will ensure even distribution of the bearing surface load on all the ball bearings.

Inspect the bearing surface of the *cones* for scoring (scratchlike marks), pitting (pencil-point dots), excessive wear (dull spots), and for stripped threads.

Inspect the bearing cup of the *hub* for scoring, pitting, or excessive wear. Check the hub spoke holes for damage or for being out-of-round. If you are working on a hub with removable bearing cups and a cup

CRACK

Inspect the hub for cracks around the outside of the ball bearing raceways. Cracks are caused by the ball bearing cone adjustment being too loose.

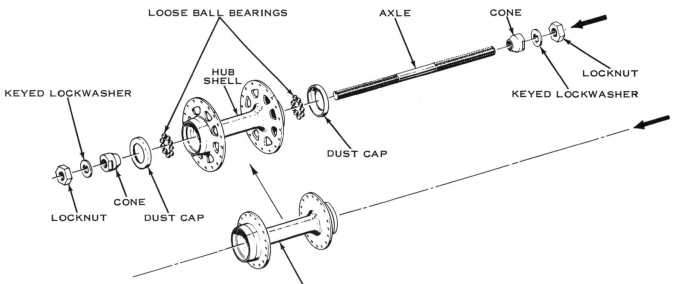

Exploded view of a Schwinn-Approved, Sprint, Normandy, and Atom front-wheel hub. All parts of these four hubs are interchangeable.

Exploded view of a typical heavy-duty front-wheel hub.

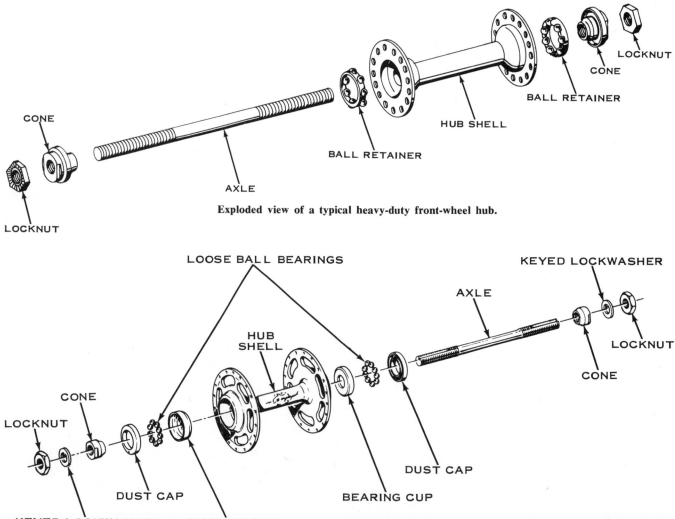

Exploded view of a Campagnolo Track, lightweight, precision front-wheel hub. Note the removable bearing cups and loose ball bearings.

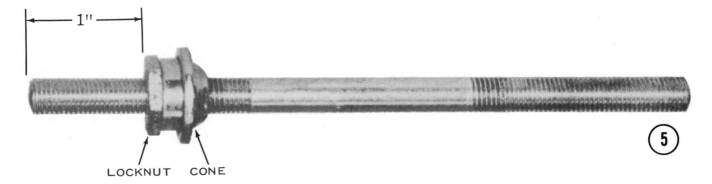

1"

LOCKNUT   CONE

⑤

needs to be replaced, remove it from the hub by tapping it out with an off-center drift punch and hammer from the other end of the hub. **CAUTION: Do not remove the cup unless it has to be replaced because it is very difficult to remove without damaging it.**

Check the *axle* and locknuts for signs of damage or stripped threads. Roll the axle slowly across a smooth flat surface and check both ends for being out-of-round or watch the center to see if it rises off the surface. Either of these indications means the axle is bent and must be replaced.

Check the *dust caps* on imported hubs to be sure they are not crimped or distorted, which could have happened during disassembly.

ASSEMBLING

⑤ Thread one of the cones onto either end of the axle until the outer edge of the cone is one inch from the end of the axle, as shown. Turn a locknut onto the axle, with the knurled side away from the cone, and then tighten it against the cone.

⑥ Pack both ball bearing assemblies with a generous amount of multipurpose lubricant. Work it throughout the bearings and the retainers with your fingers. If you are working on a hub with loose bearings, apply a generous amount of lubricant to both bearing cups of the hub. If you replaced a removable

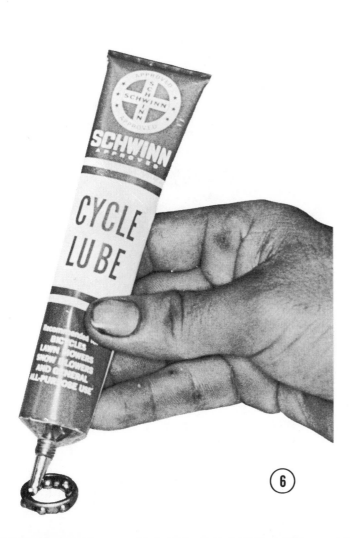

⑥

Applying multipurpose lubricant to a bearing cup of a Campagnolo precision hub. The lubricant must be inserted first to keep the loose ball bearings in place during assembly.

bearing cup, install it by using a socket the same size as the bottom of the cup, and then tapping the cup into place with a hammer. **CAUTION: Be sure the socket is the correct size; that it sets squarely on the cup; and that you tap the socket squarely to ensure that the cup goes into place evenly and without damage.**

⑦ Slip one of the caged bearing assemblies onto the cone, with the ball bearings facing toward the

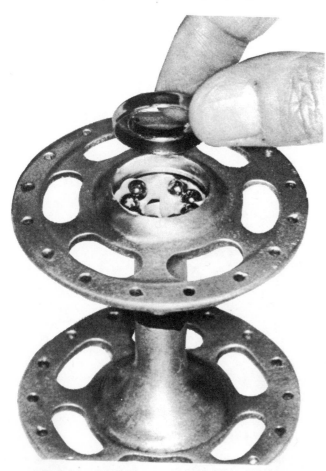

Installing the dust cap on a Campagnolo front-wheel hub. Note the one ball bearing clearance.

Installing a lightweight, precision hub on the axle. Note how the lubricant and dust cap keep the loose ball bearings from dropping out of place.

center of the axle. This will allow them to roll on the inside of the bearing cup in the hub and on the tapered part of the cone. If you are working on a lightweight hub with loose bearings, place each bearing in the lubricated bearing cup at one end of the hub with a pair of tweezers. Install the same number you counted during disassembly. If you lost count, insert bearings until they all fit snugly, and then remove one ball bearing for proper clearance. Tap the dust cap into place over the bearing cup with a mallet. Install the bearings and dust cap in the other end of the hub shell in a similar manner.

⑧ Slide the hub over the axle and into place on the bearings. The lubricant will hold the bearings in place while you slide a lightweight hub over the axle.

⑨ Push the second lubricated bearing retainer assembly into the other bearing cup of the hub.

⑩ Thread the other cone and locknut onto the axle, with the bearing race facing the bearing assembly and the knurled side of the locknut facing up. Tighten the cone finger-tight against the bearing retainer, and then back it off approximately ⅕ turn for a rough adjustment.

⑪ Hold the cone with a thin wrench or cone pliers, and then tighten the locknut against the cone. Shift the wheel in the vise so the jaws grip one of the locknuts. Grasp the rim of the wheel and try to move the wheel up and down—this is referred to as side play. Remove all but a trace of side play by adjusting the cone and then securing it with the locknut. Remove the complete and adjusted assembly from the vise.

⑫ To check the bearing adjustment, hold each end of the axle with your fingers, and then slowly twist the axle with your thumbs and forefingers—the wheel should not turn. If it does turn, the cones are too tight. Loosen one of the locknuts, back off the cone approximately ⅛ turn, and then retighten the locknut.

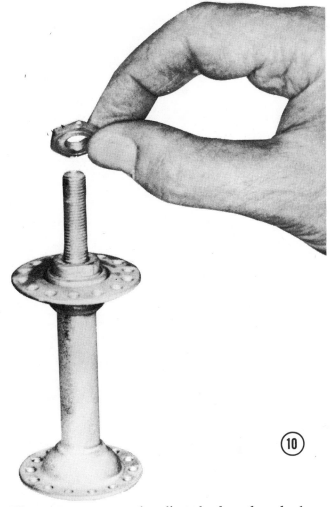

The cones are properly adjusted when the wheel rotates freely, comes to rest gradually with the valve stem at the lowest point of the wheel and there is only the slightest trace of side play. On precision-built bi-

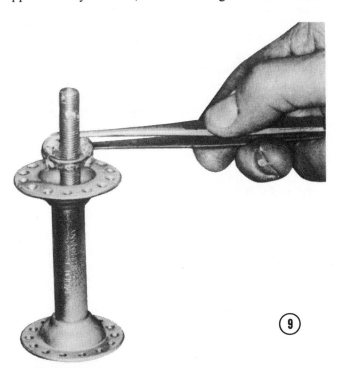

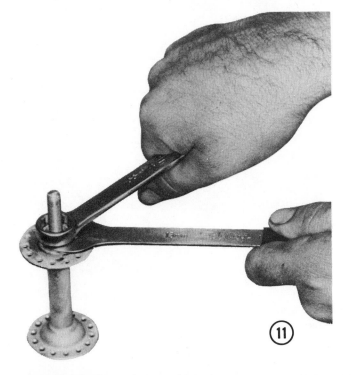

(12)

cycles, it is possible, with patience, to adjust the cones so accurately that the wheel will turn freely with no indication of side play. However, on the average bicycle, a slight trace of side play should be evident. A check of the cone adjustment must be made after the wheel is installed on the bicycle, because if care is not taken to hold the locknut while tightening the axle nuts, the cone adjustment may change. **CAUTION: If the cones are adjusted too tight, it will cause bind-**

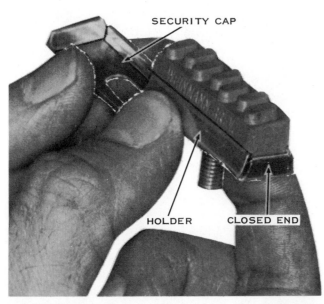

Install the brake-shoe holder with the closed end facing forward and with the beveled surface of the shoe matching the angle of the wheel rim, as discussed in the text.

ing and scoring of the hub. If the cones are adjusted too loose, it will cause fatigue, which can result in a damaged hub or broken axle.

INSTALLING THE WHEEL

Install the assembled hub and wheel in the front fork dropouts as indicated in the accompanying illustration. If you are working on a bicycle with a cone lockwasher and heavy space washer, install the lockwasher over the cone with the ears of the lockwasher facing out and aligned with the flats of the cone. Install the thick washer on the opposite side of the wheel. Guide the axle into the front fork dropout slots, with the cone lockwasher on the right side (sprocket side) of the fork, until the axle is seated against the ends of the slots.

Check to be sure the cone lockwasher and thick washer are on the inside of the fork and the cone lockwasher ears are positioned in the fork slot. If heavy washers are used against the fork to prevent the fork from twisting when the axle nuts are tightened, slide the washers onto both ends of the axle. If the bicycle has fender braces or accessory supports, slide them onto the axle. If accessory supports are installed, use a washer between the support and the axle nuts. Tighten the axle nuts, and then check to be sure the wheel turns freely with the minimum amount of side play. If the cone adjustment was disturbed during installation of the wheel, loosen the axle nut and the cone locknut on the left side of the forks; adjust the cone as necessary, with a cone wrench or cone pliers, and then retighten the locknut and the axle nut securely.

If you are working on a bicycle equipped with caliper brakes and a quick-release button on the brake handle or a quick-release lever above the brake on the cable hanger, return the lever to the operating position. If you removed one of the brake-shoe assemblies to gain tire clearance, install the holder with the closed end facing forward and with the beveled surface of the shoe matching the angle of the wheel rim. **CAUTION: The closed end of the holder must face forward to prevent the shoe from being forced out when the brakes are applied.** Adjust the brake-shoe holder in the brake-arm slot until the upper edge of the shoe makes contact just below the edge of the rim, when the brake lever on the handlebar is squeezed. Tighten the mounting nut securely.

If the tire was deflated for wheel removal, pump it up to the required pressure.

OVERHAULING A QUICK-RELEASE HUB

The Campagnolo, Sprint, Normandy, Atom, and several other quick-release front hubs are basically alike with the following exceptions: (1) Some manufacturers use eight loose ball bearings in each end of the hub shell, whereas other manufacturers use nine or more ball bearings. (2) The hub shell on some models has a bearing cup in each end of the shell to hold the bearings. On other models, the end of the hub shell forms the bearing cup. (3) Some hubs have

Typical quick-release front-wheel hub.

an oil hole in the center of the shell with an oil hole cover.

In the disassembling and assembling procedures that follow, these differences are noted in the text.

REMOVING THE WHEEL

Support the bicycle in an upright position from a bracket, a set of hooks, or a rope attached to the garage ceiling, or secure it in an automobile rear carrier rack attached to the car. Sight down over the tire to see if there is enough room for it to clear the brake shoes. If there is not sufficient clearance, it will be necessary to release the brake shoes farther than normal in order for the tire to clear. This is accomplished by first squeezing the front brake handle slightly, pushing in on the quick-release button, and then releasing the brake handle. This action releases the caliper arms farther than normal, allowing the front tire to clear the brake shoes. The only function of this button is to facilitate easy removal of the wheel for a tire change, an overhaul, or an adjustment.

If you are working on a bicycle without the quick-release button on the brake handle, there may be a quick-release lever just above the brake on the cable hanger. Turning this lever will release the brake shoes farther than normal. If neither of these quick-release mechanisms is installed, a quick way to gain the necessary clearance is to remove the mounting nut from one of the brake-shoe holders, and then remove the complete brake-shoe assembly. Still another method, provided you have a pump or air supply handy, is to deflate the tire, which will usually clear the brake shoes.

Turn the quick-release lever 180° to the full forward position. This action releases the hub so that the wheel can be removed from the front fork dropouts.

DISASSEMBLING

① Hold the quick-release lever with one hand, and then remove the quick-release adjusting nut and spring from the other end of the axle.

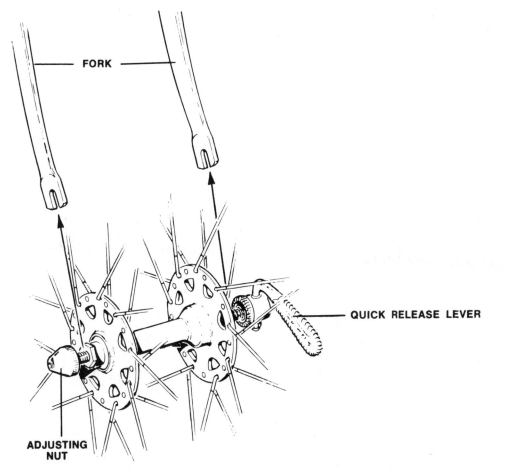

FORK

QUICK RELEASE LEVER

ADJUSTING NUT

Turning the quick-release lever allows you to remove a front-wheel hub quickly and easily without the use of tools.

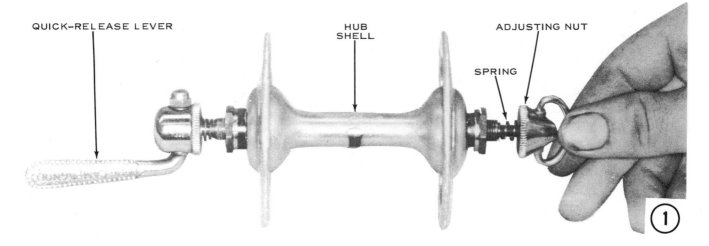

QUICK-RELEASE LEVER   HUB SHELL   ADJUSTING NUT   SPRING

② Remove the mounting stud by pulling it out of the axle. Remove the tension spring.

③ Clamp one end of the axle in a vise. **CAUTION: Protect the axle threads with soft vise jaws to keep from damaging them.** Remove the locknut, keyed lockwasher, and cone. On some foreign-built, quick-release hubs, another locknut may be installed that must be removed before you attempt to remove the cone.

④ Remove the dust cap by prying it up with a screwdriver, as shown. Work around the cap edge. Be careful not to crimp or damage it.

⑤ Reach into the hub cup with a pair of tweezers and remove each of the ball bearings. **CAUTION: Be sure to count the bearings as an aid to installation.** As mentioned, the number of ball bearings will vary, depending on the make of hub. Some front hubs may have eight ball bearings, others have nine or more. Slide the hub shell up and off the axle. If the hub shell has an oil hole and cover, snap the cover off the hub.

Carefully remove the dust cap from the other end of the hub by prying it off with a screwdriver. Remove and count the ball bearings. Reverse the axle in the vise and remove the locknut and keyed lockwasher. If you are working on a model with two locknuts, remove the second locknut.

⑥ Remove the acorn nut, lockwasher, quick-release lever, and cam lever body from the mounting stud.

CLEANING AND INSPECTING

Clean all parts in solvent and blow dry with compressed air, or wipe them dry with a lintless cloth. Keep all cleaned parts on paper towels to avoid contamination. Cover them with a clean towel to keep grit from entering the internal parts and bearings. A tiny piece of grit can do a tremendous amount of damage if allowed to work on a part over an extended period of time or while the wheel is turning at high speed.

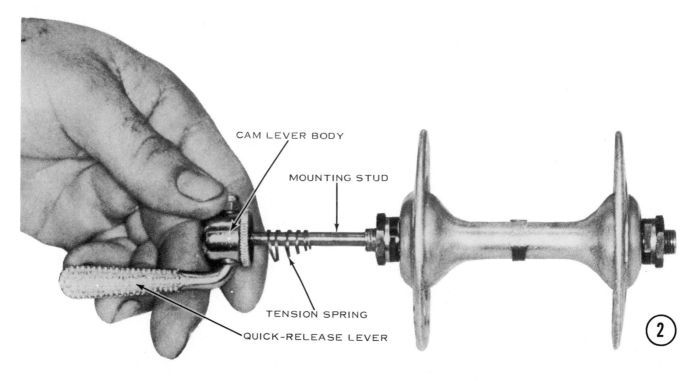

CAM LEVER BODY   MOUNTING STUD   TENSION SPRING   QUICK-RELEASE LEVER

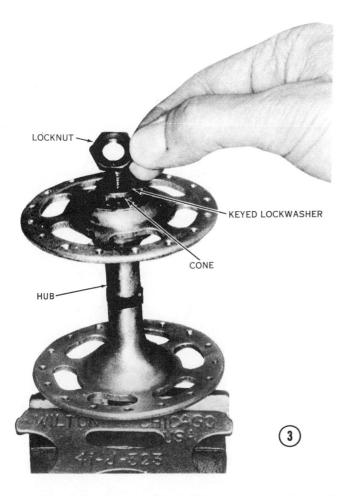

LOCKNUT

KEYED LOCKWASHER

CONE

HUB

③

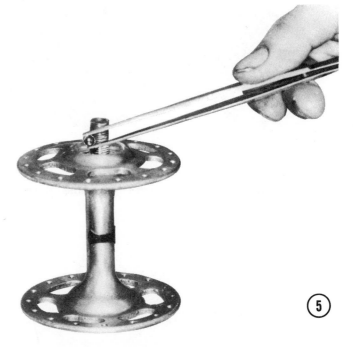

⑤

④

Carefully inspect the *ball bearings* for signs of excessive wear (dull spots, pits, or cracks) and replace the complete set if any of them are damaged. Replacing the complete set will ensure even distribution of the bearing surface load on all the ball bearings.

Inspect the bearing surfaces of the *cones* for scor-

ing (scratchlike marks), pitting (pencil-point dots), and for stripped threads.

Inspect the bearing cup of the *hub* for scoring, pitting, or excessive wear. If you are working on a hub with removable bearing cups, and a cup needs to be replaced, remove it from the hub by tapping it out with an off-center drift punch and hammer from the other end of the hub. **CAUTION: Do not remove the cup unless it has to be replaced because it is very difficult to remove without damaging it.**

Check the *axle* and locknuts for signs of damage or stripped threads. Roll the axle slowly across a smooth flat surface and check both ends for being out-of-round or watch the center of the axle to see if it rises off the surface. Either of these indications means the axle is bent and must be replaced.

Check the quick-release *mounting stud* for cracks, bends, and stripped threads.

Check both *tension springs* for cracks, breaks, or other damage.

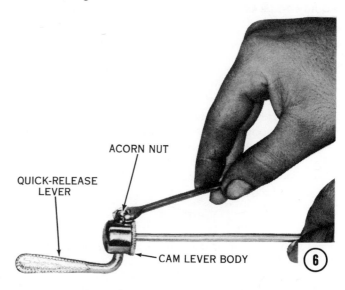

ACORN NUT

QUICK-RELEASE LEVER

CAM LEVER BODY

⑥

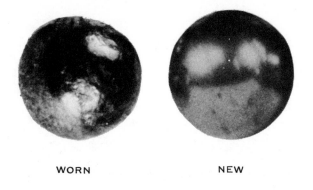

WORN   NEW

An excellent example of a pitted ball bearing alongside a new one for comparison.

ASSEMBLING

⑦ Thread one of the cones onto either end of the axle, with the bearing race facing toward the center of the axle, until the outer edge of the cone is ⅜ inch from the end of the axle, as shown. Install the locknut or keyed lockwasher with the key indexing with the keyway in the axle. If you are working on an assembly with two locknuts on the adjusting-nut end of the axle, install the keyed lockwasher, with the key indexed with the keyway in the axle. Install the second locknut, with the machined recess of the locknut facing away from the keyed lockwasher.

⑧ Apply a generous amount of multipurpose lubricant to a bearing cup of the hub shell. If you replace a removable bearing cup, install it by using a

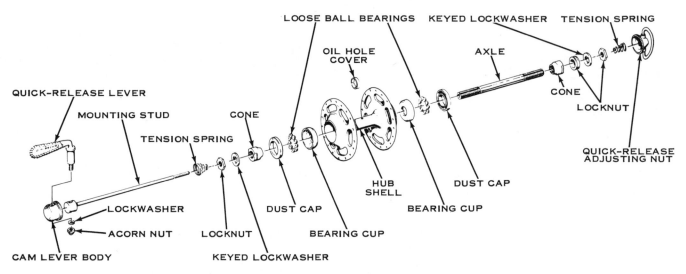

Exploded view of a Campagnolo Road precision-built hub, with removable bearing cups and loose ball bearings. Note the oil hole cover that allows you to lubricate the ball bearings periodically without disassembling the hub.

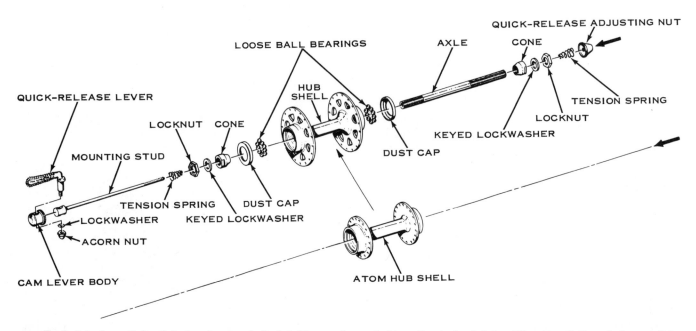

Exploded view of the Schwinn-Approved, Sprint, Normandy, and Atom front-wheel hub. All parts of these hubs are interchangeable.

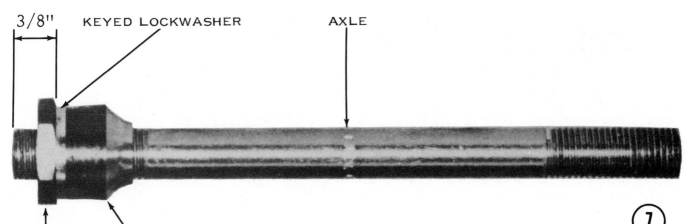

3/8" KEYED LOCKWASHER   AXLE

LOCKNUT   CONE

(7)

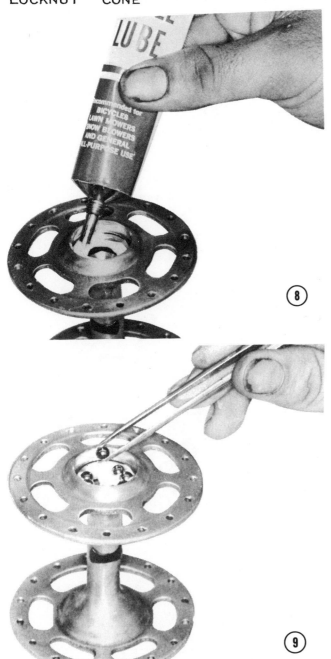

(8)

(9)

socket the same size as the bottom of the cup, and then tapping the cup into place with a hammer. **CAUTION: Be sure the socket is the correct size; that it sets squarely in the cup; and that you tap the socket squarely to ensure that the cup goes into place evenly and without damage.**

⑨ Imbed the same number of loose ball bearings in the lubricated bearing cup as you counted during disassembly. If the count was lost, place bearings in the cup until they all fit snugly around the side of the cup, and then remove one for proper clearance.

⑩ Install the dust cap. Notice the one-ball clearance between the ball bearings on the far side of the hub.

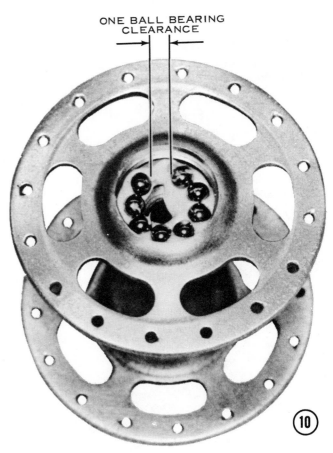

ONE BALL BEARING CLEARANCE

(10)

⑪ Tap the dust cap into place with a hammer. Lubricate the race, install the ball bearings, and replace the dust cap on the other end of the hub.

⑫ Place the assembled axle in a vise, with the soft jaws gripping the locknut. Slide the hub over the axle and into place against the cone.

⑬ Thread the other cone onto the axle finger-tight against the bearings, and then back the cone off approximately ⅛ turn for a rough adjustment. If you are working on a hub with two locknuts, install one of the locknuts.

⑭ Install the keyed lockwasher, with the key indexing with the keyway in the axle. Install the locknut, with the machined recess away from the keyed lockwasher.

⑮ To make a preliminary bearing adjustment, hold the cone with a thin wrench or cone pliers, and then tighten the locknut against the cone. Grasp the rim of the wheel and try to move the wheel up and down—this is referred to as side play. Remove all but the slightest trace of side play by adjusting the cone and then securing it with the locknut. Remove the assembly from the vise. If you are working on a hub with an oil hole and cover, snap the cover over the hub shell, and then shift the cover until the dimple on the cover pops into the oil hole to lock it in place.

⑯ To check the bearing adjustment, hold each end of the axle with your fingers, and then slowly twist the axle with your thumbs and forefingers—the

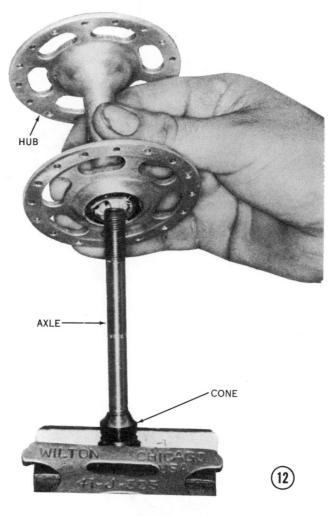

HUB

AXLE

CONE

⑫

⑪

⑬

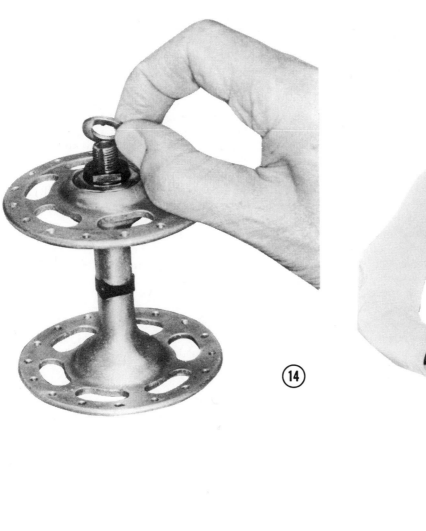

14

16

WRENCH ON LOCKNUT

WRENCH ON CONE

15

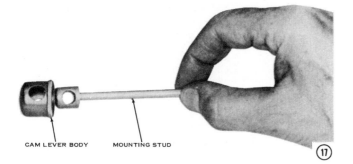

CAM LEVER BODY   MOUNTING STUD

(17)

fatigue, which can result in a damaged hub or broken axle.

⑰ Place the cam lever body on the mounting stud, and then align the holes in the body and the stud. *NOTE: The body can go on either way.*

⑱ Install the quick-release lever through the large hole in the cam lever body until it is fully seated. Rotate the quick-release lever. You should be able to move it from a forward position (90° to the mounting stud) through a full 180°, where the lever will be pointing 90° to the mounting stud in the opposite direction. If the lever cannot be rotated a full 180°, remove the lever, rotate it 180°, and then reinstall the lever back in the cam lever body.

⑲ Place the lockwasher onto the lever shaft; then thread the acorn nut on and tighten it firmly.

⑳ Slide one of the tension springs onto the mounting stud, with the small end of the spring facing toward the hub, as shown. Insert the mounting stud through the axle.

㉑ Slide the other tension spring onto the mounting stud, with the small end of the spring facing toward the hub. Start the adjusting nut onto the mounting stud by rotating it several turns.

wheel should not turn. If it does turn, the cones are too tight. Loosen one of the locknuts, back off the cone approximately ⅛ turn, and then retighten the locknut. The cones are properly adjusted when the wheel rotates freely, comes to rest gradually with the valve stem at the lowest point of the wheel and there is only the slightest trace of side play. On precision-built bicycles, it is possible, with patience, to adjust the cones so accurately that the wheel will turn freely without any indication of side play. **CAUTION: If the cones are adjusted too tight, it will cause binding and scoring of the hub. If the cones are adjusted too loose, it will cause**

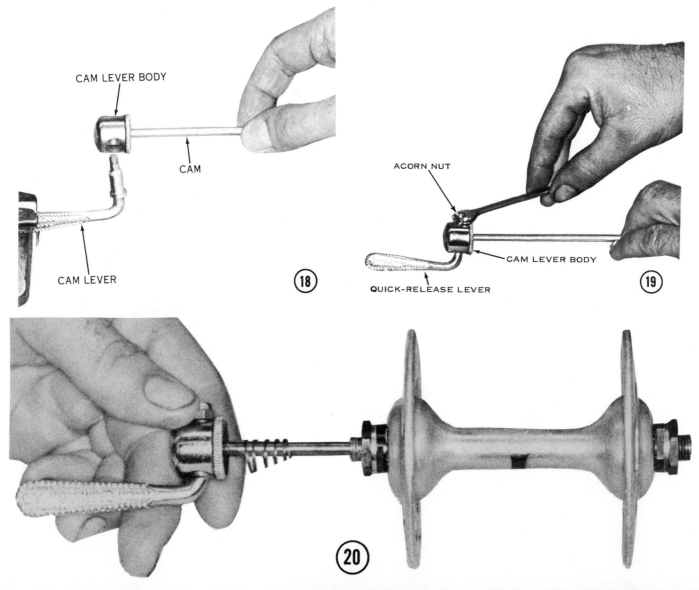

CAM LEVER BODY

CAM

CAM LEVER

(18)

ACORN NUT

CAM LEVER BODY

QUICK-RELEASE LEVER

(19)

(20)

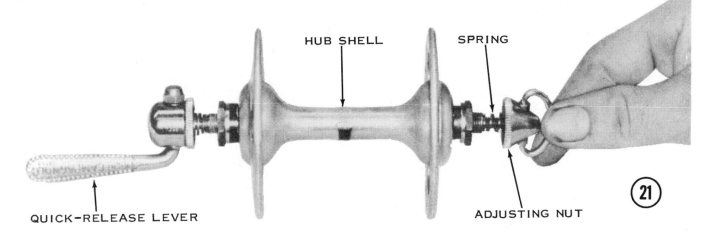

HUB SHELL

SPRING

21

QUICK-RELEASE LEVER

ADJUSTING NUT

INSTALLING THE WHEEL

Slide the wheel into place in the fork dropouts, as indicated in the accompanying illustration. Turn the cam lever from forward to the rearward position, locking the hub in place. You should meet a little resistance in turning the lever to the closed (locked) position if the adjustment is correct. To change the adjustment, turn the lever to the released position (facing forward), then tighten the acorn adjusting nut on the opposite side of the hub approximately ½ turn; now turn the lever back to the locked position. Repeat the procedure until you are satisfied with the adjustment.

Check to be sure the wheel turns freely with the desired amount of side play.

Return the caliper brakes to the operating position. If you removed one of the brake-shoe assemblies to gain tire clearance, install the holder with the closed end facing forward and with the beveled surface of the shoe matching the angle of the wheel rim. **CAUTION: Be sure the closed end of the holder is facing**

forward to prevent the shoe from being forced out when the brakes are applied and subsequent complete loss of braking ability at the front wheel. Adjust the brake-shoe holder in the brake-arm slot until the upper edge of the shoe makes contact just below the edge of the rim, when the brake lever on the handlebar is squeezed. Tighten the mounting nut securely.

If the tire was deflated for wheel removal, pump it up to the required pressure.

OVERHAULING AN ATOM FRONT-WHEEL HUB, WITH EXPANDER-TYPE BRAKE

The overhaul instructions for disassembling and assembling this type of hub are divided into two sections—one for the brake components and the other for the internal parts of the hub. However, the steps are numbered consecutively and include a complete overhaul. If the reason for working on the hub is to replace the brake shoes, only the procedures in the brake sections need to be followed. If the internal parts need attention, it is an indication the hub has had extensive use and, rarely, if ever, would the hub be reassembled without installing new brake shoes; therefore, all the procedures should be performed.

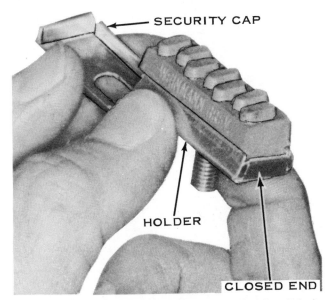

SECURITY CAP

HOLDER

CLOSED END

Install the brake-shoe holder with the closed end facing forward to keep the shoe from being forced out when the brake is applied.

This Atom hub contains an internal-expanding, double-shoe, drum-type brake assembly.

REMOVING THE WHEEL

Support the bicycle in an upright position from a bracket, a set of hooks, or a rope attached to the garage ceiling, or secure it in an automobile rear carrier rack attached to the car.

Some bicycles may have heavy washers, serrated on one side, installed on the axle between the fork members on each side to prevent the forks from twisting when the axle nuts are tightened. If basket or fender supports are attached onto the axle, a thin washer may be installed between the outside fork member and the axle nut to prevent the supports from twisting when the axle nuts are tightened.

Back off the cable anchor bolt nut by turning it counterclockwise, and then remove the cable from the anchor bolt. Loosen the locknut on the adjusting sleeve, and remove the cable and housing from the sleeve.

Remove the two axle nuts. Slide any basket or fender supports, along with any washers, off the axle, and then remove the axle from the dropouts.

DISASSEMBLING

① Clamp the axle in a vise, with the brake lever side facing up. **CAUTION: Protect the axle threads with soft vise jaws to keep from damaging them.** Remove the locknut and keyed lockwasher.

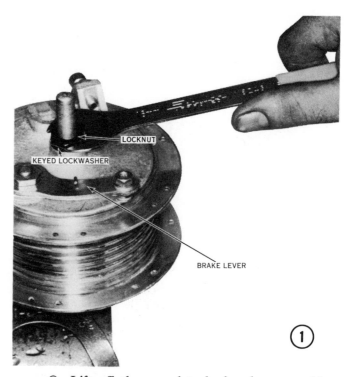

② Lift off the complete brake shoe assembly. Remove the hub and axle assembly from the vise.

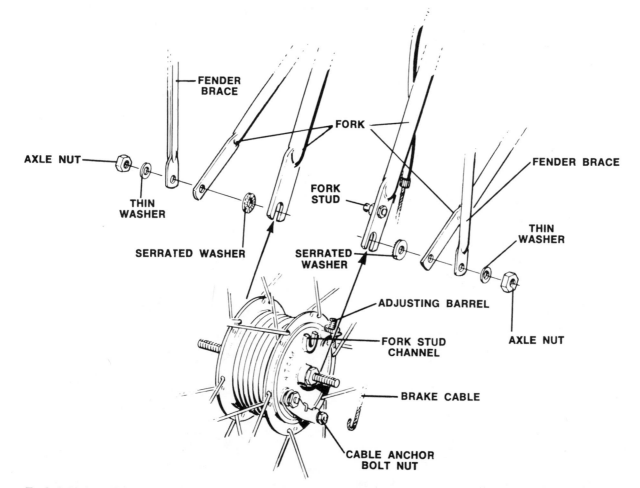

Exploded view of the Atom front-wheel hub, showing the arrangement of washers, braces, and the hub. This illustration should be used for removing and installing the parts in the proper order.

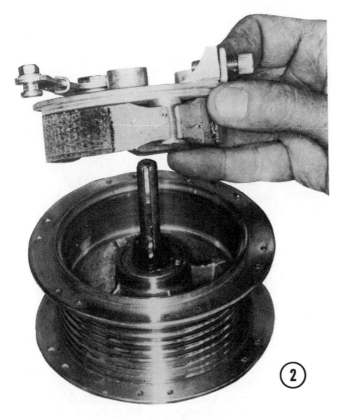

(2)

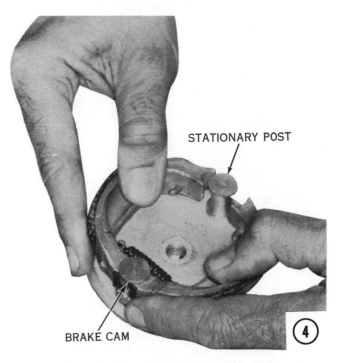

STATIONARY POST

BRAKE CAM

(4)

DISASSEMBLING THE BRAKE MECHANISM

③ Clamp a support rod in the vise, and then slide the brake assembly onto the rod, with the brake shoes facing up and the brake lever free at one end of the vise. Remove the spring on the stationary post

side by grasping the spring firmly with a pair of needle-nosed pliers and unhooking it from one of the knobs, as shown.

④ Hold one brake shoe in each hand, and then slide both shoes toward the center of the plate and off the brake cam. Remove the remaining spring from the brake shoes. *NOTE: If the only work to be performed is to replace the brake shoes, you can proceed directly to Step* ⑨ *and install a new set of shoes.*

DISASSEMBLING THE INTERNAL PARTS OF THE HUB

⑤ Clamp the hub in the vise, with the jaws gripping the axle. **CAUTION: Protect the axle threads with soft vise jaws to keep from damaging them.** Remove the locknut, keyed lockwasher, and the cone. Lift the hub up and off the axle. Turn the axle end for end in the vise. Remove the thin locknut, the two keyed lockwashers, the thick locknut, two more keyed lockwashers, and then the cone.

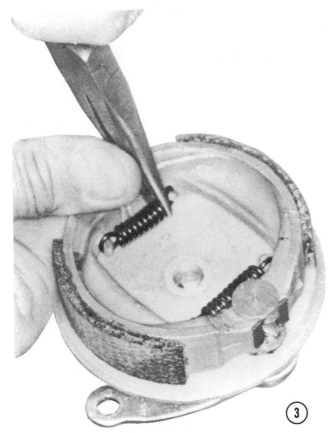

(3)

(5)

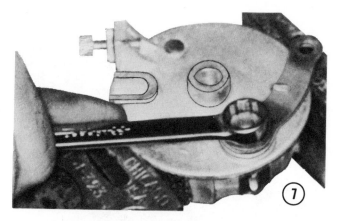

⑥ Remove the dust cap on the brake-shoe side by prying it up with a screwdriver, as shown. Work around the cap and it will pop out. Be careful not to crimp or damage it. Count and remove the loose ball bearings from the bearing cup. Turn the hub over, and then remove the dust cap on the other side by prying it up with a screwdriver as before. Count and remove the loose ball bearings from the bearing cup. There should be nine (9) loose ball bearings on each side of the hub.

⑦ Loosen the locknut on the brake cam, swing the brake lever away from the center of the brake plate, and then unhook the brake lever spring. Remove

the locknut, brake lever, and spring. Remove the cable adjusting sleeve and locknut. Remove the cable anchor nut and bolt from the brake lever.

CLEANING AND INSPECTING

Clean all parts, except the brake shoes, in solvent and blow them dry with compressed air, or wipe them dry with a lintless cloth. Keep all cleaned parts on paper towels to avoid contamination. Cover them with a clean towel to keep grit from entering the internal parts and bearings. A tiny piece of grit can do a tremendous amount of damage if allowed to work on a part over an extended period of time or while the wheel is turning at high speed.

Carefully inspect the *ball bearings*. If any of the ball bearings are pitted (pencil-point dots), show signs of excessive wear (dull spots), or are cracked, all the

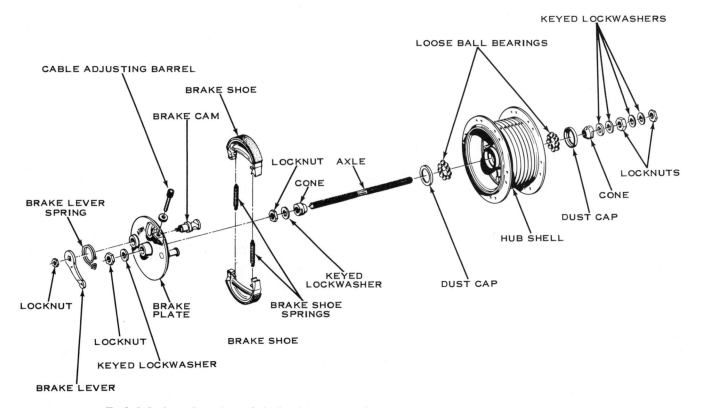

Exploded view of an Atom hub showing the two-shoe, internal-expanding type brake mechanism.

bearings in the set should be replaced. Replacing the complete set will ensure even distribution of the bearing surface load on all the ball bearings.

Inspect the bearing cups of the *hub* for scoring (scratchlike marks), pitting, or excessive wear.

Inspect the *cones* for scored or pitted bearing surfaces and for stripped threads.

Check the *axle* and locknuts for signs of damage or stripped threads. Roll the axle slowly across a smooth flat surface and check both ends for being out-of-round, or watch the center of the axle to see if it rises off the surface. Either of these indications means the axle is bent and must be replaced.

Check the *dust caps* to be sure they were not crimped, bent, or damaged when they were removed.

Check the *brake shoes* for breaks or cracks and the linings for glaze and for excessive or uneven wear. Check the brake shoe springs for damage, cracks, breaks, or weak tension. You should have had considerable difficulty unhooking the springs from the knobs, which shows that the spring tension is satisfactory.

Inspect the brake lever *spring* for cracks or breaks.

ASSEMBLING THE BRAKE MECHANISM

⑧ Place the brake plate in a vise, with the stationary post and brake cam facing up. Set the two brake shoes on the brake plate so the brake-shoe cam ends will ride on the flats of the brake cam. If the brake lever assembly was removed, install the brake cam through the brake plate so the brake cam and stationary post are on the same side of the plate. If the brake-lever assembly was not removed, reach under the plate and unhook the brake-lever spring to assist in assembly. Turn the brake cam so the flats line up toward the center of the brake plate, allowing the brake shoes to come together as closely as possible. Hook one end of either spring over a hook on one side of the cam post. Grasp the spring firmly with a pair of needle-nosed pliers, and then stretch it enough to hook it over the other brake-shoe hook. Install the other spring in a like manner. Remove the assembly from the vise. Hook the brake-lever spring over the inside edge of the lever. *NOTE: If the brake lever and spring were not removed, you can proceed directly to Step* ⑪

⑨ If the brake lever and spring were removed, place the spring over the brake-cam threaded end, with the small ear of the spring through the small hole in the plate.

⑩ Install the brake lever on the brake cam so the lever is approximately at a right-angle to the flats on the cam and the lever offset is up away from the surface of the brake plate. Thread the locknut onto the brake cam and tighten it against the brake lever. Hook the brake lever spring over the inside edge of the brake lever. Install the adjusting sleeve and locknut with approximately the same number of sleeve threads visible on either side of the flange. Install the cable anchor bolt and nut on the brake lever.

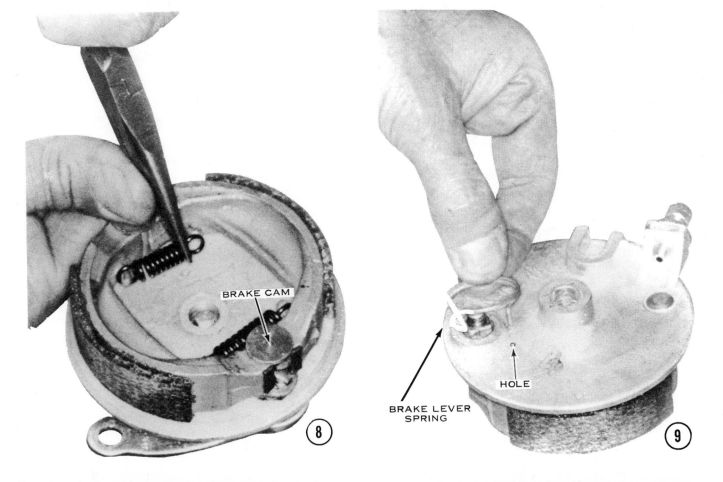

BRAKE CAM

⑧

BRAKE LEVER SPRING

HOLE

⑨

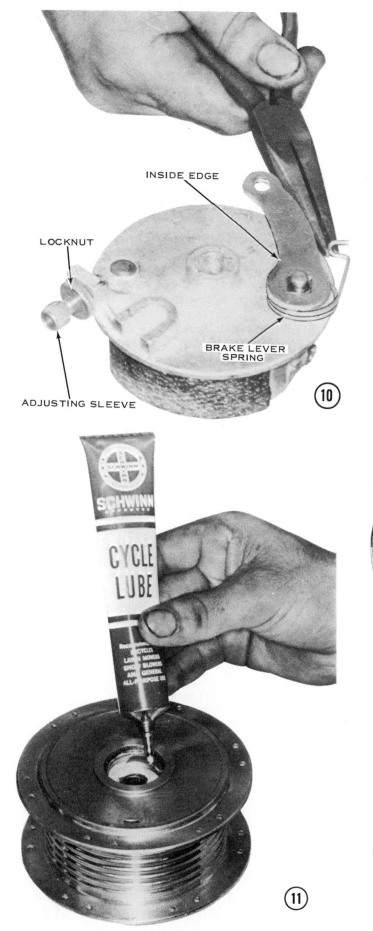

INSIDE EDGE

LOCKNUT

BRAKE LEVER SPRING

ADJUSTING SLEEVE

⑩

⑪

ASSEMBLING THE HUB

⑪ Apply a generous amount of multipurpose lubricant to the bearing cup of the hub opposite the brake shoe side.

⑫ Place nine (9) ball bearings into the lubricated bearing cup. The nine bearings should fill the cup with just a very small amount of clearance.

⑬ Position the dust cap over the ball bearings, with the flat side facing up, and then tap it into place with a hammer until the cap is fully seated in the hub shell.

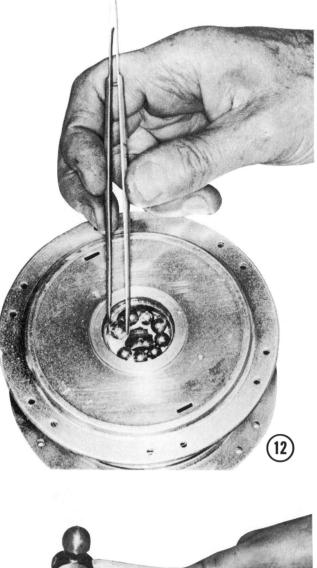

⑫

⑬

⑭ Install one of the cones on either end of the axle and turn it to the end of the axle threads. Slide two keyed lockwashers onto the axle, with the keys of the lockwashers indexing with the keyway in the axle. Next, thread a thick locknut onto the axle snugly against the lockwashers. Slide two more keyed lock-washers onto the axle with the keys indexing with the keyway in the axle, and then thread on a thin locknut. Tighten the locknut snugly against the lockwashers. Install the completed axle assembly through the hub shell from the side opposite the brake-shoe drum.

⑮ Clamp the axle in a vise, with the jaws gripping the axle locknuts and with the brake-drum side of the hub facing up. Apply a generous amount of multipurpose lubricant to the bearing cup. Place nine (9) ball bearings into the lubricated bearing cup. The nine bearings should fill the cup with just a very small amount of clearance as it did on the other end of the hub.

⑯ Slide the dust cap over the axle and ball bearings, and then tap it into place with a deep socket and hammer.

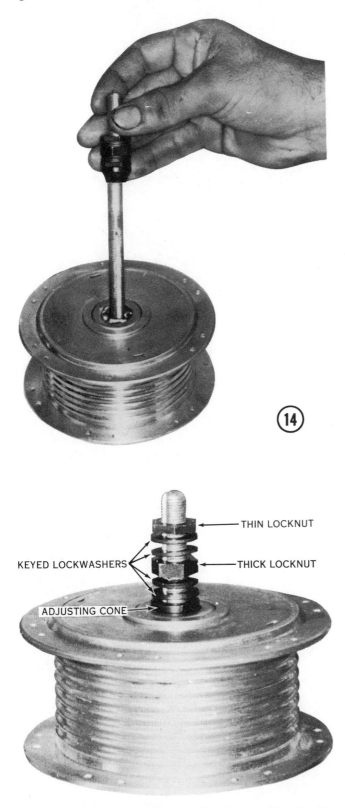

Arrangement of the washers and locknuts used on the side opposite the brake support plate of the Atom hub.

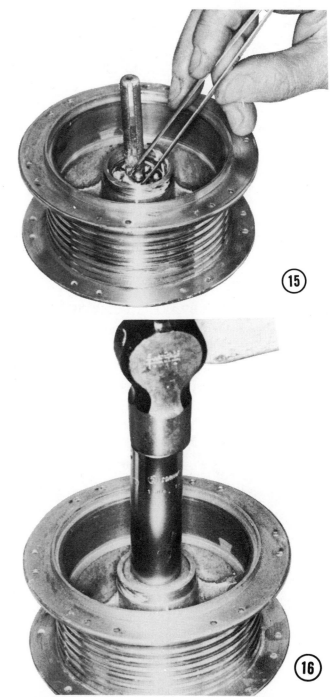

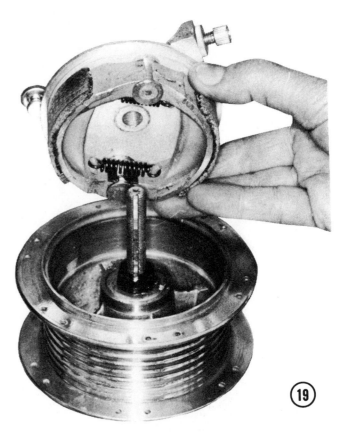

⑰ Install the cone on the axle with the bearing race facing down, and then tighten it until there is just a little drag when you turn the hub shell. Now back the cone off ⅙ turn. *NOTE: This is the only cone adjustment possible for this side because the cone is covered by the brake-shoe plate.*

⑱ Place a keyed lockwasher onto the axle, with the key indexing with the keyway in the axle. Thread a thin locknut onto the axle. Hold the cone with a thin wrench or cone pliers, and then tighten the locknut snugly.

INSTALLING THE BRAKE MECHANISM

⑲ Install the assembled brake-shoe mechanism. The springs will hold the brake shoes in the retracted position, and this should allow the assembly to slide easily into the hub shell.

⑳ Install a keyed lockwasher, with the key

indexed with the keyway in the axle. Thread a locknut onto the axle, and tighten it against the lockwasher and brake plate. Clamp the assembly in a vise, with the jaws gripping the locknut on the brake-lever side. Grasp the rim of the wheel and try to move it up and down—this is referred to as side play. Remove all but a trace of side play by backing off the locknuts and then tightening or loosening the cone. Retighten the locknuts, and then remove the assembly from the vise.

㉑ Hold each end of the axle with your fingers. Slowly twist the axle with your thumbs and forefingers —the wheel should not turn. If it does turn, the cones are too tight and must be loosened slightly. Only the exposed cone on the side opposite the brake lever can be adjusted. Back off the locknuts, loosen the cone approximately ⅛ turn, hold the cone in position with a thin wrench or cone pliers, and then retighten the locknuts. **CAUTION: If the cones are adjusted too tight, it will cause binding and scoring of the hub. If the cones are adjusted too loose, it will cause fatigue, which can result in a damaged hub or broken axle.**

INSTALLING THE WHEEL

Install the assembled hub and wheel in the front fork dropouts and secure it with the axle nuts. If the brake plate is anchored to the fork with a stud through the fork and indexing in a channel on the brake plate, rotate the wheel so the stud will slide into the channel as you move the wheel into the dropouts. If you are working on a bicycle with basket or front fender supports that attach on the axle, slide them and the proper washers onto the axle in the sequence indicated in the accompanying illustration. Be sure the serrated sides of the washers face toward the hub, as shown.

Hold the cone locknut on the inside of the fork with a thin wrench when tightening the axle nuts to prevent movement of the cone and loss of adjustment.

Details of the control levers and the parts of the Atom brake support plate.

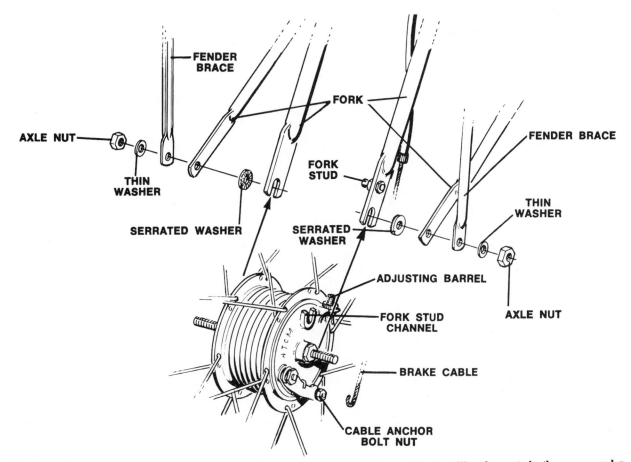

Exploded view of the Atom front-wheel hub. This illustration should be used for installing the parts in the proper order.

After the axle nuts are tight, check to be sure the wheel still turns freely with a minimum amount of side play. If the cone adjustment was disturbed while tightening the axle nuts, loosen the locknuts on the cone side opposite the brake plate just enough to allow movement of the cone, adjust the cone, and then retighten the locknuts while holding the cone in position.

If the brake plate is anchored to the fork with a brake strap, position the axle in the forks with the brake plate on the right side of the fork. Secure the brake arm to the strap with a mounting screw and nut. Guide the cable and housing into the adjusting sleeve. Insert the brake cable in the brake-lever anchor bolt. Pull the cable taut with a pair of pliers, and then secure it with the nut. Adjust the brakes by turning the wheel while you tighten the adjusting sleeve until the brake shoes just begin to rub on the drum. Back the adjusting sleeve off ⅛ turn, and then lock it in place by tightening the locknut.

For maximum enjoyment, every part of your bicycle must be properly adjusted and lubricated.

Courtesy, League of American Wheelmen

5
OVERHAULING
REAR-WHEEL HUBS

The rear-wheel hub is the most critical and complex piece of mechanism on the bicycle. If the rear hub is not functioning properly, the bicycle may not move forward, or the rider may be unable to reduce his speed or to stop properly.

Bicycles equipped with a derailleur unit and track racing bicycles with fixed rear hubs have a very simple hub, similar to the conventional and quick-release type front hubs discussed in Chapter 4. With these exceptions, the rear hub contains the most individual parts and is the most intricate part of the bicycle. This is due in part to the several functions it must perform and the fact that almost all the parts are encased in the hub shell—completely hidden from view.

Rear-wheel hubs found on today's bicycles can be grouped into one of the following six general classifications: (1) Fixed and Freewheel, (2) Freewheel with Quick-Release, (3) Single-Speed with Coaster Brake, (4) Two-Speed with Coaster Brake, (5) Three-Speed, and (6) Three-Speed with Coaster Brake.

In this chapter, you will find complete step-by-step, illustrated service instructions for disassembling, assembling, and adjusting of all six basic types of rear hubs produced by American, European, and Japanese manufacturers. Many of these firms make more than one type of hub. In some cases, because of different manufacturing techniques, one basic hub type may require a completely different set of instructions. However, hubs that are basically alike with similar service procedures or hubs that have interchangeable parts have been grouped together into one section.

Fortunately, each of the manufacturers stamps his name on the brake arm or on the hub shell and this, plus the shape of the hub, is a positive means of identification.

To assist you in identifying the type of rear wheel hub on your bike and to help you to find the proper place in the text of this chapter, each of the six types of hubs discussed above will be illustrated and reference will be made to the page number on which the service instructions begin. In effect, this chapter introduction will thus serve as a pictorial Table of Contents.

1. FIXED AND FREEWHEEL REAR HUBS

The fixed and freewheel rear hubs are very similar to the conventional front wheel hub. They have an axle passing through a hub shell (to which the spokes are attached), a set of ball bearings at each end of the hub shell, a cone at each end of the axle for adjustment, and locknuts to hold it all in place. The sprocket of the fixed wheel hub is attached directly to the hub shell, which results in the hub turning at the same speed and in the same direction as the sprocket.

The freewheel rear hub can be used with a single sprocket or with a series of varying size sprockets.

All manufacturers stamp their names on the brake arm or the hub shell, and this is an excellent method of identifying the hub that you are servicing.

A typical fixed rear-wheel hub, with the sprocket attached directly to the hub. Instructions for overhauling this type of hub begin on page 108.

A freewheel rear hub has the sprocket cluster attached to the hub through a freewheel body. Procedures for servicing this type of hub start on page 108.

The sprocket, or sprockets, are threaded onto a freewheel body, and this body is attached to the hub shell. With this type of arrangement, the hub shell moves forward at the same speed as the sprocket being driven by the chain. When the sprocket is slowed or ceases to turn, the hub shell continues to rotate, thus the term "freewheel." The combination of a freewheel body, coupled with various size sprockets and a derailleur shifting unit to move the chain from one sprocket to another, provides the rider with several gearing ratios for varying conditions.

Manufacturers of Fixed and Freewheel Rear Hubs and the page number on which the overhaul procedures begin are as follows: Atom, Schwinn-Approved Atom, Normandy, Campagnolo Track, Sprint, and Schwinn-Approved Sprint Fixed and Freewheel Rear Hubs—page 108.

2. FREEWHEEL WITH QUICK-RELEASE HUBS

The freewheel rear hub with quick-release combines the advantages of the freewheel hub with the ability to remove and install the wheel without the use of tools. A full-length mounting stud, with a cam-action-type body secured to one end, passes through the hollow axle of this hub. The other end of the stud is fitted with an adjusting nut and tension spring. This arrangement allows the wheel to be released from the rear fork dropouts by simply turning the lever away from the hub.

Manufacturers of Freewheel with Quick-Release Hubs and the page on which the overhaul procedures begin are as follows: Normandy, Atom, Sprint, and Schwinn-Approved Sprint Freewheel Rear Hubs with Quick-Release—page 118.

3. SINGLE-SPEED REAR HUBS WITH COASTER BRAKE

The single-speed rear hub with coaster brake consists of a hub that can freewheel and a sprocket-activated internal brake arrangement. The hub shell turns forward and at the same speed as the sprocket. If the speed of the rear wheel sprocket is reduced or stopped, the hub shell can continue to turn independently of the sprocket; therefore, the term "coasting." When the direction of the sprocket is reversed (turned rearward) the internal brake unit forces disks or brake shoes to bear against the interior surface of the shell, slowing or bringing the hub to a stop and preventing it from turning.

Manufacturers of Single-Speed Rear Hubs with Coaster Brake and the page number on which the overhaul procedures begin are as follows: Bendix Original, Bendix RB, Bendix RB 2, and Bendix Junior—page 126; Komet, Komet Super 161, Schwinn-Approved Komet, Pixie, and F&S Torpedo Boy–page 137. Mattatuck, Hawthorne, New Departure, Nankai, and Shimano 3.3.3—page 148.

This freewheel hub has a quick-release mechanism that allows it to be removed and installed from the rear frame dropouts without the need of tools. Overhauling instructions for this type of hub begin on page 118.

The service instructions for this Bendix single-speed rear hub with coaster brake begin on page 126.

This is a Komet single-speed rear hub with coaster brake. Rear hubs with similar internal mechanisms are: Komet, Komet 161, Schwinn-Approved Komet, Pixie, and F&S Torpedo Boy. The service instructions for this series of hubs begin on page 137.

4. TWO-SPEED REAR HUBS WITH COASTER BRAKE

The two-speed rear hub with coaster brake has freewheeling capabilities, two gearing ratios between the sprocket and the hub shell, and a sprocket-activated internal brake mechanism. The hub shell can turn independently of the sprocket, giving it the ability to coast or freewheel. One type of two-speed rear hub with coaster brake has a "low" gear in which the hub shell turns slower than the sprocket and a "normal" gear in which the hub shell turns at the same speed as the sprocket. Another type of two-speed rear hub with coaster brake has a "normal" gear and a "high" gear in which the hub shell turns faster than the sprocket. The gear ratios are changed by changing the direction of sprocket rotation slightly rearward and then forward again. When the sprocket is rotated hard rearward, the internal brake unit forces brake shoes to bear against the interior surface of the shell, slowing or bringing the hub to a stop and preventing it from turning.

The manufacturer of Two-Speed Rear Hubs with Coaster Brake and the page on which the overhaul procedures begin are as follows: Bendix Yellow Band and Bendix Blue Band—page 159.

5. THREE-SPEED REAR HUBS

The three-speed rear hub has three gearing ratios available between the sprocket and the hub shell and can freewheel or coast when the sprocket speed is reduced or stopped. The three gearing ratios are "low," when the hub shell turns slower than the sprocket; "normal," when the shell turns at the same speed as the sprocket; and "high," when the shell turns faster than the sprocket. The gearing ratios are changed by moving a control cable connected to the hub.

Manufacturers of Three-Speed Rear Hubs and the page on which the overhaul procedures begin are as follows: Shimano 3.3.3 FA—page 172 ; Sturmey-Archer AW, Styre, Schwinn-Approved Styre, Brampton, and Hercules—page 189.

The Nankai single-speed rear hub with coaster brake is similar to the Mattatuck, Hawthorne, New Departure, and Shimano 3.3.3 hubs. This series of hubs has been popular for many years and has been used on many bicycles. The service instructions for this series of hubs begin on page 148.

This is a Bendix two-speed rear hub with coaster brake. The hub is identified by the name stamped on the brake arm and by a series of yellow or blue bands encircling the hub shell. Detailed steps required for overhauling these two Bendix hubs begin on page 159.

The service instructions for the Shimano 3.3.3 FA three-speed rear hub begin on page 172.

This Sturmey-Archer AW is typical of the three-speed hubs without a coaster brake. This hub is widely used. The Styre, Schwinn-Approved Styre, Brampton, and Hercules hubs are identical to the Sturmey-Archer AW hub, with all parts being interchangeable. Overhaul procedures for these hubs begin on page 189.

6. THREE-SPEED REAR HUBS WITH COASTER BRAKE

The three-speed rear hub with coaster brake combines all the features of the three-speed rear hub, described above, plus a sprocket-activated internal brake mechanism. When the sprocket is rotated rearward, the hub shell is slowed until it stops.

The manufacturer of the Three-Speed Rear Hub with Coaster Brake and the page on which the overhaul procedures begin is as follows: Sturmey-Archer TCW III—page 204.

The Sturmey-Archer TCW III, three-speed rear hub with coaster brake. Service procedures can be found starting on page 204.

OVERHAULING A STANDARD FREEWHEEL OR FIXED REAR-WHEEL HUB

The following step-by-step illustrated instructions cover disassembling, assembling, and adjusting a typical *freewheel rear hub.* The sprocket cluster is attached to the hub through the freewheel body.

The illustrations in this section were made of a Schwinn-Approved freewheel hub that is identical to the following hubs: Normandy, Sprint, and Atom. They are typical of this type of unit.

The *fixed hub* is similar in construction to the freewheel hub, except for the method of mounting the single-drive sprocket, which is threaded directly onto the hub in this case. Because the overhaul procedures for both types of hubs are almost identical, four related illustrations of the fixed rear-wheel hub are included alongside the sequential steps.

The illustrations are of an Atom *fixed rear-wheel hub,* which is used on many track racing bicycles. They are similar to the Schwinn-Approved and Campagnolo Track rear-wheel hubs and are typical of this type of unit.

Two basic types of *freewheel bodies* are used on all bicycles utilizing the sprocket-cluster principle—the splined body and the notched body. The *splined freewheel body* is covered in these sequential steps; the *notched body* is covered in the next section that follows for the quick-release rear-wheel hub.

An exploded view showing all parts of a Normandy, Schwinn-Approved, Sprint, and Atom *freewheel rear hub* follows the Cleaning and Inspecting portion of this section. Freewheel rear hubs of other manufacturers may vary slightly, due to the number of loose ball bearings; threaded or unthreaded spacer on the sprocket end of the axle; and/or removable or fixed bearing cups in the ends of the hub shell.

Two exploded views of typical *fixed rear hubs* showing their unique features follow the Cleaning and Inspecting instructions.

For photographic clarity, the illustrations were made of a hub without the tire, rim, and spokes.

REMOVING THE WHEEL

Support the bicycle in an upright position from a bracket, hooks, or rope attached to the garage ceiling, or secure it in an automobile rear carrier rack attached to the car. Holding the bicycle rigid will make the task of removing, installing, and adjusting parts much easier.

Sight over the tire and see if it will clear the brake shoes. If there is insufficient clearance, it will be necessary to release the brake shoes farther than normal in order to remove the wheel. This is accomplished by first squeezing the rear-brake handle slightly, pushing in on the quick-release button, and then releasing the brake handle. This action releases the caliper arms farther than normal, allowing the rear wheel to clear the brake shoes. *NOTE: The only function of this button is to facilitate easy removal of the wheel for maintenance or overhaul work.*

This fixed rear-wheel hub has the sprocket attached directly to the hub.

The sprocket cluster of a freewheel rear hub is attached through a freewheel body.

If you are working on a bicycle without the quick-release button on the brake handle, there may be a quick-release lever just above the brake on the cable hanger. Turning this lever will release the brake shoes farther than normal. If neither of these quick-release mechanisms is used, a quick way to gain the necessary clearance is to remove the mounting nut from one of

the brake-shoe holders, and then remove the complete brake-shoe assembly. Still another method, provided you have a pump or air supply handy, is to deflate the tire, which will usually clear the brake shoes.

Shift the chain to the high-gear (smallest) sprocket. Remove the outside nuts from both ends of the axle. Note the washer arrangement. Some bicycles have a

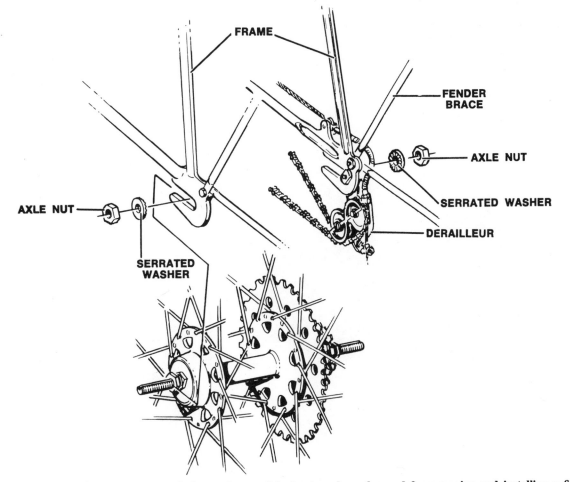

This illustration shows the arrangement of the washers and locknuts and can be used for removing and installing a fixed or freewheel rear hub to the rear frame dropouts.

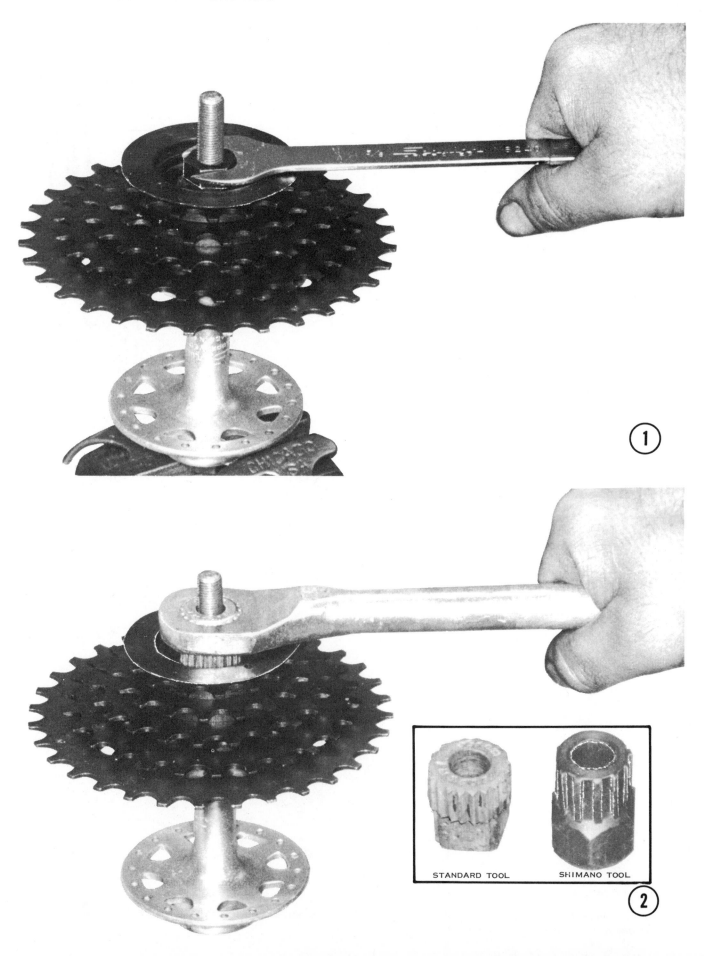

STANDARD TOOL   SHIMANO TOOL

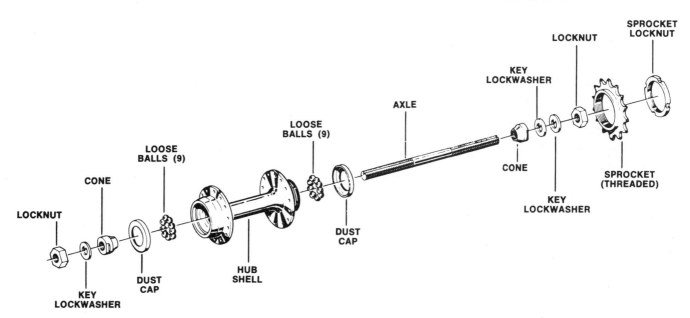

This is an exploded view of an Atom and Schwinn-Approved fixed rear-wheel hub. All parts of these two hubs are interchangeable.

serrated washer installed against the frame to prevent the wheel from moving forward under the tension of the chain.

Pull the derailleur unit toward the rear of the bicycle to obtain slack in the chain and at the same time move the wheel forward and free of the rear fork dropouts. Remove the chain from the sprocket, release the derailleur unit, and then guide the wheel clear of the frame.

DISASSEMBLING

① Clamp the hub and wheel assembly in a vise, with the jaws gripping the axle and the sprockets facing up. **CAUTION: Use soft vise jaws to protect the axle threads.** Remove the threaded spacer or the locknut and unthreaded spacer.

② Shift the hub in the vise so the jaws grip the hub. Look into the center of the freewheel body. If

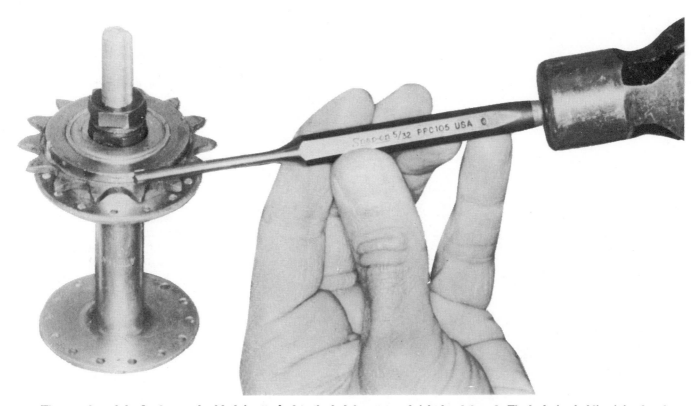

The sprocket of the fixed rear-wheel hub is attached to the hub by means of right-hand threads. The lock ring holding it in place has left-hand threads.

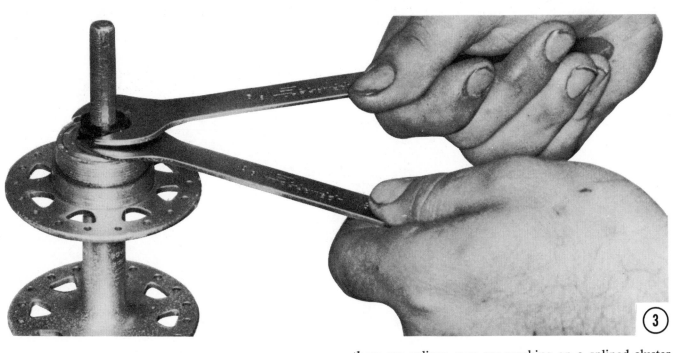

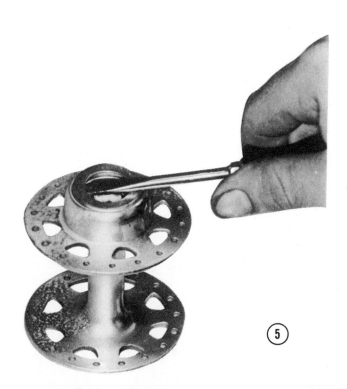

there are splines, you are working on a splined-cluster body. If the sides are smooth and there are two notches in the bottom of the opening, you are working on a notched-freewheel cluster. *NOTE: See the next section of this chapter for step-by-step procedures to remove a notched-body sprocket.* Position a deluxe freewheel tool over the axle, as shown, with the splines of the tool indexing with the splines of the cluster. Standard and Shimano splined tools are shown in the insert. If either of these is used, clamp the tool in the vise with the jaws gripping the flats. Carefully place the sprocket cluster over the tool with the splines of the freewheel body fully indexed with the splines of the tool, and the chain protector against the surface of the vise. Rotate the wheel counterclockwise to loosen the cluster. **CAUTION: Use only the proper tool for the freewheel cluster you are removing and be sure the splines of the tool and cluster remain fully engaged to prevent damaging the splines.** Remove the assembly from the vise. Hold the wheel and rotate the freewheel tool counterclockwise until the cluster body is free of the hub. Remove the spoke protector and spacer, if installed.

③ Hold the cone with a thin wrench or pair of cone pliers and remove the locknut by turning it counterclockwise. Remove the keyed lockwasher and then the cone. Lift the hub and wheel off the axle.

④ Turn the axle end for end in the vise, and then remove the locknut, keyed lockwasher, and cone.

⑤ Remove one of the dust caps by prying it up with a screwdriver. Work around the edge of the cap and be careful not to crimp or distort it. Remove and count the loose ball bearings. Turn the hub over and remove the cap and ball bearings from the other end.

CLEANING AND INSPECTING

Clean all parts in solvent and blow dry with compressed air, or wipe them dry with a lintless cloth. Keep all cleaned parts on paper towels to avoid contamination. Cover them with a clean towel to keep grit from

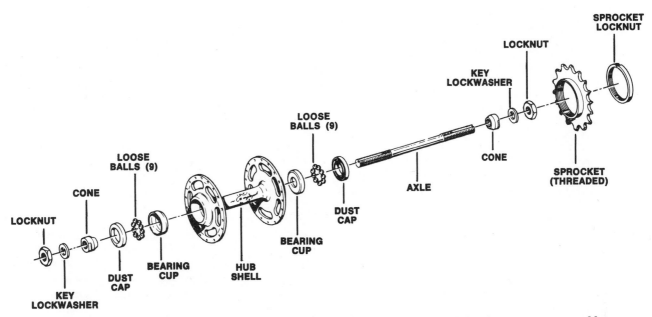

Exploded view of a Campagnolo Track fixed rear-wheel hub. Note that the ball bearing cups are removable.

entering the internal parts and bearings. A tiny piece of grit can do a tremendous amount of damage if allowed to work on a part over an extended period of time or while the wheel is turning at high speed.

Carefully inspect the ball bearings for signs of excessive wear (dull spots, pits, or cracks) and replace the complete set if any of them are damaged. Replacing the complete set will ensure even distribution of the bearing load on all the ball bearings.

Inspect the bearing surfaces of the cones for scores (scratchlike marks), pits (pencil-point dots), and for stripped threads.

Inspect the bearing cups of the hub for scores, pits, or excessive wear. If you are working on a hub with

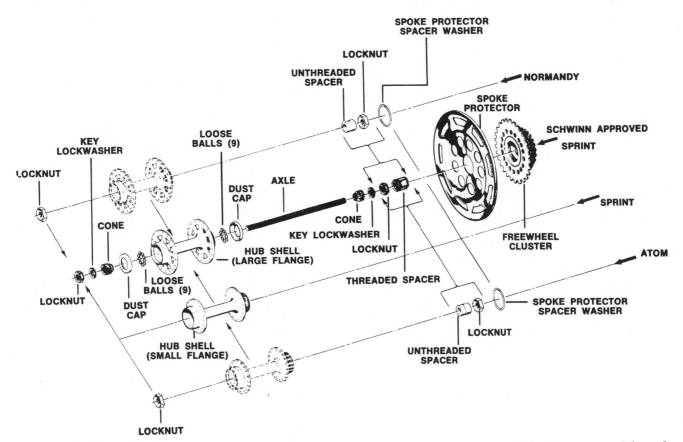

Exploded view of the Sprint, Schwinn-Approved Sprint, Atom, and Normandy freewheel rear hubs. Parts separated from the main line are not interchangeable; all others are.

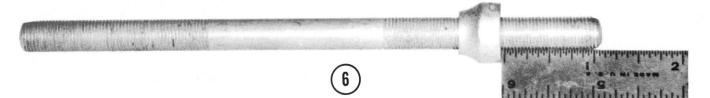

⑥

removable bearing cups and a cup needs to be replaced, remove it from the hub by tapping it out with an off-center drift punch and hammer from the other end of the hub. **CAUTION: Do not remove the cup unless it has to be replaced because removal without damage is very difficult.** Check the flanges of the hub shell for cracks, and to be sure they are not loose.

Check the axle and locknuts for stripped threads. Roll the axle slowly across a smooth flat surface and check both ends for being out-of-round or watch the center of the axle to see if it rises off the surface. Either of these indications means the axle is bent and must be replaced.

Check the dust caps to be sure they are not bent, crimped, or distorted, which could have happened during disassembly.

ASSEMBLING

⑥ Thread a cone onto one end of the axle until the outer edge is 1⅛ inch from the end of the axle, as shown.

⑦ Slide a keyed lockwasher onto the axle, with the key of the lockwasher indexing in the keyway of the axle. Thread a locknut onto the axle and tighten it

against the lockwasher. Hold the cone with a wrench while tightening the locknut to keep from disturbing the cone position on the axle.

⑧ Apply a generous amount of multipurpose lubricant in one of the bearing cups of the hub. If a bearing cup was removed, install a new one, using a socket the same size as the bottom of the cup and tapping it into position with a hammer. **CAUTION: Be sure the socket is the correct size, that it sets squarely in the cup, and that you tap the socket squarely to ensure that the cup goes into place evenly and without damage.**

⑨ Imbed the same number of loose ball bearings into the lubricated bearing cup as you removed during disassembly. If the count was lost, place bearings in the cup until they fit snugly around the side of the cup, and then remove one for proper clearance.

⑩ Place the dust cap over the bearing cup, with the flat side of the cap facing up, and then lightly tap it with a hammer until it is fully seated. Turn the hub end for end, lubricate the other bearing cup, imbed the correct number of loose ball bearings, and then install the dust cap in the same manner.

⑪ Clamp the axle in the vise, with the soft jaws

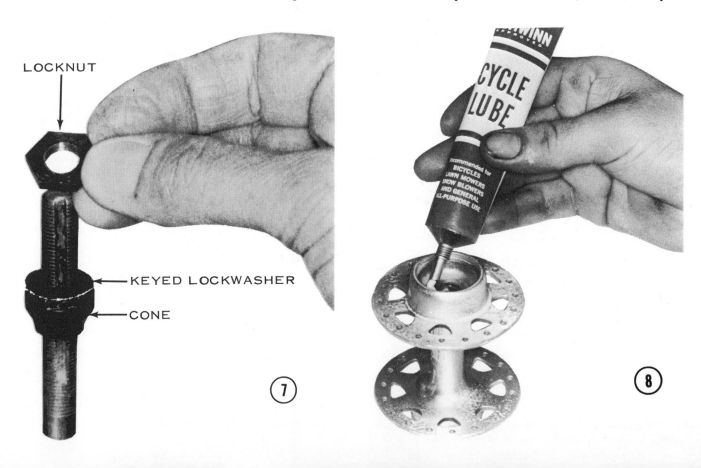

LOCKNUT

KEYED LOCKWASHER

CONE

⑦

⑧

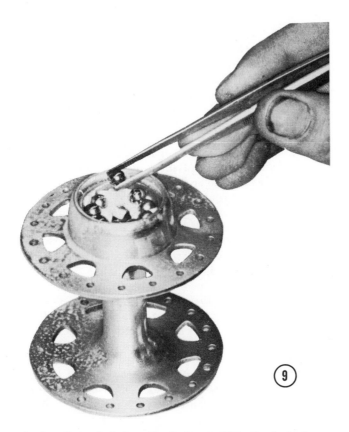

(9)

gripping the axle below the locknut. Slide the hub down the axle onto the cone, with the sprocket end facing up. Thread the other cone onto the axle snugly against the bearings, and then back it off approximately ⅛ turn for a preliminary adjustment.

(11)

⑫ Slide the keyed lockwasher over the axle, with the key of the lockwasher indexing with the keyway in the axle. Thread the locknut onto the axle. If you are working on a hub with an unthreaded spacer, slide the spacer onto the axle, and then thread the locknut on.

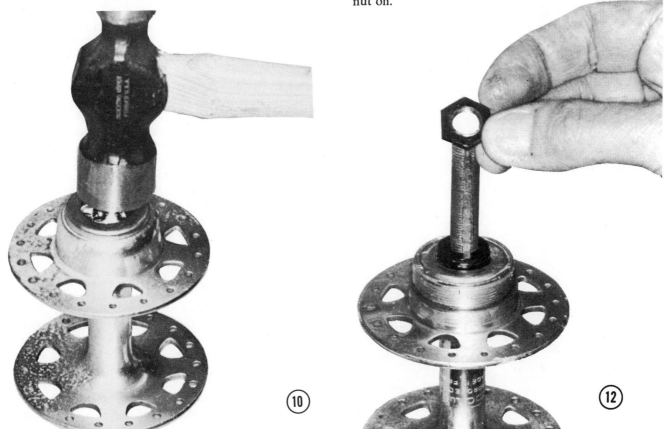

(10)

(12)

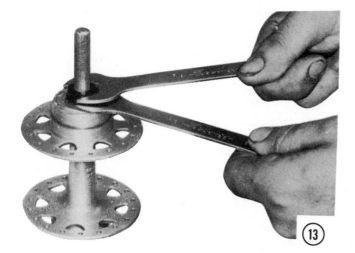

⑬ Hold the cone with a thin wrench or cone pliers, and then tighten the locknut. Shift the wheel in the vise with the vise jaws gripping one of the locknuts. Grasp the rim of the wheel and try to move the wheel up and down—this is referred to as side play. Remove all but a trace of play by adjusting the cone and then securing it with the locknut. Remove the complete and adjusted assembly from the vise.

⑭ To check the bearing adjustment, hold each end of the axle with your fingers, and then slowly twist the axle with your thumbs and forefingers—the wheel should not turn. If it does turn, the cones are too tight. Loosen one of the locknuts, back off the cone approxi-

mately ⅛ turn, and then retighten the locknut. The cones are properly adjusted when the wheel rotates freely, comes to rest gradually with the valve stem at the lowest point of the wheel, and there is *only the slightest trace of side play.* On precision-built bicycles with finely machined parts, it is possible, with patience, to adjust the cones so accurately that the wheel will turn freely with *no indication of side play.* However, on the average bicycle, a slight trace of side play should be evident. A check of the cone adjustment must be made after the wheel is installed on the bicycle, because if care is not taken to hold the locknut while tightening the axle nuts, the cone adjustment may change. **CAUTION: If the cones are adjusted too tight, it will cause binding and scoring of the hub. If the cones are adjusted too loose, it will cause fatigue, which can result in a damaged hub or broken axle.**

⑮ Turn the threaded spacer onto the axle against the locknut with the narrow end down, as shown. *NOTE: This end of the spacer does not have threads.*

⑯ Place the spoke protector spacer and spoke protector on the hub, if used. Carefully thread the sprocket cluster onto the hub by turning it clockwise. **CAUTION: Use care in starting the threads to prevent cross-threading.** The cluster does not have to be tightened with a tool because the pedaling action will work it onto the hub securely.

INSTALLING THE WHEEL

Slide an axle washer onto each end of the axle, with the serrated side toward the hub as shown in the accompanying illustration. *NOTE: On bicycles using wing nuts, the serrated washers are not used because the wing nuts must lock directly against the frame. For this reason, fender braces and accessory supports must be mounted on frame lugs and not on the axle.*

Start the axle nuts or large wing nuts onto each end of the axle. Rotate the derailleur unit toward the rear of the bicycle and simultaneously guide the wheel into the rear dropouts with the chain engaged onto the smallest sprocket and the serrated axle washers on the outside of the frame. Release the derailleur unit. If the derailleur unit is mounted on the frame with a fork end bracket, as shown, position the right side of the axle back against the bracket, and then tighten the sprocket-side axle nut. If the derailleur unit is mounted directly on the frame, position the axle approximately in the center of the dropouts, and then tighten the sprocket-side axle nut. Center the wheel in the frame, and then tighten the axle nut on the side opposite the sprocket.

Return the caliper brakes to the operating position. If you removed one of the brake-shoe assemblies to gain tire clearance, install the holder with the closed end facing forward and with the beveled surface of the shoe matching the angle of the wheel rim. The closed end of the security cap will then face rearward, as shown in the accompanying illustration. **CAUTION: Be sure the closed end of the holder is facing forward to prevent the shoe from being forced out when the brakes are applied and subsequent complete loss of braking ability at the rear wheel.**

Rotate the derailleur unit toward the rear to put slack in the chain in order to install the wheel into the rear frame dropouts. The chain must be engaged with the smallest sprocket, and the serrated axle washers must be on the outside of the frame.

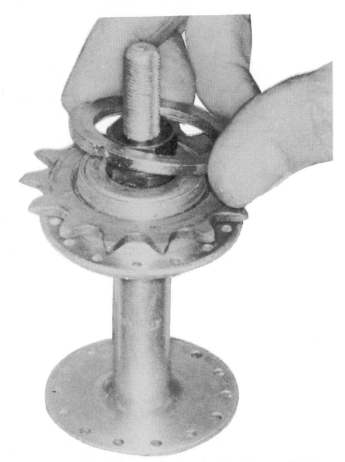

The sprocket of the fixed rear-wheel hub is attached by means of a right-hand thread. The lock ring that holds it in place has a left-hand thread.

Adjust the brake-shoe holder in the brake-arm slot until the upper edge of the shoe makes contact just below the edge of the rim when the brake lever on the handlebar is squeezed. Tighten the mounting nut securely.

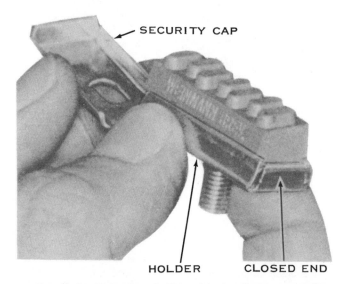

Install the brake-shoe holder with the closed end facing forward and with the beveled surface of the shoe matching the angle of the wheel rim, as discussed in the text.

OVERHAULING A QUICK-RELEASE FREEWHEEL REAR HUB

The following step-by-step illustrated instructions cover disassembling, assembling, and adjusting a Campagnolo Road hub, which is a typical quick-release rear hub with a *notched body sprocket cluster*. Removal and installation procedures for a *splined body cluster* are given in the first section of this chapter covering overhaul of a standard freewheel hub.

The illustrations in this section are almost identical to those needed to overhaul the following hubs: Normandy, Sprint, Schwinn-Approved Sprint, and Atom. Exploded views showing all parts of all these hubs follow the Cleaning and Inspecting portion of this section.

Quick-release rear-wheel hubs of other manufacturers may vary slightly in the number of loose ball bearings, a threaded or unthreaded spacer on the sprocket end of the axle, and/or removable or fixed bearing cups in the ends of the hub shell.

For photographic clarity, the illustrations were made of a hub without a tire, rim, and spokes.

REMOVING THE WHEEL

Support the bicycle in an upright position from a bracket, hooks, or rope attached to the garage ceiling, or secure it in an automobile rear carrier rack attached to the car. Holding the bicycle rigid will make the task of removing, installing, and adjusting parts much easier.

Sight over the tire and see if it will clear the brake shoes. If there is insufficient clearance, it will be necessary to release the brake shoes farther than normal in order to remove the wheel. This is accomplished by first squeezing the rear brake handle slightly, pushing in on the quick-release button, and then releasing the brake handle. This action releases the caliper arms farther than normal, allowing the rear wheel to clear the brake shoes. *NOTE: The only function of this button is to facilitate easy removal of the wheel for maintenance.*

If you are working on a bicycle without the quick-release button on the brake handle, there may be a quick-release lever just above the brake on the cable hanger. Turning this lever will release the brake shoes farther than normal. If neither of these quick-release mechanisms is used, a quick way to gain the necessary clearance is to remove the mounting nut from one of the brake-shoe holders, and then remove the complete brake-shoe assembly. Still another method, provided you have a pump or air supply handy, is to deflate the tire in order to clear the brake shoes.

Shift the chain to the high-gear (smallest) sprocket. Rotate the quick-release lever 180° to the full-forward position. This action releases the hub so that the wheel can be removed. Pull the derailleur unit toward the rear to obtain slack in the chain and at the same time move the wheel forward and free of the rear frame dropouts. Remove the chain from the sprocket, release the derailleur unit, and then guide the wheel clear of the frame.

Remove the adjusting nut from the sprocket end of the axle, and then take off the tension spring. Withdraw

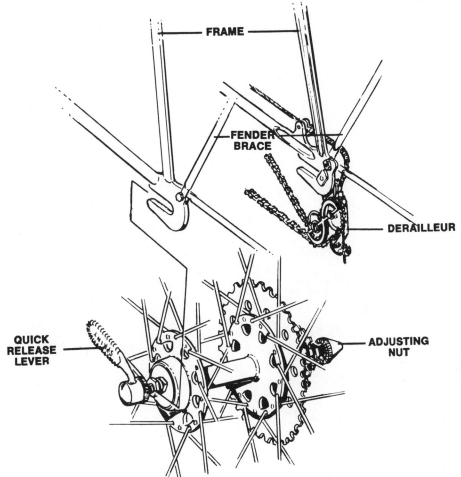

FRAME

FENDER BRACE

DERAILLEUR

QUICK RELEASE LEVER

ADJUSTING NUT

Turning the quick-release lever allows you to remove a rear-wheel hub quickly and easily without the need for tools.

UNIVERSAL FREEWHEEL TOOL

①

(2)

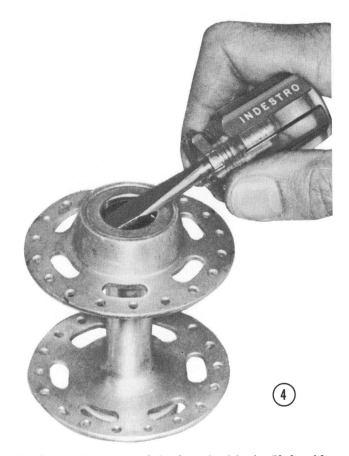

(4)

the cam lever and mounting stud from the axle, and then remove the other spring from the stud, as indicated in the accompanying illustration.

DISASSEMBLING

① Clamp the hub in a vise, with the sprocket facing up and the vise jaws gripping the axle. **CAUTION: Use soft jaws to protect the axle threads from damage.** Remove the spacer nut. *NOTE: Some bicycles may be equipped with a thick washer and locknut.*

(3)

Look into the center of the freewheel body. If the sides are smooth and there are two notches in the bottom of the opening, you are working on a *notched-body freewheel cluster*. If there are splines around the sides of the opening, you are working on a *splined-body freewheel cluster. NOTE: See the first section of this chapter for step-by-step procedures to remove a splined-body cluster.* Slide the mounting stud without the springs on it back through the axle, and then place a Universal or Atom notched-body freewheel tool over the axle and stud, with the lugs of the tool fully seated in the notches of the body. *NOTE: The Atom tool is used only on an Atom freewheel body. The Universal tool can be used on all other notched units.* Thread the adjusting nut onto the stud firmly against the tool. **CAUTION: Be sure the lugs of the tool are fully seated to prevent damage to the notches.**

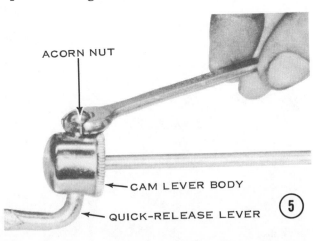

ACORN NUT

← CAM LEVER BODY

← QUICK-RELEASE LEVER

(5)

② Turn the hub and wheel over in the vise, with the jaws gripping the flats of the freewheel tool and the smallest sprocket resting on top of the vise. Grasp the wheel and turn it counterclockwise to loosen the sprocket body from the hub. As soon as you feel the wheel loosen, stop turning and remove the wheel and hub from the vise. Unthread the adjusting nut, remove the freewheel tool, and then withdraw the mounting stud from the axle. Turn the sprocket cluster counterclockwise until it is free of the hub. Remove the spoke protector and spacer.

③ Clamp the hub in the vise with the sprocket end down and the soft jaws gripping the axle. Remove the locknut and then the cone. Lift the hub up and off the axle. Turn the axle end for end in the vise and remove the other locknut, keyed lockwasher, and cone. *NOTE: The number and placement of washers and/or spacers on the sprocket end of the axle may vary, depending on the make and model of the hub. Therefore, carefully note their order during removal as an aid to assembling.*

④ Remove the dust cap from one end of the hub by prying it up with a screwdriver, as shown. Work around the edge of the cap and be careful not to crimp or distort it. Remove and count the loose ball bearings. Turn the hub over and remove the other dust cap and loose bearings in a similar manner.

⑤ Remove the acorn nut, lockwasher, quick-release lever, and cam lever body from the mounting stud.

CLEANING AND INSPECTING

Clean all parts in solvent and blow dry with compressed air, or wipe them dry with a lintless cloth. Keep all cleaned parts on paper towels to avoid contamination. Cover them with a clean towel to keep grit from entering the internal parts and bearings. A tiny piece of grit can do a tremendous amount of damage if allowed to work on a part over an extended period of time or while the wheel is turning at high speed.

Carefully inspect the ball bearings for pits (pencil-point dots), cracks, or dull spots indicating excessive wear. Replace the complete set if one is damaged to ensure even distribution of the bearing load on all the ball bearings.

Inspect the bearing surfaces of the cones for scores (scratchlike marks), pits, and for stripped threads.

Inspect the bearing cups of the hub for scores, pits, or excessive wear. If you are working on a hub with removable bearing cups and one needs to be replaced, remove it from the hub by tapping it out from the other end of the hub with an off-center drift punch and ham-

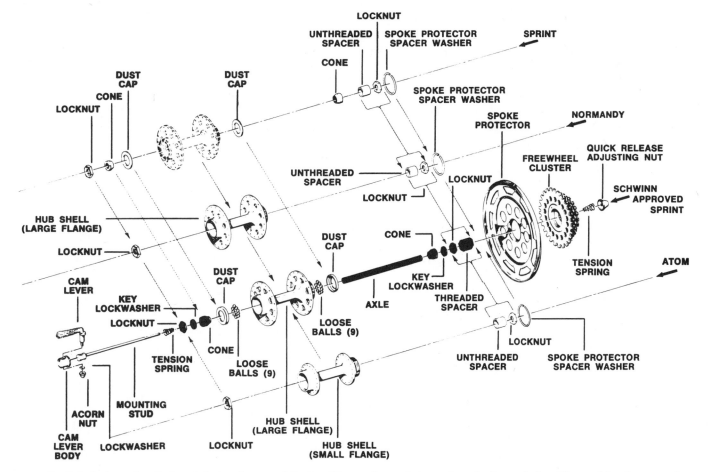

Exploded view of a Sprint, Schwinn-Approved Sprint, Normandy, and Atom freewheel rear hub with a quick-release mechanism. Parts separated from the main line of the figure are not interchangeable with the parts of the Schwinn-Approved hub; all others are.

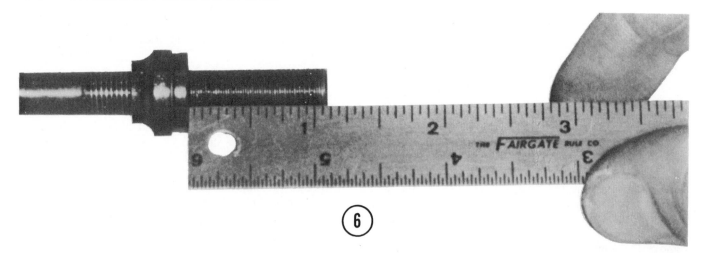

mer. **CAUTION: Do not remove the cup unless it has to be replaced because removal without damage is difficult.**

Check the dust caps to be sure they are not bent, crimped, or distorted, which could have happened during disassembly.

Check the threaded spacer, locknuts, and axle for stripped threads. Roll the axle slowly across a smooth flat surface and check both ends for being out-of-round or watch the center of the axle to see if it rises off the surface. Either of these indications means the axle is bent and must be replaced.

Check the quick-release mounting stud for cracking, bending, or having stripped threads.

Check both tension springs for cracks, breaks, or distortion.

ASSEMBLING

⑥   Thread a cone onto either end of the axle until the outer surface is 1⅛ inch from the end of the axle, as shown.

⑦   Install the thin washer, keyed lockwasher, threaded or unthreaded spacer, and locknut on the axle in the same order you noted during disassembly.

⑧   Apply a generous amount of multipurpose lubricant in one of the bearing cups of the hub. If a bearing cup was removed, install a new one using a socket the same size as the bottom of the cup and tapping it into position with a hammer. **CAUTION: Be sure the socket is the correct size, that it sets squarely in the cup, and that you tap the socket squarely to ensure that the cup goes into place evenly and without damage.**

⑨   Imbed the same number of ball bearings into the lubricated bearing cup as you removed during disassembly. If the count was lost, place bearings in the cup until they fit snugly around the side of the cup, and then remove one for the proper clearance.

⑩   Place the dust cap over the bearing cup, with the flat side of the cap facing up, and then lightly tap it with a mallet until it is fully seated. Turn the hub end for end, lubricate the other bearing cup, imbed the

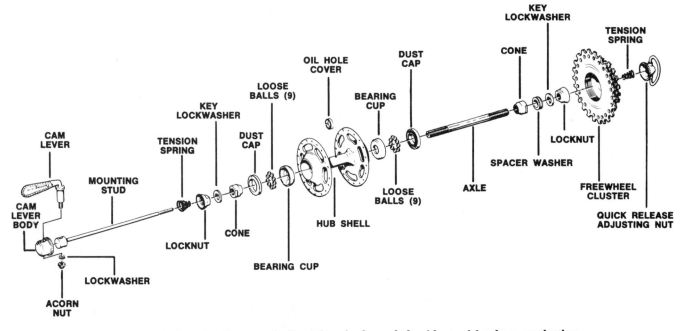

Exploded view of a Campagnolo Road freewheel rear hub with a quick-release mechanism.

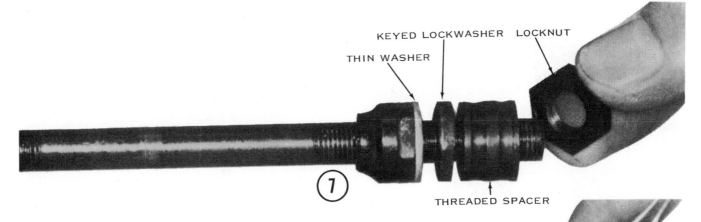

THIN WASHER
KEYED LOCKWASHER
LOCKNUT
THREADED SPACER

⑦

correct number of ball bearings, and then install the dust cap in the same manner.

⑪ Clamp the axle in the vise, with the jaws gripping the locknut. Slide the hub, with the sprocket end facing down, over the axle and onto the cone. Thread the other cone onto the axle snugly against the bearings, and then back it off approximately ⅛ turn for a preliminary adjustment.

⑫ Slide the keyed lockwasher over the axle, with the key of the lockwasher indexing with the keyway in the axle. Thread the locknut onto the axle. Check to be sure the hub and associated parts are centered on the axle. The outside surface of each locknut should be approximately ⅛ inch from each end of the axle.

⑬ Hold the cone with a thin wrench or cone pliers, and then tighten the locknut. Grasp the rim and

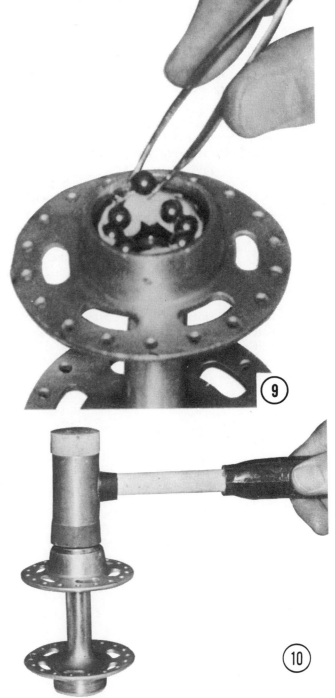

⑨

⑧

⑩

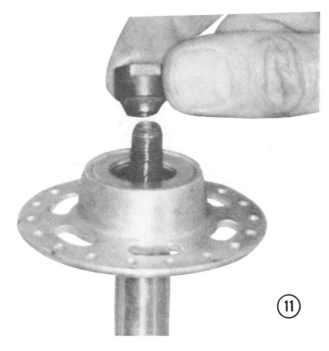

try to move the wheel up and down—this is a check for side play. Remove all but a trace of play by adjusting the cone and then securing it with the locknut. Remove the complete assembly from the vise.

⑭ To check the bearing adjustment, hold each end of the axle with your fingers, and then slowly twist the axle with your thumbs and forefingers—the wheel should not turn. If it does turn, the cones are too tight. Loosen one of the locknuts, back off the cone approximately ⅛ turn, and then retighten the locknut. The cones are properly adjusted when the wheel rotates freely, comes to rest gradually with the valve stem at the lowest point of the wheel, and there is only the slightest trace of side play. On precision-built bicycles, it is possible to adjust the cones so accurately that the wheel will turn freely with no indication of side play. However, on the average bicycle, a slight trace of side

play should be evident. **CAUTION: If the cones are adjusted too tight, it will cause binding and scoring of the hub. If the cones are adjusted too loose, it will cause fatigue, which can result in a damaged hub or broken axle.**

⑮ Place the spacer and spoke protector on the hub, with the dished side facing the wheel, as shown. Carefully thread the sprocket cluster onto the hub by turning it clockwise. **CAUTION: Use care in starting the threads to prevent cross-threading.** The cluster does

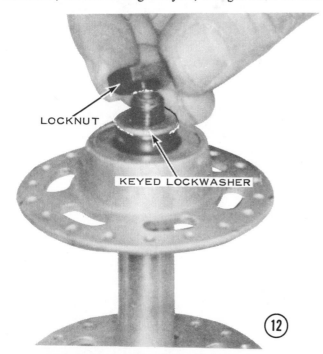

LOCKNUT

KEYED LOCKWASHER

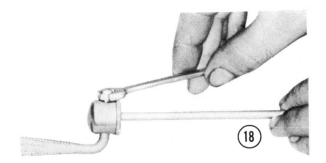

move it from a forward position (90° to the mounting stud) through a full 180°. The lever will then be pointing 90° to the mounting stud in the opposite direction. If the lever cannot be rotated a full 180°, remove the lever, rotate it 180°, and then reinstall the lever in the cam-lever body.

⑱ Place the lockwasher onto the lever shaft, and then thread on the acorn nut and tighten it firmly.

not have to be tightened with a tool because the pedaling action will work it onto the hub securely.

⑯ Place the cam-lever body on the mounting stud, and then align the holes in the body and the stud. *NOTE: The body can go on either way.*

⑰ Install the quick-release lever through the large hole in the cam-lever body until it is fully seated. Rotate the quick-release lever. You should be able to

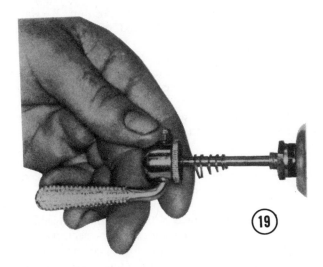

⑲ Slide one of the tension springs onto the mounting stud, with the small end of the spring facing toward the hub, as shown.

⑳ Insert the mounting stud through the axle from the end opposite the sprocket cluster. Slide the other tension spring onto the mounting stud, with the small

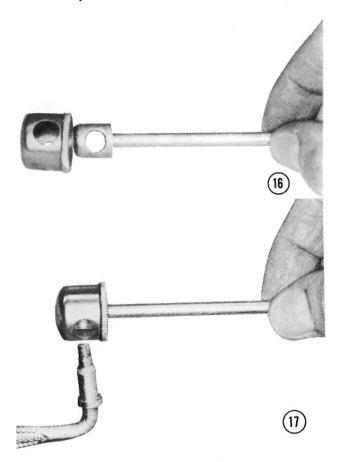

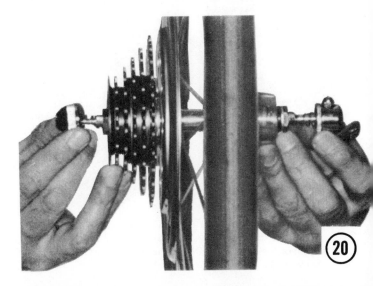

end going on first. Start the adjusting nut onto the stud by rotating it several turns.

INSTALLING THE WHEEL

Turn the quick-release lever to the open position, facing forward. Rotate the derailleur toward the rear of the bicycle and, at the same time, guide the wheel into the rear-frame dropouts with the chain engaged onto the smallest sprocket. Release the derailleur unit. If the derailleur unit is mounted on the frame with a fork-end bracket, as shown, slide the axle back against the bracket, center the wheel in the frame, and then turn the quick-release lever to the locked position, facing the rear of the bicycle. You should meet some resistance in turning the lever to the locked position and the wheel should be held firmly in place if the adjustment is correct. If it is necessary to change the adjustment, turn the lever to the released position (facing forward) and then tighten the acorn adjusting nut on the opposite side of the hub approximately ½ turn. Now turn the lever back to the locked position. Repeat the procedure until you are satisfied that the adjustment will hold the wheel securely in place.

Check to be sure the wheel turns freely with the correct amount of side play. If an adjustment is required, turn the quick-release lever to the forward position, loosen the locknut on the side opposite the sprocket cluster, loosen or tighten the cone on that side, tighten the locknut, and then return the quick-release lever to the locked position.

Return the caliper brakes to the operating position by releasing the locking device. If you removed one of the brake-shoe assemblies to gain tire clearance, install the holder with the closed end facing forward and with the beveled surface of the shoe matching the angle of the wheel rim. The closed end of the security cap will then face rearward, as shown in the accompanying illustration. **CAUTION: Be sure the closed end of the holder is facing forward to prevent the shoe from being forced out when the brakes are applied and subsequent com-**plete loss of braking ability at the rear wheel. Adjust the brake-shoe holder in the brake-arm slot until the upper edge of the shoe makes contact just below the edge of the rim when the brake lever on the handlebar is squeezed. Tighten the mounting nut securely.

OVERHAULING A BENDIX SINGLE-SPEED REAR HUB WITH COASTER BRAKE

The following step-by-step illustrated instructions cover disassembling, cleaning, inspecting, and assembling a Bendix (1946–1961), Bendix RB (1961–1963), Bendix RB2 (since 1963), and a Bendix 70J (current) rear-wheel hub with coaster brake. The hubs are identified by the name stamped on the brake arm and/or on the hub shell. Differences between these hubs are illustrated in detailed exploded drawings following the Cleaning and Inspecting portion of this section and are pointed out in the text. The following procedures apply basically to the Bendix 70J hub. Deviations from this hub that might cause problems during assembly, including specific parts that are not interchangeable, are called to your attention in the individual steps.

For photographic clarity, the illustrations were made of a hub without the tire, rim, and spokes.

REMOVING THE WHEEL

If the bicycle you are working on does not have levers mounted on the handlebars, you can turn the bicycle upside down, resting it on the seat and handlebars. A better method, and a must for bicycles with banana-type seats or "sissy" bars, is to support the bicycle in the upright position from a bracket, a set of hooks, or a rope attached to the garage ceiling, or to secure it in an automobile rear carrier rack attached to the car. Holding the bicycle rigid will make the task of removing, installing, and adjusting of parts much easier.

Remove the nut and mounting screw, securing the brake arm to the strap on the bicycle frame. Next, remove the outside axle nuts. Take note of the washer and

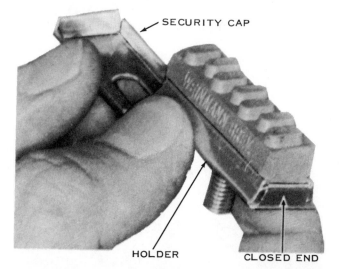

Install the brake-shoe assembly with the closed end of the holder facing forward and with the beveled surface of the shoe matching the angle of the wheel rim.

Bendix single-speed rear hub with coaster brake.

support arrangement installed on the axle. Some bicycles have a serrated washer installed against the frame to prevent the wheel from moving forward under the tension of the chain. Washers are usually installed between the fender and accessory supports to keep them from twisting when the axle nuts are tightened.

Slide any fender or accessory supports, including washers, from the axle. Move the wheel free of the dropouts, remove the chain from the rear sprocket and then hook it over the frame.

DISASSEMBLING

① Clamp the complete hub and wheel assembly in a vise, with the jaws gripping the axle nut on the brake-arm side of the hub. Remove the axle nut, washer, and serrated spacer from the other end of the axle.

② Remove the snap ring from under the drive-screw flange by prying it out and up with a screwdriver. Lift the sprocket off the drive screw. *NOTE: The Bendix hub has a locknut instead of a lock ring.* Remove the locknut by turning it counterclockwise with a spanner

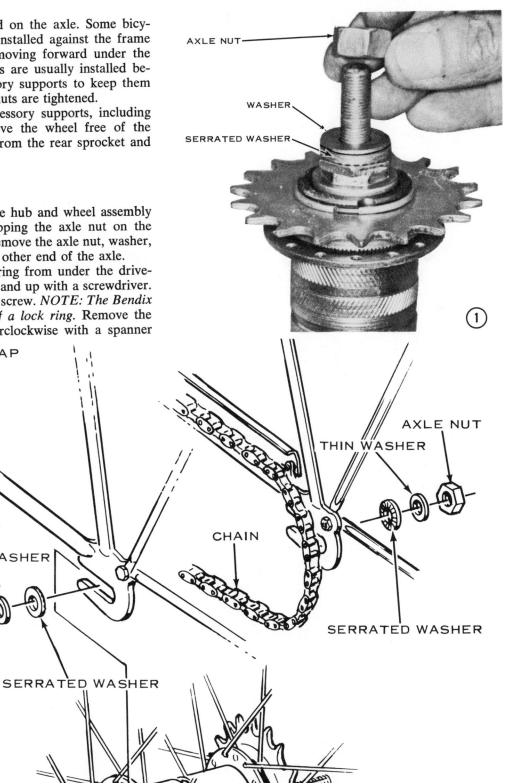

Arrangement of washers and locknuts on a typical single-speed rear hub with coaster brake.

wrench. Rotate the sprocket counterclockwise and remove it from the drive screw.

③ Remove the dust cap by prying up with a screwdriver, as shown. Work around the cap edge and it will pop out. Be careful not to crimp or distort the cap.

④ Hold the adjusting cone with a thin wrench or cone pliers, and then remove the locknut and cone.

⑤ Reach in with a pair of needle-nosed pliers, and remove the ball bearing retainer assembly. Turn the drive screw in a counterclockwise direction to remove it from the axle. Remove the second ball bearing retainer with a pair of needle-nosed pliers.

⑥ Lift up the hub shell, catch the brake shoe as the shell clears it, and then remove the shell from the axle. *NOTE: The Bendix Original, Bendix RB, and Bendix RB2 hubs each have two crescent-shaped brake shoes. On the Bendix RB2 hub, the brake-shoe keys are*

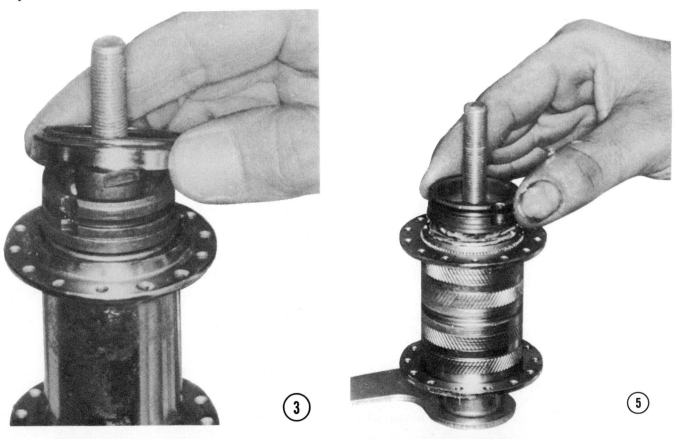

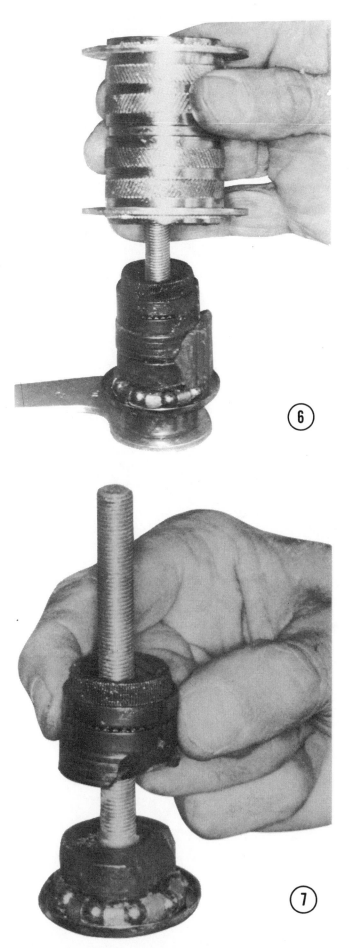

a machined part of the brake-arm and drive-side expanders. On the Bendix Original and Bendix RB hubs, the keys are loose as indicated in the exploded illustration on page 130.

⑦ Remove the complete drive-side expander unit, with the clutch, by lifting it off the axle.

⑧ Separate the drive clutch, retarder spring, and drive-side expander.

⑨ Turn the axle end for end in the vise, with the jaws gripping the axle in the center portion where there are no threads, or use a set of soft vise jaws to protect the threads. Remove the locknut, dust cap, and brake-arm side expander. Remove the ball bearing retainer from the brake-arm side expander.

CLEANING AND INSPECTING

Clean all parts in solvent and blow dry with compressed air, or wipe them dry with a lintless cloth. Keep all cleaned parts on paper towels to avoid contamination. Cover them with a clean towel to keep grit from entering the internal parts and bearings. A tiny piece of

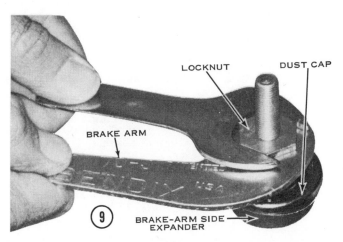

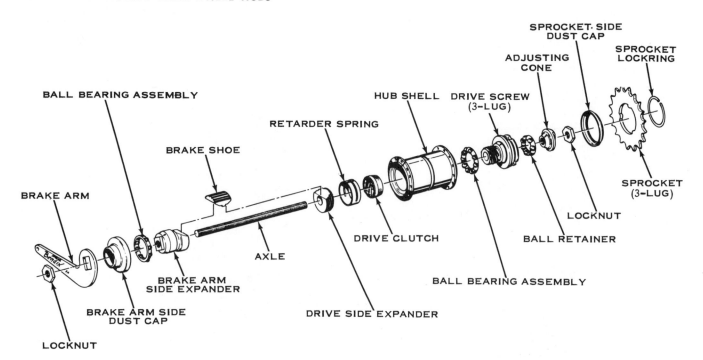

BALL BEARING ASSEMBLY

SPROCKET· SIDE
DUST CAP

ADJUSTING
CONE

SPROCKET
LOCKRING

HUB SHELL

DRIVE SCREW
(3-LUG)

RETARDER SPRING

BRAKE SHOE

BRAKE ARM

BRAKE ARM
SIDE EXPANDER

DRIVE CLUTCH

SPROCKET
(3-LUG)

AXLE

LOCKNUT

BALL RETAINER

BRAKE ARM SIDE
DUST CAP

BALL BEARING ASSEMBLY

DRIVE SIDE EXPANDER

LOCKNUT

Exploded view of a Bendix Junior single-speed rear hub with coaster brake.

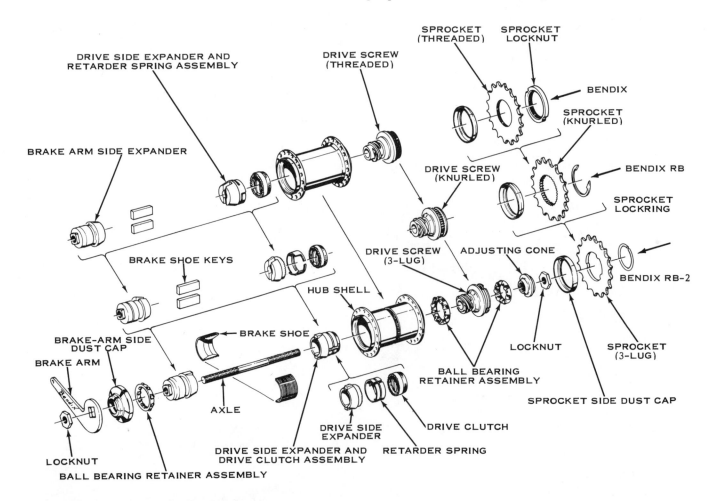

DRIVE SIDE EXPANDER AND
RETARDER SPRING ASSEMBLY

DRIVE SCREW
(THREADED)

SPROCKET
(THREADED)

SPROCKET
LOCKNUT

BENDIX

SPROCKET
(KNURLED)

BRAKE ARM SIDE EXPANDER

DRIVE SCREW
(KNURLED)

BENDIX RB

SPROCKET
LOCKRING

BRAKE SHOE KEYS

DRIVE SCREW
(3-LUG)

ADJUSTING CONE

BENDIX RB-2

HUB SHELL

BRAKE SHOE

BRAKE-ARM SIDE
DUST CAP

LOCKNUT

SPROCKET
(3-LUG)

BRAKE ARM

BALL BEARING
RETAINER ASSEMBLY

SPROCKET SIDE DUST CAP

AXLE

DRIVE SIDE
EXPANDER

DRIVE CLUTCH

RETARDER SPRING

LOCKNUT

DRIVE SIDE EXPANDER AND
DRIVE CLUTCH ASSEMBLY

BALL BEARING RETAINER ASSEMBLY

Exploded view of a Bendix RB-2, Bendix RB, and early model Bendix single-speed rear hub with coaster brake. Parts for the Bendix and Bendix RB separated from the main line of the figure are not interchangeable with those of the Bendix RB-2; all others are.

grit can do a tremendous amount of damage if allowed to work on a part over an extended period of time or while the wheel is turning at high speed.

Inspect the three ball bearing and retainer assemblies. If any of the ball bearings come out of the retainer, or are pitted (pencil-point dots), show signs of excessive wear (dull spots), or are cracked, the bearing assembly must be replaced. Check the retainers for cracks or other damage.

Check the adjusting cone bearing surface for scores (scratchlike marks), pits, or other damage. Check the cone for stripped threads.

Inspect the bearing surface of the brake-arm side expander for scores, pits, or other damage. Check the expander for stripped threads.

Inspect the drive-side expander and drive clutch for worn, chipped, or damaged teeth.

Check the splines of the drive screw for cracks, chips, or worn edges.

Replace the retarder spring with a new one to ensure proper service following assembly.

Check the axle and locknuts for signs of damage or stripped threads. Roll the axle slowly across a smooth flat surface and check both ends for being out-of-round or watch the center of the axle to see if it rises off the surface. Either of these indications means the axle is bent and must be replaced.

Check both dust caps to be sure they are not crimped or distorted, which could have happened during disassembly.

Inspect the bearing surfaces of the hub shell for scores, pits, or excessive wear. Check the flanges of the hub shell for cracks, and to be sure they are not loose.

Inspect the brake shoe or shoes for damage, burrs, or glazed lining surfaces.

Check the brake arm to be sure it is not bent or damaged. *NOTE: All parts of the Bendix RB2 and Bendix 70J hubs are interchangeable except for the brake arm, brake-side expander, drive-side expander, and the brake shoes, one of which is used on the 70J and two on the RB2. Parts that are not interchangeable between the Bendix Original, Bendix RB, and Bendix RB2 are noted in the exploded illustration on page 130.*

ASSEMBLING

⑩ Pack one of the outside ball bearing retainer

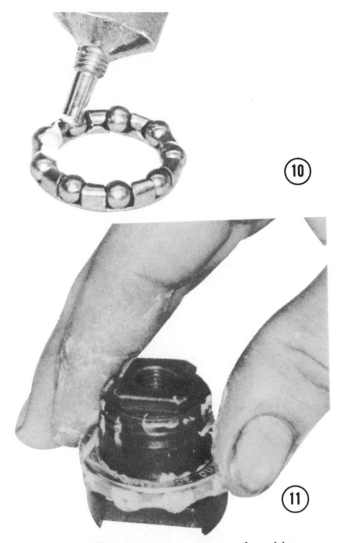

assemblies with a generous amount of multipurpose lubricant. Work the lubricant throughout the bearings and retainer with your fingers.

⑪ Place the lubricated ball bearing assembly on the brake-arm side expander, with the ball bearings facing the bearing race of the brake-arm side expander, as shown.

⑫ Thread the brake-arm side expander onto the axle until the outside edge of the expander is 1⅛ inches from the end of the axle.

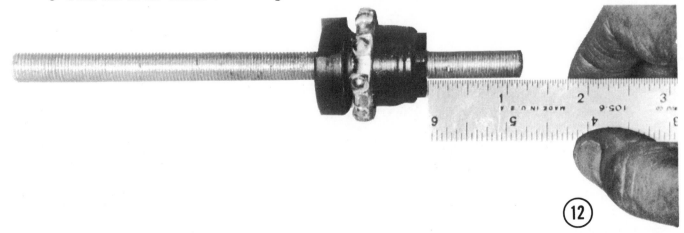

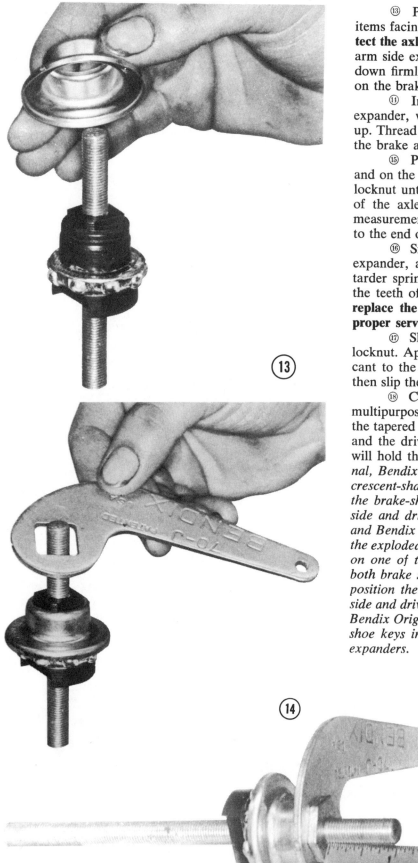

⑬ Position the axle in a vise, with the installed items facing up. **CAUTION: Use soft vise jaws to protect the axle threads.** Place the dust cap over the brake-arm side expander and bearing assembly. Push the cap down firmly to seat the ball bearing retainer assembly on the brake expander.

⑭ Install the brake arm on the brake-arm side expander, with the manufacturer's identification facing up. Thread the axle nut onto the axle finger-tight against the brake arm.

⑮ Position a cone locknut gauge over the axle and on the locknut. Hold the brake arm and tighten the locknut until the end of the gauge is even with the end of the axle. If a cone gauge is not available, use a measurement of one inch from the surface of the locknut to the end of the axle.

⑯ Snap a new retarder spring on the drive-side expander, and then install the drive clutch in the retarder spring, with the teeth of the expander engaging the teeth of the clutch, as shown. **CAUTION: Always replace the retarder spring with a new one to ensure proper service after assembly.**

⑰ Shift the axle in the vise so the jaws grip the locknut. Apply a liberal amount of multipurpose lubricant to the outside surface of the retarder spring, and then slip the complete unit onto the axle.

⑱ Coat the inside surface of the brake shoe with multipurpose lubricant. Position the brake shoe against the tapered ramps of the brake side of the expander unit and the drive side of the expander unit. The lubricant will hold the shoe in place. *NOTE: The Bendix Original, Bendix RB, and Bendix RB2 hubs each have two crescent-shaped brake shoes. On the Bendix RB2 hub, the brake-shoe keys are a machined part of the brake-side and drive-side expanders. On the Bendix Original and Bendix RB hubs, the keys are loose, as indicated in the exploded illustration on page 130. If you are working on one of these three hubs, coat the inside surface of both brake shoes with multipurpose lubricant, and then position them against the tapered ramps of the brake-side and drive-side expanders. If you are working on the Bendix Original or Bendix RB hub, place the two brake shoe keys in the slots of the brake-side and drive-side expanders.*

Locate the outside surface of the locknut one inch from the end of the axle if a gauge is not available.

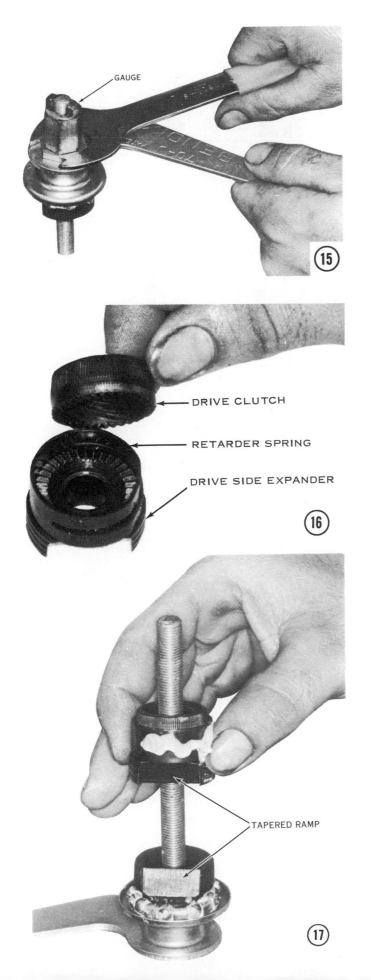

GAUGE

(15)

DRIVE CLUTCH

RETARDER SPRING

DRIVE SIDE EXPANDER

(16)

TAPERED RAMP

(17)

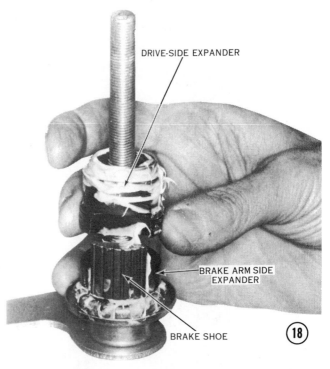

DRIVE-SIDE EXPANDER

BRAKE ARM SIDE EXPANDER

BRAKE SHOE

(18)

⑲ Apply a moderate amount of premium-quality cycle oil to the inside surface of the hub shell.

⑳ Slide the oiled hub shell over the axle, with the large opening facing the brake, and simultaneously

SCHWINN PREMIUM QUALITY CYCLE OIL

(19)

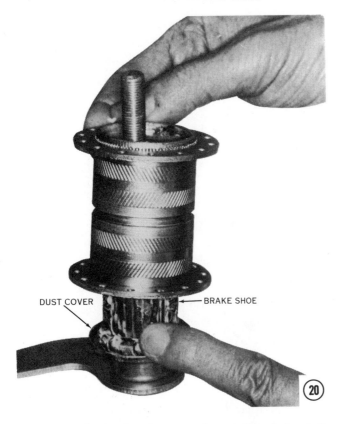

DUST COVER   BRAKE SHOE

20

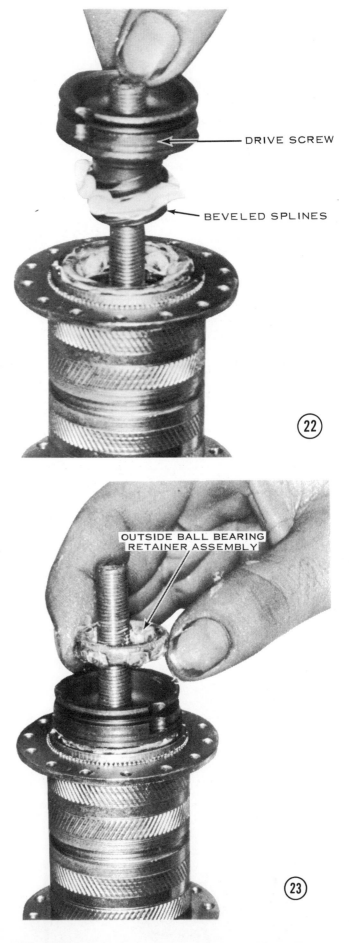

DRIVE SCREW

BEVELED SPLINES

22

push in on the brake shoe, as shown. The hub shell should slide into place against the dust cap.

㉑ Apply a generous coating of multipurpose lubricant to the sprocket-side ball bearing retainer assembly. Work the lubricant throughout the ball bearings

SPROCKET-SIDE
BALL BEARING
RETAINER ASSEMBLY

21

OUTSIDE BALL BEARING
RETAINER ASSEMBLY

23

and the retainer. Install the bearing assembly over the axle, with the flat side of the retainer facing up. Push the retainer into place onto the bearing race of the drive-side expander.

㉒ Apply a generous amount of multipurpose lubricant to the beveled splines of the drive screw. Twist the lubricated drive screw clockwise into place until it is seated against the ball bearing retainer.

㉓ Pack the outside ball bearing assembly with a generous amount of multipurpose lubricant. Work the lubricant throughout the bearings and the retainer with your fingers. Install the bearing assembly in the drive screw, with the flat side of the retainer facing up.

㉔ Thread the adjusting cone onto the axle. Bring the cone down snug, and then back it off approximately ⅜ turn, or until there is just a discernible amount of side play when you move the wheel rim up and down.

㉕ Install the locknut on the axle and tighten it against the adjusting cone. Hold the adjusting cone with a thin wrench or cone pliers, and then tighten the locknut securely.

㉖ Remove the assembled hub and wheel from the vise. Hold each end of the axle with your fingers. Slowly twist the axle with the thumb and forefinger of each hand—the wheel should not turn. If it does turn, the cones are too tight and must be loosened slightly. Back off the locknut on the axle end opposite the brake arm. Loosen the cone approximately ⅛ turn, and then retighten the locknut. The cones are properly adjusted when the wheel rotates freely, comes to rest gradually with the valve stem at the lowest point of the wheel

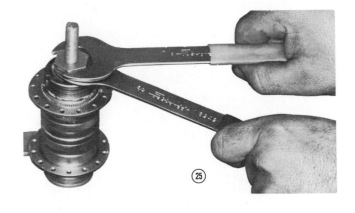

and there is only the slightest trace of side play. A check with the valve stem at the lowest point of the wheel, is installed on the bicycle, because if care is not taken to hold the locknut while tightening the axle nuts, the cone adjustment may change. **CAUTION: If the cones are adjusted too tight, it will cause binding and scoring of the hub. If the cones are adjusted too loose, it will cause fatigue, which can result in a damaged hub or broken axle.**

㉗ Position the dust cap over the drive screw.

㉘ Install the sprocket, with the lugs on the inner surface of the sprocket indexing with the recesses in the drive screw, and then slide the sprocket into place on top of the dust cap. If you are working on the Bendix Original hub, thread the sprocket onto the drive screw in a clockwise direction.

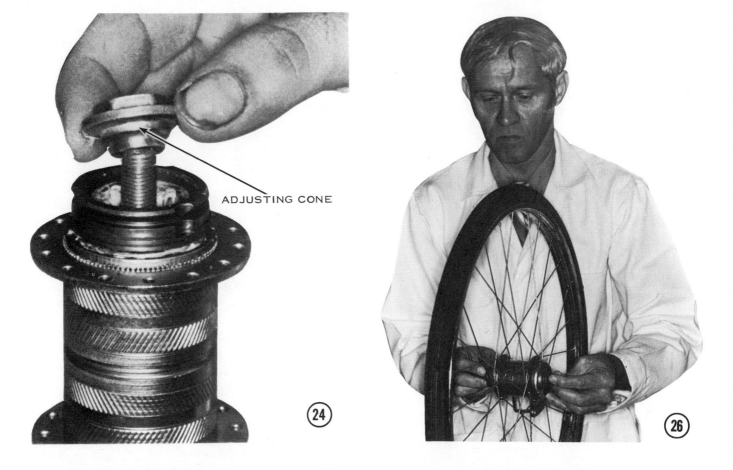

ADJUSTING CONE

㉔

㉖

(27)

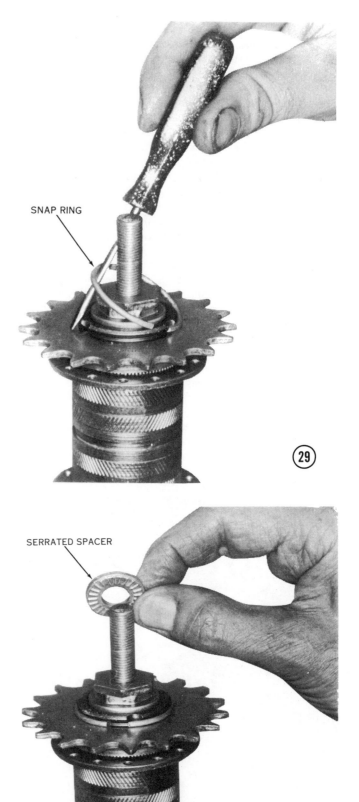

SNAP RING

(29)

SPROCKET

DRIVE SCREW

(28)

SERRATED SPACER

(30)

㉙ Spread the snap ring over the flange of the drive screw, locking the sprocket in place. If you are working on a Bendix Original hub, thread the locknut on the drive screw in a clockwise direction, and then tighten it with a hook-type spanner wrench.

㉚ Place the serrated spacer onto the axle, with the serrations facing down.

㉛ Install the flat washer on the axle, and then thread on the axle nut.

INSTALLING THE WHEEL

Engage the chain onto the sprocket, and then slide the axle into the dropouts as indicated in the accompanying illustration. Slide any carriage or fender supports onto the axle in the same order as you noted when removing the wheel. If a serrated washer is used, place the washer on the axle with the serrations toward the hub—against the frame.

Thread the outside axle nuts onto the axle finger-tight. Take up the slack in the chain by pulling the axle back until the chain is snug. Tighten the axle nut on the sprocket side until it is snug, and then align the wheel so it rotates midway between the rear frame members by pulling the axle back on the side opposite the sprocket. Adjust the chain tension until it can be depressed approximately ⅜ inch at a point midway between the hanger and rear sprocket.

Tighten both axle nuts firmly. Slip the brake lever into the strap on the frame, and then secure it with the mounting screw and nut. If the brake strap has several mounting holes, bend the strap around the frame so the brake lever will be as close to the frame as possible.

Turn the crank in the forward direction and observe that the chain and wheel turn freely without binding or rubbing on the frame. Reverse the crank direction and the wheel should stop almost immediately.

OVERHAULING A KOMET, KOMET SUPER 161, SCHWINN-APPROVED KOMET, F&S TORPEDO BOY, AND PIXIE SINGLE-SPEED REAR-WHEEL HUB WITH COASTER BRAKE

The following step-by-step illustrated instructions cover disassembling, assembling, and adjusting the Komet, Komet Super 161, Schwinn-Approved Komet, F&S Torpedo Boy, and Pixie single-speed rear-wheel hub with coaster brake. Each hub is identified by the name stamped on the brake arm and/or on the hub shell. Many of the components in the Komet series are interchangeable. All the F&S Torpedo Boy parts are interchangeable with those of the Pixie hub. However, none of the parts from these two hubs are interchangeable with the Komet series. Differences between the five hubs, including interchangeable Komet parts, are illustrated in detailed exploded drawings following the Cleaning and Inspecting portion of this section, and are pointed out in the text.

The following procedures apply basically to the Schwinn-Approved Komet hub. Deviations from this hub that might cause problems during assembly, including specific parts that are not interchangeable, are called to your attention in the individual steps.

For photographic clarity, the illustrations were made of a hub without the tire, rim, and spokes.

REMOVING THE WHEEL

If the bicycle you are working on does not have levers mounted on the handlebars, you can turn the bicycle upside down, resting it on the seat and handlebars. A better method is to support the bicycle in an upright position from a bracket, a set of hooks, or a rope attached to the garage ceiling, or to secure it in

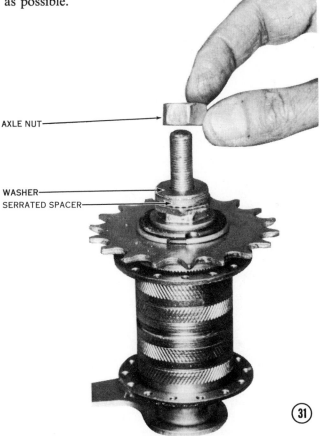

AXLE NUT

WASHER
SERRATED SPACER

㉛

Komet single-speed rear hub with coaster brake. Rear hubs with similar internal parts are: Komet, Komet 161, Schwinn-Approved Komet, Pixie, and F&S Torpedo Boy.

an automobile rear carrier rack attached to the car. Holding the bicycle rigid will make the task of removing, installing, and adjusting parts much easier.

Remove the nut and mounting screw securing the brake arm to the strap on the bicycle frame. Next, remove the outside axle nuts. Take note of the washer and support arrangement installed on the axle. Some bicycles have a serrated washer installed against the frame to prevent the wheel from moving forward under the tension of the chain. Washers are usually installed between fender and accessory supports to keep them from twisting when the axle nuts are tightened.

Slide off any carriage or fender supports, including washers, from the axle. Move the wheel free of the dropouts, remove the chain from the rear sprocket, and then hook it over the frame.

DISASSEMBLING

① Clamp the complete hub and wheel assembly in a vise, with the jaws gripping the locknut on the brake-arm side of the hub. Remove the sprocket lock ring by prying it up with a screwdriver, and then lift the sprocket up and off the drive screw. *NOTE: The Pixie and F&S Torpedo Boy hubs use two thick sprocket washers. Note their position to facilitate installation.*

② Lift the dust cap off the drive screw.

③ Turn the hub assembly end for end in the vise, with the jaws gripping the axle. **CAUTION: Use a set of soft vise jaws to protect the axle threads.** Remove the locknut from the axle by turning it in a counterclockwise direction. If you are working on a Komet or Komet Super 161 hub, use a hook-spanner type wrench to remove the locknut. *NOTE: The F&S Torpedo Boy hub has two hook-spanner locknuts.* Remove the keyed lockwasher.

④ Grasp the brake arm and turn it in a counterclockwise direction until the brake-arm side expander is clear of the axle. The brake arm, dust cap, and brake-arm side expander will come out together. The ball bearing retainer assembly will come out with the expander assembly. Remove the ball bearing retainer assembly from the expander. Hold the retainer assembly

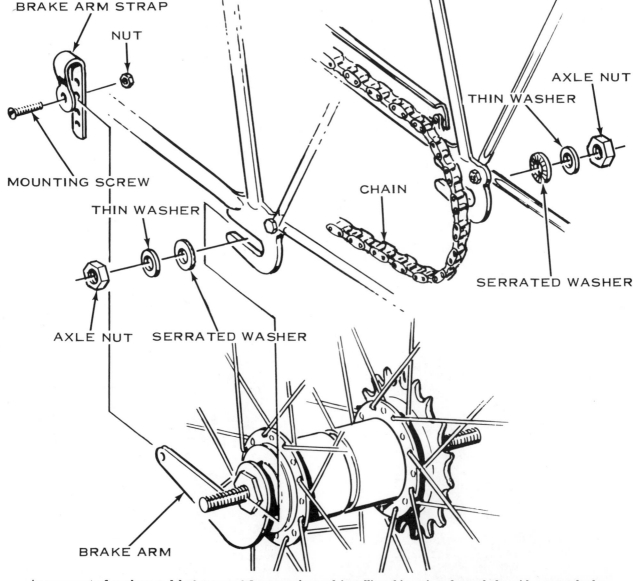

Arrangement of washers and locknuts used for removing and installing this series of rear hubs with coaster brake.

with the fingers of both hands, push on the open end of the expander with your thumbs and the retainer assembly will slide off the expander. *NOTE: The bearing retainer assembly cannot be removed from the expander of the Komet Super 161 hub.*

⑤ Remove the hub shell by lifting and turning it in a counterclockwise direction.

⑥ Remove the brake cylinder assembly and drive clutch from the hub shell.

⑦ Lift the ball bearing retainer assembly off the drive screw, and then remove the drive screw from the axle.

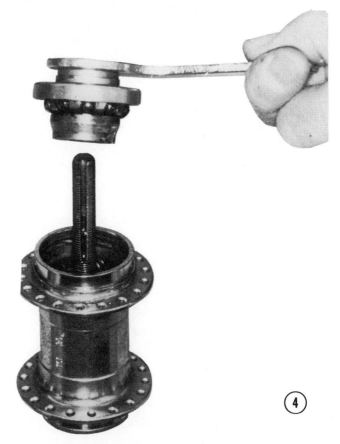

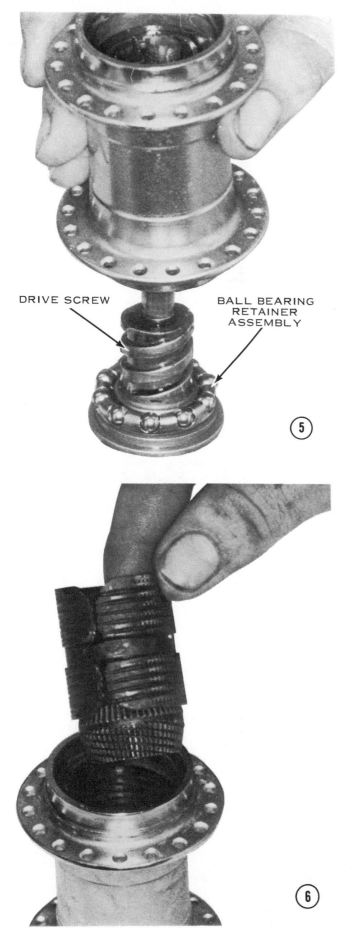

DRIVE SCREW

BALL BEARING RETAINER ASSEMBLY

(5)

(6)

(7)

⑧ Remove the dust cap off the drive screw by prying up with a screwdriver, as shown, and the cap will pop out. Work around the cap edge and be careful not to crimp or distort it. Remove the 10 loose ball bearings from the drive screw. *NOTE: The ball bearings are held in a retainer on the Komet Super 161 hub.*

⑨ Shift the axle in the vise so the jaws grip the flats on the end of the axle. Loosen the stationary cone by turning it in a clockwise direction. *NOTE: The Pixie and F&S Torpedo Boy hubs have a locknut against the stationary cone, which must be loosened before the cone can be rotated.* Turn the axle end for end in the vise,

(8)

and then remove the cone. Remove the axle from the vise, and then clamp the brake arm in the vise, as shown. Drive the brake-arm side expander from the brake arm with a hammer and drift punch. **CAUTION: Tap lightly with the hammer and work the drift punch around the opening in the brake arm to keep from damaging the expander or distorting the brake arm.**

CLEANING AND INSPECTING

Clean all parts in solvent and blow dry with compressed air, or wipe them dry with a lintless cloth. Keep all cleaned parts on paper towels to avoid contamination. Cover them with a clean towel to keep grit from entering the internal parts and bearings. A tiny piece of grit can do a tremendous amount of damage if allowed to work on a part over an extended period of time or while the wheel is turning at high speed.

Inspect the ball bearing retainer assemblies. If any of the ball bearings come out of the retainer, are pitted (pencil-point dots), show signs of excessive wear (dull spots), or are cracked, the bearing assembly must be replaced. Check the retainers for cracks or other damage. If you are working on a Komet Super 161 hub, and the captive ball bearing retainer assembly on the brake-arm side expander is damaged and needs to be replaced, the complete expander assembly, including the ball bearing assembly, must be replaced as a unit.

If you are working on a Komet, Schwinn-Approved Komet, Pixie, or F&S Torpedo Boy hub, carefully inspect the loose ball bearings for signs of excessive wear and replace the complete set if any of them are damaged. Replacing the complete set will ensure distribution of the bearing surface load equally on all the ball bearings.

Check both ends of the hub shell for pitted or worn bearing surfaces. Check the flanges of the hub shell for cracks and to be sure they are not loose.

Inspect the drive screw for pitted or worn bearing surfaces and the splines for wear or chipped edges.

Check the outer surface of the drive clutch for worn dentils. Check for chipped or worn threads.

Inspect the brake cylinder assembly for worn or glazed surfaces.

Check the dust caps to be sure they are not crimped or distorted, which could have happened during disassembly.

Check the brake arm to be sure it is not bent or damaged.

Inspect the axle and locknuts for signs of damage or stripped threads. Roll the axle slowly across a smooth flat surface and check both ends for being out-of-round, or watch the center of the axle to see if it rises off the

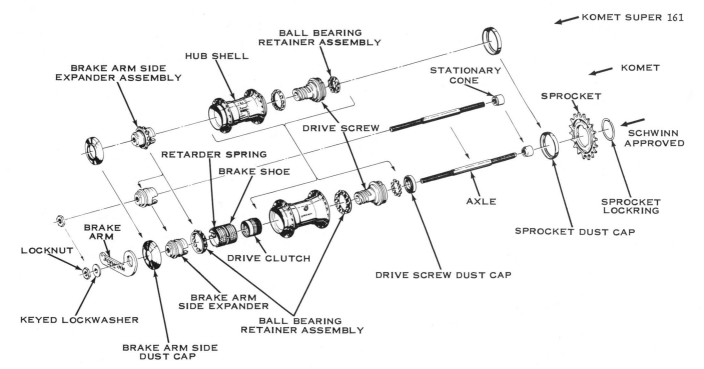

Exploded view of a Schwinn-Approved, Komet, and Komet Super 161 single-speed rear hub with coaster brake. Parts of the Komet and Komet 161 separated from the main line of the figure are not interchangeable with those of the Schwinn-Approved; all others are.

⑩

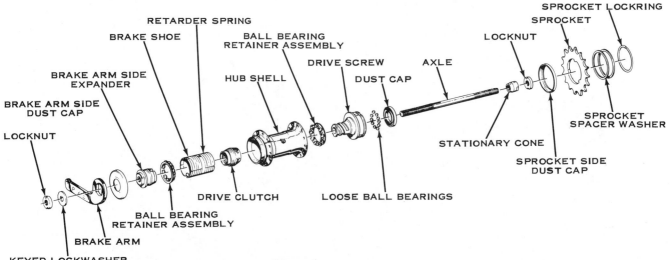

surface. Either of these indications means the axle is bent and must be replaced.

Check the key of the keyed lockwasher to be sure it is not broken or cracked.

Check the stationary cone for stripped or damaged threads. Inspect the bearing surface of the cone for pits or excessive wear.

Inspect the brake-arm side expander for worn flats.

The ball bearings for the Komet Super 161 are in a retainer. All other hubs in this series use loose ball bearings.

ASSEMBLING

⑩ Spread a generous amount of multipurpose lubricant on the bearing race of the drive screw. Imbed the 10 loose ball bearings in the lubricant. The bearings will not fit snugly because of the one-ball bearing clear-

SPROCKET LOCKRING
SPROCKET
RETARDER SPRING
BRAKE SHOE
BALL BEARING
RETAINER ASSEMBLY
LOCKNUT
BRAKE ARM SIDE
EXPANDER
DRIVE SCREW
HUB SHELL
AXLE
BRAKE ARM SIDE
DUST CAP
DUST CAP
LOCKNUT
STATIONARY CONE
SPROCKET
SPACER WASHER
SPROCKET SIDE
DUST CAP
DRIVE CLUTCH
LOOSE BALL BEARINGS
BALL BEARING
RETAINER ASSEMBLY
BRAKE ARM
KEYED LOCKWASHER

Exploded view of a Pixie and F&S Torpedo Boy single-speed rear hub with coaster brake. All parts of these two hubs are interchangeable.

ance required. If you are working on a Komet Super 161 hub, pack the ball bearing retainer assembly with a generous amount of multipurpose lubricant. Work the lubricant throughout the bearings and retainer with your fingers. Install the lubricated bearing assembly into the drive screw. If these bearings need replacing, and you are unable to obtain the type required for your particular hub, you may use loose ball bearings in the Komet Super 161, or the ball bearing retainer assembly in the Komet and Schwinn-Approved Komet hubs.

⑪ Cover the loose ball bearings with another coating of multipurpose lubricant.

⑫ Position the dust cap over the ball bearings, with the flat side facing up and tap into place with a hammer until it is fully seated in the drive screw.

⑬ Apply a generous coating of multipurpose lubricant onto the inside ridge of the brake cylinder assembly and around the recess of the drive clutch, as shown. Insert the drive clutch into the brake cylinder assembly, with the smooth machined surface of the drive clutch down. This will allow the dentils of the drive clutch to engage the dentils of the brake cylinder.

⑭ Coat the brake shoe surface of the brake cylinder assembly with multipurpose lubricant. Insert the assembled brake cylinder and drive clutch into the end of the hub shell that has the small external flange, as shown.

⑮ Pack one of the large ball bearing retainer assemblies with a generous amount of multipurpose

⑫

lubricant. Work the lubricant throughout the bearings and the retainer.

⑯ Place the lubricated bearing assembly onto the brake-arm side expander, with the flat side of the retainer down. If you are working on the Komet Super

⑪

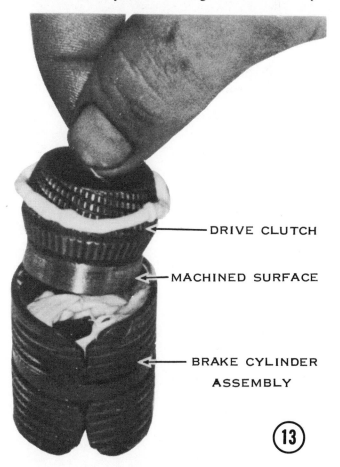

DRIVE CLUTCH

MACHINED SURFACE

BRAKE CYLINDER ASSEMBLY

⑬

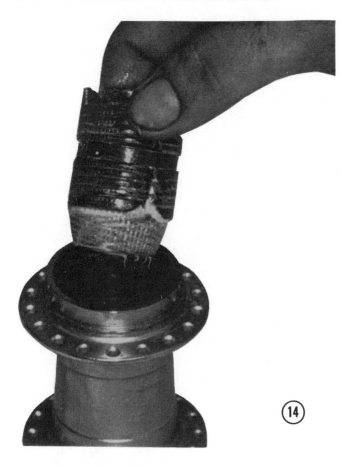

(14)

(16)

the Komet or Schwinn-Approved Komet hubs. Refer to the exploded illustration on page 141.

⑰ Position the dust cap over the brake-arm side expander. **CAUTION: The dust cap of the Komet Super 161 is not interchangeable with the cap of the Komet or Schwinn-Approved Komet hubs.** Place the brake arm on the brake-arm side expander, with the flats of the brake arm indexing with the flats on the end of the expander and with the manufacturer's identification facing up. Tap the brake arm lightly, working around the end of the expander until the arm is fully seated against the dust cap.

161 hub, apply a generous amount of multipurpose lubricant to the captive bearing assembly. Work the lubricant throughout the bearings and the retainer. **CAUTION: The brake-arm side expander of the Komet Super 161 is not interchangeable with the expander of**

(15)

The ball bearings for the brake-arm side expander of the Komet Super 161 hub are part of the expander assembly and cannot be removed for service.

⑱ Insert the assembled brake-arm side expander in the hub shell. Set the hub on the bench in the vertical position, resting on the brake arm. Pack the ball bearing retainer assembly with a generous amount of multi-purpose lubricant. Work the lubricant throughout the bearings and retainer. Insert the lubricated bearing as-

sembly into the hub, with the flat side of the retainer facing up.

⑲ Install the assembled drive screw in the hub by rotating it in a clockwise direction until it is fully seated. **CAUTION: The drive screw of the Komet Super 161 is not interchangeable with the drive screw of the**

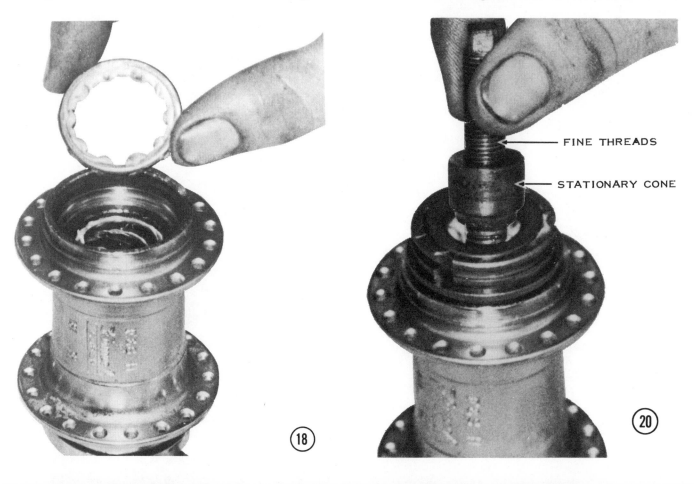

FINE THREADS

STATIONARY CONE

HOOK SPANNER
LOCKNUT

KEYED
LOCKWASHER

㉑

Komet and Schwinn-Approved Komet hubs.

⑳ Thread the stationary cone onto the axle end, which has the flats. Tighten it firmly to the end of the fine threads. If you are working on a Pixie or F&S Torpedo Boy hub, thread the locknut onto the axle and tighten it against the cone. Insert the axle through the assembled hub, as shown.

㉑ Slide the keyed lockwasher onto the axle against the brake arm, with the key indexing with the keyway of the axle. Thread the hook spanner locknut onto the axle finger-tight. *NOTE: The Schwinn-Approved Komet hub has a conventional locknut. The F&S Torpedo Boy hub has two hook-spanner locknuts.*

㉒ Clamp the assembly in the vise, with the jaws gripping the axle at the brake arm end. **CAUTION: Use soft vise jaws to protect the axle threads.** Install the sprocket, with the dished (concave) side facing up and the lugs on the inside surface of the sprocket indexing with the recesses in the drive screw.

㉓ Snap the lock ring into place with a screwdriver. *NOTE: Install the thick sprocket washers on the Pixie and F&S Torpedo Boy in the same position as you noted during disassembly.*

㉔ Turn the assembly end for end in the vise with the jaws gripping the flats on the end of the axle. Turn the brake arm in a clockwise direction until it is barely snug, and then back it off slightly. Rotate the sprocket in a counterclockwise direction and at the same time raise the drive-screw assembly and hub until the brake cylinder keys are aligned in the brake-arm side expander keyways. When this alignment is reached, you will be

SPROCKET
LUG

RECESSES IN DRIVE SCREW

㉒

㉓

able to feel the hub rise slightly. Hold the hub in this position and rotate the brake arm in a clockwise direction until it is finger-tight, then back the arm off approximately one full turn.

㉕ Hold the brake arm and tighten the locknut. If you are working on a Komet, Komet Super 161, Pixie, or F&S Torpedo Boy hub, use a hook-type spanner wrench. The Schwinn-Approved Komet hub uses a conventional locknut. Grasp the rim of the wheel and try to move the wheel up and down—this is referred to as side play. Remove all but a trace of side play by first loosening the locknut, then tightening the brake arm by turning it in a clockwise direction, and then securing it with the locknut.

㉖ Remove the assembled hub and wheel from the vise. Hold each end of the axle with your fingers. Slowly twist the axle with the thumb and forefinger of each hand—the wheel should not turn. If it does turn, the cones are too tight and must be loosened slightly. Back off the locknut on the brake arm side. *NOTE: The F&S Torpedo Boy hub has two locknuts.* Loosen the cone by turning the brake arm in a counterclockwise direction approximately ⅛ turn, and then retighten the locknut. The cones are properly adjusted when the wheel rotates freely, comes to rest gradually with the valve stem at the lowest point of the wheel, and there is only the slightest trace of side play. A check of the cone adjustment must be made after the wheel is installed on the bicycle, because if care is not taken to hold the locknut while tightening the axle nuts, the cone adjustment may change. **CAUTION: If the adjustment is made too tight, it will cause binding and scoring of the hub. If the adjustment is too loose, it will cause fatigue, which can cause serious damage to internal parts, a damaged hub, or a broken axle.**

INSTALLING

Engage the chain onto the sprocket, and then slide the axle into the dropouts as indicated in the accompanying illustration. Slide any carriage or fender sup-

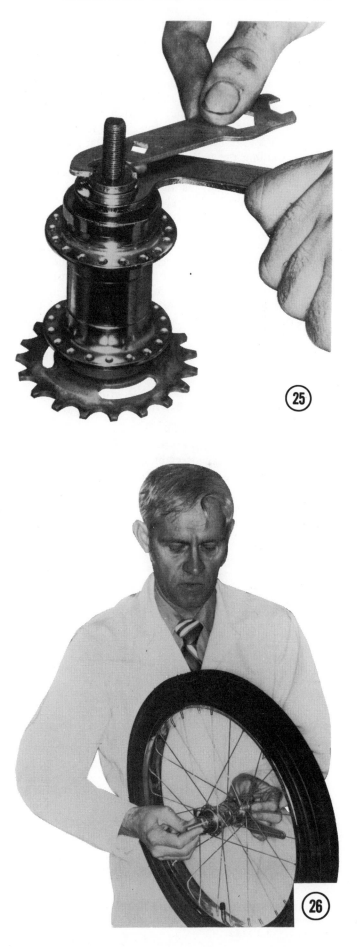

㉕

㉔

㉖

ports onto the axle in the same order as you noted when removing the wheel. If a serrated washer is used, place the washer on the axle with the serrations toward the hub—against the frame.

Thread the outside axle nuts onto the axle finger-tight. Take up the slack in the chain by pulling the axle back until the chain is snug. Tighten the axle nut on the sprocket side until it is snug, and then align the wheel so it rotates midway between the rear frame members by pulling the axle back on the side opposite the sprocket. Adjust the chain tension until it can be depressed approximately ⅜ inch at a point midway between the hanger and rear sprocket.

Tighten both axle nuts firmly. Slip the brake lever into the strap on the frame, and then secure it with the mounting screw and nut. If the brake strap has several mounting holes, bend the strap around the frame so the brake lever will be as close to the frame as possible.

Turn the crank in the forward direction and observe that the chain and wheel turn freely without binding or rubbing on the frame. Reverse the crank direction and the wheel should stop almost immediately.

OVERHAULING A MATTATUCK, HAWTHORNE, NEW DEPARTURE, NANKAI, AND SHIMANO 3.3.3 SINGLE-SPEED REAR-WHEEL HUB WITH COASTER BRAKE

The following step-by-step illustrated instructions cover disassembling, assembling, and adjusting the Mattatuck, Hawthorne, New Departure, Nankai, and Shimano 3.3.3 single-speed rear-wheel hubs with coaster brake. Each hub is identified by the manufacturer's name stamped on the brake arm and/or on the hub shell. These five hubs are basically alike, with many

of the parts of the first four hubs being interchangeable. The Shimano 3.3.3 components cannot be interchanged with any other hub.

Differences between the hubs are illustrated in detailed exploded drawings following the Cleaning and Inspecting portion of this section, and are pointed out in the text. The following procedures apply basically to the Mattatuck hub. Deviations from this hub that might cause problems during assembly, including specific parts that are not interchangeable, are called to your attention in the individual steps.

For photographic clarity, the illustrations were made of a hub without the tire, rim, and spokes.

REMOVING THE WHEEL

If the bicycle you are working on does not have levers mounted on the handlebars, you can turn the bicycle upside down, resting it on the seat and handlebars. A better method is to support the bicycle in an upright position from a bracket, a set of hooks, or a rope attached to the garage ceiling, or to secure it in an automobile rear carrier rack attached to the car. Holding the bicycle rigid will make the task of removing, installing, and adjusting parts much easier.

Remove the nut and mounting screw that hold the brake arm to the strap on the bicycle frame. Next, remove the outside axle nuts. Take note of the washer and support arrangement installed on the axle. Some bicycles have a serrated washer installed against the frame to prevent the wheel from moving forward under

The Nankai single-speed rear hub with coaster brake is similar to the Mattatuck, Hawthorne, New Departure, and Shimano 3.3.3 hubs.

the tension of the chain. Washers are usually installed between fender and accessory supports to keep them from twisting when the axle nuts are tightened.

Slide off any carriage or fender supports, including washers, from the axle. Move the wheel free of the dropouts, and then remove the chain from the rear sprocket and hook it over the frame.

DISASSEMBLING

① Clamp the complete hub assembly in a vise, with the jaws gripping the axle nut on the brake arm side of the hub. If you are working on a Mattatuck or Shimano 3.3.3 hub, remove the sprocket lock ring by prying it up with a screwdriver and then lifting the sprocket up and off the drive screw. If you are working on a Hawthorne, New Departure, or Nankai hub, remove the locknut, and then unscrew the sprocket by turning it counterclockwise.

② Remove the dust cap by prying up with a screwdriver, as shown. Work around the cap edge and it will pop out. Be careful not to crimp or distort the cap.

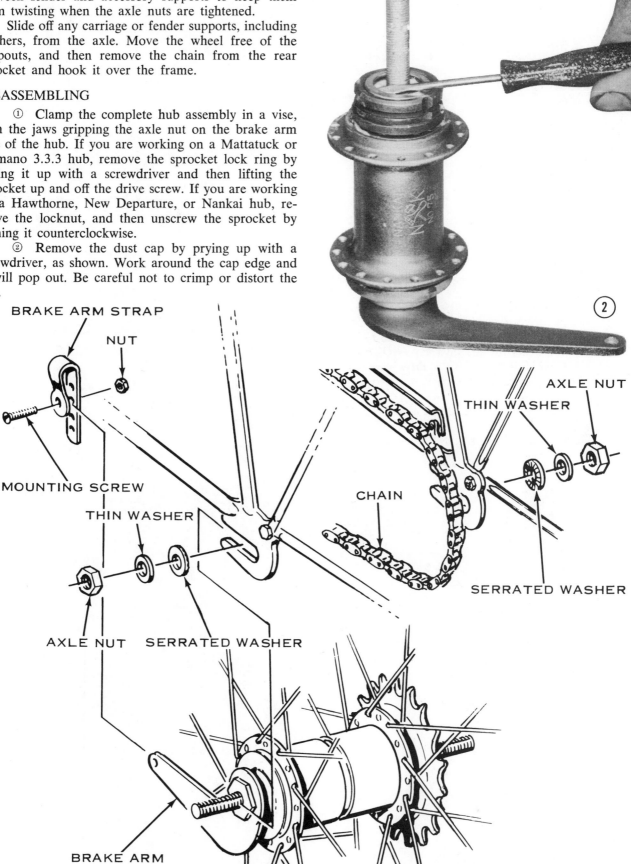

Arrangement of washers and locknuts used for removing and installing this series of rear hubs with coaster brake.

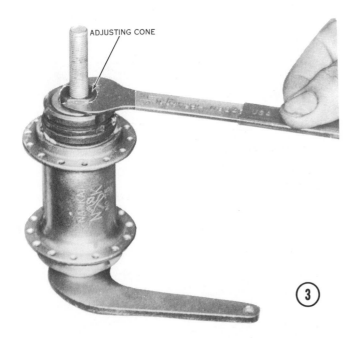

ADJUSTING CONE

③

③ Remove the locknut and adjusting cone.

④ Pry the drive-screw dust cap out with a screwdriver. Work the screwdriver around the axle to keep from crimping or distorting the dust cap. *NOTE: The Shimano 3.3.3 hub does not have a drive-screw dust cap. On the New Departure hub this dust cap is a part of the sprocket locknut.*

⑤ Lift out the ball bearing retainer assembly from the drive screw.

⑥ Remove the drive screw from the axle by

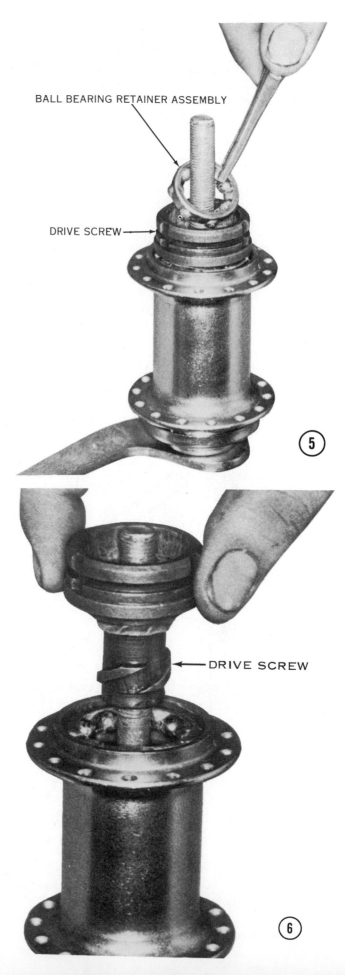

BALL BEARING RETAINER ASSEMBLY

DRIVE SCREW

⑤

DUST CAP

④

DRIVE SCREW

⑥

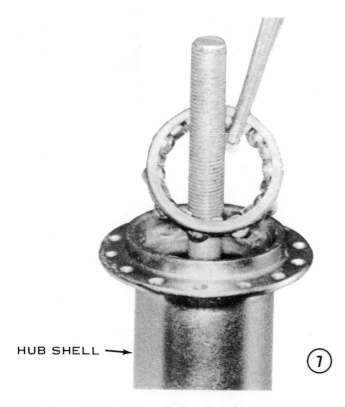

HUB SHELL →

⑦

turning it in a counterclockwise direction.

⑦ Lift the ball bearing retainer assembly out of the hub shell.

⑧ Lift the hub shell up and off the axle.

⑨ Remove the drive clutch.

⑩ Slide the brake clutch off the axle.

DRIVE CLUTCH

⑨

BRAKE CLUTCH

⑧

⑩

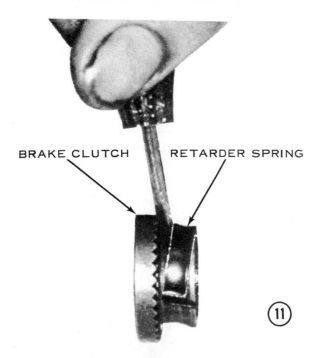

BRAKE CLUTCH   RETARDER SPRING

(11)

⑪ Remove the retarder spring from the brake clutch. If you are working on a Mattatuck hub, pry the spring off the brake clutch by inserting a narrow-bladed screwdriver through the spring slots, and then prying the spring off the brake clutch. If you are working on a Hawthorne, New Departure, Nankai, or Shimano 3.3.3 hub, insert a narrow-bladed screwdriver under the lower edge of the spring and pry it off the brake clutch.

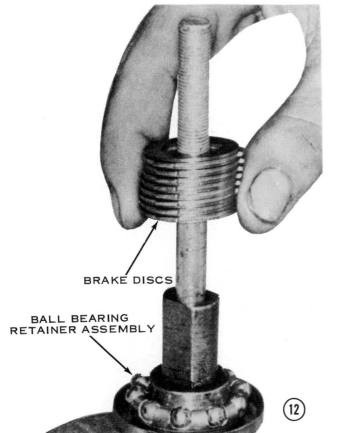

BRAKE DISCS

BALL BEARING
RETAINER ASSEMBLY

(12)

(13)

⑫ Remove the steel and bronze brake disks, and then lift out the ball bearing and retainer assembly. *NOTE: On the Shimano 3.3.3 hub, remove the spacer with the brake disks.*

⑬ Turn the axle end for end in the vise, with the jaws gripping the center (unthreaded portion) of the axle, or use a set of soft vise jaws to protect the axle threads. Remove the locknut by turning it in a counterclockwise direction. If you have trouble loosening the locknut, lower the axle in the vise until the jaws grip the flats of the disk support sleeve for a better bite, and then loosen and remove the locknut. Shift the axle in the vise so the jaws grip the center portion of the axle or use soft vise jaws.

⑭ Remove the brake arm and dust cap. Remove the disk support sleeve by turning it in a counterclockwise direction until it is clear of the axle.

CLEANING AND INSPECTING

Clean all parts in solvent and blow dry with compressed air, or wipe them dry with a lintless cloth. Keep all cleaned parts on paper towels to avoid contamination. Cover them with a clean towel to keep grit from entering the internal parts and bearings. A tiny piece

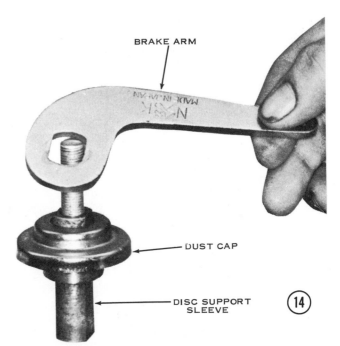

BRAKE ARM

DUST CAP

DISC SUPPORT
SLEEVE

(14)

of grit can do a tremendous amount of damage if allowed to work on a part over an extended period of time or while the wheel is turning at high speed.

Inspect the three ball bearing retainer assemblies. If any of the ball bearings come out of the retainer, are pitted (pencil-point dots), show signs of excessive wear (dull spots), or are cracked, the bearing and retainer assembly must be replaced. Check the retainers for cracks or visible signs of damage.

Check the adjusting cone bearing surface for scoring (scratchlike marks), pits, or other damage. Check for stripped cone threads.

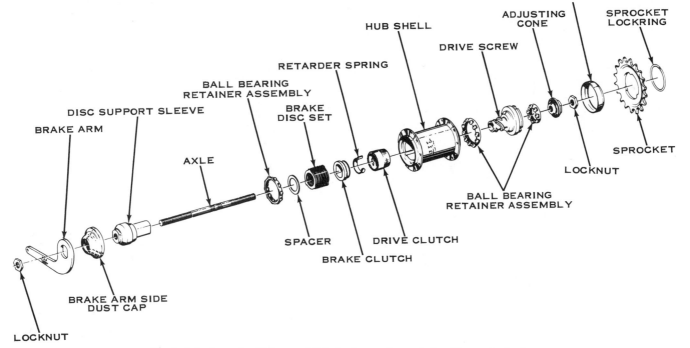

Exploded view of a Shimano 3.3.3 single-speed rear hub with coaster brake.

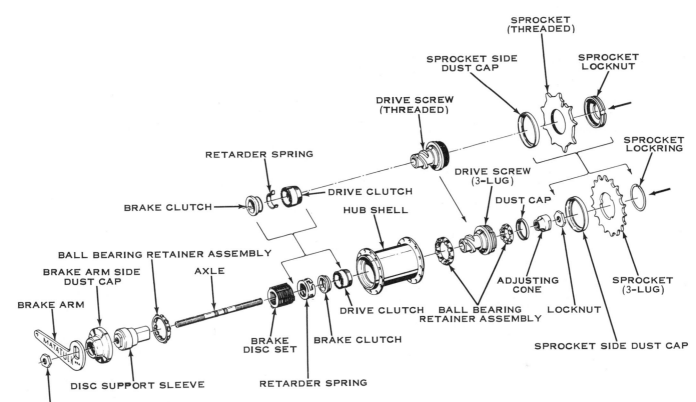

Exploded view of a Mattatuck single-speed rear hub with coaster brake. Parts separated from the main line of the figure apply to Hawthorne, New Departure, and Nankai hubs and are not interchangeable with those of the Mattatuck; all others are.

Inspect the bearing surface of the disk support sleeve for scores, pits, or other damage. Check for stripped threads.

Inspect the drive clutch and the brake clutch for worn, chipped, or damaged teeth.

Check the splines of the drive screw for cracks, chips, or worn edges.

Check the axle and locknuts for signs of damage or stripped threads. Roll the axle slowly across a smooth flat surface and check both ends for being out-of-round, or watch the center of the axle to see if it rises off the surface. Either of these indications means the axle is bent and must be replaced.

Check the three dust caps to be sure they are not crimped or distorted, which could have happened during disassembly.

Inspect the bearing surfaces of the hub shell for scores, pits, or excessive wear. Check the flanges of the hub shell for cracks and to be sure they are not loose.

Inspect the steel and bronze brake disks for worn surfaces or broken ears.

Check the brake arm to be sure it is not bent or damaged.

CAUTION: Use only Shimano 3.3.3 parts when replacing components on that hub. Do not attempt to use Shimano 3.3.3 parts on the Mattatuck, Hawthorne, New Departure, and Nankai hubs.

ASSEMBLING

⑮ Thread the disk support sleeve onto either end of the axle until the outer edge of the sleeve shoulder is 1⅛ inches from the end of the axle, or the inner edge is midway between the double-threaded section in the center of the axle. If you are working on the Shimano 3.3.3 hub, thread the disk support sleeve on the end of the axle farthest from the double-threaded section.

⑯ Clamp the axle in a vise, with the disk support sleeve facing up. **CAUTION: Use soft vise jaws to protect the axle threads from damage.** Slide the brake-side dust cap over the axle and down onto the disk support sleeve. Place the brake arm on the dust cap, with the flats on the arm indexing with the flats on the disk support sleeve and the manufacturer's identification facing up.

⑰ Thread the locknut onto the axle, and then tighten it against the brake arm securely by holding the arm and turning the locknut clockwise.

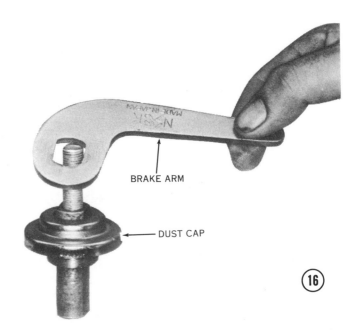

BRAKE ARM

DUST CAP

⑯

⑱ Pack one of the large ball bearing retainer assemblies with a generous amount of multipurpose lubricant. Work the lubricant throughout the bearings and retainer with your fingers.

⑲ Remove the axle from the vise and turn it end for end, with the jaws gripping the locknut. Install the lubricated ball bearing assembly on the disk support sleeve, with the flat side of the retainer facing down—the ball bearings facing up.

⑳ Slide one of the steel disks onto the axle and disk support sleeve, with the flats of the disk indexing

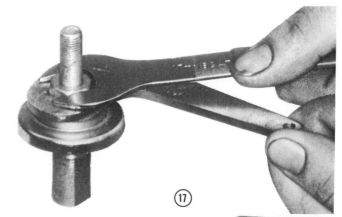

⑰

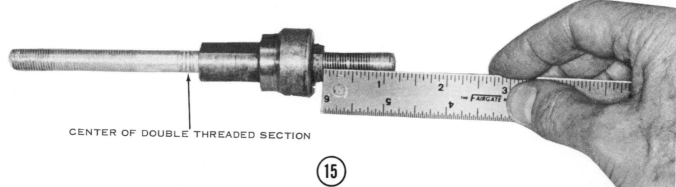

CENTER OF DOUBLE THREADED SECTION

⑮

(18)

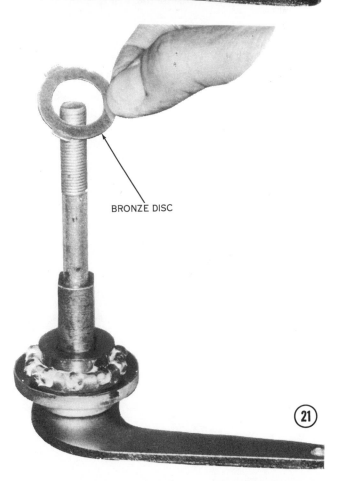

STEEL DISC

(20)

with the flats on the sleeve. *NOTE: If you are working on a Shimano 3.3.3 hub, install the spacer onto the axle before the first steel disk.*

㉑ Install one of the bronze disks on top of the steel disk.

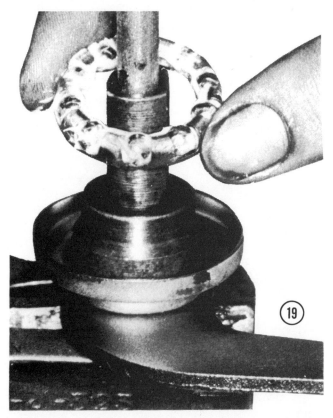

(19)

BRONZE DISC

(21)

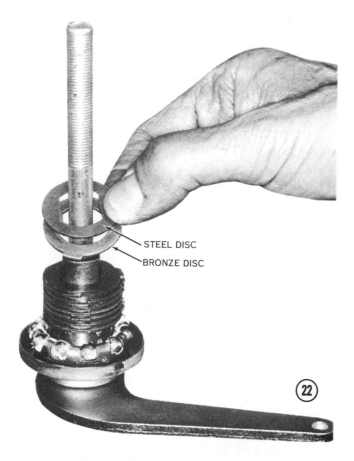

STEEL DISC
BRONZE DISC

㉒

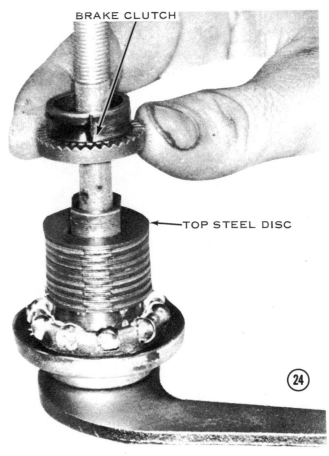

BRAKE CLUTCH

TOP STEEL DISC

㉔

㉒ Continue to install the disks, alternating between a bronze and a steel disk. Align the ears of the bronze disks.

㉓ Snap a new retarder spring onto the brake clutch. **CAUTION: Always replace the retarder spring with a new one to ensure proper service after assembly.**

The illustrated retarder spring and brake clutch are common to a Hawthorne, New Departure, Nankai, and Shimano 3.3.3 hub. The brake clutch on the Mattatuck hub is similar, but the retarder spring is quite different in shape, although it performs the same function. If you are working on a Mattatuck hub, install the retarder

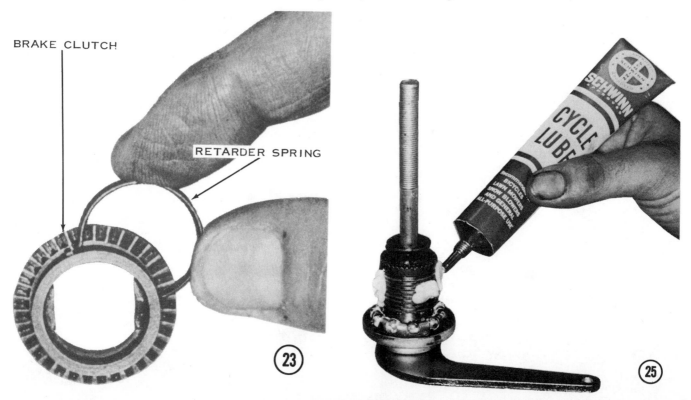

BRAKE CLUTCH

RETARDER SPRING

㉓

㉕

spring by snapping it onto the large end of the brake clutch. **CAUTION: The retarder spring, brake clutch, and drive clutch of the Mattatuck hub are not interchangeable with the Hawthorne, New Departure, and Nankai hubs.**

㉔   Slide the brake clutch onto the axle, with the teeth facing up and the flats on the inside surface of the clutch indexing with the flats on the disk support sleeve. This will allow the clutch to set on the top steel disk.

㉕   Coat the brake disks and brake clutch with a generous amount of multipurpose lubricant.

㉖   Slip the drive clutch over the axle, with the teeth facing down in order to index with the teeth of the brake clutch.

㉗   Install the hub shell over the assembled parts, with the largest opening facing down so the recesses on the inside surface of the shell index with the four rows of bronze disk ears. When properly installed, the lip on the lower flange of the hub shell will seat in the brake arm dust cap.

㉘   Pack the other large ball bearing and retainer assembly with a generous amount of multipurpose lubricant. Work the lubricant throughout the bearings and retainer with your fingers. Insert the lubricated bearing assembly into the hub shell, with the flat side of the retainer facing up.

㉙   Apply a coating of multipurpose lubricant to the splines of the drive screw, and then thread the drive screw onto the axle in a clockwise direction as far as possible by hand. **CAUTION: If the drive screw has**

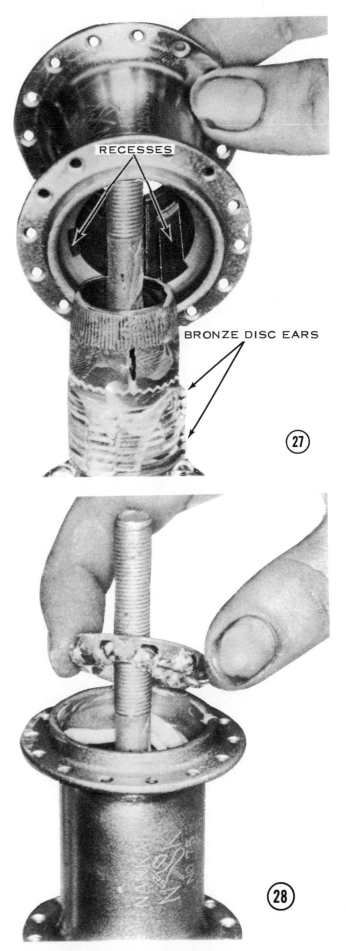

RECESSES

BRONZE DISC EARS

㉗

DRIVE CLUTCH

㉖

㉘

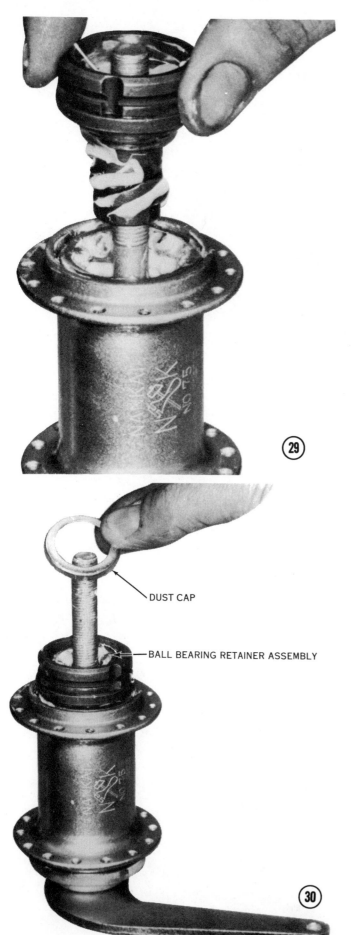

DUST CAP

BALL BEARING RETAINER ASSEMBLY

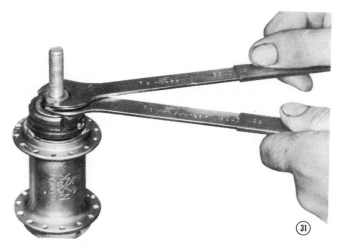

to be replaced be sure to purchase the proper one for the hub you are working on. The drive screw of the Mattatuck hub is not interchangeable with the drive screw of the Hawthorne, New Departure, and Nankai hubs, although they appear similar.

㉚ Pack the remaining ball bearing assembly with a generous amount of multipurpose lubricant. Work the lubricant throughout the bearings and retainer. Insert the lubricated bearing assembly into the bearing cup of the drive screw, with the flat side of the retainer facing up. Install the dust cap over the bearing assembly with the flat side facing up and then tap it into place with a hammer. **CAUTION: The dust cap of the**

Mattatuck hub is not interchangeable with that of the Hawthorne, New Departure, and Nankai hubs. If you have to buy a new cap, be sure to specify the hub you are working on. *NOTE: The Shimano 3.3.3 hub does not have this dust cap. On the New Departure hub this cap is part of the sprocket locknut.*

㉛ Thread the cone and locknut onto the axle. Tighten the cone until it is snug, and then back it off approximately ¼ turn or until there is just a discernible amount of side play when you move the wheel rim up and down. Hold the cone with a thin wrench or cone pliers, and then tighten the locknut. Place the sprocket-side dust cap in position with the flat side facing up, and then tap it with a hammer until it is fully seated in the hub shell.

㉜ Remove the assembled hub and wheel from the vise. Hold each end of the axle with your fingers. Slowly twist the axle with the thumb and forefinger of each hand—the wheel should not turn. If it does turn, the cones are too tight and must be loosened slightly. Back off the locknut on the axle end opposite the brake arm. Loosen the cone approximately ⅛ turn, and then retighten the locknut. The cones are properly adjusted when the wheel rotates freely, comes to rest gradually with the valve stem at the lowest point of the wheel, and there is only the slightest trace of side play. A check of the cone adjustment must be made after the wheel is installed on the bicycle, because if care is not taken to hold the locknut while tightening the axle nuts, the cone adjustment may change. **CAUTION: If the cones are adjusted too tight, it will cause binding and scoring of the hub. If the cones are adjusted too loose, it will**

cause fatigue, which can result in a damaged hub or broken axle.

㉝ Install the sprocket. If you are working on a Hawthorne, New Departure, or Nankai hub, thread the sprocket onto the drive screw, and then secure it with the sprocket locknut. If you are working on a Mattatuck or Shimano 3.3.3 hub, install the sprocket onto the drive screw, with the lugs on the inside surface of the sprocket indexing with the recesses in the drive screw. Secure it by snapping the sprocket locknut ring over the lip on the drive screw. Install the axle washer and axle nut.

INSTALLING THE WHEEL

Engage the chain onto the sprocket, and then slide the axle into the dropouts as indicated in the accompanying illustration. Slide any carriage or fender supports onto the axle in the same order as you noted when removing the wheel. If a serrated washer is used, place the washer on the axle with the serrations toward the hub—against the frame. Thread the outside axle nuts onto the axle finger-tight. Take up the slack in the chain by pulling the axle back until the chain is taut. Tighten the axle nut on the sprocket side snugly, and then align the wheel so it rotates midway between the rear frame members by pulling the axle back on the side opposite the sprocket. Adjust the chain tension until it can be depressed about ⅜ inch at a point midway between the hanger and rear sprocket. Tighten both axle nuts firmly. Slip the brake lever into the strap on the frame, and then secure it with the mounting screw and nut. If the brake strap has several mounting holes, bend the strap around the frame so the brake lever will be as close to the frame as possible.

Turn the crank in the forward direction and observe that the chain and wheel turn freely without binding or rubbing on the frame. Reverse the crank direction and the wheel should stop almost immediately.

OVERHAULING A BENDIX YELLOW BAND AND BENDIX BLUE BAND TWO-SPEED REAR HUB WITH COASTER BRAKE

The following step-by-step illustrated instructions cover disassembling, assembling, and adjusting the Bendix Yellow Band and Bendix Blue Band two-speed rear hub with coaster brake. The hubs are identified by the word BENDIX stamped on the brake arm and a series of yellow or blue bands circling the center of the hub. These two hubs are basically alike with many of the parts being interchangeable. Differences between the hubs, including interchangeable parts, are illustrated in a detailed exploded drawing following the Cleaning and Inspecting portion of this section, and are pointed out in the text. The following procedures apply basically to the Bendix Blue Band hub. Deviations from this hub that might cause problems during assembly, including specific parts that are not interchangeable, are called to your attention in the individual steps.

For photographic clarity, the illustrations were made of a hub without the tire, rim, and spokes.

㉝

Bendix two-speed rear hub with coaster brake. The hub can be identified by the name stamped on the brake arm and by a series of yellow or blue bands encircling the hub shell.

REMOVING THE WHEEL

If the bicycle you are working on does not have levers mounted on the handlebars, you can turn the bicycle upside down, resting it on the seat and handlebars. A better method is to support the bicycle in an upright position from a bracket, a set of hooks, or a rope attached to the garage ceiling, or to secure it in an automobile rear carrier rack attached to the car. Holding the bicycle rigid will make the task of removing, installing, and adjusting parts much easier.

Remove the nut and mounting screw that hold the brake arm to the strap on the bicycle frame. Next, remove the outside axle nuts. Take note of the washer and support arrangement installed on the axle. Some bicycles have a serrated washer installed against the frame to prevent the wheel from moving forward under the tension of the chain. Washers are usually installed between fender and accessory supports to keep them from twisting when the axle nuts are tightened.

Slide off any carriage or fender supports including washers from the axle. Move the wheel free of the dropouts, remove the chain from the rear sprocket, and then hook it over the frame.

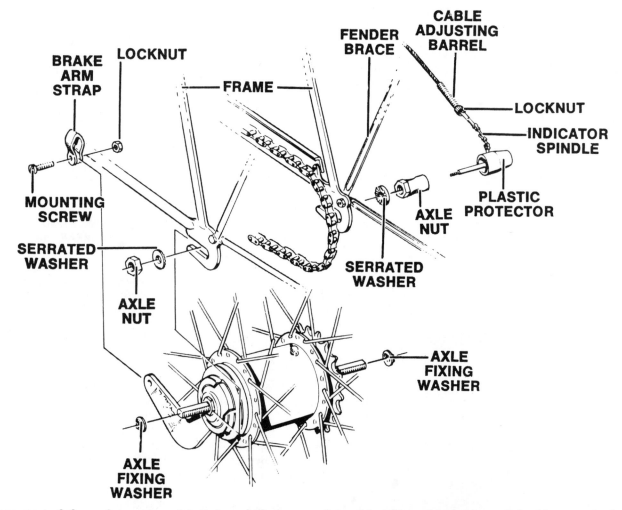

Arrangement of the washers, nuts, and indicator spindle for removing and installing a two-speed rear hub with coaster brake.

DISASSEMBLING

① Clamp the complete hub assembly in a vise, with the jaws gripping the axle on the sprocket side, as shown. **CAUTION: Use soft vise jaws to protect the axle threads.** Hold the brake arm and remove the locknut by turning it in a counterclockwise direction.

② Lift off the brake arm, and then the dust cap.

③ Remove the brake-arm side expander, and then the ball bearing retainer assembly. Hold the retainer assembly with your fingers, push on the square head of the expander with your thumbs, and the retainer assembly will slide off the expander.

④ Grasp the hub shell and lift it straight up and off the axle.

BRAKE SHOES

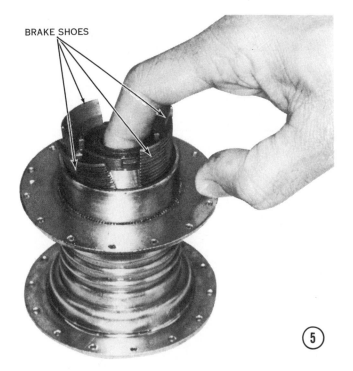

⑤ Reach into the hub shell with your forefinger, lift the expander and clutch assembly slightly, and remove the four brake shoes as they rise.

⑥ Remove the complete expander and clutch assembly.

⑦ Remove the ball bearing retainer assembly from the drive screw.

⑧ Unsnap and remove the indexing spring from the drive screw, using a screwdriver, as shown.

⑨ Remove the low-speed and high-speed drive screw assemblies, and then the ball bearing retainer assembly.

⑩ Lift the high-speed drive screw and catch the loose ball bearings as the drive screw begins to rise.

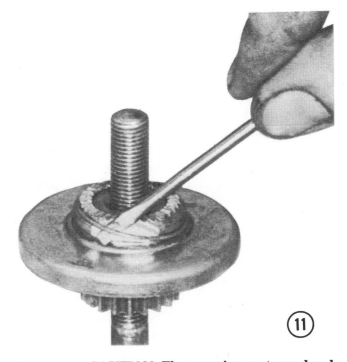

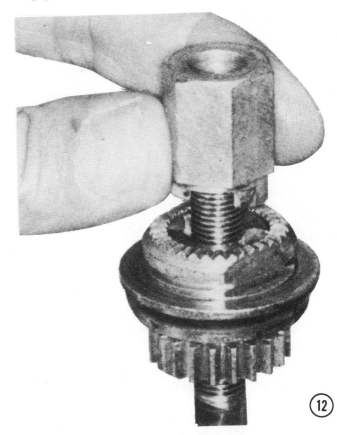

NOTE: *On the Bendix Blue Band hub, the sprocket is welded to the low-speed drive screw. On the Bendix Yellow Band hub, the drive screw is welded to the high-speed drive screw as indicated in the exploded drawing on page 167.* The planetary gears can be removed by driving the gear pin out with a drift punch and hammer from the side opposite the splined shaft of the low-speed

drive screw. **CAUTION: The gear pins are tapered and can be driven out in only one direction.** These gears are usually not removed because the low-speed drive screw is sold as a complete unit with the gears installed.

⑪   Turn the axle end for end in the vise with the jaws gripping the center unthreaded portion. Remove the dust-cap lock ring by prying it up with a screwdriver. Lift off the dust cap.

⑫   Place a cone locknut tool over the axle and engage the ears of the tool with the slots in the locknut.

HIGH SPEED
DRIVE SCREW

LOOSE BALL
BEARINGS

PLANET GEAR

TAPERED GEAR PIN
(DRIVE OUT FROM OTHER SIDE)

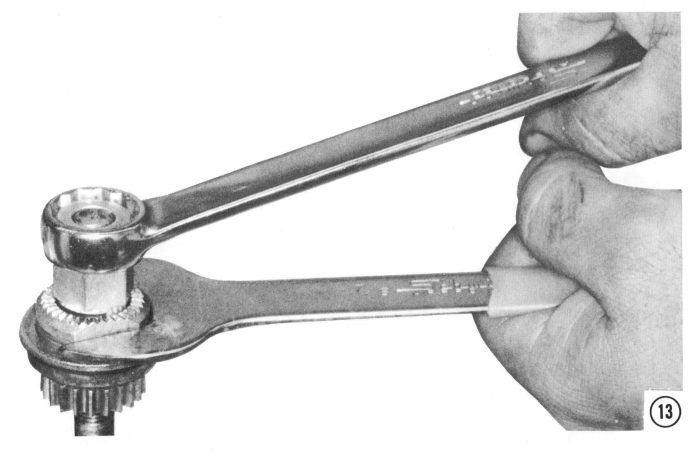

⑬ Hold the adjusting-cone sun gear assembly with one wrench and loosen the locknut with another wrench on the cone tool. Remove the locknut, and then the sun gear assembly.

⑭ Separate the high-speed drive clutch assembly from the low-speed drive clutch retarder assembly by pulling them apart. The high-speed clutch will release from the high-speed coupling.

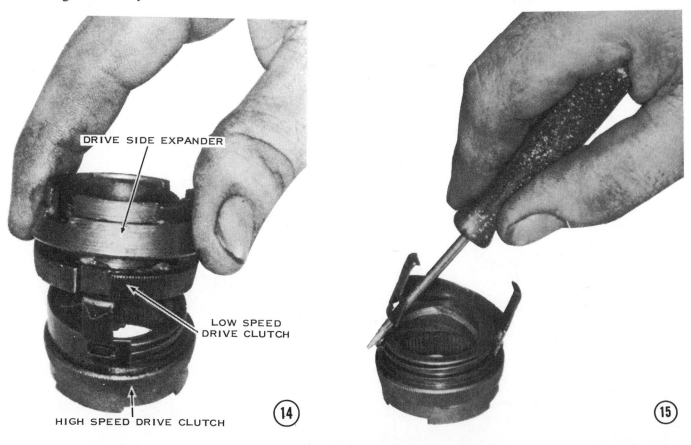

DRIVE SIDE EXPANDER

LOW SPEED DRIVE CLUTCH

HIGH SPEED DRIVE CLUTCH

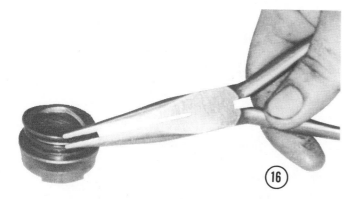

(16)

⑮ Snap the coupling off the high-speed clutch assembly with a screwdriver.

⑯ Remove the high-speed retarder spring by first working it up with a narrow-bladed screwdriver and then removing the spring with a pair of needle-nosed pliers.

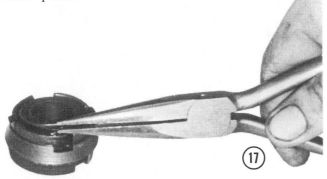

(17)

⑰ Insert a narrow-bladed screwdriver under the low-speed retarder spring, pry it up and grasp it with a pair of needle-nosed pliers, and then remove the spring from the low-speed drive clutch.

⑱ Separate the low-speed drive clutch and drive-side expander.

(18)

CLEANING AND INSPECTING

Clean all parts in solvent and blow dry with compressed air, or wipe them dry with a lintless cloth. Keep all cleaned parts on paper towels to avoid contamination. Cover them with a clean towel to keep grit from entering the internal parts and bearings. A tiny piece of grit can do a tremendous amount of damage if allowed to work on a part over an extended period of time or while the wheel is turning at high speed.

Carefully inspect the loose ball bearings for signs of excessive wear (dull spots, pits, or cracks) and replace the complete set if any of them are damaged. Replacing the complete set will ensure distribution of the bearing load equally on all the ball bearings.

Inspect the two ball bearing retainer assemblies. If any of the ball bearings come out of the retainer, are pitted (pencil-point dots), show signs of excessive wear (dull spots), or are cracked, the bearing and retainer assembly must be replaced. Check the retainers for cracks or visible signs of damage.

Inspect the bearing surface of the adjusting cone for scores (scratchlike marks), pits, and stripped threads.

Inspect the bearing cups of the hub for scores, pits, or excessive wear. Check the flanges of the hub shell for cracks, and to be sure they are not loose.

Check the dust caps to be sure they are not bent, crimped, or distorted, which could have happened during disassembly.

Check the axle and locknuts for signs of damage or stripped threads. Roll the axle slowly across a smooth flat surface and check both ends for being out-of-round or watch the center of the axle to see if it rises off the surface. Either of these indications means the axle is bent and must be replaced.

Inspect the bearing surface of the brake-arm side expander for scores, pits, or other damage. Check for stripped threads.

Check the indexing slots of the drive-side expander for wear or rounded edges.

Inspect the low-speed drive clutch for chipped and worn threads or worn dentils on the outer surfaces.

Inspect the brake shoes for a worn or glazed condition. Check the tapered surface for burrs.

Inspect the high-speed drive clutch for chipped or worn threads.

Inspect the high-speed coupling for damaged windows and hooks.

Inspect the planetary gears and adjusting-cone sun gear for worn or damaged gear teeth.

If you are working on a Bendix Yellow Band hub, inspect the weld between the sprocket and the high-speed drive-screw portion for cracks or signs of fatigue. If you are working on a Bendix Blue Band hub, inspect the weld between the sprocket and low-speed drive-screw portion.

Check the brake arm to be sure it is not bent or damaged.

ASSEMBLING

⑲ Thread the adjusting-cone sun gear assembly onto either end of the axle until the outside edge is

⅞ inch from the end of the axle, as shown.

⑳ Thread the locknut onto the axle, with the slots facing up. Place a cone locknut tool over the axle and engage the ears of the tool with the slots in the locknut.

㉑ Hold the adjusting-cone sun gear assembly with a wrench and tighten the locknut with another wrench on the tool. Remove the tool.

㉒ Set the drive-side expander over the low-speed drive clutch, with the slots in the expander facing up.

㉓ Slide a narrow-bladed screwdriver between the spiral of the low-speed retarder spring at the lower end. Place the lower end of the retarder spring into the machined recess of the low-speed drive clutch, with the upper end of the spring winding downward in a clockwise spiral and the lower end catching in the drive-side expander slot. Rotate the screwdriver in a counterclockwise direction (at the same time pushing down on the screwdriver blade) to roll the low-speed retarder spring completely into the machined recess.

DRIVE SIDE
EXPANDER

LOW SPEED DRIVE CLUTCH

㉒

LOW SPEED RETARDER SPRING

DRIVE SIDE EXPANDER

㉓

CAUTION: Always install new retarder springs when overhauling this type of hub to ensure satisfactory service. Install the high-speed retarder spring in the

recess of the high-speed drive clutch in a similar manner, rotating the screwdriver in a counterclockwise direction.

㉔ Coat the inside and outside surfaces of the high-speed drive clutch with multipurpose lubricant. Install the high-speed coupling on the high-speed drive clutch, with the lower window indexing with the lower

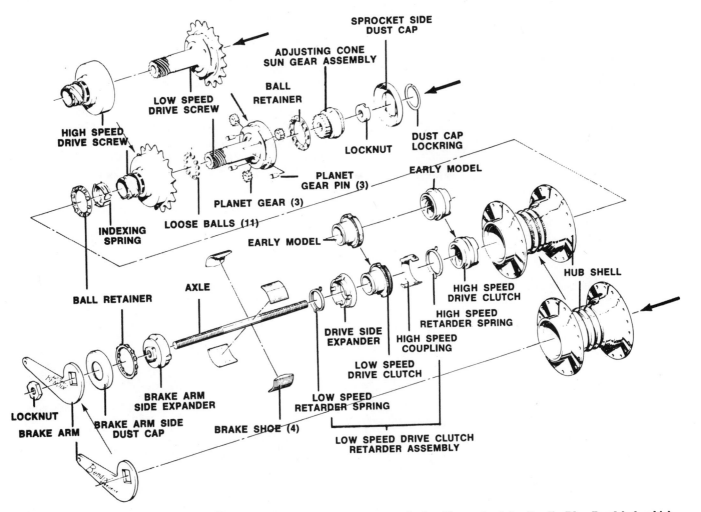

Exploded view of a Bendix Yellow Band two-speed rear hub with coaster brake. The parts of the Bendix Blue Band hub which are not interchangeable are separated from the main line of the drawing.

HIGH SPEED COUPLING

(24)

end of the high-speed retarder spring. Stretch the upper window of the coupling over the other end of the high-speed retarder spring hook. **CAUTION: The high-speed coupling can be installed properly in only one way to allow the ears of the high-speed retarder spring to index properly in the windows of the coupling.**

㉕ Join the high-speed and low-speed drive clutch assemblies by sliding one leg of the high-speed coupling

(27)

into either slot of the low-speed drive clutch assembly with the hook on the bottom of the leg catching the low-speed drive clutch. Push the high-speed drive clutch down with the other leg of the coupling, indexing with the high-speed clutch slot and the hook catching the high-speed drive clutch.

㉖ Apply a generous coating of multipurpose lubricant around the shaft of the low-speed drive screw, on top of the planetary pinion, as shown. **CAUTION: The low-speed drive screw of the Bendix Blue Band**

(25)

(26)

(28)

hub is not interchangeable with the drive screw of the Yellow Band hub. Place the loose ball bearings around the shaft and imbed them in the lubricant. *NOTE: After all the ball bearings are in place, there should be approximately one ball bearing clearance left.*

㉗ Coat the inside surface of the high-speed drive screw with multipurpose lubricant. **CAUTION: The high-speed drive screw of the Bendix Blue Band hub is not interchangeable with the drive screw of the Bendix Yellow Band hub.** Slide the high-speed drive screw onto the shaft of the low-speed drive screw and over the loose ball bearings. Rotate the high-speed drive screw in a clockwise direction to set it down in place and to index the teeth of the planetary gears with the internal teeth of the ring gear.

㉘ Cover the inside surface of the indexing spring with premium-quality cycle oil. Spread the ends of the indexing spring and install it under the shoulder of the high-speed drive screw. Coat the outside surface with cycle oil. **CAUTION: Always install a new indexing spring when overhauling this hub to ensure proper service after assembly.**

㉙ Apply a thin coating of premium-quality cycle oil to the inside surface of the hub shell. **CAUTION: The hub shell of the Bendix Blue Band hub is not interchangeable with the shell of the Bendix Yellow Band hub.** Insert the low-speed and high-speed drive clutch assemblies into the tapered end of the shell, with the high-speed drive clutch going in first, as shown.

㉚ Cover the inside surfaces of the four brake shoes with multipurpose lubricant. Apply a very thin coating of lubricant to the outside surfaces of the shoes. Insert the brake shoes into the hub between the ears of the drive-side expander. The brake shoes will then

㉚

be in pairs on either side of the two expander ears, as shown.

㉛ Pack one of the large sets of ball bearing assemblies with multipurpose lubricant. Work the lubricant throughout the bearings and retainer with your

㉙

㉛

㉜ Apply a coating of multipurpose lubricant to the bearing race, as shown.

㉝ Pack one of the large sets of ball bearing assemblies with a generous amount of multipurpose lubricant. Work the lubricant throughout the bearings and retainer. Place the lubricated bearing assembly into the hub shell, with the flat side of the retainer facing up.

㉞ Hold the brake-arm side expander in place with one hand and with the other hand insert the assembled drive screws into the opposite end of the hub. Rotate the sprocket in a clockwise direction until the assembly is fully seated in the hub shell.

㉟ Apply a generous amount of multipurpose lubricant to the bearing race of the drive assembly. Pack the other ball bearing retainer assembly with multipurpose lubricant, and then install it with the flat side of the retainer facing up.

㊱ Slide the axle through the hub while holding the brake-arm expander firmly in place. The axle will go partway, and then it must be rotated in a clockwise direction. As the axle is being threaded into place, the sun gear will mesh with the planetary gears and allow the dust cap to seat against the shoulder of the sprocket. Rotate the axle until it is finger-tight.

㊲ Install the brake-arm-side dust cap and then the brake arm, with the flats of the brake arm indexing with the flats on the brake-arm side expander and with the manufacturer's identification facing up. **CAUTION: The brake arm of the Bendix Blue Band hub is not interchangeable with the brake arm of the Bendix Yellow Band hub.** Thread the locknut onto the axle and tighten it by holding the brake arm with one hand and

fingers. Place the lubricated bearing assembly onto the brake-arm side expander, with the flat side facing up and then press it into place using the brake-arm-side dust cap. Remove the dust cap. Insert the brake-arm side expander into the hub shell. Hold the expander in place, and then turn the hub shell end for end on the bench.

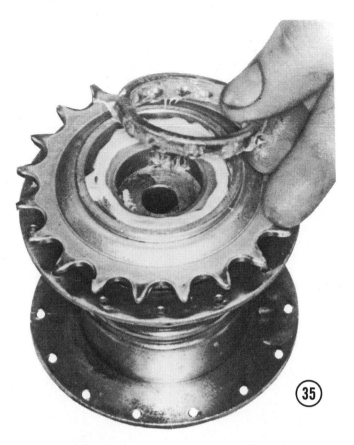

tightening the locknut with a wrench. Place the completed assembly in a vise, with the jaws gripping the axle on the brake-arm end. Place a cone locknut wrench over the axle, with the ears of the wrench indexing with the notches in the locknut. Loosen the locknut slightly, and then back off the adjusting cone approximately ⅓ turn, or until there is just a discernible amount of side play when you move the wheel rim up and down. Hold the adjusting cone with a wrench and tighten the

locknut with a wrench on the locknut tool.

㊳ Remove the assembled hub and wheel from the vise. Hold each end of the axle with your fingers. Slowly twist the axle with the thumb and forefinger of each hand—the wheel should not turn. If it does turn, the cones are too tight and must be loosened slightly. Back off the locknut using the locknut tool, loosen the adjusting cone approximately ⅛ turn, and then retighten the locknut. The cones are properly adjusted when the wheel rotates freely, comes to rest gradually with the valve stem at the lowest point of the wheel, and there is only the slightest trace of side play. **CAUTION: If the cones are adjusted too tight, it will cause binding and scoring of the hub. If the cones are adjusted too loose, it will cause fatigue, which can result in a damaged hub or broken axle.**

INSTALLING

Engage the chain onto the sprocket, and then slide the axle into the dropouts as indicated in the accompanying illustration. Slide any accessory or fender supports onto the axle in the same order as you noted when removing the wheel. If a serrated washer is used, place the washer on the axle with the serrations toward the hub—against the frame. Thread the outside axle nuts onto the axle finger-tight. Take up the slack in the chain by pulling the axle back until the chain is snug. Barely tighten the axle nut on the sprocket side, and then align the wheel so it rotates midway between the rear frame members by pulling the axle back on the side opposite the sprocket. Adjust the chain tension until it can be depressed about ⅜ inch at a point midway between the hanger and rear sprocket. Tighten both axle nuts firmly. Slip the brake lever into the strap on the frame, and then secure it with the mounting screw and nut. If the brake strap has several mounting holes, bend the strap around the frame so the brake lever will be as close to the frame as possible.

Turn the crank in the forward direction and observe that the chain and wheel turn freely without binding or rubbing on the frame. Reverse the crank direction and the wheel should stop almost immediately.

OVERHAULING A SHIMANO 3.3.3 FA THREE-SPEED REAR HUB

The following step-by-step illustrated instructions cover disassembling, assembling, and adjusting a Shimano 3.3.3 FA three-speed rear hub. The hub is identified by the name stamped on the hub shell. A detailed exploded drawing of this hub, showing all internal parts, follows the Cleaning and Inspecting portion of this section.

For photographic clarity, the illustrations were made of a hub without the tire, rim, and spokes.

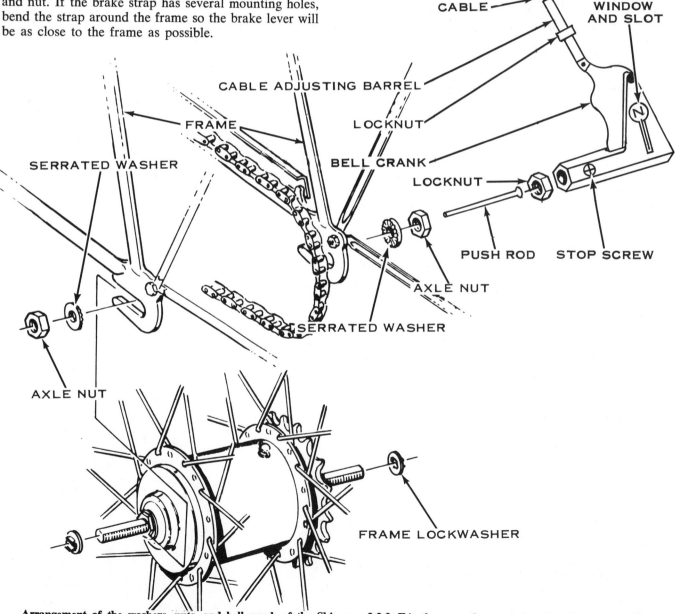

Arrangement of the washers, nuts, and bell crank of the Shimano 3.3.3 FA three-speed rear hub. This illustration will be helpful in removing and installing the wheel.

Shimano 3.3.3 FA three-speed rear hub.

REMOVING THE WHEEL

If the bicycle you are working on does not have levers mounted on the handlebars, you can turn the bicycle upside down, resting it on the seat and handlebars. A better method is to support the bicycle in an upright position from a bracket, a set of hooks, or a rope attached to the garage ceiling, or to secure it in an automobile carrier rack attached to the car. Holding the bicycle rigid will make the task of removing, installing, and adjusting parts much easier.

Sight over the tire and see if it will clear the brake shoes. If there is not sufficient clearance, it will be necessary to release the brake shoes farther than normal in order to remove the wheel. This is accomplished by first squeezing the rear-brake handle slightly, pushing in on the quick-release button, and then releasing the brake handle. This action releases the caliper arms farther than normal, allowing the rear wheel to clear the brake shoes. The only function of this button is to facilitate easy removal of the wheel for a tire change, an overhaul, or an adjustment.

If you are working on a bicycle without the quick-release button on the brake handle, there may be a quick-release lever just above the brake on the cable hanger. Turning this lever will release the brake shoes farther than normal. If neither of these quick-release mechanisms is installed, you can obtain the necessary clearance by removing one of the brake shoes. This is accomplished by removing the mounting nut on the outside of the brake arm, and then removing the brake shoe, including the holder. Still another method, provided you have an air supply or pump handy, is to deflate the tire, which will usually clear the brake shoes.

Remove the cable adjusting barrel from the bell crank by turning it counterclockwise, and then withdrawing the shift rod from the axle. Remove the thin bell-crank locknut from the axle. Take note of the washer and support arrangement installed on the axle. Some bicycles have serrated washers installed against the frame to prevent the wheel from moving forward under the tension of the chain. Washers are usually installed between fender and accessory supports to keep them from twisting when the axle nuts are tightened. However, on bicycles equipped with this type of hub, the usual method is to mount accessory supports on frame lugs and not on the axle.

Slide any fender or accessory supports, including washers, from the axle. Move the wheel forward in the

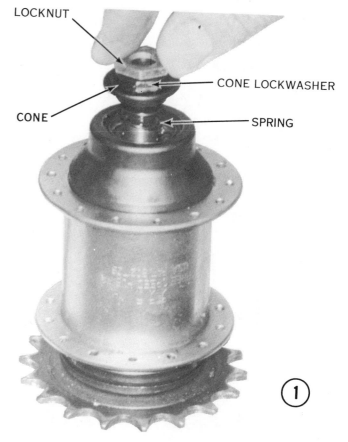

①

dropouts, and then remove the chain from the sprocket and hook it over the frame. Remove the frame lockwasher from the sprocket side of the axle. Guide the wheel free of the frame.

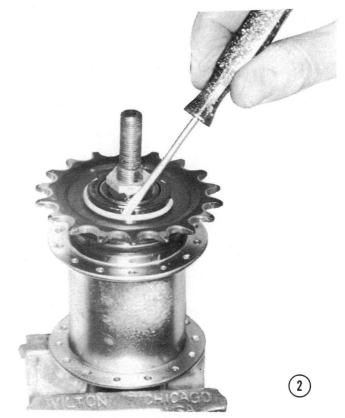

②

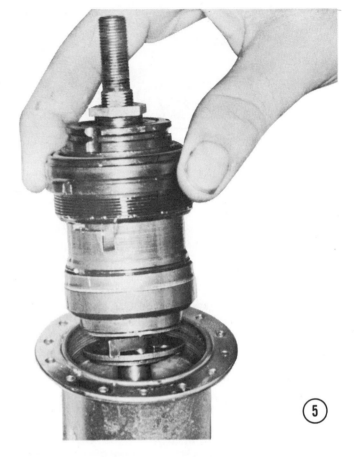

DISASSEMBLING

①   Clamp the complete hub assembly in a vise, with the jaws gripping the axle on the sprocket side, as shown. **CAUTION: Use soft vise jaws to protect the axle threads.** Remove the locknut, cone lockwasher, cone, and then the spring.

②   Carefully turn the hub assembly end for end in the vise with the jaws gripping the hub shell, not the axle. Snap the sprocket lock ring out of its recess with a narrow-bladed screwdriver, and then lift off the sprocket.

③   Remove the dust cap.

④   Loosen the driver in a counterclockwise di-

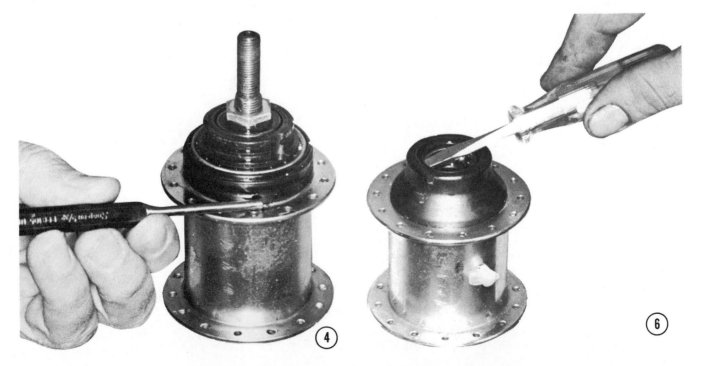

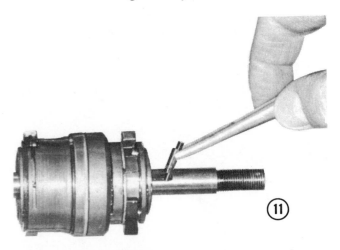

rection by using a drift punch and hammer, as shown, or a hook-spanner type wrench.

⑤ Lift the complete internal assembly out of the hub.

⑥ Remove the hub shell from the vise, turn it end for end, and pop the dust cap out with a screwdriver. Work around the edge of the cap and be careful not to crimp or distort it.

⑦ Remove the ball bearing retainer assembly.

⑧ Clamp the internal assembly in the vise in a horizontal position with the jaws gripping the axle at the unthreaded portion opposite the sprocket end. Hold the adjusting cone with a cone wrench, loosen it, and then remove the nut and the cone.

⑨ Remove the driver unit and ball bearing retainer assembly from the axle.

⑩ Remove the right-hand ball cup.

⑪ Remove the axle from the vise, and then pull out the short and long axle keys.

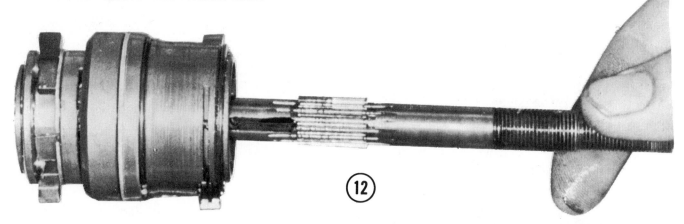

⑫

⑫ Withdraw the axle from the gear-ring ratchet and planetary-cage ratchet assemblies.

⑬ Pry the cartridge retaining ring out of the slot in the gear-ring ratchet assembly using a narrow-bladed screwdriver, and then remove it.

⑭ Remove the retaining pin sleeve. Lightly tap and rotate the entire assembly on the bench at an angle to remove the four cartridge retaining pins.

⑬

⑭

⑮ Separate the gear ratchet assembly from the planetary cage.

⑯ Remove the low-gear pawl pin retaining ring by prying it out and up with a narrow-bladed screwdriver, as shown, or use a pair of snap-ring pliers. Turn the planetary cage end for end, hold it with your thumb and fingers, and then jar the back of your hand on the bench; the two pawl pins will come out, releasing the low-gear pawls and pawl springs.

⑰ Remove the two planetary gear pin retaining plates. Turn the planetary cage end for end in your hand, hold it with your thumb and fingers, and then jar the back of your hand on the bench; the four planetary gear pins will come out, releasing the planetary gears.

⑱ Remove the high-gear pawl-pin retaining ring by prying it out and up with a screwdriver, as shown, or use a pair of snap-ring pliers. When the ring is re-

⑮

moved, the high-gear pawls can be lifted out of their slots in the gear ring ratchet. Turn the assembly end for end, hold it with your thumb and fingers, and then jar the back of your hand on the bench; the two pawl spring pins will come out, releasing the springs.

⑲ Remove the pawl-pin retaining ring from the driver assembly by prying it up with a screwdriver, as shown. Turn the assembly end for end, hold it with your thumb and fingers, and then jar the back of your hand on the bench; the two long pawl pins will come out, releasing the four pawls and pawl springs.

CLEANING AND INSPECTING

Clean all parts in solvent and blow dry with compressed air, or wipe them dry with a lintless cloth. Keep all cleaned parts on paper towels to avoid contamination. Cover them with a clean towel to keep grit from entering the internal parts and bearings. A tiny piece of grit can do a tremendous amount of damage if allowed to work on a part over an extended period of time or while the wheel is turning at high speed.

Inspect the three ball bearing retainer assemblies. If any of the ball bearings come out of the retainer, are pitted (pencil-point dots), show signs of excessive wear (dull spots), or are cracked, the bearing and retainer assembly must be replaced. Check the retainers for cracks or visible signs of damage.

Inspect the bearing surface of both cones for scores (scratchlike marks), pits, and for stripped threads.

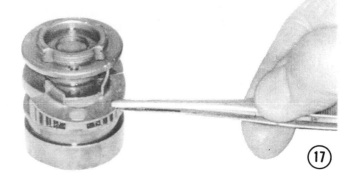

Inspect the axle for stripped threads, and for worn or chipped teeth on the sun gear. Check the two axle slots for wear (rounded edges).

Check the dust caps to be sure they are not bent, crimped, or distorted, which could have happened during disassembly.

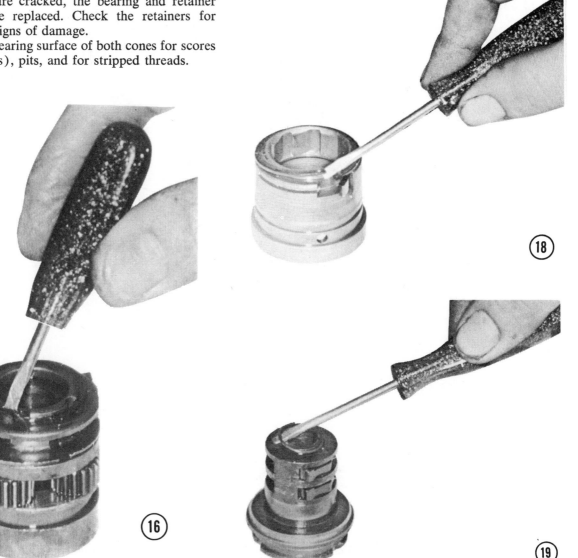

Inspect the hub shell for damage including chipped or worn ratchet teeth. Inspect the bearing cup for scores, pits, or excessive wear. Check the flanges of the hub shell for cracks and to be sure they are not loose.

Inspect all the pawls for worn or damaged driving edges.

NOTE: If the hub has been completely disassembled, all the pawl springs should be replaced to ensure proper service. The thrust spring should also be replaced.

Inspect the gear-ring ratchet, planetary-cage ratchet, and planetary gears for chipped or worn teeth.

Inspect the right-hand ball cup for chipped or worn ratchet teeth. Check the bearing surface for scores or pits. Check for stripped threads.

Inspect the bearing surface of the driver for scores or pits.

Check both axle keys to be sure they are not bent or damaged.

Inspect the axle nuts for stripped or damaged threads.

ASSEMBLING

㉒ Lay the driver on the bench, resting on its side. Place a new pawl spring on the machined recess side of one of the pawls, with the hooked end of the

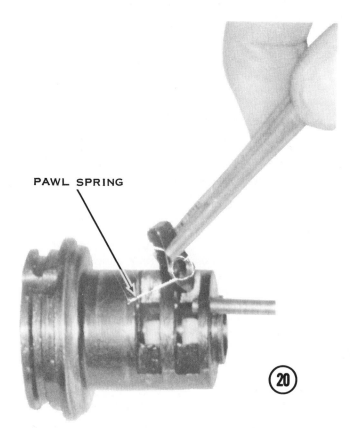

PAWL SPRING

㉒

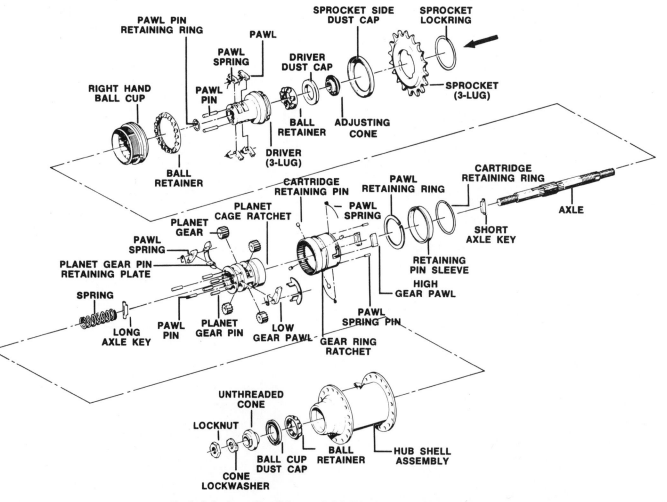

Exploded view of a Shimano 3.3.3 FA three-speed rear hub.

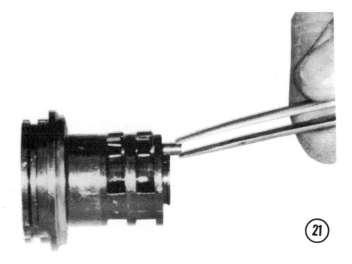

(21)

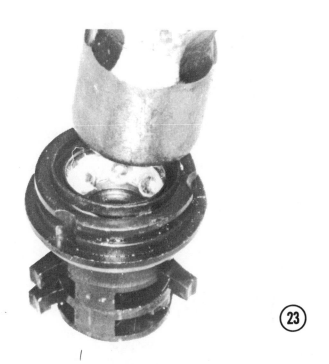

(23)

spring catching over the edge of the pawl and the straight end of the spring perpendicular to the pawl. Align the spring coil over the hole in the pawl. **CAUTION: Be sure both ends of the spring are on the same side of the pawl and that the straight end of the spring faces in a counterclockwise direction.** Insert one of the pawl pins partway into position until it is just barely through the first flange of the driver. Hold the spring and pawl with a pair of tweezers and insert them into one of the upper slots of the driver. When the hole in the pawl aligns with the pin, push the pin through just far enough to retain the pawl and the spring. When properly installed, the pawl can be depressed until it is almost flush with the outside surface of the driver.

㉑ Place another spring on the machined recess of the second pawl, and then insert it into the lower slot of the driver exactly as you did with the first pawl. When the hole in the pawl aligns with the pin, push the pin all the way in to retain the pawl and spring. Install the second set of pawls and springs in the driver in the same manner as for the first set. *NOTE: Late-model Shimano*

rear hubs use four right-hand wound springs. Early model hubs used two right-hand and two left-hand wound springs. Whether right-hand or left-hand springs are used, be sure the spring is on the recessed surface of the pawl, both ends of the spring are on the same side of the pawl, and the straight end of the spring faces in a counterclockwise direction.

㉒ Snap the pawl-pin retaining ring into position using a narrow-bladed screwdriver. Rotate the ring, if necessary, so the opening in the ring is not centered over one of the pins.

㉓ Pack the driver ball bearing retainer assembly with a generous amount of multipurpose lubricant. Work the lubricant throughout the bearings and retainer with your fingers. Insert the lubricated bearing assembly into the driver, with the flat surface of the retainer facing up. Place the dust cap in the driver, with the flat side facing down. Tap the dust cap lightly with a hammer until it is flush with the surface of the driver. Set the assembled driver aside.

㉔ Stand the planetary gear ratchet on the bench, with the planetary gear pin holes facing up. Place the

(22)

(24)

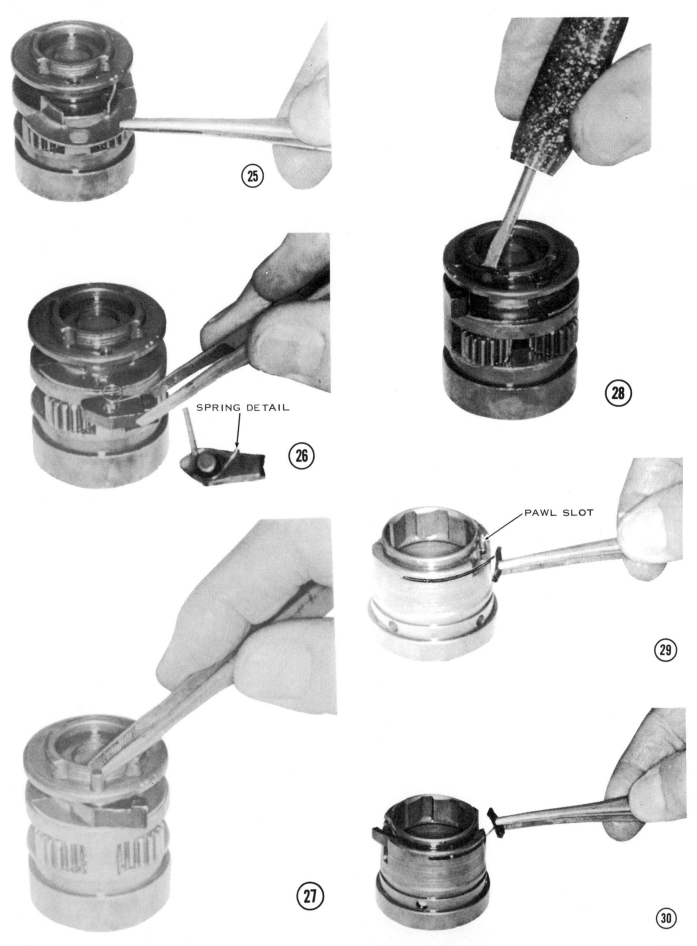

25

26   SPRING DETAIL

27

28

PAWL SLOT

29

30

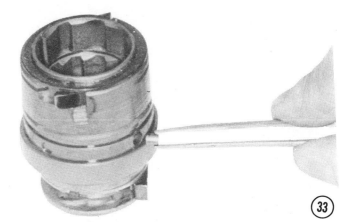

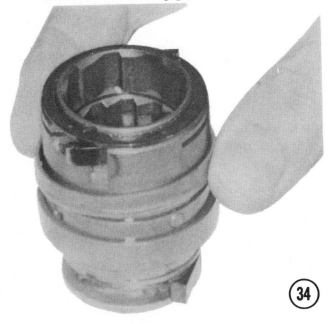

(31)

(33)

Install the other pawl in the same manner.

㉘ Snap the pawl-pin retaining ring into place using a thin-bladed screwdriver or pair of snap-ring pliers. Rotate the ring, if necessary, so the opening in the ring is not over one of the pawl pins.

㉙ Place one of the high-gear pawl springs into position in the recess of the gear-ring ratchet housing, with the coil of the spring facing out and aligned with the spring-pin hole. Insert the spring pin. Position one of the pawls against the spring with the spring in the pawl slot. Push in on the pawl against the force of the spring, and then slide the knobbed end of the pawl into the retaining slot in the housing.

㉚ Install the second pawl and spring in the same manner as you did for the first one.

㉛ Snap the pawl retaining ring into place using a thin-bladed screwdriver or pair of snap-ring pliers. Rotate the ring, if necessary, so the opening in the ring is not directly over one of the pins.

㉜ Lower the assembled gear-ring ratchet unit down over the assembled planetary-cage ratchet, as shown.

㉝ Insert the four cartridge retaining pins using a small amount of multipurpose lubricant on the ends of the pins to hold them in place.

㉞ Slide the retaining pin sleeve over the gear-

four planetary gears in position, and then insert the gear pins.

㉕ Insert the two planetary-gear-pin retainer plates into position, with the holes in the plate aligned with the holes in the housing.

㉖ Place one of the pawl springs on the machined recess side of a low-gear pawl, with the hook end of the spring over the inside edge of the pawl, and the straight edge perpendicular to the pawl, as shown.

㉗ Push the pawl into place against the force of the spring until the hole in the pawl aligns with the hole in the housing flange, and then insert the pawl pin.

(32)

(34)

(35)

(36)

ring ratchet, with the flange side down on the lip of the housing.

㉟ Depress the two high-gear pawls and slide the cartridge retaining ring over the gear-ring ratchet until it indexes with the recess in the retaining pin sleeve.

㊱ Clamp the axle in a vise with the short threaded end up. Slide the completed subassembly onto the axle, with the low-gear pawls up, as shown.

㊲ Lift the assembly slightly and insert the short axle key into the axle slot with the flat side up. While you are holding the assembly, the key should fall to the bottom of the slot. Lower the assembly and you should be able to see the key flats fully indexed against the inner flanges of the planetary-cage ratchet assembly. If the key has not dropped into position properly, raise the assembly just a little bit more until the key does drop into place.

㊳ Rotate the assembly on the axle and lubricate the internal mechanism with premium-quality cycle oil.

㊴ Shift the axle in the vise to a horizontal position with the jaws gripping the unthreaded portion.

CAUTION: Do not allow the assembly to move on the axle during this operation to prevent the installed key from slipping out of position. Lubricate the high-speed pawls with premium-quality cycle oil.

㊵ Depress the high-speed pawls and slide the right-hand ball cup into position on the gear-ring ratchet assembly.

㊶ Pack the large ball bearing retainer assembly with a generous amount of multipurpose lubricant. Work the lubricant throughout the bearings and retainer with your fingers.

㊷ Push the lubricated ball bearing assembly into the bearing race of the ball cup, with the flat side of the retainer facing out.

SHORT THREADED END

LONG AXLE KEY

SHORT AXLE KEY

LARGE THREADED SECTION

STANDARD THREADS

Details of the axle used in the Shimano 3.3.3 FA hub. Note the long and short axle key placement as well as the positions of the notches.

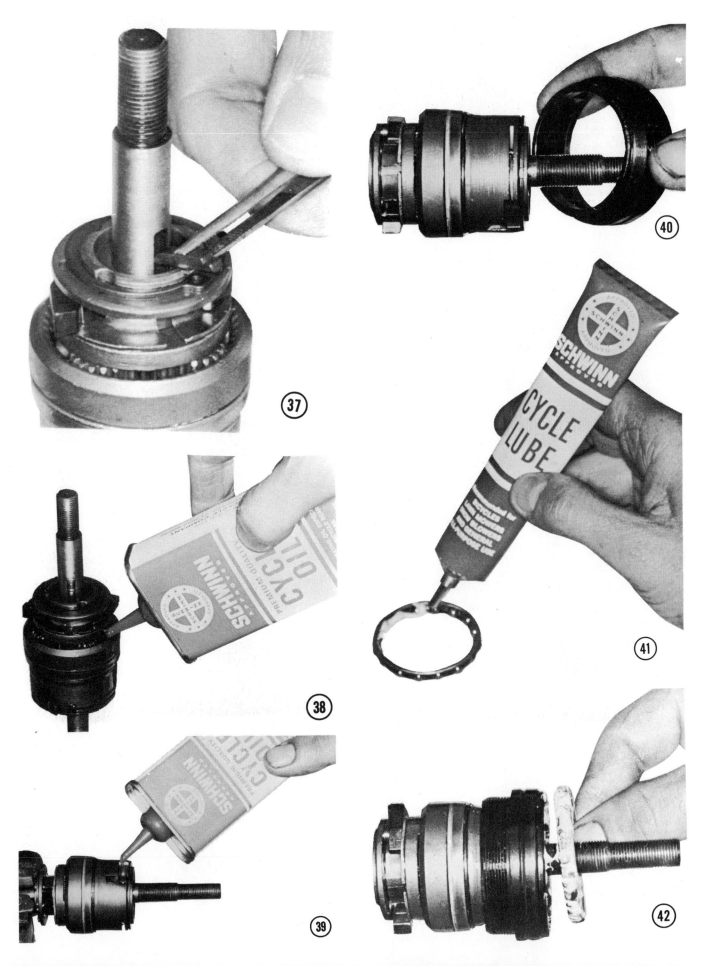

37

38

39

40

41

42

⁴³ Slide the driver assembly onto the axle.

⁴⁴ Depress the driver pawls. Push and rotate the driver into the gear-ring assembly, allowing the pawls to index with the internal ratchets.

⁴⁵ Slide the threaded cone onto the axle until it engages the large threaded portion, and then rotate it clockwise until it is finger-tight.

⁴⁶ Thread the locknut onto the axle against the cone finger-tight.

⁴⁷ Shift the assembly in the vise, with the keyway in the axle up. **CAUTION: Use soft vise jaws to protect the threads.** Install the long axle key in the keyway with the flat side down. The cutouts in the ends of the key should lie against the shoulder of the planetary-cage ratchet assembly.

⁴⁸ Pack the remaining ball bearing retainer assembly with a generous amount of multipurpose lubricant. Work the lubricant throughout the bearings and retainer. Install the lubricated bearing assembly in the bearing race of the ball cup, with the flat side of the retainer facing up.

⁴⁹ Place the dust cap in the ball cup with the flat side down. Tap the cap lightly with a hammer until the cap is flush with the top surface of the ball cup.

⁵⁰ Install a new thrust spring on the axle—either end down. Remove the assembly from the vise. Place the hub (wheel) in a horizontal position, with the tire against your chest and the left-hand ball cup of the hub facing up, as shown. *NOTE: For photographic clarity, the wheel and spokes are not shown.* Insert the assembled unit into the threaded end of the shell. Turn the internal-drive assembly counterclockwise to allow the low-gear pawls to index with the ratchet inside of the hub shell. When the pawls index, you will feel the assembly move farther into the hub, and the threads of the right-hand ball cup will engage the internal threads of the hub shell. When this occurs, turn the right-hand ball cup clockwise until it is finger-tight.

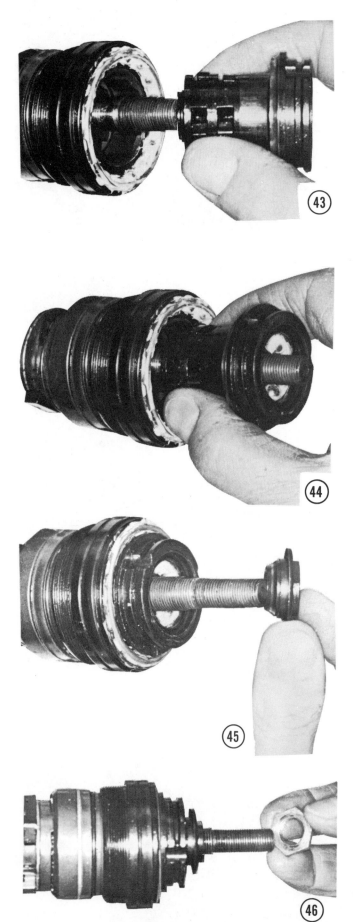

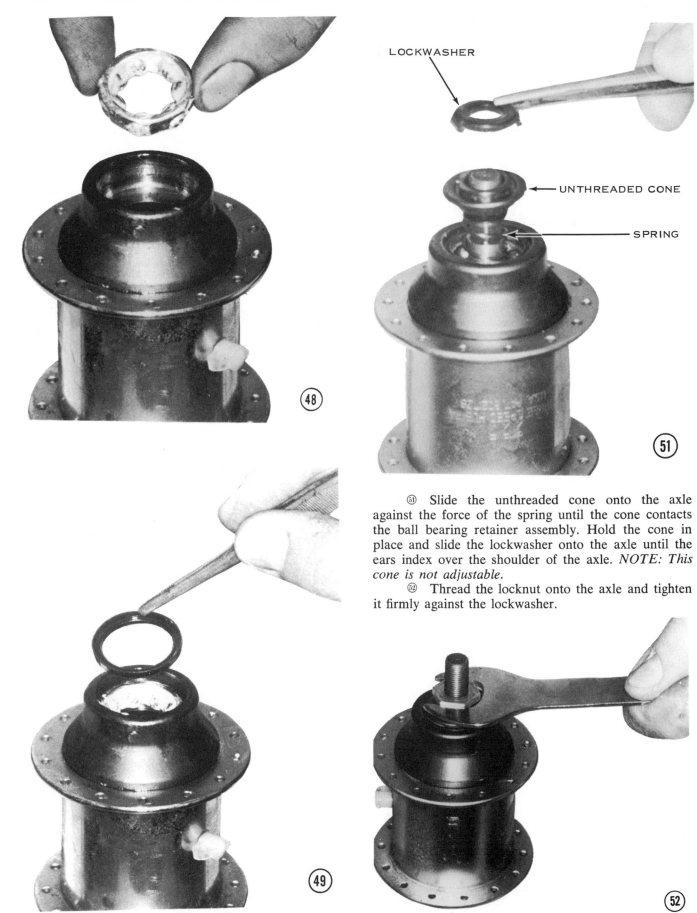

LOCKWASHER

UNTHREADED CONE

SPRING

⑤ Slide the unthreaded cone onto the axle against the force of the spring until the cone contacts the ball bearing retainer assembly. Hold the cone in place and slide the lockwasher onto the axle until the ears index over the shoulder of the axle. *NOTE: This cone is not adjustable.*

⑤ Thread the locknut onto the axle and tighten it firmly against the lockwasher.

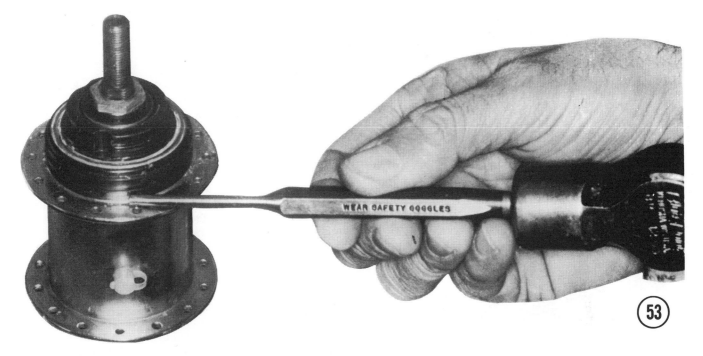

(53)

Turn the complete assembly end for end in the vise. **CAUTION: Use soft vise jaws to protect the axle threads.** Tighten the right-hand ball cup by rotating it clockwise using a drift punch indexed in one of the cup notches, or with a hook-spanner type wrench.

Hold the locknut with a wrench and tighten the adjusting cone with a thin wrench or cone pliers until the cone is snug, and then back it off approximately ¼ turn, or until there is just a discernible amount of side play when you move the wheel rim up and down. Tighten the locknut securely. Remove the assembled hub and wheel from the vise. Hold each end of the axle with your fingers. Slowly twist the axle with the thumb and forefinger of each hand—the wheel should not turn. If it does turn, the cones are too tight and must be loosened slightly. Back off the locknut on the sprocket end of the axle. Loosen the cone approximately ⅛ turn, and then retighten the locknut. The cones are properly

adjusted when the wheel rotates freely, comes to rest gradually with the valve stem at the lowest point of the wheel, and there is only the slightest trace of side play. **CAUTION: If the cone is adjusted too tight, it will cause binding and scoring of the hub. If the cone is adjusted too loose, it will cause fatigue, which can result in a damaged hub or broken axle.**

Clamp the assembly back in the vise with the right-hand ball cup up. Slide the frame lockwasher onto the axle with the ear facing up and the flats indexing with the flats on the axle.

(54)

(55)

㊽ Install the dust cap on the right-hand ball cup, with the flat side of the cap facing up.

㊼ Install the sprocket, with the lugs on the inner surface of the sprocket indexing with the recesses in the right-hand ball cup.

㊾ Spread the snap ring over the flange of the ball cup, locking the sprocket in place.

INSTALLING THE WHEEL

Engage the chain onto the sprocket. Slide the axle into the dropouts with the key of the frame lockwasher indexing with the slot on the inside of the frame on the sprocket side, as indicated in the accompanying illustration. If serrated washers are used, place the washers on the axle with the serrations toward the hub—against the frame. Slide any carriage or fender supports, including washers, onto the axle in the order you noted when removing the wheel. **CAUTION: On bicycles equipped with this type of hub, the best method is to mount accessory supports on frame lugs and not on the axle.**

Thread the outside axle nuts onto the axle finger-tight. Take up the slack in the chain by pulling the axle back until the chain is snug. Tighten the axle nut on the sprocket side until it is snug, and then align the wheel so it rotates midway between the rear frame members by pulling the axle back on the side opposite the sprocket. Adjust the chain tension until it can be depressed approximately ⅜ inch at a point midway between the hanger and rear sprocket.

Tighten both axle nuts firmly. Check the cone adjustment. The wheel should spin freely with just a discernible amount of side play at the wheel rim. If an adjustment is required because of binding or excessive side play, loosen the axle nut and locknut on the sprocket side, adjust the cone with a thin cone wrench or cone pliers, and then retighten the locknut and axle nut.

Thread the thin bell-crank locknut onto the axle. Slide the shift rod into the axle. Turn the bell crank onto the axle in a clockwise direction until the stop screw contacts the axle. Back off the bell crank until

the threaded arm of the bell-crank assembly is pointing in the direction of the shifting cable. Place the gear-shift control in the high-gear position. Thread the cable adjusting barrel onto the bell-crank arm until the cable is taut. Move the shift lever on the handlebar to the neutral (N) position. Turn the adjusting barrel on the cable housing until the N appears in the window, and the index line appears in the slot. Tighten the locknut to hold the cable adjusting barrel in this position.

If you are working on a bicycle with a quick-release button on the brake handle or a quick-release lever above the brake on the cable hanger, return the lever to the operating position. If you are working on a bicycle without these quick-release mechanisms and you re-moved one of the brake pads and holder to gain tire clearance for removal, install the holder with the closed

end of the holder facing forward. **CAUTION: The closed end of the holder must face forward to prevent the pad from being forced out by the wheel rim when the brakes are applied.** Secure the brake holder with the locknut. Naturally, if you deflated the tire to gain clearance, pump it up to the required pressure.

OVERHAULING A STURMEY-ARCHER AW, STYRE, SCHWINN-APPROVED STYRE, BRAMPTON, AND HERCULES THREE-SPEED REAR HUB

The following step-by-step illustrated instructions cover disassembling, assembling, and adjusting a Sturmey-Archer AW, Styre, Schwinn-Approved Styre, Brampton, and Hercules three-speed rear hub. These hubs are identified by the name stamped on the hub

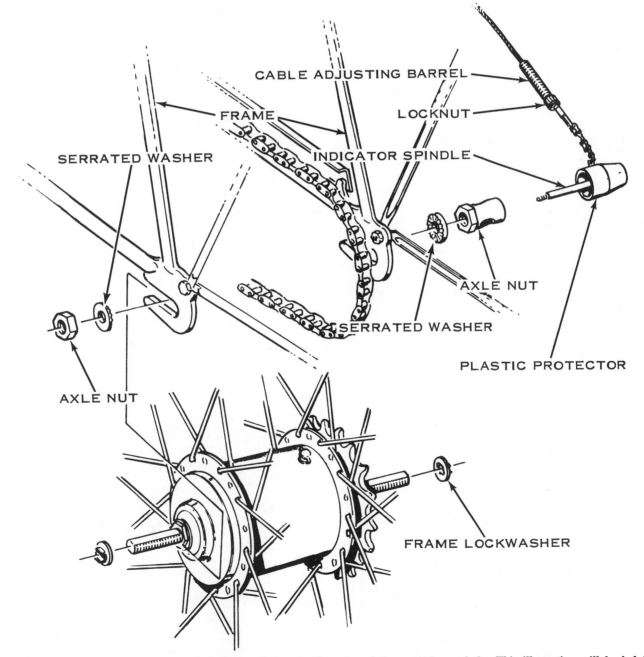

Arrangement of washers, nuts, and indicator spindle of this series of three-speed rear hubs. This illustration will be helpful in removing and installing the wheel.

Sturmey-Archer AW three-speed rear hub.

shell and on the brake arm. All the parts of these five hubs are interchangeable. A detailed exploded drawing of these hubs, showing internal parts, follows the Cleaning and Inspecting portion of this section.

For photographic clarity, the illustrations were made of a Sturmey-Archer AW hub without the tire, rim, and spokes.

REMOVING THE WHEEL

If the bicycle you are working on does not have levers mounted on the handlebars, you can turn the bicycle upside down, resting it on the seat and handlebars. A better method is to support the bicycle in an upright position from a bracket, a set of hooks, or a rope attached to the garage ceiling, or to secure it in an automobile rear carrier rack attached to the car. Holding the bicycle rigid will make the task of removing, installing, and adjusting parts much easier.

Sight over the tire and see if it will clear the brake shoes. If there is not sufficient clearance, it will be necessary to release the brake shoes farther than normal in order to remove the wheel. This is accomplished by first squeezing the rear-brake handle slightly, pushing in on the quick-release button, and then releasing the brake handle. This releases the caliper arms farther than normal, allowing the rear wheel to clear the brake shoes.

If you are working on a bicycle without the quick-

release button on the brake handle, there may be a quick-release lever just above the brake on the cable hanger. Turning this lever will release the brake shoes farther than normal. If neither of these quick-release mechanisms is installed, you can obtain the necessary clearance by removing one of the brake shoes. This is accomplished by removing the mounting nut on the outside of the brake arm and then removing the brake shoe, including the holder. Still another method, provided you have an air supply or pump handy, is to deflate the tire, which will then clear the shoes without disturbing the brakes.

To remove the wheel, loosen the three-speed cable adjusting barrel locknut, and then remove the barrel from the indicator spindle. If a plastic protector is used on the right-hand axle nut, remove the protector. Loosen both axle nuts by turning them in a counterclockwise direction. Remove the indicator spindle from the hub. Take off both axle nuts.

Note the washer and support arrangement installed on the axle. Some bicycles have serrated washers positioned against the frame to prevent the wheel from moving forward under the tension of the chain. Washers are usually installed between the fender and accessory supports to keep them from twisting when the axle nuts are tightened.

Slide any fender or accessory supports, including washers, from the axle. Move the wheel forward in the dropouts, and then remove the chain from the sprocket; hook it over the frame. Remove the frame lockwasher from both ends of the axle. Guide the wheel free of the frame.

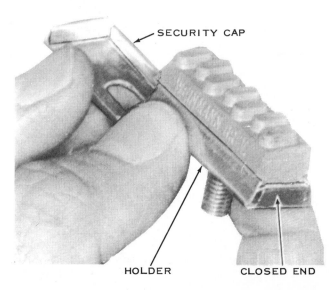

SECURITY CAP

HOLDER   CLOSED END

①

(2)

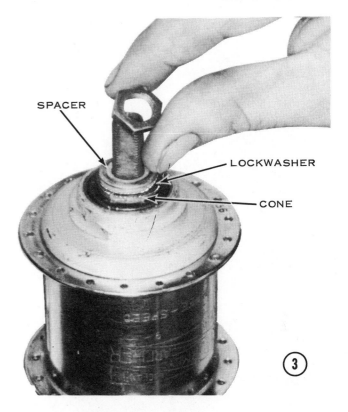

SPACER

LOCKWASHER

CONE

(3)

DISASSEMBLING

① Clamp the complete hub assembly in a vise, with the sprocket end up and the jaws of the vise gripping the flats on the axle. **CAUTION: Use soft vise jaws to protect the axle threads.** Remove the sprocket lock ring by prying it out of its recess in the driver with a narrow-bladed screwdriver, and then lift off the sprocket.

② Remove the two spacers.

③ Turn the assembly end for end in the vise, with the jaws gripping the flats of the axle. Remove the locknut by turning it in a counterclockwise direction. Remove the spacer washer, cone lockwasher, and cone from the axle.

④ Turn the assembly end for end in the vise, with the jaws gripping the flats of the hub crown.

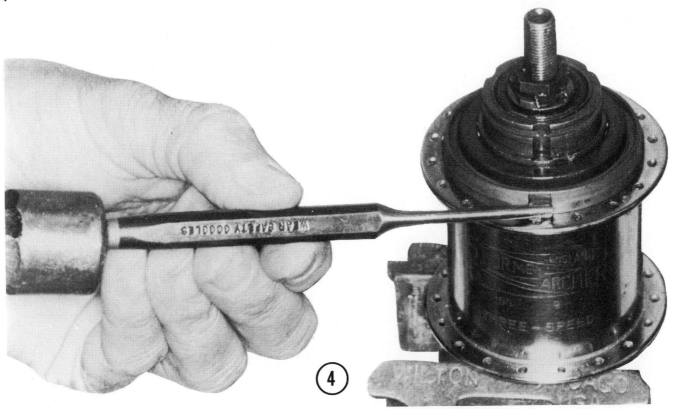

(4)

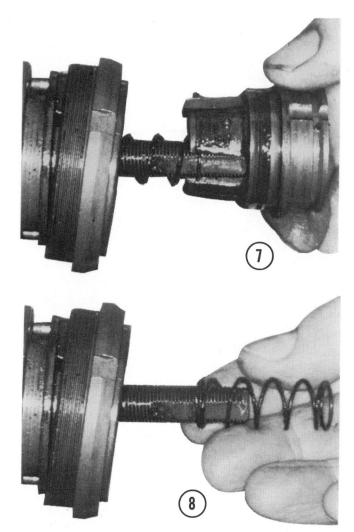

Loosen the right-hand ball cup by turning it in a counterclockwise direction with a drift punch and hammer, as shown. Continue to rotate the ball cup until it is free of the threads in the hub shell.

⑤ Lift the complete assembly straight up and out of the hub shell. **CAUTION: Be careful to keep the pawl pins, pawls, and springs from falling out and becoming lost.**

⑥ Clamp the assembly in the vise in a horizontal position, with the soft jaws gripping the axle flats at the planetary cage end. Remove the locknut, lockwasher, and cone from the axle.

⑦ Slide the driver off the axle.

THRUST RING

THRUST WASHER

⑩

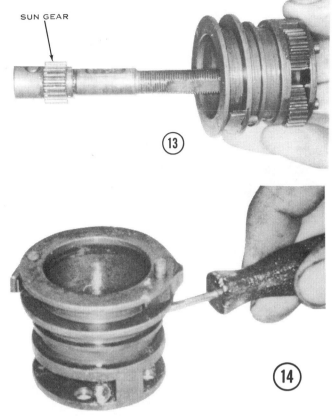

SUN GEAR

⑬

⑭

⑧ Remove the clutch spring. Take off the spring cap, if so equipped.

⑨ Pull the right-hand ball cup free of the gear ring.

⑩ Disengage and remove the gear ring from the planetary gears by pulling the ring straight off.

⑪ Remove the thrust washer and thrust ring, and then pull out the axle key.

⑫ Slide the clutch off the axle and then the clutch sleeve.

⑬ Disengage the internal teeth of the planetary cage from the sun gear by pulling the cage straight off, and then withdraw it from the axle.

⑭ Hold the planetary cage in your hand, with the gears facing down, and then jar the back of your hand on the bench; the four planetary-gear pins will come out, releasing the planetary gears. Place the cage on the bench and use a scrwdriver to push out the two pawl pins, which will release the pawls and the pawl springs. Hold the ring gear in your hand, with the pawls facing down, and then jar the back of your hand on the bench; the high-gear pawl pins will slide out, releasing the pawls and the pawl pins.

⑮ Pry the dust cap from the right-hand ball cup

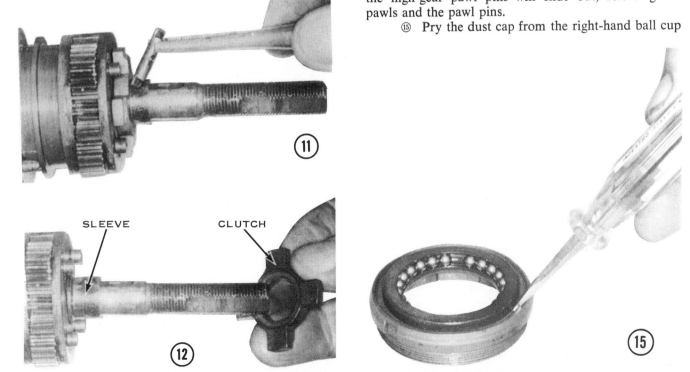

⑪

SLEEVE   CLUTCH

⑫

⑮

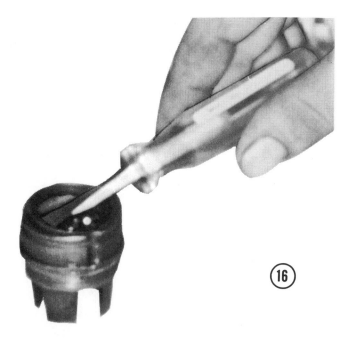

(16)

with a screwdriver. Work around the cap edge and be careful not to crimp or damage it. Remove the loose ball bearings. **CAUTION: Count them for assembly purposes.**

⑯ Remove the dust cap from the driver with a screwdriver, and then remove the ball bearing retainer assembly.

⑰ Pop the dust cap out of the left-hand ball cup of the hub shell with a screwdriver, and then remove the ball bearing retainer assembly.

(17)

CLEANING AND INSPECTING

Clean all parts in solvent and blow dry with compressed air, or wipe them dry with a lintless cloth. Keep all cleaned parts on paper towels to avoid contamination. Cover them with a clean towel to keep grit from entering the internal parts and bearings. A tiny piece of grit can do a tremendous amount of damage if allowed to work on a part over an extended period of time or while the wheel is turning at high speed.

Inspect the two ball bearing retainer assemblies. If any of the ball bearings fall out of the retainer, are pitted (pencil-point dots), show signs of excessive wear (dull spots), or are cracked, the entire bearing and retainer assembly must be replaced. Check the retainers for cracks or visible signs of damage.

Carefully inspect the loose ball bearings for signs of excessive wear and replace the complete set if any of them are damaged. Replacing the complete set will ensure distribution of the bearing load equally on all the ball bearings.

Inspect the bearing surface of the left-hand ball cup in the hub shell, both cones, the driver, and the right-hand ball cup for scores (scratchlike marks), and pits. Check both cones for stripped threads.

Inspect the axle for damaged or stripped threads. Check the sun gear on the axle for chipped or worn teeth. Check the axle slot to be sure the edges have not been rounded.

Inspect the planetary gears for chipped or worn teeth. Check the small end of the planetary-gear pins for wear.

Inspect the clutch for worn driving arms.

Inspect the high- and low-gear pawls for worn driving edges.

Check the dust caps to be sure they are not bent, crimped, or distorted, which could have happened during disassembly.

Inspect the high- and low-gear pawl cage assemblies for cracks around the rivets. Check both assemblies for worn driving edges. Inspect the internal gear of the high-gear cage for worn or chipped teeth.

Check the axle key to be sure it is not bent, the edges are not rounded, or the threads in the key are not stripped.

Inspect the hub shell for chipped or worn ratchet teeth. Check the flanges of the shell for cracks and to be sure they are not loose.

If the hub has been completely disassembled, the clutch spring and pawl springs must be replaced to ensure proper service.

Inspect the exterior splines on the ring gear for a worn or glazed condition.

Inspect the locknuts for stripped or damaged threads. Check the ears of the right-hand lockwasher to be sure they are not cracked.

ASSEMBLING

⑱ Insert a low-gear pawl and new spring into the cage slot, with the long leg of the spring riding against the planet cage, as shown, and the hook end pushing against the pawl. **CAUTION: New pawl springs must be installed to ensure proper service.** Push the pawl

LONG LEG OF SPRING

⑱

⑲

and spring into the slot until the hole in the pawl aligns with the hole in the cage flange, and then push the pawl pin into position, with the flat end of the pin facing up. When properly installed, the head of the pin will be flush with the surface of the cage flange; the pawl will be forced outward by spring tension; and the long end of the pawl will be facing out. Install the second pawl in a similar manner. Cover the ends of the pins with a light coating of multipurpose lubricant to hold them in place.

⑲ Carefully turn the cage body end for end on the bench to keep from jarring out the pins. Slide one of the planetary gears into place, with the pin hole aligned with the hole in the cage flange. Insert one of the gear pins into position, with the shoulder end of the pin facing up, as shown. Install the other three planetary gears in a similar manner.

⑳ Position a new pawl spring on one of the high-gear pawls, with the loop of the spring aligned over the pawl hole. The long leg of the spring must be

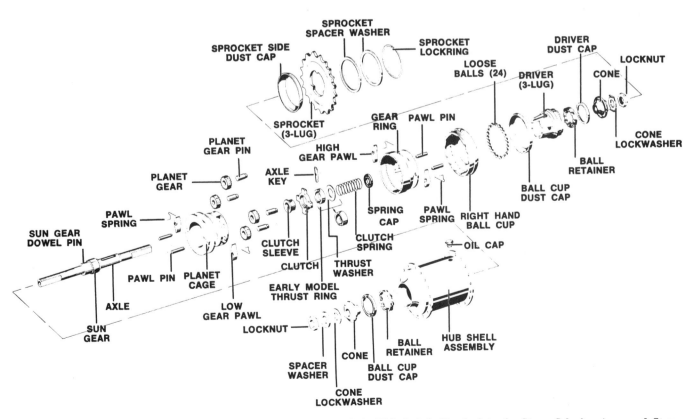

Exploded view of the Sturmey-Archer AW three-speed rear hub. This hub is identical to the Styre, Schwinn-Approved Styre, Brampton, and Hercules hubs. All parts of these five hubs are interchangeable.

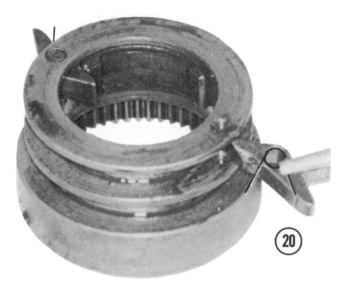

(20)

(23)

(21)

(22)

facing toward the ring slot, and the hook end must be over the pawl, as shown. **CAUTION: Always use new pawl springs to ensure proper service.**

㉑ Push in on the pawl, against the tension of the spring, and then insert one of the pins, with the tapered end facing down. Install the other pawl, spring, and pin in a similar manner. Cover the ends of the pins with a light coating of multipurpose lubricant to hold them in place.

㉒ Apply a light coating of multipurpose lubricant to the bearing race of the right-hand ball cup.

㉓ Place the same number of loose ball bearings into the lubricated bearing race of the right-hand ball cup as you counted during disassembly. If the count was lost, insert enough bearings until they fit snugly, and then remove one bearing for running clearance.

㉔ Position the dust cap on the right-hand ball cup, with the flat side up, and then tap it with a hammer until it is fully seated. Note the one-ball clearance, which is clearly shown in this illustration.

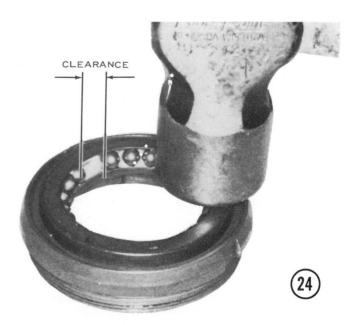

CLEARANCE

(24)

㉕ Pack the small ball bearing retainer assembly with a generous amount of multipurpose lubricant. Work the lubricant throughout the bearings with your fingers. Insert the lubricated bearing assembly into the driver, with the flat side of the retainer facing up. Spread another light coating of lubricant over the bearing assembly.

㉖ Install the dust cap over the bearing assembly, with the flat side of the cap facing *down*. Tap the cap lightly with a hammer until it is fully seated. **CAUTION: Any damage to the cap will cause the cone to drag and prevent a proper bearing adjustment.**

㉗ Clamp the axle in the vise in a horizontal position, with the slotted end facing out and the jaws gripping the axle flats. **CAUTION: Use soft vise jaws to protect the axle threads from damage.** Slide the as-

sembled planetary-cage assembly onto the axle, with the planetary gears facing out, as shown. Work the cage back and forth until the internal gear of the cage meshes with the teeth of the sun gear on the axle, and then push the cage on as far as it will go.

㉘ Apply a small amount of premium-quality cycle oil to the pawls and to the planetary gears.

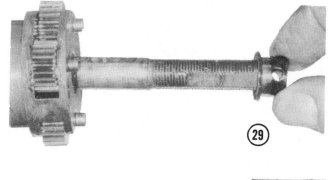

㉙ Slide the clutch sleeve onto the axle, with the flanged end toward the planetary cage.

㉚ Install the clutch, with the notched ends of the ears facing away from the planetary cage. Turn the clutch so the ears are flat against the surface of the planetary cage between the planetary gear pins.

㉛ Insert the axle key through the hole in the clutch sleeve and through the slot in the axle, with the flat ends facing away from the clutch.

㉜ Slide the solid shaft end (with the short threads) of the indicator spindle assembly through the hollow axle, and then thread it into the axle key by turning it clockwise. After you have tightened the indicator spindle assembly finger-tight, check to be sure it is threaded properly into the axle key by pulling out

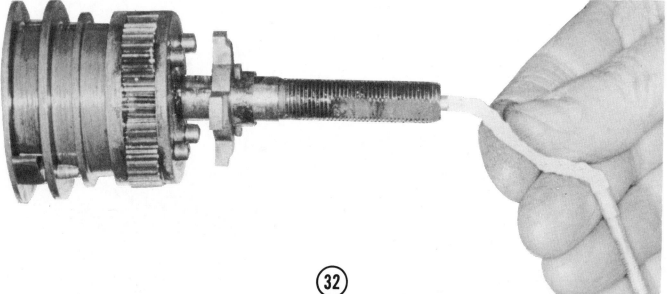

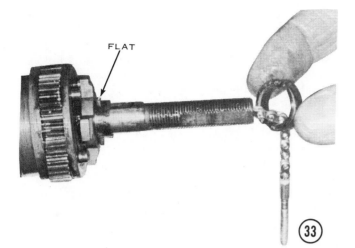

FLAT

PLANET GEAR THRUST WASHER

THRUST RING

㉟

㉝

on the spindle. It must not come out. This is necessary to assure that the axle key will remain in its correct position and it will not be disturbed during installation of the remaining parts.

㉝ Install the thrust ring, with the cutouts indexed over the flats of the axle key.

㉞ Hold the thrust ring firmly in place, and then check for 0.005–0.008″ clearance between the thrust ring and the surface of the clutch. If the clearance is less than 0.005″, install a new axle key.

㉟ Slip the thrust washer onto the axle. *NOTE: Some Sturmey-Archer AW hubs do not have a thrust washer. If the thrust ring has a smaller opening at one end, a thrust washer is not required. If the thrust ring*

has the same size openings at both ends, a thrust washer must be installed. Push the gear ring over the planetary-cage assembly as far as it will go, with the internal teeth indexing with the teeth of the planetary gears.

㊱ Depress the two high-gear pawls, and then twist the right-hand ball cup clockwise into place over the pawls. The ball cup should ratchet as it is turned clockwise and should engage the pawls when turned counterclockwise.

㊲ Slide the assembled driver unit onto the axle, and then turn it clockwise while pushing it into place. When the slots in the driver index over the ears of the

㉞

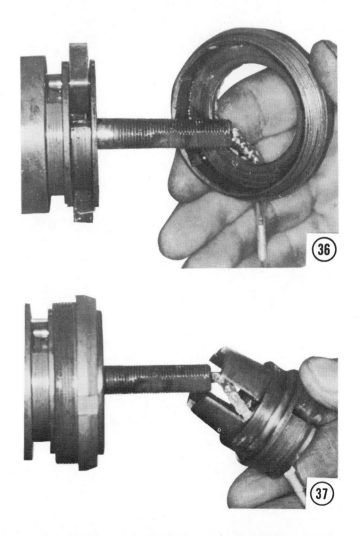

㊱

㊲

(38)

clutch, you will feel the driver engage and move slightly farther into the ball cup and ring-gear assembly.

③⑧ Install a new clutch spring onto the axle and then the spring cap, if you removed a cap during disassembly. **CAUTION: A new clutch spring must be installed to ensure proper service.**

(39)

EAR

EAR

(40)

(41)

③⑨ Thread one of the cones onto the axle finger-tight, and then back it off ¼ turn. *NOTE: This is the final adjustment to this cone because it is locked in place and covered with the hub shell; therefore, it is not accessible.* Remove the indicator spindle assembly from the axle by twisting it counterclockwise until it is free of the axle key and then pulling it out.

④⓪ Slide the cone lockwasher onto the axle, with the internal flats of the washer indexing with the axle flats. Twist the cone not more than ¼ turn counterclockwise to enable the ears of the lockwasher to contact the flats of the cone.

④① Thread the locknut onto the axle, and then tighten it securely against the cone lockwasher.

④② Pack the left-hand ball bearing retainer assembly with a generous amount of multipurpose lubricant. Work the lubricant throughout the bearings with your fingers. Insert the retainer assembly into the ball cup, with the flat side of the retainer facing up. Place the dust cap into the ball cup, with the flat side facing *down*. **CAUTION: Tap the cap lightly with a hammer until it is fully seated. Any damage to the cap will cause the cone to rub and prevent accurate adjustment.**

④③ Remove the assembly from the vise. Place the hub (wheel) in a horizontal position, with the tire against your chest and the left-hand ball cup of the hub facing up, as shown. *NOTE: For photographic clarity, the wheel and spokes are not shown.* Insert the assembled unit into the hub shell, with the low-gear pawls facing up. Turn the internal-drive assembly counterclockwise to allow the low-gear pawls to index with the ratchet inside the hub shell. When the pawls index,

BALL BEARING
RETAINER

DUST CAP

RIGHT-HAND BALL CUP

(42)

you will feel the assembly move farther into the hub, and the threads of the right-hand ball cup will engage the internal threads of the hub shell. When this occurs, turn the right-hand ball cup clockwise until it is finger-tight.

④④ Clamp the assembled unit in the vise, with the open end of the hub shell facing up and the soft vise jaws gripping the flats of the axle. Thread the cone onto the axle finger-tight.

④⑤ Install the cone lockwasher, with the internal flats indexing with the flats of the axle. Slide the thick washer down the axle, with the flat side of the washer against the surface of the lockwasher.

④⑥ Thread the locknut onto the axle finger-tight.

④⑦ Turn the complete assembly end for end in the vise, with the jaws gripping the flats on the left-hand ball cup portion of the hub shell. Tighten the right-hand ball cup firmly by turning it in a clockwise direction with a drift punch and hammer, as shown.

④⑧ Reverse the assembly in the vise, with the jaws gripping the flats of the axle. Adjust the cone by tightening or loosening it with a cone wrench to obtain a trace of side play when the wheel rim is moved up and down, and then tighten the locknut. Remove the assembled wheel and hub from the vise. Hold each end

④④

④③

SPACER WASHER

LOCKWASHER

④⑤

of the axle with your fingers. Slowly twist the axle with the thumb and forefinger of each hand—the wheel should not turn. If it does, the adjusting cone is too tight and must be loosened slightly. Clamp the assembly in the vise, with the left-hand ball cup end of the hub shell facing up and the soft vise jaws gripping the axle flats. Loosen the locknut, and then rotate the cone counterclockwise approximately ⅛ turn. Retighten the locknut while holding the cone with a cone wrench. Remove the assembly from the vise, and then recheck

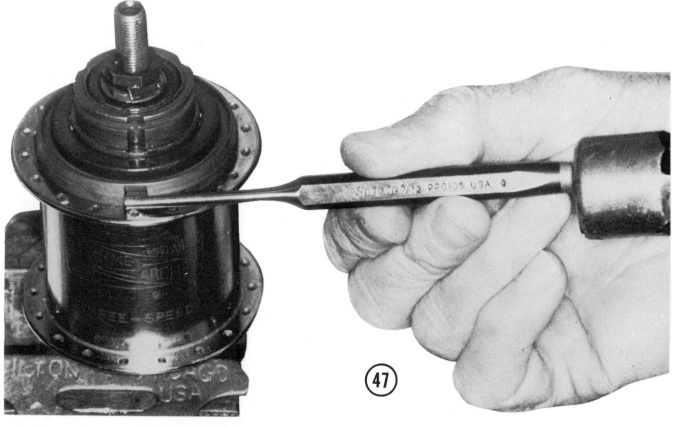

for side play and rotation as before. The cone is properly adjusted when the wheel rotates freely, comes to rest gradually, with the valve stem at the lowest point of the wheel, and there is only the slightest trace of side play. **CAUTION: If the cone is adjusted too tight, it will cause binding and scoring of the hub. If the cone is adjusted too loose, it will cause fatigue, which can result in a damaged hub or broken axle.**

④⑨ After cone adjustment is completed, clamp the assembly in the vise, with the driver end facing up and the jaws gripping the flats of the axle. Install the same number of spacers you noted during disassembly.

⑤⓪ Place the sprocket on top of the spacers, with the concave side facing up and with the lugs indexing with the notches in the driver.

⑤① Snap the lock ring into the recess of the driver to lock the sprocket in place.

INSTALLING THE WHEEL

Slide the axle frame lockwashers onto both ends of the axle, with the flats of the washers indexing with the flats of the axle and the keys of the washers facing *away* from the hub. Guide the wheel into the rear forks, engage the chain over the sprocket teeth, and then slide the axle back into the rear dropouts with the lockwasher keys indexing with the slots on the *in-*

⑤⓪

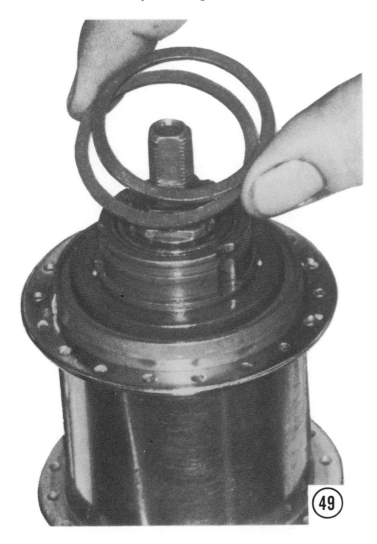

④⑨

⑤①

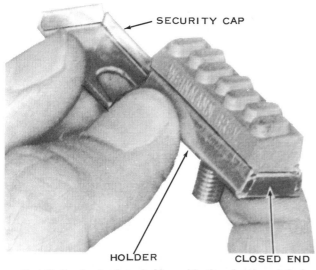

SECURITY CAP

HOLDER   CLOSED END

Install the brake-shoe holder with the closed end facing forward and with the beveled surface of the shoe matching the angle of the wheel rim, as discussed in the text.

side of the frame. If serrated washers are used, place the washers on the axle with the serrations *toward* the hub—against the frame, as shown in the accompanying illustration. Slide any carriage or fender supports, including washers, onto the axle in the order you noted when removing the wheel. **CAUTION: On bicycles equipped with this type of hub, it is best to mount accessory supports on frame lugs and not on the axle.**

Thread both axle nuts onto the axle finger-tight, with the long nut (the one with the hole in it) on the sprocket side end. Take up the slack in the chain by pulling the axle back until the chain is snug. Tighten the axle nut on the sprocket side until it is snug, and then align the wheel so that it rotates midway between the rear frame members by pulling the axle back on the side opposite the sprocket. Adjust the chain tension until it can depressed approximately ⅜ inch at a point midway between the hanger and rear sprockets, and then tighten both axle nuts securely.

Turn the crank in the forward direction to see that the chain and wheel turn freely without binding or rubbing on the frame.

Check the cone adjustment. The wheel should spin freely with just a trace of side play at the wheel rim. If an adjustment is required because of binding or excessive side play, loosen the axle nut on the side opposite the sprocket. Adjust the cone on that side, and then retighten the nut.

Slide the solid shaft (with the short threads) of the indicator spindle assembly into the axle, and then thread it into the axle key by turning the assembly in a clockwise direction as far as possible. If necessary, back it off not over ½ turn to align the threaded portion of the spindle with the shifting cable. If the shift mechanism is equipped with a plastic protector, slide the protector over the indicator spindle and axle nut.

Place the shift control in high gear (No. 3 position). Turn the cable adjusting barrel onto the indicator

spindle until the cable is snug. Check the indicator spindle adjustment as follows: Place the shift control lever in the No. 2 position. Slide the plastic protector back off the axle nut. Sight through the hole in the long axle nut to see if the end of the indicator rod is even with the end of the axle. If it is not, loosen the locknut, and then adjust the knurled section of the cable until the end of the rod is even with the end of the axle. Tighten the locknut and replace the plastic protector.

If you are working on a bicycle with a quick-release button on the brake handle or a quick-release lever above the brake on the cable hanger, return the lever to the operating position. If you removed one of the brake-shoe assemblies to gain tire clearance, install the holder with the closed end facing forward. **CAUTION: The closed end of the holder must face forward to prevent the shoe from being forced out when the brakes are applied.** Secure the brake holder with the mounting nut. If you deflated the tire for clearance, inflate it to the required pressure.

OVERHAULING A STURMEY-ARCHER TCW III THREE-SPEED REAR HUB WITH COASTER BRAKE

The following step-by-step illustrated instructions cover disassembling, assembling, and adjusting a Sturmey-Archer TCW III three-speed rear hub with coaster brake. The hub is identified by the name stamped on the hub shell and on the brake arm. A detailed exploded drawing of this hub, showing all internal parts, follows the Cleaning and Inspecting portion of this section.

For photographic clarity, the illustrations were made of a hub without the tire, rim, or spokes.

REMOVING THE WHEEL

If the bicycle you are working on does not have levers mounted on the handlebars, you can turn the bicycle upside down, resting it on the seat and handlebars. A better method is to support the bicycle in an upright position from a bracket, set of hooks, or rope attached to the garage ceiling, or to secure it in an automobile rear carrier rack attached to the car. Holding the bicycle rigid will make the task of removing, installing, and adjusting parts much easier.

Loosen the three-speed cable adjusting barrel locknut, and then remove the barrel from the indicator spindle. Remove the mounting screw from the brake-arm strap, and then slide the brake arm free of the strap. If a plastic protector is used on the right-hand axle nut, remove the protector. Loosen both axle nuts by turning them in a counterclockwise direction. Remove the indicator spindle from the hub. Remove both axle nuts.

Take note of the washer and support arrangement on the axle. Some bicycles have serrated washers installed against the frame to prevent the wheel from moving forward under tension of the chain. Washers are usually installed between the fender and accessory supports to keep them from twisting when the axle nuts are tightened.

Slide any fender or accessory supports, including washers, from the axle. Move the wheel forward in the dropouts, and then remove the chain from the sprocket; hook it over the frame. Remove the frame lockwasher from both ends of the axle. Guide the wheel free of the frame.

DISASSEMBLING

① Clamp the complete hub assembly in a vise, with the jaws gripping the axle flats on the brake arm end. **CAUTION: Use soft vise jaws to protect the axle threads.** Remove the sprocket lock ring by prying it out of its recess with a narrow-bladed screwdriver and then lifting it off the sprocket.

② Remove the spacers. *NOTE: Count the number of spacers under the snap ring, as they are used to align the rear sprocket with the hanger sprocket.*

③ Turn the assembly end for end in the vise, with the soft jaws gripping the flats of the axle. Remove the locknut and then the lockwasher. Remove the ad-

A Sturmey-Archer TCW III three-speed rear hub with coaster brake.

justing cone by turning it counterclockwise with a hook-spanner type wrench or a drift punch and hammer.

④ Rotate the brake arm in a counterclockwise direction until the brake-arm side expander is clear of the axle. The brake cylinder will come off with the assembly, as shown.

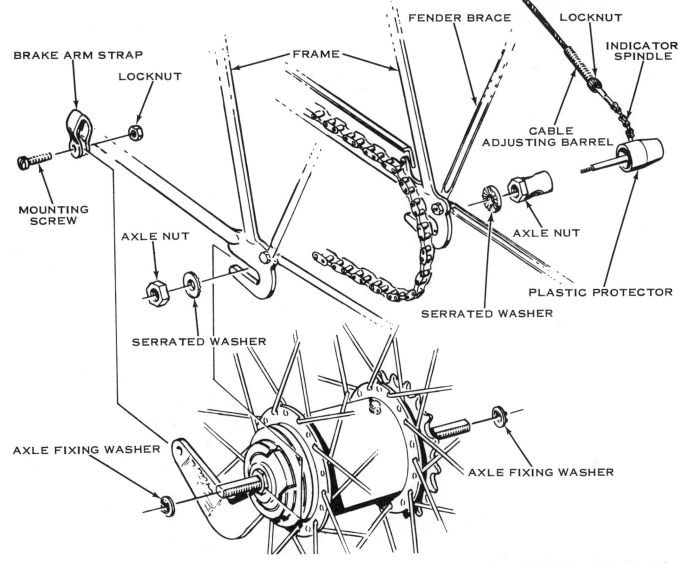

Arrangement of washers, nuts, indicator spindle, and brake arm strap of a Sturmey-Archer TCW III hub. This illustration will be helpful in removing and installing the wheel.

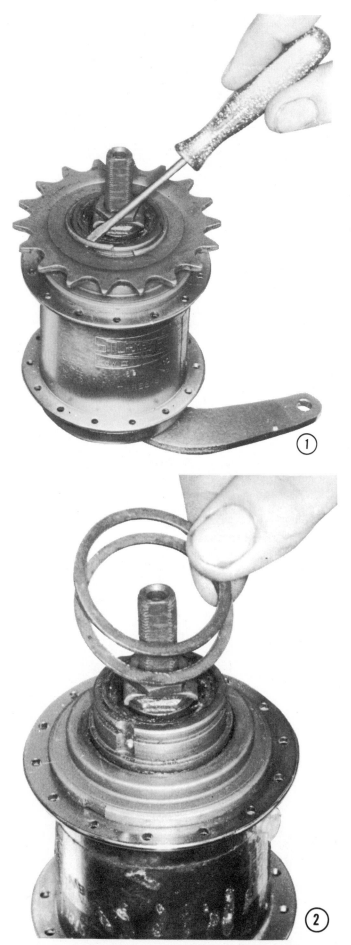

ADJUSTING CONE

⑤ Lift out the drive-side expander, until you engage the threads, and then thread it off the axle in a counterclockwise direction until it is clear.

⑥ Remove the low-gear pawl cage assembly from the hub shell.

⑦ Shift the assembly end for end in the vise, with the jaws gripping the flange of the hub, not the axle. Rotate the right-hand ball cup counterclockwise, using a drift punch and hammer, as shown, until it is free of the threads.

⑧ Lift the complete assembly out of the hub, and then remove the hub from the vise.

⑨ Clamp the assembly in the vise, with the soft jaws of the vise gripping the flats of the axle and the locknut facing up. Remove the locknut. Lift off the cone lockwasher, and then remove the cone.

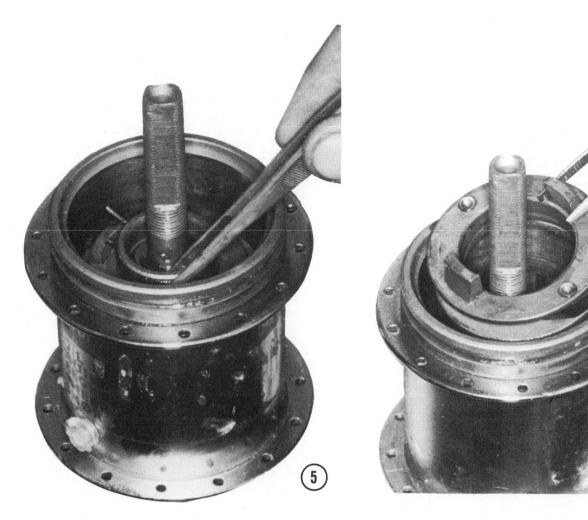

⑤   ⑥

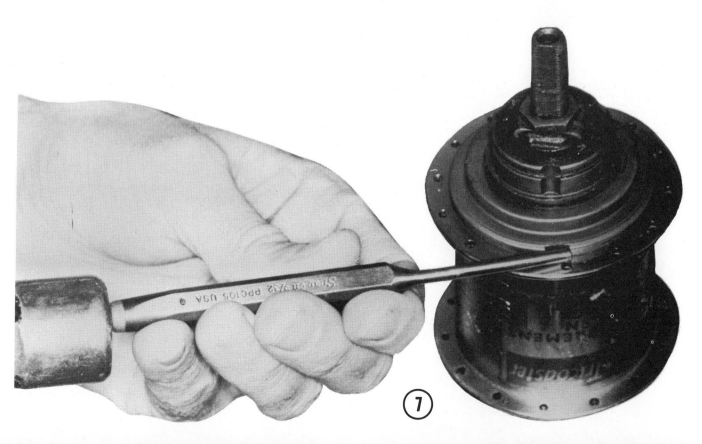

⑦

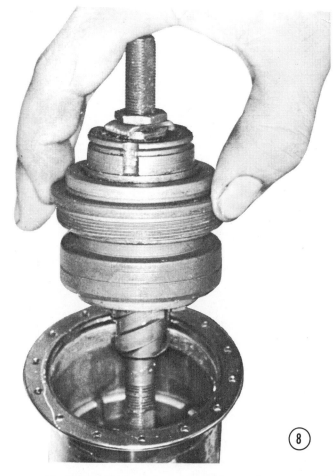

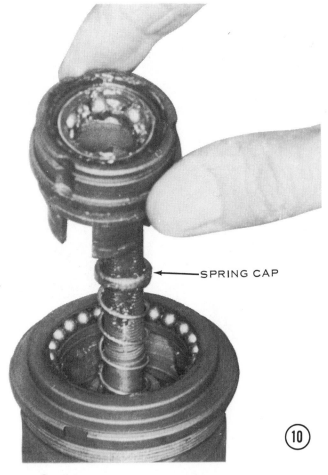

SPRING CAP

⑧

⑩

⑩ Remove the driver assembly, spring cap, and spring from the axle.

⑪ Lift the right-hand ball cup off the high-gear pawl assembly.

⑫ Remove the high-gear pawl cage assembly from the ring gear.

⑬ Lift the ring gear straight up to disengage the teeth from the planetary gears, and then remove it from the axle.

⑭ Slide the thrust ring off the axle.

⑮ Pull the axle key out of the keyway in the axle.

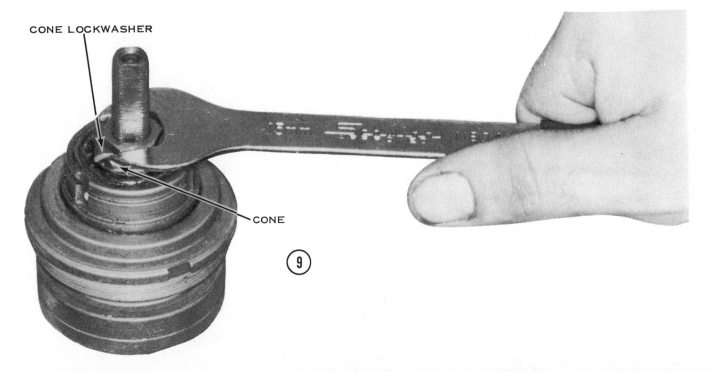

CONE LOCKWASHER

CONE

⑨

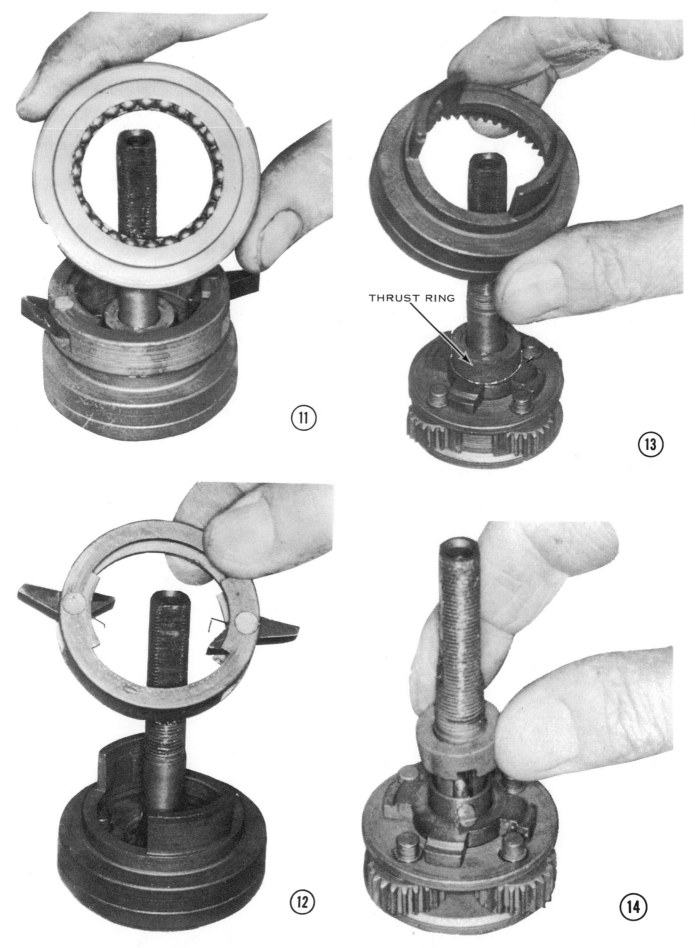

THRUST RING

⑪

⑫

⑬

⑭

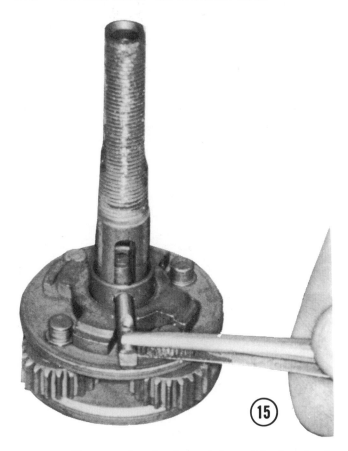

(15)

PLANET CAGE

(17)

⑯ Remove the clutch, and then slide the clutch sleeve off the axle. Lift out the planetary gear pins, and then slide the planetary gears out of the planetary cage assembly.

⑰ Turn the remaining assembly end for end in the vise, with the soft jaws gripping the flats of the axle. Pry the planetary cage retaining ring from the axle with a narrow-bladed screwdriver, and then remove the planetary cage from the axle.

⑱ Pry the dust cap from the right-hand ball cup with a screwdriver. Work around the cap edge and be careful not to crimp or damage it. Remove the loose ball bearings. **CAUTION: Count them for assembly purposes.**

⑲ Remove the brake cylinder from the brake-arm side expander.

⑳ Pry the brake arm off the dust cap, using a wide-bladed screwdriver, as shown.

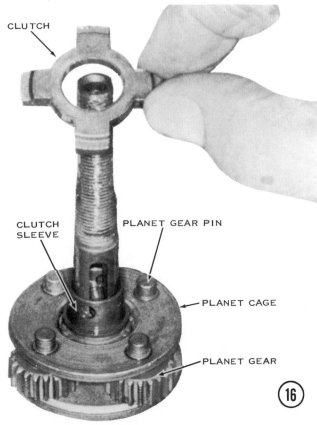

CLUTCH

CLUTCH SLEEVE

PLANET GEAR PIN

PLANET CAGE

PLANET GEAR

(16)

(18)

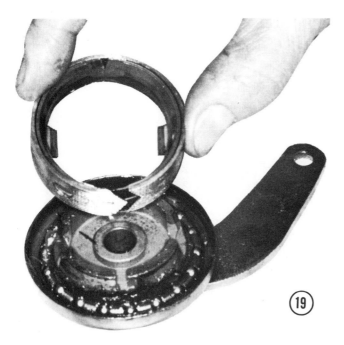

㉑ Hold the brake-arm side dust cap in one hand, with the rounded surface up, as shown, and then separate it from the brake-arm side expander by striking the center of the expander with a hammer.

㉒ Turn the brake-arm side expander over, and then remove the ball bearing retainer assembly.

㉓ Pry the dust cap from the driver with a screwdriver, as shown. Work around the cap edge and it will pop out. **CAUTION: Be careful not to crimp or damage the cap.** Remove the ball bearing retainer assembly.

CLEANING AND INSPECTING

Clean all parts in solvent and blow dry with compressed air, or wipe them dry with a lintless cloth. Keep all cleaned parts on paper towels to avoid contamination. Cover them with a clean towel to keep grit from entering the internal parts and bearings. A tiny piece of grit can do a tremendous amount of damage if

allowed to work on a part over an extended period of time or while the wheel is turning at high speed.

Inspect the two ball bearing retainer assemblies. If any of the ball bearings fall out of the retainer, are pitted (pencil-point dots), show signs of excessive wear (dull spots), or are cracked, the bearing retainer assembly must be replaced. Check the retainers for cracks or visible signs of damage.

Carefully inspect the loose ball bearings for signs of excessive wear and replace the complete set if any of them are damaged. Replacing the complete set will ensure distribution of the bearing load equally on all the ball bearings.

Inspect the bearing surface of the brake-arm side

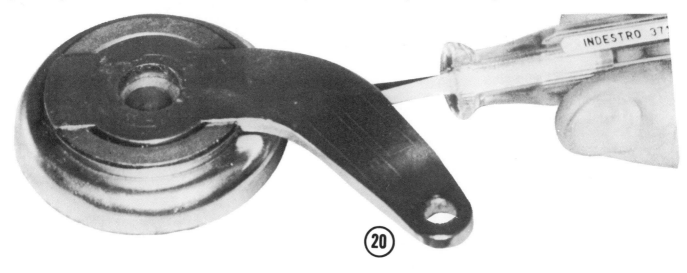

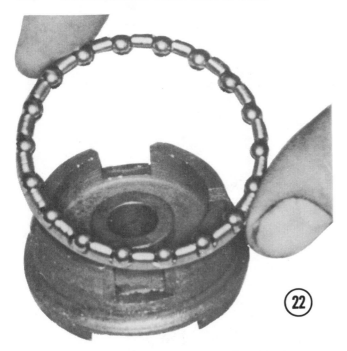

expander, cone, driver, and the right-hand ball cup for scores (scratchlike marks), and pits. Check the brake-arm side expander and the cone for stripped threads.

Inspect the axle for damaged or stripped threads. Check the sun gear on the axle for chipped or worn teeth.

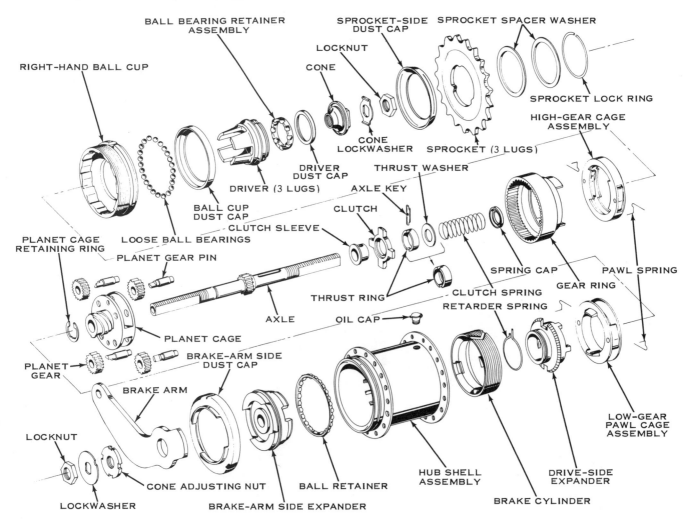

Exploded view of a Sturmey-Archer TCW III three-speed rear hub with coaster brake.

Inspect the planetary gears for chipped or worn teeth. Check the small end of the planetary-gear pins for wear.

Check the dust caps to be sure they are not bent, crimped, or distorted, which could have happened during disassembly.

Inspect the gear ring for chipped or worn teeth and for damaged or worn splines.

Inspect the high- and low-gear pawl cage assemblies for cracks around the rivets. Check both assemblies for worn driving edges.

Inspect the locknuts and the cone adjusting nut for stripped or damaged threads.

Inspect the clutch for worn driving arms.

If the hub has been completely disassembled, the clutch spring must be replaced to ensure proper service.

Check the axle key to be sure it is not bent, the edges not rounded, or the threads in the key are not stripped.

Inspect the brake cylinder and the right-hand ball cup for a worn or glazed condition.

Inspect the planetary cage retaining ring for worn ears.

Inspect the hub shell for chipped or worn ratchet teeth. Inspect the bearing cup for scores, pits, or excessive wear. Check the flanges of the shell for cracks and to be sure they are not loose.

ASSEMBLING

㉔ Clamp the axle in the vise, with the jaws gripping the flats of the axle and the slot facing down. **CAUTION: Use soft vise jaws to protect the axle threads from damage.** Slide the planetary cage onto the axle as far as it will go with the splines facing up and the internal teeth of the cage indexing with the sun gear on

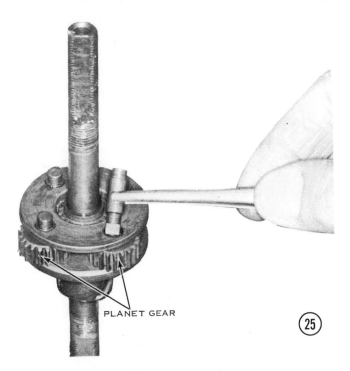

PLANET GEAR

㉕

the axle. Press the planetary-cage retaining ring into the axle groove to secure the planetary cage.

㉕ Turn the axle end for end in the vise, with the soft jaws gripping the axle flats. Slide one of the planetary gears into the planetary cage, with the teeth of the gear indexing with the teeth of the sun gear. Insert the gear pin, with the flat-shaped end down and facing out, as shown. Install the other three planetary gears in a similar manner.

㉖ Slide the clutch sleeve onto the axle, with the flanged end facing down.

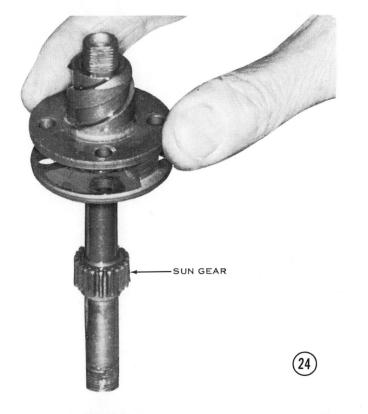

SUN GEAR

㉔

㉖

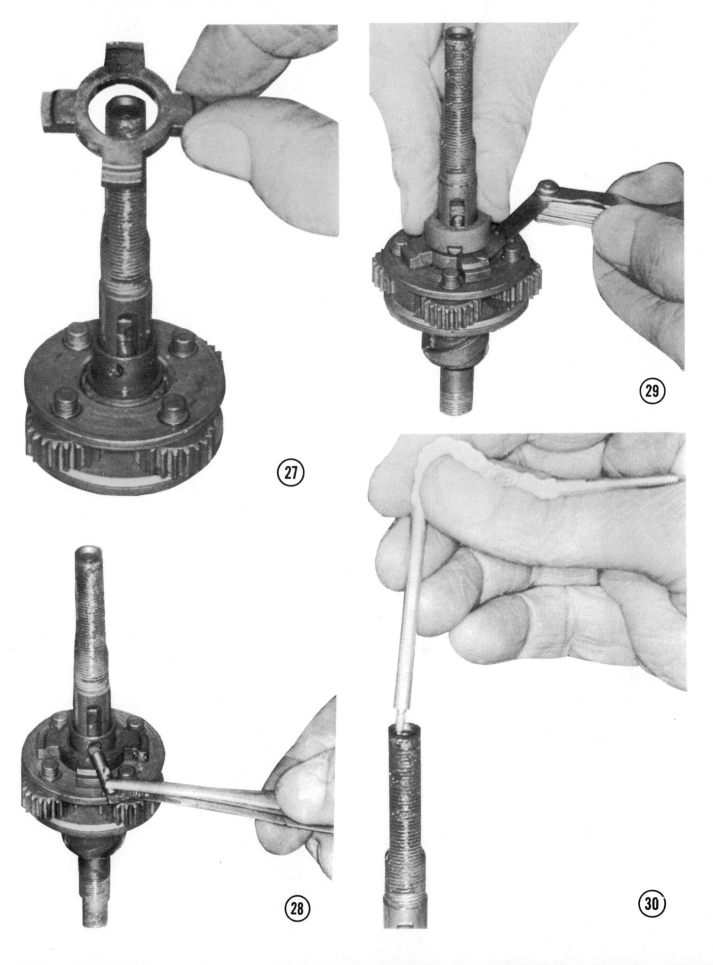

㉗ Install the clutch, with the notched ends of the ears facing up, as shown.

㉘ Insert the axle key through the hole in the clutch sleeve, with the flats at the ends of the key facing up.

㉙ Install the thrust ring, with the slots of the ring indexed over the flats of the axle key. Check for 0.005–0.008" clearance between the thrust ring and the surface of the clutch. If the clearance is less than 0.005", install a new axle key.

㉚ Slide the solid shaft end (with the short threads) of the indicator spindle assembly down the hollow axle, and then thread it into the axle key by turning it clockwise.

㉛ After you have tightened the indicator spindle assembly finger-tight, check to be sure it is threaded properly into the axle key by pulling up on the spindle. This is necessary to assure you the axle key will remain in its correct position and that it will not be disturbed during installation of the remaining parts.

㉜ Install the thrust ring with the cutouts in the ring indexed over the flats of the axle key. Place the gear ring over the planetary assembly, with the internal teeth indexing with the teeth of the planetary gears.

㉝ Install the high-gear pawl cage assembly on the gear ring, with the smooth surface of the pawl rivets facing up and the internal shoulders indexing with the cutouts in the gear ring. You can tell that the high-gear pawl cage assembly is fully seated when the top of the gear ring is flush with the top surface of the pawl cage assembly.

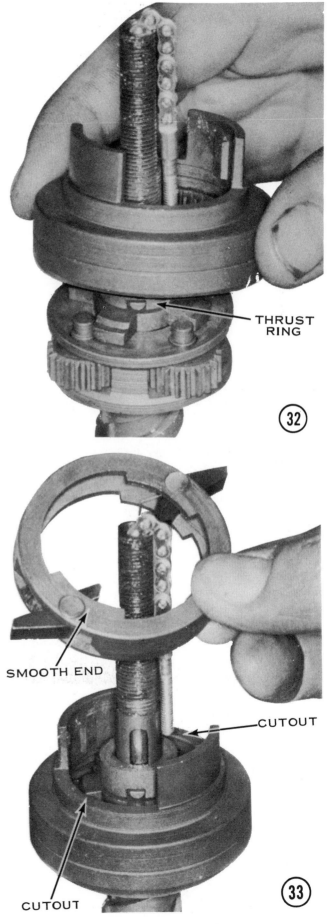

THRUST RING

㉜

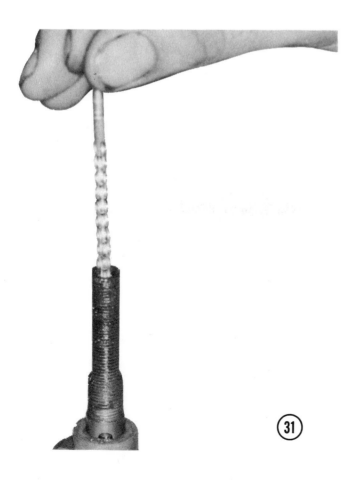

SMOOTH END

CUTOUT

CUTOUT

㉛

㉝

(34)

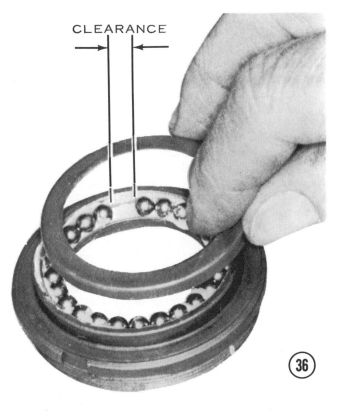

CLEARANCE

(36)

③④ Apply a light coating of multipurpose lubricant to the bearing race of the right-hand ball cup.

③⑤ Place the same number of loose ball bearings into the lubricated bearing race of the right-hand ball cup as you counted during disassembly. If the count was lost, insert enough bearings until they all fit snugly, and then remove one bearing for running clearance.

③⑥ Place the ball cup dust cap in position over the flange of the ball cup with the flat side facing up. Lightly tap the cap with a hammer until it is fully seated.

(35)

(37)

㊲ Install the assembled right-hand ball cup, with the dust cap side facing up, as shown. Depress the pawls to enable the ball cup assembly to seat on the shoulder of the high-gear pawl cage assembly. Note the one-ball clearance, which is necessary for proper service life.

㊳ Install the clutch spring and spring cap onto the axle, with the spring seated in the cap and the cap end facing up.

㊴ Pack the driver ball bearing retainer assembly with a generous amount of multipurpose lubricant. Work the lubricant throughout the bearings with your fingers. Install the lubricated bearing assembly into the driver with the flat side of the retainer facing up. Install the dust cap over the ball bearing retainer assembly with the flat side of the cap facing *down*. Tap the edge of the cap with a hammer until it is fully seated. Slide the driver down the axle over the spring until the slots engage over the lugs of the clutch assembly.

㊵ Thread the cone onto the axle until it is finger-tight, and then back it off ¼ turn for a preliminary adjustment. Remove the indicator assembly from the axle by twisting it in a counterclockwise direction until it is free of the axle key, and then pulling it out.

㊶ Guide the cone lockwasher over the axle, with the ears facing down and the flats indexing with the flats of the axle. If necessary, back off the cone no more than ¼ turn to align the flats of the cone with the ears of the lockwasher.

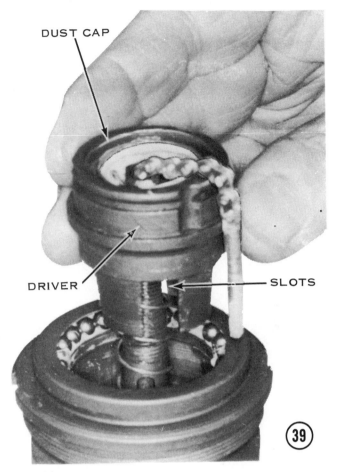

DUST CAP

DRIVER

SLOTS

39

38

40

ing with the slots of the expander. Turn each planetary gear pin until the flat sides of all the pins face out, as shown. Turn the assembled drive-side expander and low-gear pawl cage unit onto the planetary cage assembly clockwise until the low-gear cage seats flush on the surface of the planetary cage. *NOTE: The flats of the planetary gear pins must face out to allow the low-gear pawl cage assembly to seat squarely on the surface of the planetary cage.*

⑭ Remove the assembly from the vise. Place the hub (wheel) in an approximate horizontal position, with the tire against your chest and the brake side up. (For photographic clarity the wheel and spokes are not shown in the illustration.) Insert the assembled unit into the hub shell with the drive-side expander up, as shown. Turn the internal-drive assembly in a counterclockwise direction to allow the pawls on the low-gear cage assembly to index with the ratchet inside the hub shell. When the pawls index, you will be able to feel the assembly move farther into the hub, and the threads of the right-hand ball cup will engage the internal threads of the hub shell. When this occurs, turn the right-hand ball cup clockwise until it is finger-tight.

⑮ Clamp the assembled unit in the vise, with the open end of the hub shell facing up and the soft jaws gripping the flats of the axle. Install the brake cylinder into the hub shell with the cylinder keys facing up.

41

⑫ Thread the locknut onto the axle, and then tighten it securely against the cone lockwasher.

⑬ Turn the axle end for end in the vise, with the soft jaws gripping the flats of the axle. Insert the drive-side expander into the low-gear pawl cage assembly, with the shoulders of the cage assembly index-

42

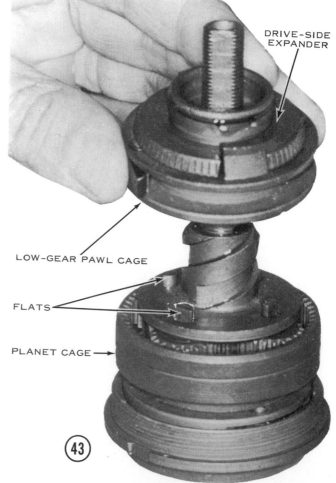

DRIVE-SIDE EXPANDER

LOW-GEAR PAWL CAGE

FLATS

PLANET CAGE

43

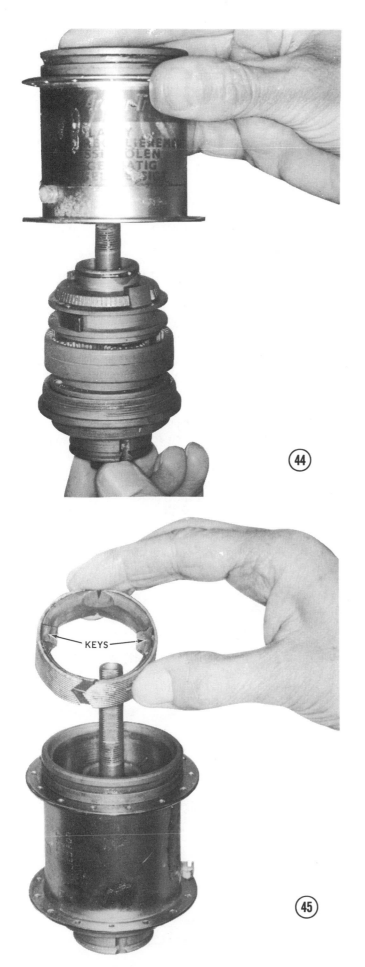

④⑥ Pack the brake-side ball bearing retainer assembly with a generous amount of multipurpose lubricant. Work the lubricant throughout the retainer with your fingers. Install the lubricated bearing assembly, with the flat side of the retainer facing up. Apply a second light coating of multipurpose lubricant to the inside surfaces of the ball bearings.

④⑦ Place the dust cap over the brake-arm side expander, with the cutouts in the cap aligned with the cutouts in the expander. Lightly tap the dust cap with a hammer until it is fully seated on the expander.

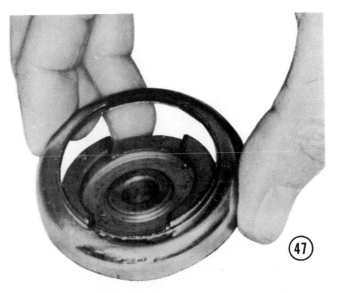

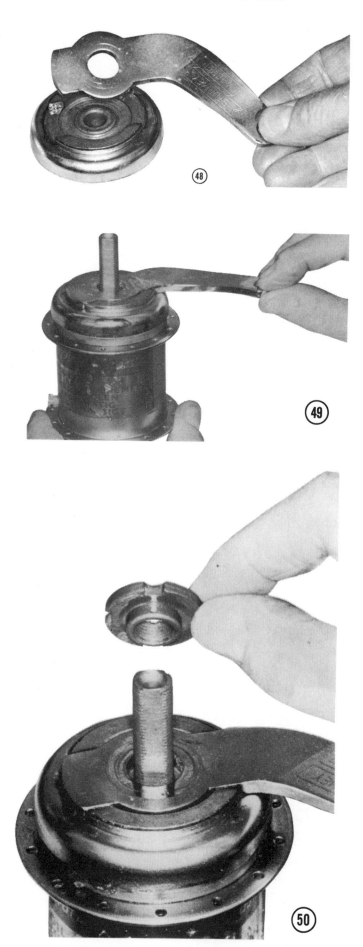

48

49

50

④ Position the brake arm in the cutouts of the dust cap and expander, with the manufacturer's identification facing up, and then lightly tap it into place with a hammer.

④ Slide the brake-arm assembly onto the axle. Rotate the brake arm clockwise and counterclockwise until the lugs of the brake cylinder engage the slots of the brake-arm side expander. When this occurs, you will feel the assembly drop into place.

⑤ Thread the cone adjusting nut onto the axle finger-tight.

⑤ Turn the complete unit end for end in the vise, with the soft jaws gripping the brake-side dust cap. Tighten the right-hand ball cup by turning it clockwise, using a drift punch and hammer, as shown.

⑤ Reverse the assembly in the vise, with the brake arm facing up and the soft jaws gripping the flats of the axle. Rotate the cone adjusting nut with a hook-spanner wrench to obtain just a trace of side play when the wheel rim is moved up and down.

⑤ Remove the assembled wheel and hub from the vise. Hold each end of the axle with your fingers. Slowly twist the axle with the thumb and forefinger of each hand—the wheel should not turn. If it does, the adjusting cone is too tight and must be loosened slightly. Clamp the assembly back in the vise with the brake arm facing up and the soft jaws gripping the axle flats. Loosen the locknut, and then rotate the cone counterclockwise approximately ⅛ turn. Retighten the locknut. Remove the assembly from the vise, and then recheck for side play and rotation as before. The cone is properly adjusted when the wheel rotates freely, comes to rest gradually with the valve stem at the

51

52

(53)

(55)

lowest point of the wheel, and there is only the slightest trace of side play. **CAUTION: If the cone is adjusted too tight, it will cause binding and scoring of the hub. If the cone is adjusted too loose, it will cause fatigue, which can result in a damaged hub or broken axle.**

⑬ After cone adjustment has been made, clamp the assembly in the vise, with the brake arm facing up and the soft jaws gripping the axle flats. Install the lockwasher on the axle, with the internal flats of the washer indexing with the flats on the axle. Rotate the cone-adjusting nut slightly to allow the ear of the washer to index with the closest slot in the adjusting nut. Thread the locknut onto the axle tightly against the lockwasher.

⑭ Install the same number of spacers you noted during disassembly.

⑮ Place the sprocket on top of the spacers, with the concave side facing up and the lugs indexing with the slots in the driver.

(54)

SLOT

(56)

⑤⑦ Snap the lock ring into the recess of the driver to lock the sprocket in place.

INSTALLING THE WHEEL

Slide the axle frame lockwashers onto both ends of the axle, with the flats of the washers indexing with the flats of the axle and the keys of the washers facing *away* from the hub, as indicated in the accompanying illustration. Guide the wheel into the rear forks, engage the chain over the sprocket teeth, and then slide the axle back into the rear dropouts, with the lockwasher keys indexing with the slots on the *inside* of the frame. If serrated washers are used, place the washers on the axle with the serrations *toward* the hub—against the frame. Slide any carriage or fender supports, including washers, onto the axle in the order you noted when removing the wheel. Thread the long axle nut (with the hole in it) finger-tight onto the sprocket end of the axle. **CAU-**

TION: Be sure to use this nut on the sprocket end because the hole is used to sight through when alignment of the indicator spindle is made. Thread the other axle nut onto the axle finger-tight. Take up the slack in the chain by pulling the axle back until the chain is snug. Tighten the axle nut on the sprocket side until it is snug, and then align the wheel so it rotates midway between the rear frame members by pulling the axle back on the brake-arm side. Adjust the chain tension until it can be depressed approximately ⅜ inch at a point midway between the hanger and rear sprockets, and then tighten the sprocket side nut securely.

Tighten the other axle nut firmly. Slip the brake lever into the strap on the frame, and then secure it with the mounting screw and nut. If the brake strap has several mounting holes, bend the strap around the frame so the brake lever will be as close to the frame as possible.

Turn the crank in the forward direction to see that the chain and wheel turn freely without binding or rubbing on the frame. Reverse the crank direction, and the wheel should stop almost immediately.

Check the cone adjustment. The wheel should spin freely with just a trace of side play at the wheel rim. If an adjustment is required because of binding or excessive side play, loosen the axle nut on the brake-arm side. Adjust the cone on that side, and then retighten the nut.

Slide the solid shaft (with the short threads) of the indicator spindle assembly into the axle, and then thread it into the axle key by turning the assembly clockwise as far as possible. If necessary, back off the assembly not more than ½ turn to align the threaded portion of the spindle with the shifting cable. If the shift mechanism is equipped with a plastic protector, slide the protector over the indicator spindle and axle nut.

Place the shift control in the high-gear (No. 3) position. Turn the cable adjusting barrel onto the indicator spindle until the cable is snug. Check the indicator spindle adjustment as follows: Place the shift control lever in the No. 2 position, and then slide the plastic protector back off the axle nut and sight through the hole in the long axle nut to see if the end of the indicator rod is even with the end of the axle. If it is not, loosen the locknut, and then adjust the knurled section of the cable until the end of the rod is even with the end of the axle. Tighten the locknut and replace the plastic protector.

6
OVERHAULING A FREEWHEEL BODY AND SPROCKET CLUSTER

The hub shell with a freewheel body attached, including single or multiple sprockets, is driven forward at the same speed as the sprocket. If more than one sprocket is used, it is referred to as a "cluster." When the sprocket speed is reduced or stopped, the freewheel body allows the hub to continue turning, thus the term "freewheel." This freewheel action is accomplished through a pair of pawls and an internal-ratchet arrangement within the freewheel body. Turning the exterior portion of the body forward causes the pawls to catch in the ratchets and rotate the hub. When the sprocket or cluster rotation is reversed (turned rearward), the pawls ride over the ratchets, enabling the rider to hold the pedals stationary or reverse their rotation while the bicycle is moving forward. In the early days of the freewheel body and sprocket cluster, it was quite mystifying to see a rider come to a stop using the hand brakes while simultaneously pedaling backwards.

Splined- or notched-sprocket clusters are used on virtually all bicycles equipped with a freewheel mechanism, regardless of the manufacturer. The only difference between the two types is the method of removing the complete cluster assembly from the hub and the method of attaching the individual sprockets to the freewheel body.

SERVICE PROCEDURES

All freewheel bodies are identical, except for material, workmanship, number of loose ball bearings, and number and arrangement of spacers or shims. Therefore, carefully note the placement of spacers and count loose ball bearings during disassembly to ensure proper assembly and alignment.

The internal ball bearings, pawls, and pawl spring of the freewheel cluster body are protected by dust rings that minimize the entrance of dirt. However, using the bicycle at the beach or in excessively dusty areas will require frequent disassembling, cleaning, lubricating, and/or overhauling to prevent damaging wear. Precision-built units are expensive; therefore the time and effort spent in cleaning, replacing a broken pawl spring, or replacing worn bearings is well justified.

The young owner of a bicycle who maintains his machine in proper working condition develops a sensitivity for making adjustments, gains an awareness of how mechanical things work, and realizes the importance of adequate lubrication to moving parts.

The first section of this chapter provides complete instructions for removing and installing the rear wheel, including aligning the sprocket cluster on the axle. These procedures begin on page 224.

The second section contains detailed illustrated instructions for complete overhaul of a splined-sprocket cluster; they begin on page 226.

The third section covers disassembly and installation of the sprockets on a notched-freewheel body, which begins on page 233.

The last section of this chapter contains fully illustrated step-by-step procedures for complete overhaul of a freewheel body. The instructions begin on page 236.

REMOVING AND INSTALLING A REAR WHEEL

This section provides illustrated instructions for removing and installing a rear wheel equipped with a freewheel sprocket cluster, including alignment of the cluster on the axle.

REMOVING THE WHEEL

Support the bicycle in the upright position from a bracket, a set of hooks, or a rope attached to the garage ceiling, or secure it in an automobile rear carrier rack attached to the car. Holding the bicycle rigid will make the task of removing, installing, and adjusting the rear wheel and sprocket cluster much easier.

Sight over the tire to see if it will clear the brake shoes. If there is insufficient clearance, it will be necessary to release the brake shoes farther than normal in order to remove the wheel. This is accomplished by first squeezing the rear brake handle slightly, pushing in on the quick-release button, and then releasing the brake handle. This action spreads the caliper arms farther

than normal, allowing the rear wheel to clear the brake shoes. If you are working on a bicycle without the quick-release button, there may be a quick-release lever just above the brake on the cable hanger. Turning this lever will release the brake shoes farther than normal. If neither of these mechanisms is installed, you can remove one of the brake-shoe assemblies by first removing the mounting nut and then pulling out on the brake arm until the shoe and holder clear the wheel and brake arm.

Shift the chain to the smallest (high-gear) sprocket on the rear cluster. On bicycles equipped with a quick-release hub, turn the release lever outward, away from the frame, or from the rearward position to the full forward (unlocked) position. On bicycles without the quick-release mechanism, remove the outside axle nuts.

Rotate the derailleur unit toward the rear to obtain slack in the chain; simultaneously slide the wheel out of the dropouts. Remove the chain from the sprocket. Release the derailleur unit and guide the wheel free of the frame.

For bicycles equipped with a quick-release hub, hold the release lever on one end of the mounting stud, and then remove the adjusting nut from the other end. Remove the tension spring, withdraw the mounting stud from the axle, and then slide off the other spring.

Look into the center of the freewheel body. If there

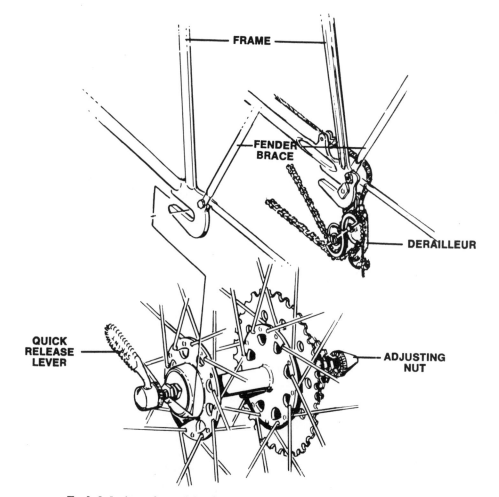

Exploded view of a quick-release rear hub with a sprocket cluster.

are splines around the sides of the opening, you are working on a splined-body freewheel cluster, and the next section of this chapter gives complete instructions for overhauling this type of cluster. If the sides of the interior of the freewheel body are smooth and there are two notches in the bottom of the opening, you are working on a notched-body freewheel cluster. The third section of this chapter provides detailed steps for overhauling this type of cluster.

INSTALLING THE WHEEL

If serrated washers are used, place the washers on each end of the axle, with the serrations facing the hub. Start the axle nuts onto the axle.

For bicycles equipped with a quick-release mechanism, slide one of the tension springs onto the mounting stud against the quick-release body, with the small end of the spring facing the center of the stud. Insert the mounting stud through the axle from the side opposite the sprocket cluster. Install the other tension spring, with the small end facing the hub. Start the adjusting nut onto the stud.

Position the wheel between the frame members, and then engage the chain over the smallest sprocket of the cluster. Pull the derailleur unit rearward and, simultaneously, move the wheel up and into the rear dropouts, with the axle washers positioned on the outside of the frame and outside the derailleur fork-end bracket. Center the wheel in the frame, and then tighten both axle nuts finger-tight. If you are working on a bicycle with a quick-release mechanism, turn the quick-release lever toward the rear to the locked position.

Check the alignment of the sprocket cluster with the chain wheels on the hanger set. If double wheels are used, the center line of the third sprocket of the rear cluster must be aligned midway between the two chain wheels. If three chain wheels are used, the center sprocket of the cluster must be aligned with the center line of the middle chain wheel. If only one chain wheel is installed (as on five-speed bicycles) the center line of the third sprocket of the cluster must be aligned with the center line of the chain wheel. Securely tighten the axle nuts.

If the sprocket cluster is not properly aligned, the hub must be shifted on the axle through movement of the cones. This adjustment requires removing the wheel, removing the sprocket cluster, loosening one cone and tightening the other, reinstalling the cluster, and then mounting the wheel back in the frame.

Pull the derailleur unit rearward to obtain slack in the chain as you move the axle into the dropouts.

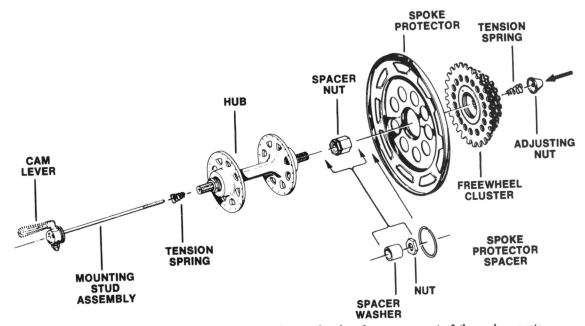

Exploded view of a rear hub with a freewheel cluster, showing the arrangement of the various parts.

On rear hubs equipped with a quick-release mechanism, the axle should extend approximately ⅛ inch beyond the locknuts on each side of the hub. If necessary, remove the wheel, remove the sprocket cluster, shift the hub on the axle (through movement of the

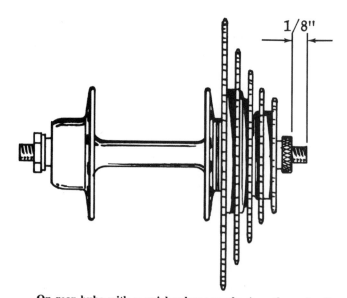

On rear hubs with a quick-release mechanism, the ends of the axle should extend approximately ⅛ inch from the locknuts, as shown. If an adjustment is needed, remove the freewheel cluster and shift the hub on the axle by moving the cones, as discussed in the text.

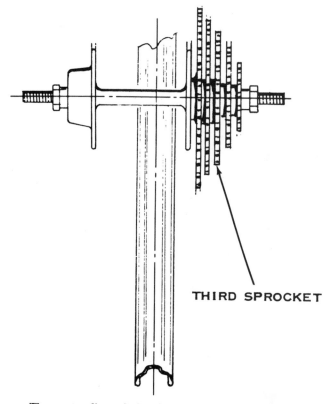

THIRD SPROCKET

The center line of the third sprocket of the rear-wheel cluster must be aligned with the chain wheel(s) at the hanger set, as discussed in the text.

cones), reassemble the complete unit, and then mount it in the frame. Bear in mind when shifting the hub and sprocket cluster that you must maintain proper alignment with the chain wheels mounted on the hanger set.

Return the caliper brakes to the operating position by releasing the locking device. If you removed one of the brake shoe assemblies to gain tire clearance, install the holder, with the closed end facing forward and with the beveled surface of the shoe matching the angle of the wheel rim. The closed end of the security cap will then face rearward, as shown in the accompanying illustration. **CAUTION: Be sure the closed end of the holder is facing forward to prevent the shoe from being forced out when the brakes are applied with subsequent complete loss of braking ability at the rear wheel.**

Adjust the brake shoe holder in the brake-arm slot until the upper edge of the shoe makes contact just below the edge of the rim when the brake lever on the handlebar is squeezed. Tighten the mounting nut securely.

OVERHAULING A SPLINED-BODY SPROCKET CLUSTER

This section contains complete step-by-step illustrated procedures for overhauling a splined-body sprocket cluster. In the text, the sprockets are identified as first, second, third, fourth, and fifth, with the first being the smallest (high-gear) sprocket and the fifth being the largest (low-gear) sprocket. The first and second sprockets have standard right-hand threads. On early model splined clusters (prior to about 1968), the third sprocket also has right-hand threads and the fourth and fifth sprockets have left-hand threads. The third, fourth, and fifth sprockets on almost all splined-body clusters since 1968 slide onto the freewheel body with the internal lugs indexing in slots in the body. The following procedures apply basically to the late model cluster; however, differences between it and the early model are pointed out in the text with supporting illustrations.

For photographic clarity the illustrations were made of a hub without a tire, rim, and spokes. *NOTE:*

②

The procedures begin with the wheel removed from the bicycle.

DISASSEMBLING

① Clamp the complete hub and wheel assembly in a vise, with the jaws gripping the axle and the sprocket cluster facing up. **CAUTION: Use soft vise jaws to protect the axle threads.** Remove the locknut by turning it counterclockwise. Lift the unthreaded spacer off the axle. If you are working on a late-model hub, the spacer is threaded and can be removed by turning it counterclockwise.

② Shift the hub in the vise so that the soft jaws grip the hub. Position a freewheel tool over the axle, with the splines of the tool indexing with the cluster splines. A deluxe freewheel tool shown in the illustration may be used or a less expensive standard one can be used in combination with an end wrench. **CAUTION: Be sure to use the correct tool for the make of sprocket cluster you are working on and check carefully that the tool is fully seated to provide a solid grip in order to prevent damage to the internal splines of the cluster body.** Rotate the tool counterclockwise to loosen the

③

Some clusters use a snap ring to hold the chain protector in place. The snap ring can be pried out with a screwdriver.

cluster. Remove the sprocket cluster and the spoke protector from the hub. Lift off the spoke protector washer, and then take the hub out of the vise.

③ Clamp the sprocket cluster in the vise, with the jaws holding the fifth (largest) sprocket, as shown. Remove the high-gear chain protector using a pin spanner wrench. Rotate it counterclockwise. The protector can also be removed by using a hammer and a drift punch in one of the protector's holes. If you use this method, keep the punch in the same plane as the surface of the protector and use quick, sharp blows of the hammer to jar the protector loose. If the chain protector does not have two holes on its surface, then it is held in place with a snap ring. Pry the ring out of its recess with a screwdriver.

④ Remove the first (smallest) sprocket using a sprocket tool or chain wrench and turning it counterclockwise. An effective chain wrench can be made by attaching a short piece of discarded chain to a length of strap iron, as shown. Remove the second sprocket by turning it counterclockwise with the chain or sprocket wrench.

⑤ Check the interior perimeter of the third sprocket to see if it has three lugs indexed with slots in the freewheel body. If it has the lugs shown, you are working on a late-model unit, and the sprocket can be pulled straight out and off the body. If the sprocket does not have the three lugs, you have an early-model unit and the sprocket must be removed with a chain or sprocket wrench.

④

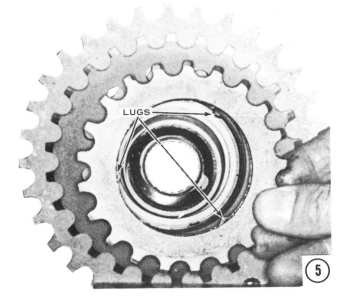

⑥ On the late-model units, pry the spacer ring off the freewheel body with a thin-bladed screwdriver. On early-model units, clamp the freewheel body horizontally in the vise, with the soft jaws gripping the small threaded portion and with the largest sprocket facing up. Remove the fifth and then the fourth sprocket, using a chain or sprocket wrench and turning it clockwise. **CAUTION: The fourth and fifth sprockets have left-hand threads.**

⑦ On late-model units, pull the fourth sprocket, and then remove the spacer ring with a screwdriver. Remove the freewheel body from the back side of the fifth sprocket. Remove the fifth sprocket from the vise.

CLEANING AND INSPECTING

Clean the sprockets, spacers, and exterior surface of the freewheel body with solvent and wipe them dry with a clean lintless cloth.

On early models, the fourth and fifth sprockets are threaded on the cluster body with left-hand threads.

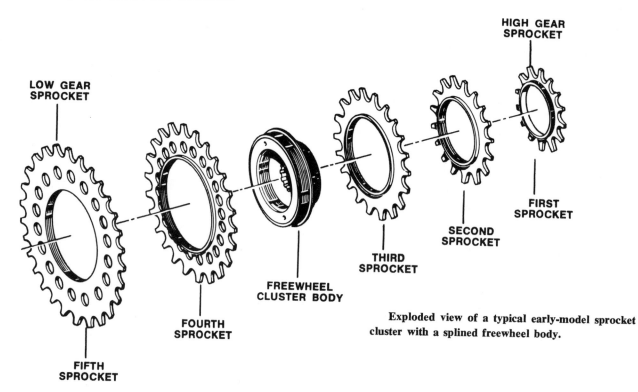

LOW GEAR
SPROCKET

HIGH GEAR
SPROCKET

FIRST
SPROCKET

SECOND
SPROCKET

THIRD
SPROCKET

FREEWHEEL
CLUSTER BODY

FOURTH
SPROCKET

FIFTH
SPROCKET

Exploded view of a typical early-model sprocket cluster with a splined freewheel body.

Carefully inspect each sprocket and the freewheel body for stripped or damaged threads.

Check the teeth of each sprocket for worn edges and for being out of alignment. If any of the teeth are out of line, carefully bend them back with a wrench. Apply even pressure. Try not to bend the teeth back and forth too much as this could cause metal fatigue. The tooth may snap off later under the strain of use.

ASSEMBLING

⑧ Clamp the largest sprocket in the vise, with the jaws gripping the sprocket near its outer edge, as shown. Insert the freewheel body through the opening with the lugs of the sprocket indexing with the slots in the body. If you are working on an early-model unit without the lugs on the inner surface of the sprocket

Installing the fourth and fifth sprockets on an early model, with left-hand threads.

or the slots in the freewheel body, clamp the body in the vise with the soft jaws gripping the smaller set of threads. Turn the fourth (next to the largest) sprocket clockwise onto the freewheel body with the shoulder of the sprocket facing up. **CAUTION: The fourth and fifth sprockets have left-hand threads. Use care when starting to turn the sprocket onto the body to prevent cross-threading.** Turn the fifth sprocket onto the body with the shoulder facing down. *NOTE: The shoulders of the fourth and fifth sprockets must face each other for proper chain clearance.*

⑨ Slide one of the spacer rings onto the freewheel body until it is flush against the fifth sprocket.

⑩ Install the fourth sprocket against the spacer ring, with the lugs indexing with the slots of the freewheel body. Place the other spacer ring on the freewheel body, and then push it flush against the fourth sprocket.

⑪ Position the third sprocket on the freewheel body against the spacer ring. If you are working on an early-model cluster, remove the body from the vise and reclamp it, with the jaws gripping the outer area of the fifth sprocket and with the freewheel body facing

you. Turn the third sprocket onto the body in a clockwise direction.

⑫ Thread the second sprocket onto the freewheel body in a clockwise direction and then the first sprocket. Snugly tighten each sprocket in turn, using a chain or sprocket tool. If you are working on an early-model cluster, check for equal distance between the first, second, and third sprockets. If the distance is not equal, remove the first and second sprockets, and then turn the sprockets around. Reinstall the parts.

⑬ Clamp the sprocket cluster in the vise, with the jaws gripping the fifth sprocket, as shown. Turn the high-gear chain protector clockwise onto the freewheel body, and then firmly tighten it using a pin spanner wrench or a drift punch and hammer. If the chain protector does not have two holes in its surface, then it is held in place with a snap ring. Place the protector in position on the freewheel body, and then force the ring into the recess in the body with a screwdriver.

Prying the snap ring into its recess to hold the chain protector in place.

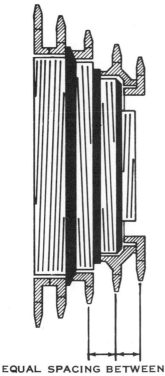

EQUAL SPACING BETWEEN
FIRST, SECOND, AND THIRD SPROCKETS

The center lines of the sprockets will be equally spaced, as shown in this drawing, if the parts have been assembled properly. If not, the sprockets must be disassembled and reassembled as discussed in the text.

⑪ Remove the sprocket cluster from the vise and clamp the hub and wheel in it, with the soft jaws gripping the hub and with the threaded portion of the hub facing up. Place a spoke protector spacer on the hub, and then the spoke protector, with the flat side facing down. Thread the freewheel body onto the hub in a clockwise direction until it is snug. *NOTE: Rotation of the cluster while cycling will tend to tighten it securely on the hub; therefore, a special tool is not needed.* Shift the hub and wheel in the vise, with the soft jaws gripping the axle. Install the spacer and then the locknut.

INSTALLING THE WHEEL

Detailed steps for installing and aligning the wheel are given in the first section of this chapter.

OVERHAULING A NOTCHED-BODY SPROCKET CLUSTER

The following step-by-step illustrated procedures cover overhauling a notched-body sprocket cluster. The sprockets of the cluster are identified as first, second, third, fourth, and fifth, with the first being the smallest (high-gear) sprocket and the fifth being the largest (low-gear) sprocket. The first, second, and third sprockets have standard right-hand threads. The fourth and fifth sprockets have left-hand threads.

For photographic clarity, the following illustra-

tions were made of a hub without the tire, rim, and spokes. *NOTE: The procedures begin with the wheel removed from the bicycle.*

DISASSEMBLING

① Clamp the hub and wheel assembly in a vise equipped with soft jaws, with the jaws gripping the hub and with the sprocket cluster facing up. Place the notched tool (insert) over the axle, with the ears

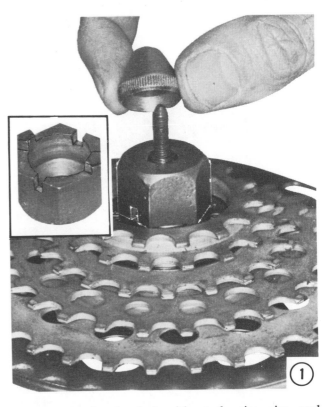

③

clockwise. An effective chain wrench can be made by attaching a short piece of discarded chain to a length of strap iron, as shown. Remove the second and third sprockets by turning them counterclockwise with the sprocket or chain wrench.

① Shift the assembly in the vise to a horizontal position, with the jaws gripping the freewheel body. **CAUTION: Use soft jaws in the vise to protect the threads of the body.** Remove the fifth sprocket by turning it clockwise using the sprocket or chain wrench. **CAUTION: The fourth and fifth sprockets have left-hand threads.** Remove the fourth sprocket in a similar manner.

CLEANING AND INSPECTING

Clean the sprockets and the exterior surface of the freewheel body with solvent and wipe them dry with a clean cloth.

Carefully inspect each sprocket and the freewheel body for stripped or damaged threads.

Check the teeth of each sprocket for worn edges and for being out of alignment. If any of the teeth are out of line, carefully bend them back with a wrench. Apply even pressure. Try not to bend them back and forth too much as this could cause metal fatigue. The teeth may snap off later under the strain of use.

ASSEMBLING

⑤ Clamp the freewheel body in the vise, with the jaws gripping the smaller set of threads. **CAUTION: Use soft vise jaws to protect the threads of the body.** Turn the fourth (next to the largest) sprocket counterclockwise onto the freewheel body, with the shoulder of the sprocket facing up. Tighten the sprocket firmly using a sprocket or chain wrench. **CAUTION: The fourth and fifth sprockets have left-hand threads.** Use care when starting the sprockets onto the body to prevent cross-threading. Turn the fifth sprocket onto the body, with the shoulder facing down. *NOTE: The shoulders of the fourth and fifth sprockets must face each other for the proper chain clearance.*

of the tool fully indexed in the slots of the freewheel body. Turn the adjusting nut onto the axle finger-tight against the tool, and then back it off approximately ½ turn to allow the cluster body to "break loose" from the hub.

② Turn the wheel over in the vise, with the jaws gripping the flats of the notched tool. Turn the quick-release lever to the locked position. If standard axle nuts are used, thread the nuts onto the axle in the normal manner to keep the tool from slipping out of the slots of the freewheel body. Grasp the wheel and turn it counterclockwise to loosen the freewheel body from the hub. When you feel it loosen, remove the hub from the vise, remove the axle or adjusting nuts, and then rotate the cluster counterclockwise until it is free of the hub.

③ Clamp the sprocket cluster in a vise, with the jaws gripping the largest (low-gear) sprocket, as shown. Remove the first (smallest) sprocket using a sprocket tool or a chain wrench and turning it counter-

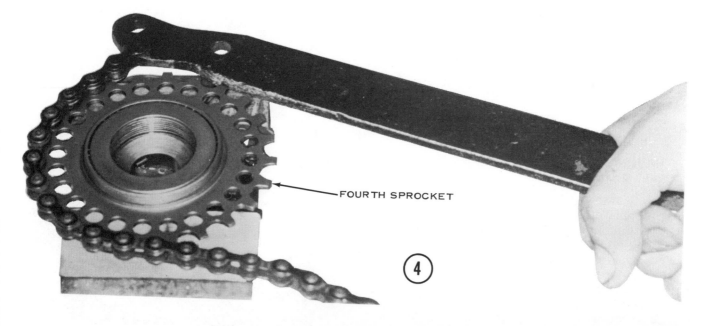

FOURTH SPROCKET

④

FIFTH SPROCKET

⑤

This holding jig is available for clamping the freewheel body and sprocket cluster in the vise without damaging the threads.

⑥

⑥ Shift the sprocket assembly in the vise to a vertical position, with the jaws gripping the largest sprocket. Carefully thread the third, second, and first sprockets clockwise onto the freewheel body, with the shoulder of each facing the fourth sprocket. *NOTE: The sprockets must be installed with one shoulder between each sprocket for the proper chain clearance.* Tighten each sprocket in turn using a sprocket or chain wrench. Remove the sprocket cluster from the vise,

and then clamp the hub and wheel in it, with the soft jaws gripping the hub, and with the threaded portion of the hub facing up. Place a spoke protector spacer on the hub, and then the spoke protector, with the flat side facing down. Thread the freewheel body onto the hub in a clockwise direction until it is snug. *NOTE: Rotation of the cluster while cycling will tend to tighten it securely on the hub; therefore, a special tool is not needed.* Shift the hub and wheel in the vise, with the soft jaws gripping the axle. Install the spacer and then the locknut.

INSTALLING THE WHEEL

Detailed steps for installing and aligning the wheel are given in the first section of this chapter.

OVERHAULING A FREEWHEEL BODY

This section provides complete step-by-step illustrated instructions for overhauling a splined- or notched-freewheel cluster body. The following procedures apply basically to the splined-freewheel body; however, differences between it and the notched-freewheel body are pointed out in the text with supporting illustrations.

For photographic clarity, the illustrations were made of a hub without the tire, rim, and spokes. *NOTE: The procedures begin with the wheel removed from the bicycle.*

DISASSEMBLING

① Clamp the complete hub and wheel assembly in a vise, with the jaws gripping the axle and with the sprocket cluster facing up. **CAUTION: Use soft vise jaws to protect the axle threads.** Remove the locknut by turning it counterclockwise. Lift the unthreaded spacer off the axle. If you are working on a late-model hub, the spacer is threaded and can be removed by turning it counterclockwise. Look into the center of the freewheel body. If there are splines around the sides of the opening, you are working on a splined-body

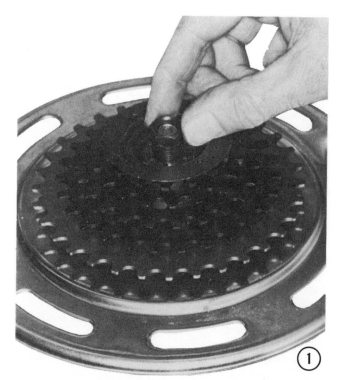

①

②

freewheel cluster. If the sides of the interior of the freewheel body are smooth and there are two notches in the bottom of the opening, you are working on a notched-body freewheel cluster.

② *For the splined-body sprocket cluster,* proceed as follows: Shift the hub in the vise so the soft jaws grip the hub. Position the proper freewheel tool over the axle, with the splines of the tool indexing with the internal splines of the freewheel body. The illustration shows a deluxe freewheel tool being used; however, a less expensive standard tool is available and can be used in combination with an end wrench. **CAUTION: Be sure the tool is the correct one for the make of sprocket you are working on and check carefully that the tool is fully seated to provide a solid grip in order to prevent damage to the internal splines of the cluster body.** Rotate the tool counterclockwise to loosen the cluster. Take off the sprocket cluster and spoke protector. Remove the spoke protector washer, and then lift the hub out of the vise.

③ *For the notched-body sprocket cluster,* proceed as follows: Clamp the hub and wheel assembly in a vise equipped with soft jaws, with the jaws gripping the hub and with the sprocket cluster facing up. Place the notched tool over the axle, with the ears of the tool fully indexed in the slots of the freewheel body. Turn an axle or adjusting nut onto the axle finger-tight against the tool, and then back it off approximately ½ turn to allow the cluster body to "break loose" from the hub. Turn the wheel over in the vise, with the jaws gripping the flats of the notched tool. Turn the quick-release lever to the locked position. If standard axle nuts are used, thread the nuts onto the axle in a normal manner to keep the tool

To remove a notched body sprocket, turn the wheel over in the vise, and then turn the quick-release lever to the locked position.

from slipping out of the slots of the freewheel body. Grasp the wheel and turn it counterclockwise in order to loosen the freewheel body from the hub. Remove the hub from the vise, take off the axle or adjusting nut, and then rotate the cluster counterclockwise until it is free of the hub.

④ Clamp the freewheel tool in a vise, with the jaws gripping the flats, as shown. Place the cluster over the tool, with the largest sprocket facing down, until the splines of the freewheel body index with the splines of the tool.

③

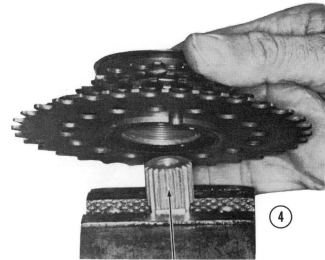

④

STANDARD FREEWHEEL TOOL

⑤

⑤ Remove the chain protector by turning it counterclockwise with a pin spanner wrench. It can also be removed by using a hammer and drift punch set in one of the protector's holes. If you use this method, keep the punch as horizontal as possible and use quick sharp blows with the hammer to jar the protector loose. If the chain protector does not have two holes on its surface, then it is held in place with a snap ring, which can be pried out of its recess with a screwdriver.

⑥ Rotate the bearing race in a clockwise direction with a pin spanner wrench, or drift punch and hammer. **CAUTION: The bearing race has left-hand threads and must be turned clockwise to remove it.** Remove the cluster assembly from the vise. Turn it

over; catch and count the loose ball bearings and spacers. Pay particular attention to the number of spacers because they provide the adjustment for the freewheel body.

⑦ Pry out the dust ring with a screwdriver. Work around the freewheel body and be careful not to crimp or distort the ring. Turn the cluster over; catch and count the loose ball bearings. Remove the main freewheel body from the cluster assembly.

⑧ Pry the pawl spring out of its recess with a screwdriver, and then remove the pawls.

CLEANING AND INSPECTING

Clean all parts in solvent and blow dry with compressed air, or wipe them dry with a lintless cloth.

⑥

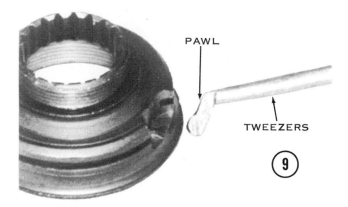

Keep all cleaned parts on paper towels to avoid contamination. Cover them with a clean towel to keep grit from entering the internal areas of the main cluster body or settling on the ball bearings. A tiny piece of grit can do a tremendous amount of damage if allowed to work on a part over an extended period of time or while the wheel is turning at high speed.

Carefully inspect the ball bearings for signs of excessive wear (dull spots), pits (pencil-point dots), or cracks and replace the complete set of bearings if any one of them is damaged. Replacing the entire set will ensure even distribution of the bearing load on all the bearings.

Thoroughly inspect the main cluster body. Check the internal and external parts for stripped threads;

bearing surfaces for scratchlike scores or pits; and the internal splines for cracks, chips, or broken edges.

Check the pawls for broken edges, cracks, or signs of excessive wear.

Inspect the pawl spring for a crack or loss of tension.

Inspect the dust ring to be sure it is not bent or distorted, something that could have happened during disassembly.

Check the bearing race for stripped threads. Bear in mind that it has left-hand threads. Check the bearing surface for scores, pits, or corrosion.

Check the shims for cracks, distortion, or signs of excessive wear from damaged bearings.

ASSEMBLING

⑨ Place the pawls into the recesses of the main cluster body, with the contour of the pawl following that of the body, as shown.

⑩ Secure the pawls in place with the pawl spring. Check to be sure the spring is fully seated in the slots of the pawls, with one end of the spring on each side of the projection, as shown in the accompanying illustration.

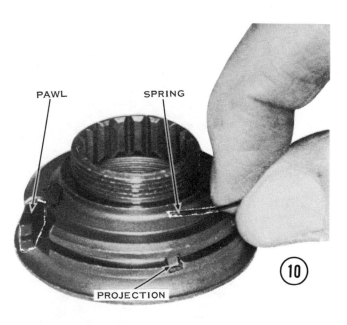

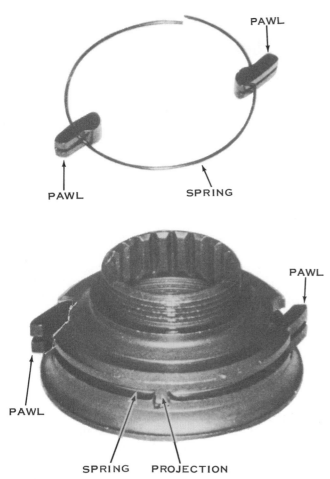

PAWL

PAWL

SPRING

PAWL

PAWL

SPRING   PROJECTION

Arrangement of the pawls and spring (top), with the parts assembled to the freewheel body. Note that the ends of the spring must straddle the projection, as shown in the bottom view.

⑪ Lay the cluster on the bench with the largest sprocket facing up. Apply a generous amount of multi-purpose lubricant to the bearing race.

⑫ Imbed the same number of loose ball bearings into the lubricant as you counted during disassembly. *NOTE: The number of bearings may vary with different models of freewheel bodies.*

⑬ If the count was lost during disassembly, insert enough ball bearings to fill the perimeter of the bearing race snugly, and then take one out for clearance.

⑭ Place the main freewheel body in position on top of the bearings, with the external threads facing down.

⑮ Depress each of the pawls to their retracted position, and then push the main freewheel body down until its upper surface is below the surface of the outer body by approximately the thickness of the dust ring.

⑯ Place the dust ring on top of the main freewheel body, and then tap it into position with a mallet. The ring must seat flush with the surface of the outer body flange to hold the main body and the bearings.

⑰ Turn the complete cluster unit over and apply a light coating of multipurpose lubricant to the bearing cup of the main body.

⑱ Insert the same number of shims you counted during disassembly. *NOTE: The shims provide the bearing adjustment.*

⑲ Spread a thin coating of multipurpose lubricant on top of the shims. Imbed the same number of loose ball bearings into the lubricant as you counted

during disassembly. *NOTE: The number of bearings on this side may also vary with different models of freewheel bodies.* If the count was lost, insert enough ball bearings to fill the cup snugly, and then remove one bearing for clearance.

⑳ Thread the bearing race into the main body by turning it counterclockwise. **CAUTION: The bearing race has left-hand threads.** Securely tighten the bearing race with a pin spanner wrench or a drift punch and hammer. Check the assembly and bearing

adjustment as follows: Hold the freewheel body in your left hand and rotate the sprocket cluster in both directions. The sprocket cluster should rotate freely and without side play when it is turned counterclockwise. You should be able to hear the pawls riding over the internal ratchets. The pawls should catch when you attempt to turn the cluster clockwise, also causing the body to rotate in your left hand. If the body is too tight, remove the bearing race and add a shim. If the body has side play, remove the bearing race, take out a shim, and then reinstall the race. Recheck the adjustment again. Remove or install shims until the cluster rotates freely, but without side play.

㉑ Turn the high-gear chain protector clockwise onto the main body until it is snug. *NOTE: The notched-body sprocket cluster does not have a chain protector.*

㉒ Clamp the hub and wheel assembly in the vise, with the soft jaws gripping the hub and with the threaded portion of the hub facing up. Place a spoke protector spacer on the hub, and then position the spoke protector so that the flat side faces down. Thread the cluster unit clockwise onto the hub until it is snug. *NOTE: Rotation of the cluster while cycling will tend to tighten it securely; therefore, no special tool is needed.*

㉓ Shift the hub and wheel in the vise so the

soft jaws grip the axle. Install the spacer and then the locknut.

INSTALLING THE WHEEL

Detailed steps for installing and aligning the wheel are given in the first section of this chapter.

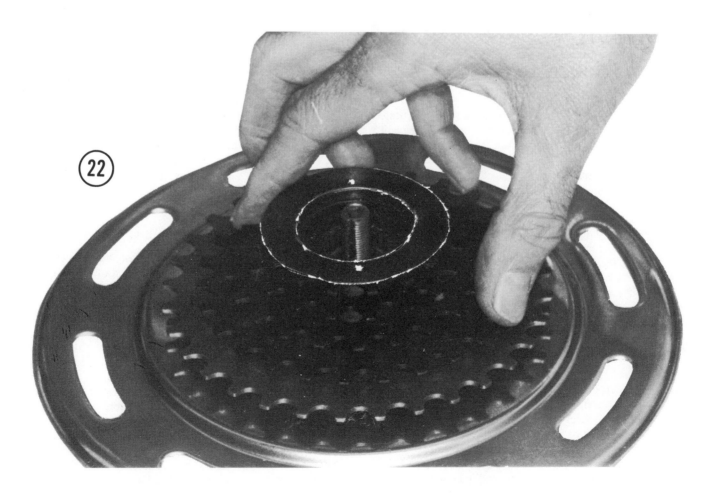

7
OVERHAULING
REAR DERAILLEURS

The term *derailleur* is derived from the French "to derail," and means simply a device to move the chain on a bicycle from one sprocket to another.

Actually, the rear derailleur unit has two important functions to perform. First, it must move the chain back and forth from one sprocket to another and, second, it must keep the chain under constant tension. The length of the chain required when it is engaged on the smallest sprocket at the rear wheel and on the smaller chain wheel at the hanger set is much less than the opposite combination, when the chain is engaged on both of the largest sprockets—front and rear.

All rear derailleurs, regardless of make, style, or the precision of parts used in their construction, operate on the same basic principle. Two small pulleys, housed in a cage assembly, move by means of two traversing arms under spring tension and are actuated through connecting cable linkage to an operating shift lever, mounted at the front of the bicycle. The traversing arms, together with the cage holding the pulleys, form and maintain a perfect parallelogram. It is this principle that allows the upper or "jockey" pulley to stay in vertical alignment with each sprocket of the cluster and thus shift the chain from one sprocket to another. The pulley cage is under spring tension to keep the lower pulley forced toward the rear of the bicycle and the chain tight when it is engaged on any possible combination of front and rear sprockets.

Limit screws are installed to restrict the amount of jockey pulley travel for the largest (low-gear) sprocket and the smallest (high-gear) sprocket.

SERVICE PROCEDURES

Because the derailleur is exposed, it is easily damaged if the bicycle should fall on its right side. Sand, dirt, and other abrasive materials thrown onto it by the rear wheel and chain cause the mechanism to require periodic cleaning, lubricating, adjustment, or overhaul.

To the owner of a five-, ten-, or fifteen-speed bicycle equipped with a five-sprocket cluster attached to the rear hub, the rear derailleur unit is one of the most critical pieces of equipment on his bike. If the derailleur is not adjusted correctly, or is not functioning properly to give him the changes of gear ratios required on a tour or during a race, his machine may be reduced to a single-speed unit.

The first section of this chapter provides complete procedures for removing, installing, and adjusting a rear derailleur unit. The location of adjustment screws, method of attachment to the bicycle, and control cable hookup may vary among manufacturers, but the principles are basically alike and the following instructions cover typical units.

The second section gives detailed procedures for complete overhaul of a Sprint, Huret Alvit, Huret Svelto, Schwinn-Approved, Shimano 3.3.3, Shimano Lark, and Sun Tour derailleur and begins on page 250.

The third section contains instructions for overhauling a Campagnolo Record, Campagnolo Gran Sport, Campagnolo Nuovo Record, and Simplex Prestige unit, and begins on page 258.

The fourth section has the illustrated procedures for overhauling a Shimano Sun Tour GT derailleur, and begins on page 266.

REMOVING THE DERAILLEUR UNIT

The following step-by-step illustrated instructions cover removal of a typical derailleur unit. Though the method of attachment to the bicycle, and control cable hookup may vary, the principle is similar for all derailleurs and the following procedures can be easily used for all such units.

① Support the bicycle in an upright position with the rear wheel clear of the floor. Holding the bicycle rigid will make the task of removing, installing, and adjusting much easier. Sight over the tire to see if it will clear the brake shoes. If there is insufficient clearance, it will be necessary to release the brake shoes farther than normal in order to remove the wheel. This can be accomplished by first squeezing the rear-brake handle slightly, pushing in on the quick-release button, and then releasing the brake handle.

This action releases the caliper arms farther than normal, allowing the rear wheel to clear the brake shoes. If the bicycle is not equipped with a quick-release button on the brake handle, there may be a quick-release lever just above the brake bridge on the cable hanger. Turning this lever will release the brake shoes farther than normal. If neither of these quick-release mechanisms is used, take off the mounting nut from one of the brake-shoe holders as shown, and then remove the complete brake-shoe assembly.

② Hold the wheel and loosen both axle nuts. If the bicycle you are working on is equipped with a quick-release mechanism, turn the lever 180° from the locked position.

③ Pull the derailleur unit rearward and, while holding it in this position, push the wheel forward and down, to clear it of the rear frame dropouts.

④ Look at the inside arm of the cage assembly. If one end of the arm has a hook, as installed on a Sun Tour GT derailleur, loosen the spindle nut slightly at the hook, pivot the arm, and then lift the chain free

of the tension pulley. If the inside arm does not pivot, remove the tension pulley spindle and the pulley from the cage. This simple step eliminates the need for breaking (separating) the chain in order to remove the derailleur.

⑤ Loosen the cable anchor nut, pull the cable free of the anchor bolt, and then draw it out of the cable adjusting barrel. Loosen the mounting bolt securing the derailleur fork-end bracket to the frame. Slide the bracket free of the rear frame dropout. If the derailleur is attached directly to the frame, hold the pivot bolt with the correct size Allen wrench, and then remove the locknut. Turn the pivot bolt counterclock-

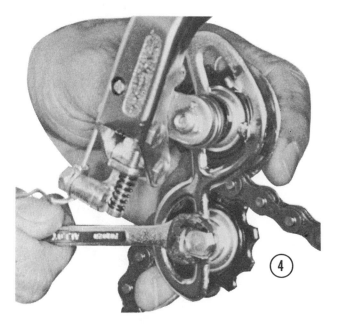

wise until it is free of the frame, and then remove the derailleur, shim washer, stop plate, and spacer, as shown in the accompanying illustration.

INSTALLING THE DERAILLEUR UNIT

The following illustrated procedures provide step-by-step instructions for installing a derailleur unit on the bicycle.

⑥ Guide the fork-end bracket of the derailleur into the rear-frame dropout, with the nut on one side of the frame and the bracket on the other side, until the shoulder of the nut seats against the end of the dropout slot. Align the slot in the bracket with the slot of the dropout, and then tighten the nut securely. To install a Shimano Lark derailleur unit, line up the vertical line across the name on the fork-end bracket with the chain stay. To install a derailleur unit without a fork-end bracket, insert the pivot bolt into the outer arm. Slide a thick spacer onto the pivot bolt with the rounded side facing the derailleur, as shown in the accompanying illustration. Install the stop plate on the pivot bolt, with the small pin facing outward, and then install the shim washer. Thread the pivot bolt into the mounting hole on the fork-end of the bicycle frame securely, and then back it off about ¼ turn, or until the derailleur unit pivots freely without side play. Hold the pivot bolt adjustment and thread the locknut on tightly. Check the pivot bolt adjustment and tighten or loosen it as required by first backing off the locknut

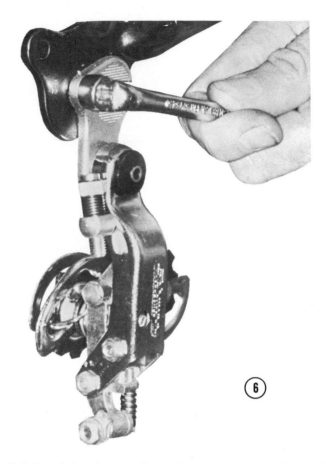

⑥

slightly, tightening or loosening the pivot bolt, and then retightening the locknut.

⑦ Check the pivot bolt adjustment. The derailleur unit should pivot freely without side play. If an adjustment is required after it is mounted on the bicycle, hold the pivot bolt with an Allen wrench and loosen the locknut. Tighten or loosen the pivot bolt, and then retighten the locknut.

Arrangement of the parts on the pivot bolt of a derailleur unit attached directly to the bicycle frame.

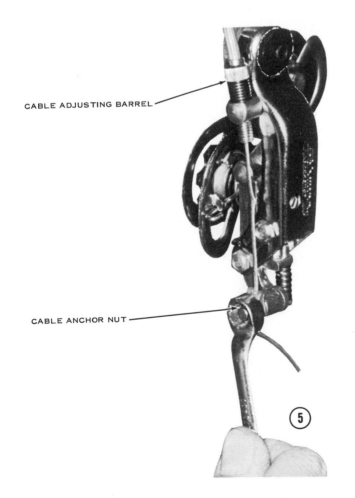

CABLE ADJUSTING BARREL

CABLE ANCHOR NUT

⑤

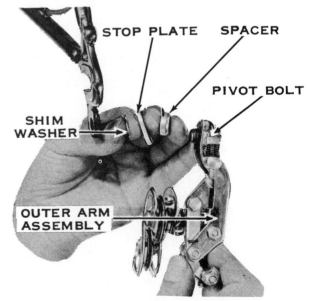

STOP PLATE   SPACER

PIVOT BOLT

SHIM WASHER

OUTER ARM ASSEMBLY

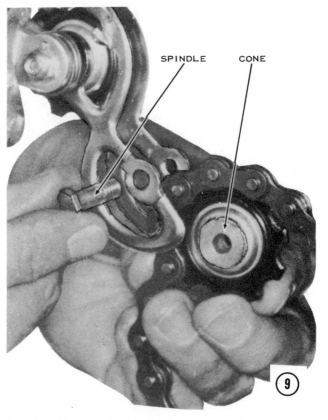

⑧ Feed the control cable through the guide, adjusting barrel, and anchor bolt. Secure the anchor bolt finger-tight to hold the cable in place.

⑨ Engage the chain on the tension pulley, and

then install the pulley into the cage with the spindle. Tighten the spindle, and then lift the chain clear of the pulley. Check the pulley for free rotation without side play. If an adjustment is required, loosen the spindle slightly, tighten or loosen the cone of the pulley, and then retighten the spindle. If the inner arm of the cage assembly is a pivot type, engage the chain on

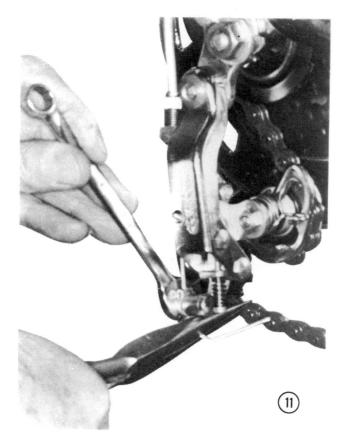

(11)

until resistance is experienced in turning the lever to the locked position.

⑪ Place the rear shift lever in the full-forward position, and then check to see that the chain is still engaged on the smallest sprocket. Pull the control cable taut, and then secure it by tightening the anchor nut. Install a plastic cap over the end of the cable.

⑫ Replace the brake shoe assembly with the closed end of the holder facing forward. **CAUTION: The closed end of the holder must face forward to prevent the shoe from working out when the brakes are applied, which would result in a complete loss of braking ability at the rear wheel.** If the bicycle is equipped with a brake-release lever or button, return the lever or the brake handle to the normal operating position.

ADJUSTING THE DERAILLEUR UNIT

⑬ Place the chain on the smallest sprocket and the shift lever in the high-gear (full-forward) position. Rotate the high-gear adjusting screw clockwise or counterclockwise until the center line of the jockey pulley is aligned with the center line of the smallest sprocket.

⑭ Move the chain to the largest (low-gear) sprocket either by hand or by using the shift lever. Set the shift lever to the low-gear (full-rearward) position. Adjust the low-gear screw until the center line of the jockey pulley is aligned with the center line of the largest sprocket.

⑮ To make an alternate adjustment for the high-gear sprocket, proceed as follows: Position the chain onto the second smallest sprocket by hand. Turn in the high-gear limit screw until it contacts the main traversing arm and holds the chain on the second

the pulley, pivot the arm until the hook engages over the spindle nut, and then tighten the nut.

⑩ Position the wheel between the frame members, and then engage the chain over the smallest sprocket. Pull the derailleur unit rearward and, simultaneously, move the wheel up and into the rear dropouts, with the axle washers on the outside of the frame and outside the derailleur fork-end bracket. Center the wheel in the frame, and then tighten both axle nuts. If you are working on a bicycle with a quick-release mechanism, turn the quick-release lever toward the frame to lock the wheel in place. If the lever does not turn with some effort, tighten the adjusting nut

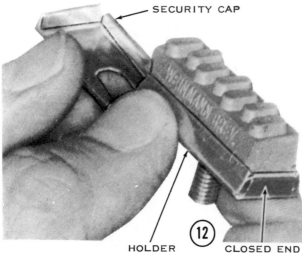

SECURITY CAP

HOLDER   (12)   CLOSED END

PULLEYS ALIGNED
WITH SMALL SPROCKET   (13)

smallest sprocket. Place the control lever in the high-gear position, and then loosen the cable anchor bolt slightly. Rotate the cranks in the driving direction and, at the same time, turn out the high-gear limit screw until the chain drops down onto the smallest sprocket. Pull the cable through the anchor bolt until it is taut, and then tighten the bolt firmly. Force the shift lever down several times to prestress the cable.

MAKING A MAJOR ADJUSTMENT

NOTE: The following four steps are considered major adjustments and should be performed only if necessary and with caution to prevent damage to the derailleur. Steps ⑯ and ⑰ apply to the Sprint, Huret Alvit, Huret Svelto, Schwinn-Approved, Shimano 3.3.3, Shimano Lark, and Sun Tour derailleurs. Steps ⑱ and ⑲ apply to the Campagnolo Record, Campagnolo Gran Sport, Campagnolo Nuovo Record, and Simplex Prestige derailleurs.

SPRINT, HURET ALVIT, HURET SVELTO, SCHWINN APPROVED, SHIMANO 3.3.3, SHIMANO LARK, AND SUN TOUR

⑯ Check the *vertical* alignment of the derailleur by sighting along the plane of the pulleys while the pulleys are in a *vertical* position. The vertical center line of the pulleys should be parallel with the plane of the sprockets. If the derailleur is out of line, twist the outer arm with a wrench until the pulleys are properly positioned.

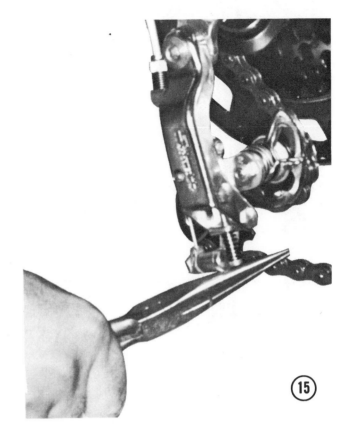

⑮

⑰ Check the *horizontal* alignment of the derailleur by sighting along the plane of the pulleys while the pulleys are in a *horizontal* position. The center line of the pulleys should be parallel with the plane of the sprockets. If the derailleur is out of line, twist the outer arm with a wrench until the pulleys are properly positioned.

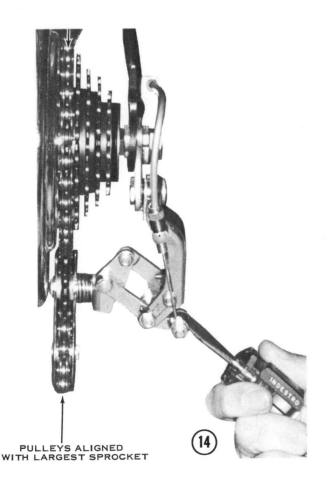

PULLEYS ALIGNED
WITH LARGEST SPROCKET

⑭

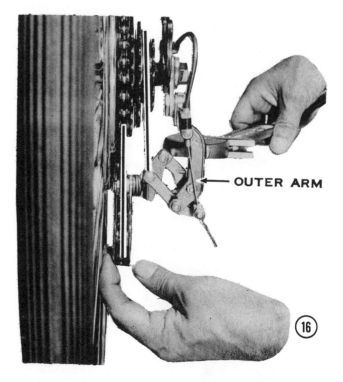

← OUTER ARM

⑯

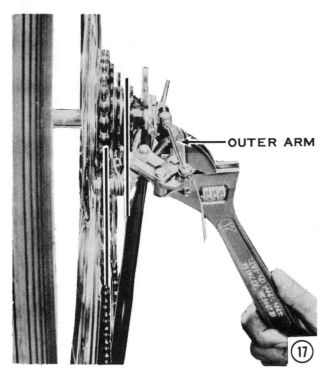

OUTER ARM

(17)

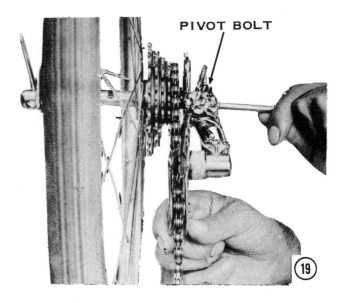

PIVOT BOLT

(19)

⑲ Check the *horizontal* alignment of the derailleur by sighting along the plane of the pulleys while the pulleys are in the *horizontal* position. The center line of the pulleys should be parallel with the plane of the sprockets. If the derailleur is out of line bend the derailleur by using the correct size Allen wrench in the pivot bolt for leverage.

Campagnolo Record, Campagnolo Gran Sport, Campagnolo Nuovo Record, and Simplex Prestige

⑱ Check the *vertical* alignment of the derailleur by sighting along the plane of the pulleys while the pulleys are in the *vertical* position. The vertical center line of the pulleys should be parallel with the plane of the sprockets. If the derailleur is out of line, bend the derailleur into position using a wrench, or better still, use an Allen wrench fitted in the pivot bolt as a lever to bend the unit. Using the Allen wrench will prevent damage to the finished surfaces.

OVERHAULING A SPRINT, HURET ALVIT, HURET SVELTO, SCHWINN-APPROVED, SHIMANO 3.3.3, SHIMANO LARK, AND SUN TOUR REAR DERAILLEUR

The following step-by-step illustrated instructions cover disassembling, cleaning and inspecting, and as-

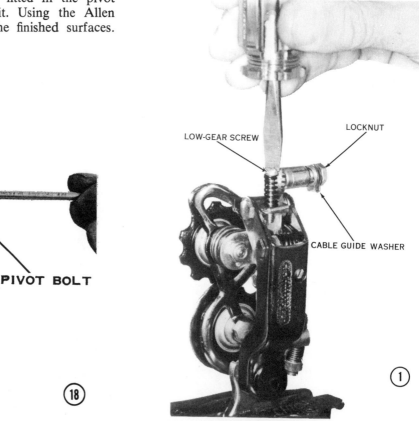

LOW-GEAR SCREW

LOCKNUT

CABLE GUIDE WASHER

PIVOT BOLT

(18)

(1)

sembling a Sprint, Huret Alvit, Huret Svelto, Schwinn-Approved, Shimano 3.3.3, Shimano Lark, and Sun Tour rear derailleur unit. The illustrations were made of a Schwinn-Approved rear derailleur, which is similar to the other units.

The first section of this chapter gives complete procedures for removing, installing, and adjusting the derailleur.

Each derailleur assembly can be identified by the manufacturer's name embossed on the exposed surface of the outer arm. An exploded drawing showing all parts of the derailleurs listed for this section follows the Cleaning and Inspecting instructions. The instructions begin with the derailleur removed from the bicycle.

DISASSEMBLING

① Clamp the derailleur unit in a vise, with the jaws gripping the fork-end bracket. **CAUTION: Use soft vise jaws to keep from damaging the finish on the fork-end bracket.** Remove the low-gear limit screw and spring. Remove the locknut, cable guide washer, and cable anchor bolt. *NOTE: Numerous shims, spacers, washers, and bushings are used throughout this derailleur unit and they vary in number and placement, depending on the manufacturer. Remove the parts slowly and carefully in order to bear in mind their arrangement as an aid to assembly.*

② Remove the locknut from the long pulley cage spindle. Use a wide-bladed screwdriver to turn the spindle counterclockwise out of the outer arm. Remove the complete cage assembly, pulley cage spring, bushing, and shims from the mounting plate.

③ Remove the locknuts from the three pivot

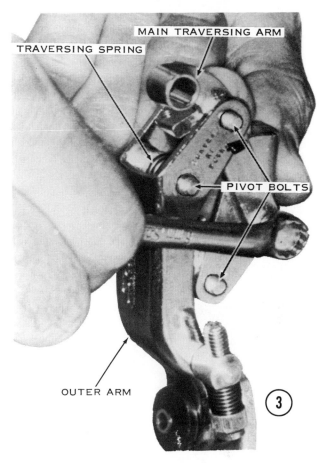

PULLEY CAGE SPRING

MOUNTING PLATE

②

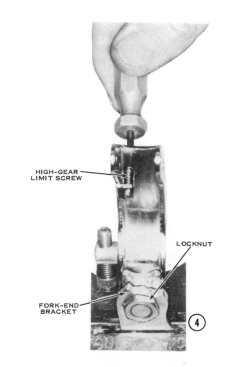

MAIN TRAVERSING ARM

TRAVERSING SPRING

PIVOT BOLTS

OUTER ARM

③

bolts. Unhook the traversing spring from the outer arm. Turn the two pivot bolts out, and then remove the main traversing arm and mounting plate. Back out the pivot bolt passing through the traversing spring, and then remove the spring and bushings.

④ Take off the high-gear limit screw and spring. Remove the locknut from the fork-end bracket pivot bolt.

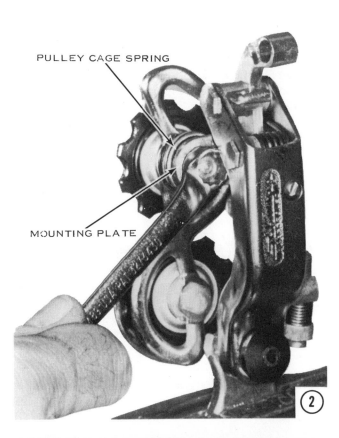

HIGH-GEAR LIMIT SCREW

LOCKNUT

FORK-END BRACKET

④

CABLE ADJUSTING BARREL

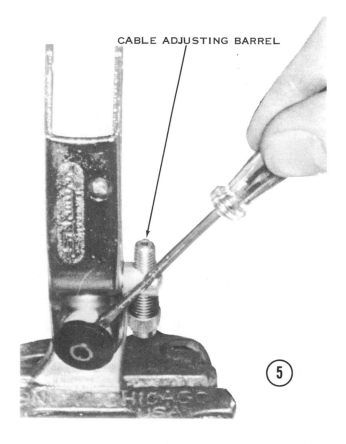

⑤

⑥

⑤ Snap the cap off the pivot bolt. Turn the pivot bolt counterclockwise with an Allen wrench until the bolt is clear of the fork-end bracket. Separate the outer arm and the pivot bolt from the bracket. Lift the outer arm off the pivot bolt. The shim washer, stop plate, and spacer will come off with it. Remove the cable adjusting barrel and spring.

⑥ Remove the remaining spindle from the inner cage assembly and separate the two halves, which will free the pulleys. Remove the cone bushing from each pulley. Remove and count the loose ball bearings.

CLEANING AND INSPECTING

Clean all parts in solvent and blow them dry with compressed air, or wipe them dry with a lintless cloth. Keep all cleaned parts on paper towels to avoid contamination. Cover them with a clean towel to keep grit from entering the internal parts and bearings.

Carefully inspect the loose ball bearings for signs of excessive wear (dull spots), pits (pencil-point dots), or cracks. Replace the complete set if any of them are damaged to ensure even distribution of the bearing load on all the ball bearings.

Check all threaded parts for stripped threads.

Inspect the springs for cracks, lost tension, or corrosion.

Inspect the bearing surface of the pulleys for pits or scores (scratchlike marks). Check the teeth of the pulleys for cracks or worn edges, indicating excessive wear.

Inspect the bearing surface of the cone bushings for pits or scores.

Check the arms to be sure they are not bent or damaged.

Check the inner and outer sides of the cage assembly for bending, distortion, or damage.

ASSEMBLING

CAUTION: The derailleur assembly has many threaded aluminum parts. Use care when installing bolts or spindles to prevent stripping the threads by over-tightening.

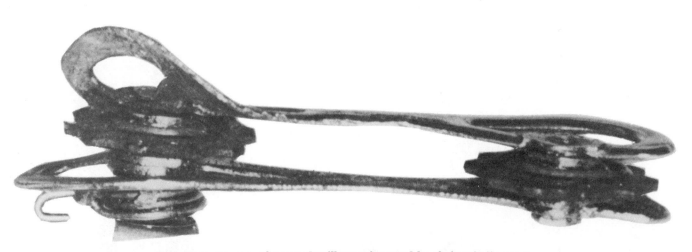

Damage to the cage of a rear derailleur unit caused by chain misalignment.

⑦ Place the same number of loose ball bearings in the bearing race of each pulley as you counted during disassembly. If the count was lost, insert half the total number you have in each pulley, or until they fit with a small amount of clearance between each bearing, but not enough so you could insert another one. Apply a thin coating of multipurpose lubricant over the bearings.

⑧ Thread a cone bushing finger-tight into each pulley. Hold each side of the cone bushing with your thumb and forefinger and spin the pulley to be sure it rotates freely. It must not have any side play when you attempt to wiggle the pulley on the cone bushing. If the pulley drags or has side play, loosen or tighten the cone bushing as required.

⑨ Arrange the inner and outer cage sides and

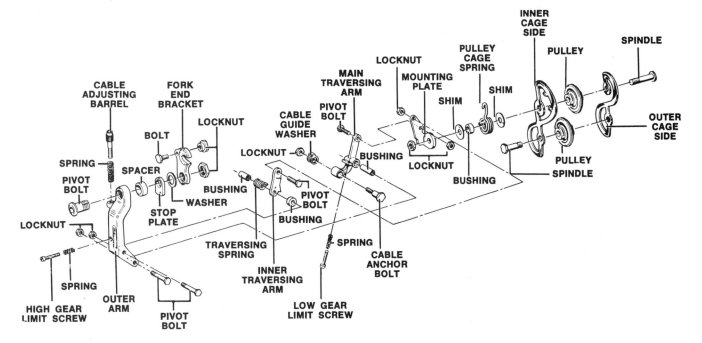

Exploded view of a Sprint, Huret-Alvit, Huret Svelto, Schwinn-Approved, Shimano 3.3.3, Shimano Lark, and Sun Tour rear derailleur unit.

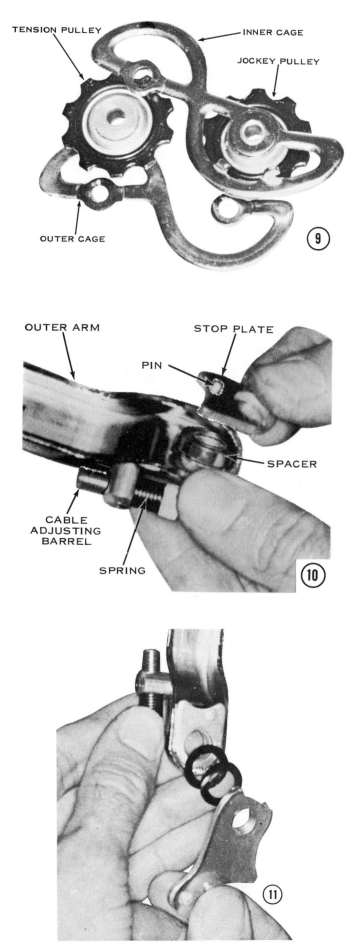

the two pulleys in the pattern shown, with the extended threaded area of the jockey pulley facing up, and the spring hooks on the inner cage side facing away from the pulleys. Turn the jockey pulley tightly into the inner cage. Check the pulley for freedom of rotation, with just a discernible amount of side play. Back the pulley out of the cage and adjust the cone bushing, if necessary. Insert the short spindle through the inner cage, through the tension pulley, and into the threaded hole in the closed loop of the outer cage. *NOTE: If the tension pulley was removed to keep from breaking (separating) the chain for removal of the derailleur from the bicycle, do not install it at this time. It will be installed later.* Tighten the spindle securely, and set the assembly to one side.

⑩   Slide the spring onto the cable-adjusting barrel, and then thread it partway into the outer arm. Place the spacer in position on the outer arm, with the rounded edge facing the arm. Install the stop plate on the spacer, with the pin facing away from the outer arm.

⑪   Install the same number of shims you noted during disassembly, and then the fork-end bracket, with the knurled surface facing down, in the position shown. Insert the pivot bolt from the manufacturer's identification side of the outer arm, and then thread it into the fork-end bracket.

⑫   Clamp the fork-end bracket in a vise with soft jaws. Tighten the pivot bolt with an Allen wrench, and then back it off approximately ¼ turn or until the outer arm moves freely without side play. Adjust the pivot bolt, if necessary.

⑬   Hold the pivot bolt adjustment with an Allen wrench; install and tighten the locknut. Check the outer arm again for freedom to rotate without side play.

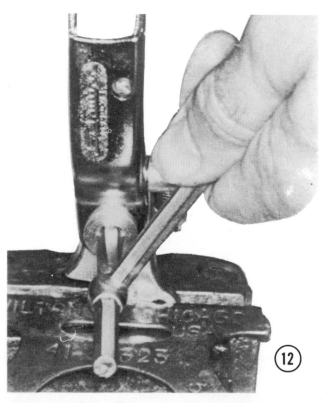

SPRING

HIGH-GEAR LIMIT SCREW

⑬

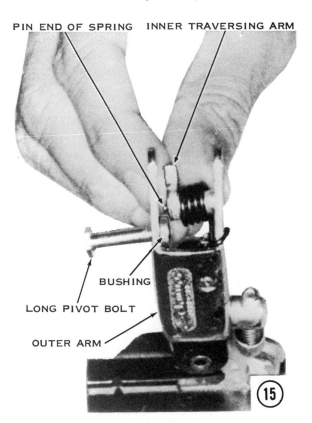

PIN END OF SPRING   INNER TRAVERSING ARM

BUSHING

LONG PIVOT BOLT

OUTER ARM

⑮

Adjust the pivot bolt as required by first loosening the locknut slightly, making the adjustment, and then retightening the locknut. Snap the cap over the pivot bolt head. Place the high-gear limit spring between the outer arm and the flange. Thread the high-gear limit screw about five turns into the flange as a preliminary setting.

⑭ Connect the inner traversing arm to the mounting plate, as shown. Insert the shorter pivot bolt through the recessed end of the inner traversing arm. Turn the pivot bolt snugly into the threaded hole of the mounting plate, and then back it off approximately ¼ turn. Hold the pivot bolt with this adjustment, and then tighten the locknut securely. Check the movement of the traversing arm, which should move freely with only a discernible amount of side play. Readjust the pivot bolt as required by first loosening the locknut, adjusting the pivot bolt, and then retightening the locknut.

⑮ Insert the long pivot bolt through the hole at the bend of the outer arm, with a small bushing in place on the inside of the arm. Slide the long bushing through the spring. Position the spring over the hole in the inner traversing arm, with the short pin end of the spring indexed through the small hole in the arm. Place the assembled unit between the sides of the outer arm, with the hook end of the spring over the side of the outer arm, as shown.

⑯ Rotate the mounting plate upward until the

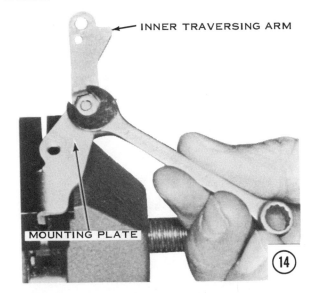

INNER TRAVERSING ARM

MOUNTING PLATE

⑭

MOUNTING PLATE

⑯

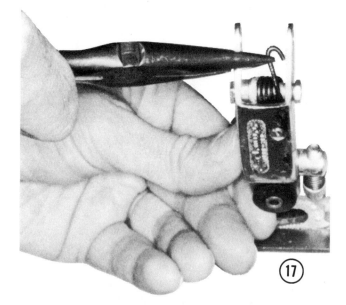

(17)

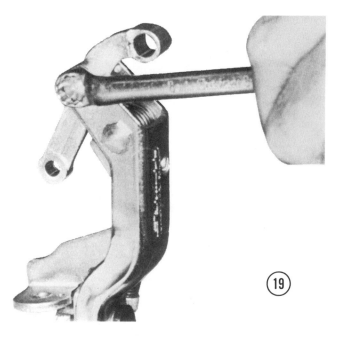

(19)

spring bushing aligns with the long pivot bolt. Push the bolt through the bushing and thread it into the outer arm. Tighten the pivot bolt, and then back it off approximately ¼ turn or until the inner arm and mounting plate turn freely with just a discernible amount of side play. Hold the pivot bolt with this adjustment and then tighten the locknut securely. Check the movement of the arms and adjust the pivot as required by first loosening the locknut, adjusting the pivot bolt, and then retightening the locknut.

⑰ Wind the spring around the spring bushing, and then hook it over the inside edge of the outer arm.

⑱ Insert the bushing through the pivot hole of the main traversing arm. Guide the main traversing arm between the sides of the outer arm, with the curved end up until the bushing hole aligns with holes in the sides of the outer arm, and then slide the pivot bolt through. Thread it into the hole on the opposite side, and then tighten it securely.

⑲ Back off the pivot bolt approximately ¼ turn and check that the main traversing arm turns freely with just a trace of side play. Hold the pivot bolt with this adjustment, and then install and tighten the lock-

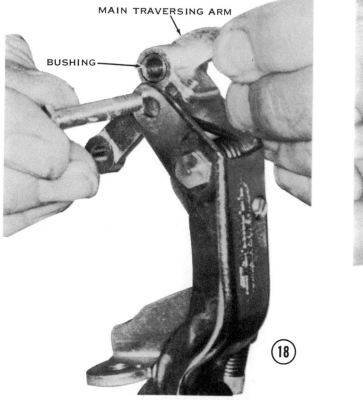

MAIN TRAVERSING ARM

BUSHING

(18)

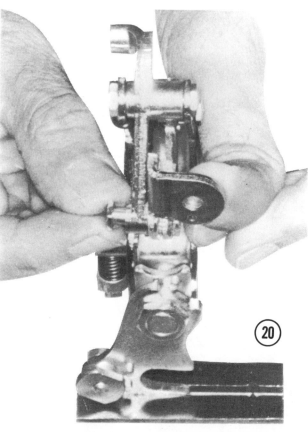

(20)

nut. Adjust the pivot bolt as required by first loosening the locknut slightly, adjusting the pivot bolt, and then retightening the locknut.

㉑ Push upward on the flange of the mounting plate until the hole through the plate and the main traversing arm align, and then insert the pivot bolt through from the side of the outer arm with the cable-adjusting barrel, as shown. Carefully thread the pivot bolt into the mounting plate, and then back it off approximately ¼ turn, or until the arms move freely with no side play. Install the locknut tightly onto the pivot bolt. Check the pivot bolt adjustment by forcing the flange of the mounting plate up and down and attempting to move it sideways. Adjust the bolt as required by first loosening the locknut slightly, adjusting the pivot bolt, and then retightening the locknut.

㉑ Slide the spindle through the upper pulley from the outer cage side. Place a shim, the bushing, and then the pulley cage spring on the spindle, with the short pin end of the spring facing out. Install the other shim on the spindle, with the small hole in the shim indexed over the pin end of the spring, as shown in the accompanying illustration. Thread the spindle into the mounting plate snugly, and then back it off approximately ¼ turn, or until the cage assembly moves freely with no side play.

㉒ Hold the pivot bolt adjustment with a screwdriver while you thread the locknut onto the spindle. Tighten it securely. Wrap the spring around the bushing to tighten it, and then hook it over the flange of the inner cage. Check the pivot bolt adjustment to be

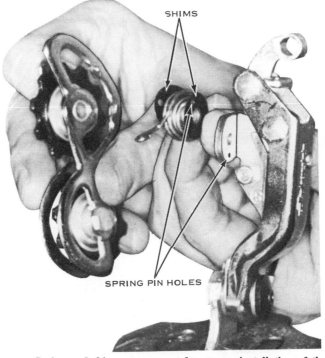

Spring and shim arrangement for proper installation of the pulley cage assembly to the mounting plate.

sure the cage assembly is free to rotate with no side play. Adjust the pivot bolt, if necessary, by first loosening the locknut slightly, tightening or loosening the

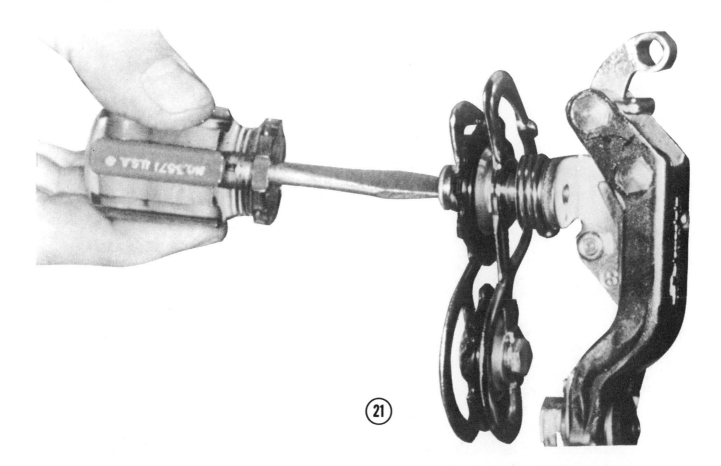

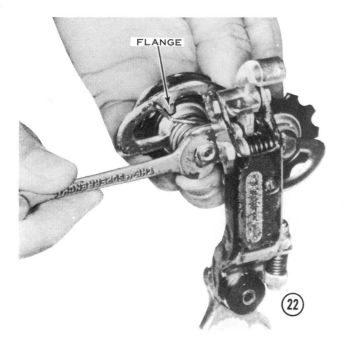

FLANGE

(22)

pivot bolt, and then retightening the locknut.

㉓ Install the cable anchor bolt through the main traversing arm, with the flat of the bolt aligned with the flat of the traversing arm. Slide the cable guide washer onto the bolt, with the closed end of the washer facing down toward the adjusting barrel. Thread the locknut onto the cable anchor bolt, and then tighten it firmly.

㉔ Slide the long spring on the low-gear limit screw, and then thread the screw about five turns into the main traversing arm for a preliminary setting.

INSTALLING

Refer to the first section of this chapter for detailed steps required for installation and adjustment of the derailleur.

OVERHAULING A CAMPAGNOLO RECORD, CAMPAGNOLO NUOVO RECORD, CAMPAGNOLO GRAN SPORT, AND SIMPLEX PRESTIGE REAR DERAILLEUR

The following step-by-step illustrated instructions cover disassembling, cleaning and inspecting, and assembling a Campagnolo Record, Campagnolo Nuovo Record, Campagnolo Gran Sport, and Simplex Prestige rear derailleur unit.

The illustrations were made of a Campagnolo Nuovo Record rear derailleur assembly, which is almost identical to the others. The instructions begin with the derailleur removed from the bicycle.

The first section of this chapter gives complete procedures for removing, installing, and adjusting the derailleur.

Each derailleur assembly can be identified by the manufacturer's name embossed on the exposed surface of the outer arm. A detailed exploded drawing of these derailleurs, showing all internal parts, follows the Cleaning and Inspecting section.

DISASSEMBLING

① Take out the low-gear adjusting screw by turning it counterclockwise, and then remove the spring. Back out the high-gear adjusting screw completely, and then remove the spring.

② Clamp the derailleur in a vise, with the jaws gripping the fork-end bracket. Remove the cable anchor bolt and the cable guide washer.

③ Rotate the derailleur cage assembly slightly to relieve pressure on the stop stud, and then remove

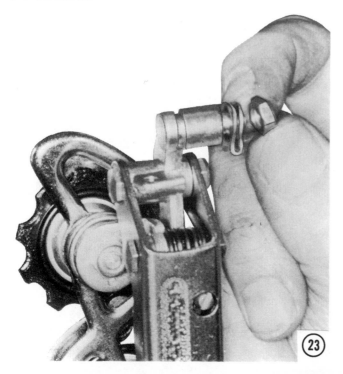

(23)

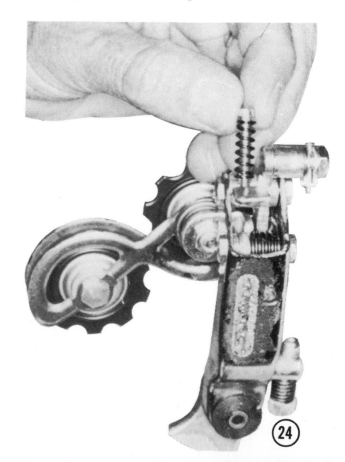

(24)

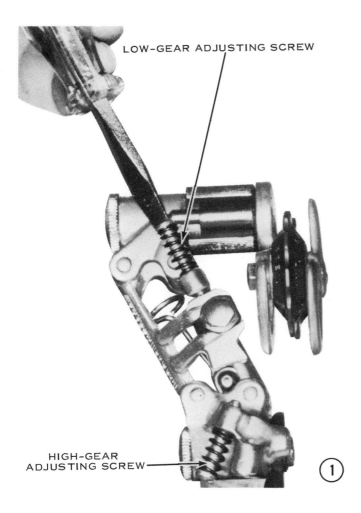

LOW-GEAR ADJUSTING SCREW

HIGH-GEAR ADJUSTING SCREW

(1)

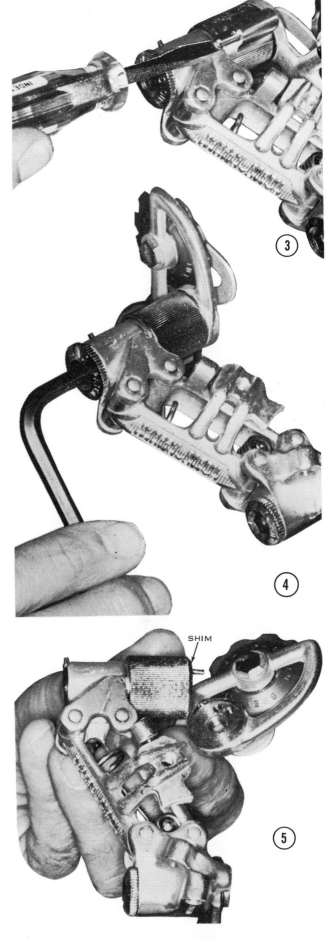

(3)

(4)

SHIM

(5)

the stud. Allow the cage to rotate until the tension on the pulley cage spring is released.

④ Remove the pulley cage spindle using a correct size Allen wrench.

⑤ Disengage the pulley cage assembly from the spring. Note which hole in the cage was used for the spring leg as an aid to assembly. Be sure to save the shim installed between the spring cap and the cage.

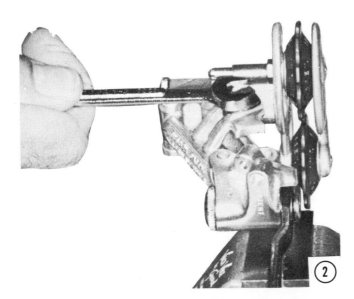

(2)

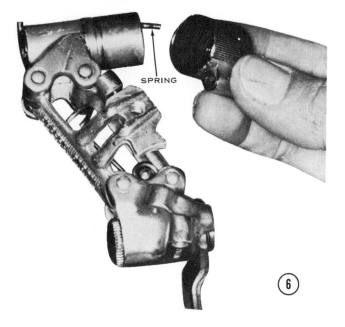

⑥ Withdraw the spring cap from the end of the traversing arm assembly, and then slide the spring out of the other end.

⑦ Grasp the traversing spring firmly with a pair of needle-nosed pliers; pull it out of the arm and relieve the tension.

⑧ Remove the spring pivot bolt and the traversing spring.

⑨ Remove the pivot bolt, using an Allen wrench, and then separate the fork-end bracket from the traversing arm assembly.

⑩ Disassemble the cages by removing the spindles.

⑪ Pry out the dust caps with a screwdriver, and then push the bushing out of the center of each pulley.

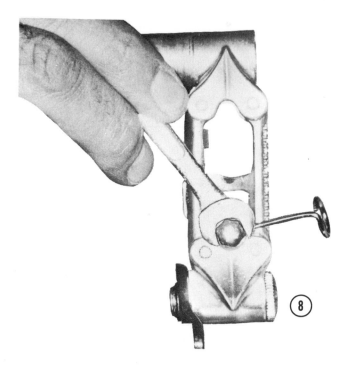

CLEANING AND INSPECTING

Clean all parts in solvent and blow them dry with compressed air, or wipe them dry with a lintless cloth. Keep all cleaned parts on paper towels to avoid contamination. Cover them with a clean towel to keep grit from entering the internal parts or sticking to the bushings.

Check all threaded parts for stripped threads.

Inspect the springs for cracks, loss of tension, or corrosion.

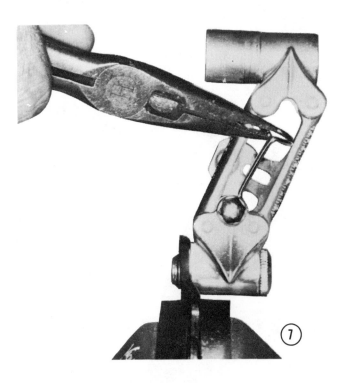

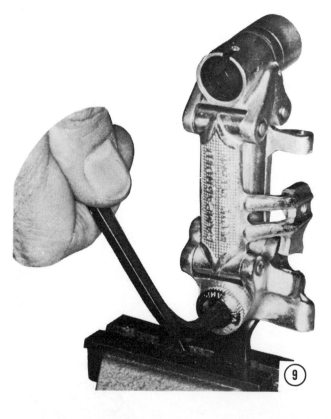

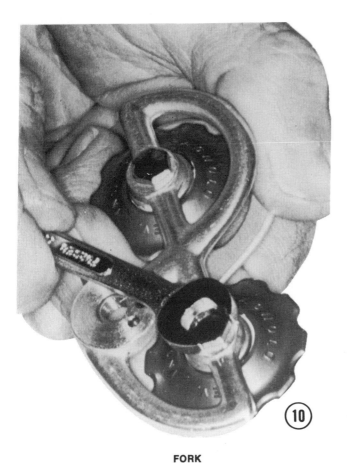

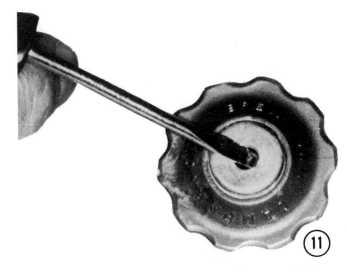

Check the inner and outer sides of the cage assembly for bending, distortion, or damage.

Inspect the teeth of the pulleys for cracks or worn edges, indicating excessive wear. Check the bushings for scratchlike scores or pencil-point type pits. If any part of the pulley is damaged, replace the pulley, including the bushing, and both dust caps as a unit.

ASSEMBLING

CAUTION: The derailleur assembly has many threaded aluminum parts. Use care when installing bolts and spindles to prevent stripping the threads by overtightening.

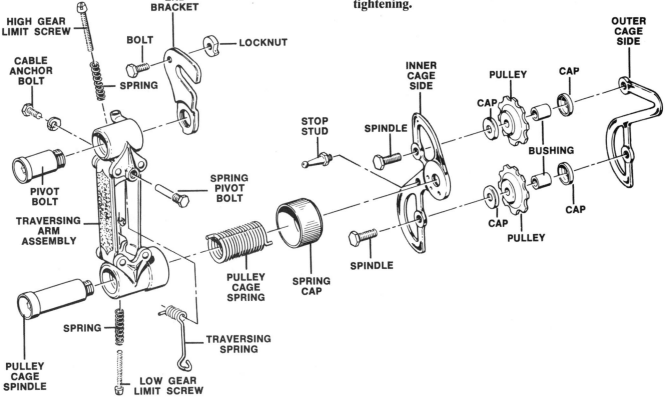

Exploded view of a Campagnolo Record, Campagnolo Nuovo Record, Campagnolo Gran Sport, and Simplex Prestige rear derailleur.

(12)

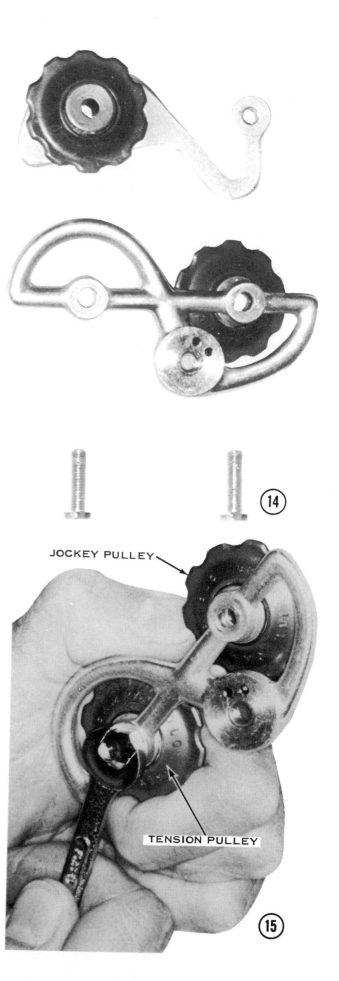

⑫ Coat both bushings with a small amount of multipurpose lubricant, and then insert them into the center of the pulleys.

⑬ Place the dust caps in position on both sides of each pulley.

⑪ Arrange the cage parts in the pattern shown for ease in assembly.

(14)

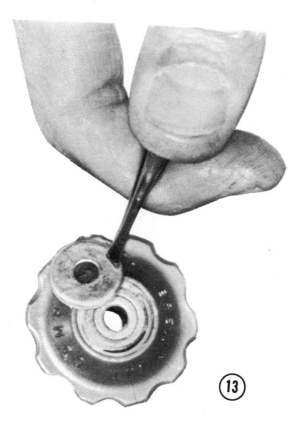

(13)

JOCKEY PULLEY

TENSION PULLEY

(15)

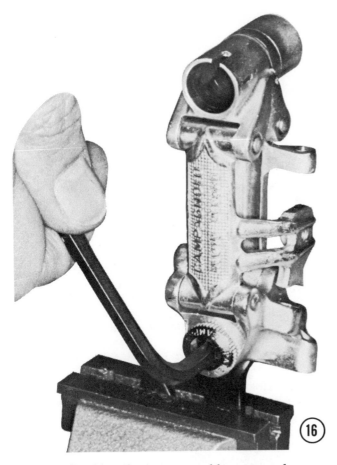

⑯

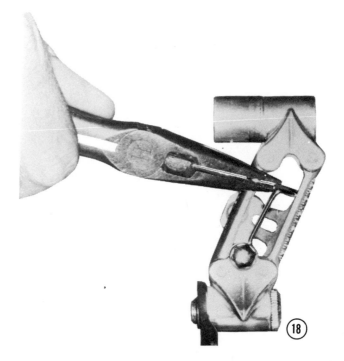

⑱

⑮ Combine the cage assembly parts and secure them with the spindles. *NOTE: If the tension pulley was removed to keep from breaking (separating) the chain when you took the derailleur unit off the bicycle, do not install it at this time; it will be installed later.*

⑯ Clamp the fork-end bracket in a vise, with the jaws gripping the hooked end. Attach the traversing arm assembly to the bracket, with the pivot bolt and the hook of the bracket facing away from the side with the adjusting screws, as shown. The bolt has a shoulder that will "bottom out" when fully tightened.

⑰ Apply a thin coating of multipurpose lubricant to the traversing spring, and then lay it in position behind the flange of the traversing arm assembly, with the loop of the spring facing toward the arm assembly body. Slide the spring pivot bolt through the flange and spring. Tighten it securely.

⑱ Grasp the loop end of the spring firmly with a pair of needle-nosed pliers, and then force it into the traversing arm assembly body.

⑲ Coat the pulley cage spring with a thin layer of multipurpose lubricant, and then insert it through the traversing arm body so the small hook-end of the spring indexes in the slot, as shown.

⑳ Slide the spring cap over the assembly body, with the spring leg through the same hole as you noted during disassembly. If you are unable to recall which

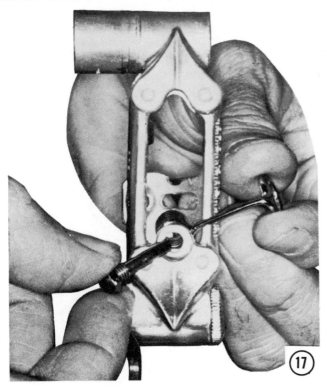

⑰

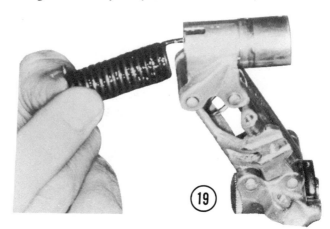

⑲

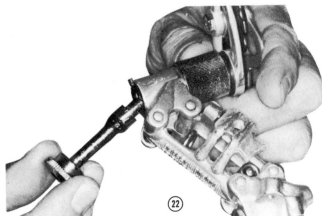

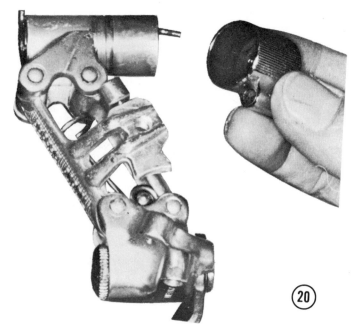

(20)

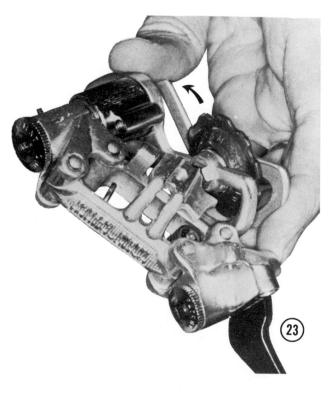

(22)

hole was used, insert the spring leg through the hole that will give the least spring tension. If more tension is desired later on, the cage assembly can be removed and the other hole used.

㉑ Place the thin shim in position, with the spring leg through the matching hole used for the cap. Mate the cage assembly to the traversing arm assembly using the same matching hole for the spring leg as you used for the cap and shim.

㉒ Insert the pulley spindle through the traversing arm body, and then thread it into the cage assembly. Tighten the spindle securely, using an Allen wrench. The shoulder on the spindle will "bottom out" to prevent you from tightening it too much or stripping the threads.

㉓ Rotate the pulley cage assembly one full turn in the direction shown to put tension on the spring.

㉔ Hold the pulley cage with tension on the spring and the hole for the stop stud clear of the traversing arm body. Thread the stop stud into place securely, and then let the cage spring back until the stop stud bears against the body.

㉕ Place the cable anchor guide in position, with the ear of the guide indexed between the two frame members of the traversing arm assembly, as shown. Thread the cable anchor bolt finger-tight into the flange of the traversing body.

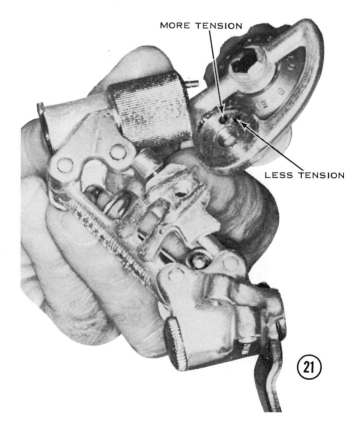

MORE TENSION

LESS TENSION

(21)

(23)

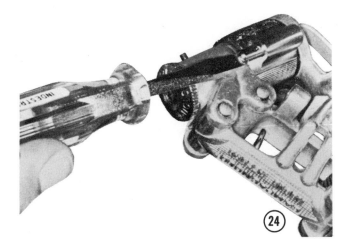

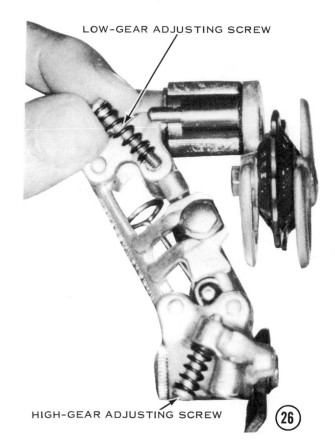

LOW-GEAR ADJUSTING SCREW

HIGH-GEAR ADJUSTING SCREW

㉖ Slide one of the springs onto one of the adjusting screws, and then thread the screw approximately five turns into the high-gear adjusting hole for a preliminary setting. Slide the other spring onto the remaining adjusting screw, and then thread the screw about five turns into the low-gear adjusting hole for a preliminary setting.

㉗ Guide the short bolt through the fork-end bracket, and then thread the locknut about two full turns onto the bolt, with the small flange side of the nut facing the bracket, as shown.

INSTALLING

Refer to the first section of this chapter for detailed instructions covering installation and adjustment of the derailleur unit.

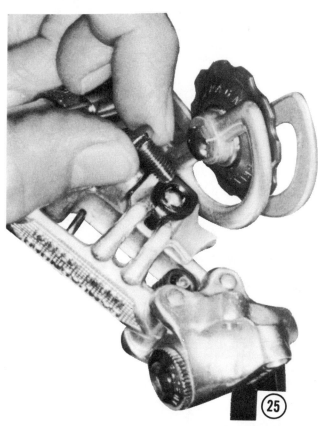

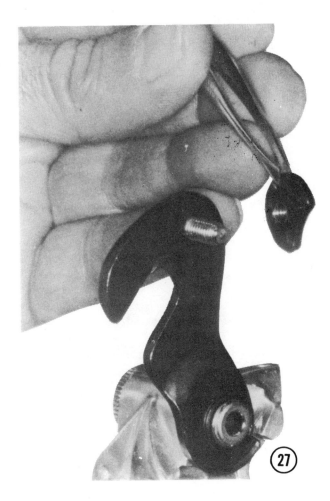

CABLE ADJUSTING BARREL

①

③

OVERHAULING A SUN TOUR GT REAR DERAILLEUR

The following step-by-step illustrated instructions cover disassembling, cleaning and inspecting, and assembling a Sun Tour GT rear derailleur unit. The instructions begin with the derailleur removed from the bicycle. The first section of this chapter gives complete procedures for removing, installing, and adjusting this model of derailleur.

The assembly can be identified by the manufacturer's name embossed on the exposed surface of the main body. Many of the major parts are riveted and

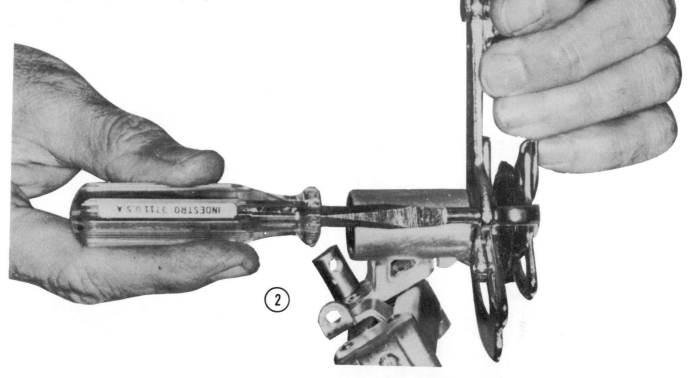

②

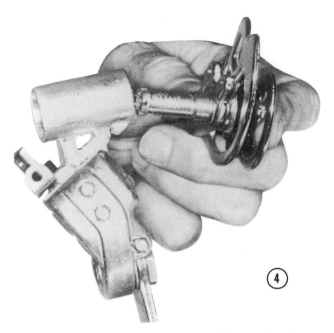

(4)

(6)

cannot be disassembled. The traversing spring is enclosed within the main body and cannot be removed.

DISASSEMBLING

① Clamp the derailleur in a vise, with the jaws gripping the fork-end bracket. Back out the fork-end bracket stop screw. Remove the cable adjusting barrel.

② Rotate the derailleur cage assembly slightly to relieve pressure on the stop stud, and then remove the stud. Allow the cage assembly to rotate until the

tension on the spring is released.

③ Remove the pulley cage spindle cap, using an Allen wrench.

④ Remove the pulley cage and spindle assembly. *NOTE: The spindle and jockey pulley cage are an integral unit and cannot be taken apart. Be careful not to lose the thin shim installed at the base of the spindle.*

⑤ Remove the pulley cage spring.

⑥ Remove the locknut from the pivot bolt.

⑦ Back out the pivot bolt, using an Allen wrench. Note the arrangement of the spacer and any shims between the fork-end bracket and the main body for assembly purposes.

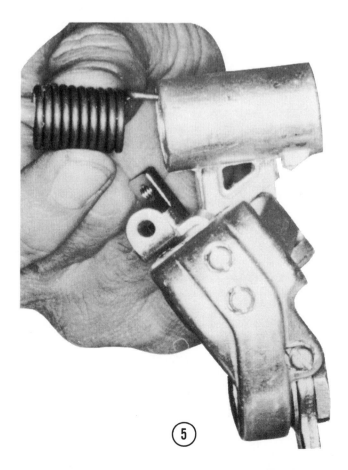

(5)

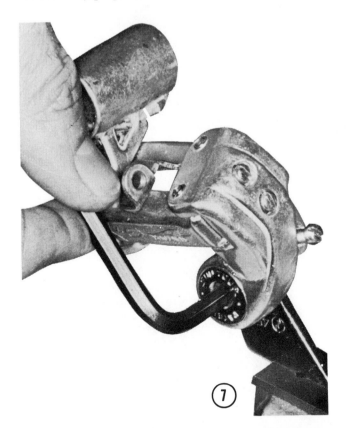

(7)

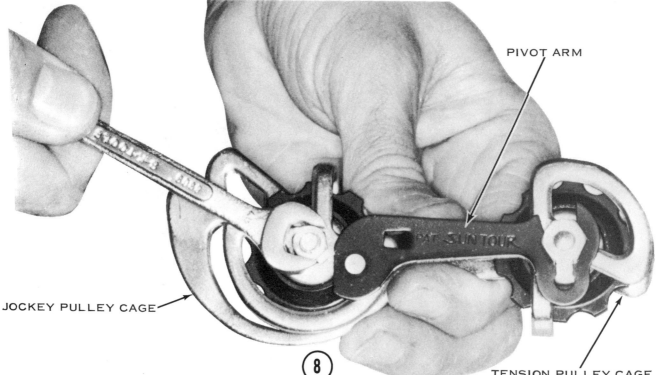

PIVOT ARM

JOCKEY PULLEY CAGE

TENSION PULLEY CAGE

⑧

⑧ Remove the spindle nuts and spindles from the pulley cages, and then take off the pulleys. Unsnap the pivot arm from the jockey pulley cage.

⑨ Pry the dust caps out of both sides of each pulley, and then remove the bushings.

CLEANING AND INSPECTING

Clean all parts in solvent and blow them dry with compressed air, or wipe them dry with a lintless cloth. Keep all cleaned parts on paper towels to avoid contamination. Cover them with a clean towel to keep grit from entering the internal parts or sticking to the bushings.

Check all threaded parts for stripped threads.

Inspect the springs for cracks, loss of tension, or corrosion.

⑨

⑩

⑪

Check both parts of the cage assembly for bending, distortion, or damage.

Inspect the teeth of the pulleys for cracks or worn edges indicating excessive wear. Check the bushings for scratchlike scores or pencil-point type pits. If any part of the pulley is damaged, replace the complete pulley, including the bushing and both dust caps as a unit.

ASSEMBLING

⑩ Coat each bushing with a small amount of multipurpose lubricant, and then insert the bushings into the center of the pulleys.

⑪ Place the dust caps in position on both sides of each pulley.

⑫ Place one of the assembled pulleys in the jockey pulley cage, and then slide the assembly onto the spindle, with the hole in the cage indexed over the pin on the fixed arm.

⑬ Thread the small nut firmly onto the spindle, with the shoulder of the nut facing down. **CAUTION: Each cage has a hole that must index over a matching pin on the fixed arm before the spindle nuts are tightened in order to keep from distorting the cages.**

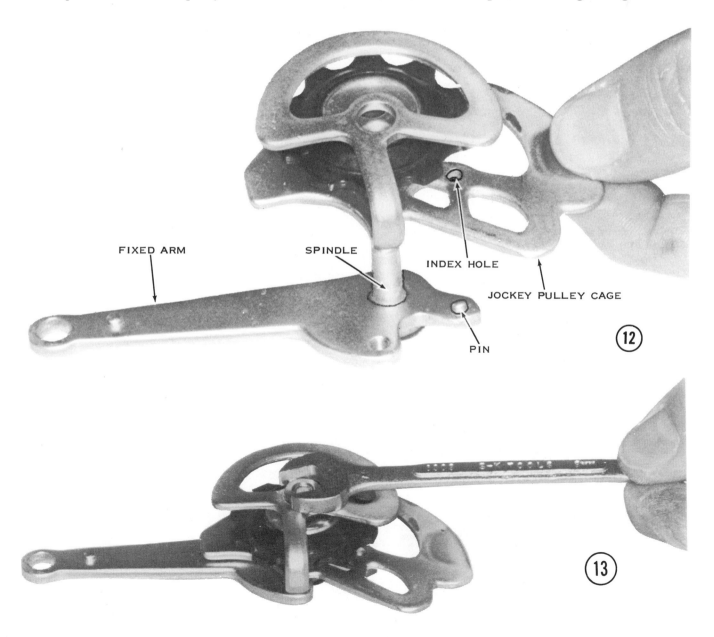

FIXED ARM   SPINDLE   INDEX HOLE   JOCKEY PULLEY CAGE   PIN   ⑫

⑬

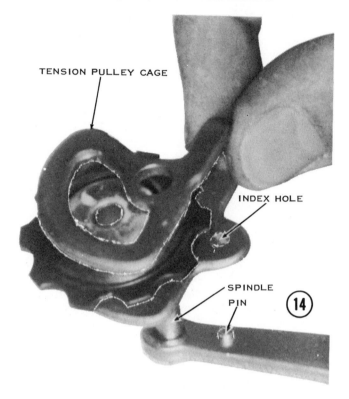

TENSION PULLEY CAGE

INDEX HOLE

SPINDLE PIN

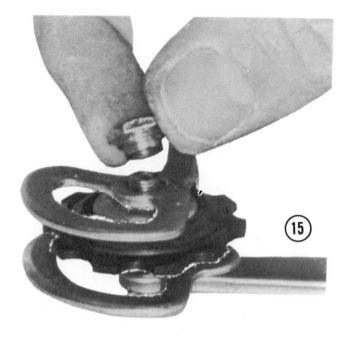

⑭ Insert the tension pulley spindle through the fixed arm, as shown. Place the other assembled pulley in the tension cage, and then slide the assembly onto the spindle, with the hole in the cage indexed over the pin on the fixed arm.

⑮ Thread the large nut with the double shoulder approximately two full turns onto the tension spindle. This will leave room for the pivot arm to swing into place on the shoulder of the nut after the derailleur is installed on the bicycle and the chain is in place on the tension pulley.

⑯ Snap the pivot arm into the opening of the jockey cage, with the hook of the arm over the outer edge of the cage, as shown in the illustration.

⑰ Slide the pivot bolt through the traversing arm, and then install the shim and washer, with the washer on the outside, as shown. Turn the pivot bolt into the fork-end bracket until it is snug but loose enough for the bracket to pivot. Secure this adjustment with the locknut.

⑱ Insert the pulley cage spring into the traversing arm assembly, as shown. Rotate the spring until the leg of the spring indexes into the hole closest to the upper edge of the body.

⑲ Slide the same number of shims onto the cage spindle as you noted during disassembly. Install the cage spindle through the pulley cage spring, with the short leg of the spring indexed in one of the slots in the spindle, when the cage assembly is approximately at right angles to the traversing arm and the tension pulley

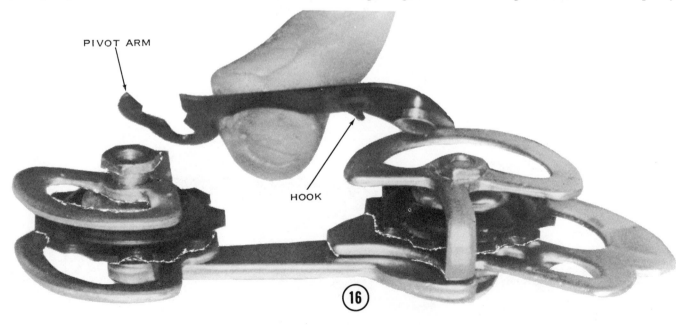

PIVOT ARM

HOOK

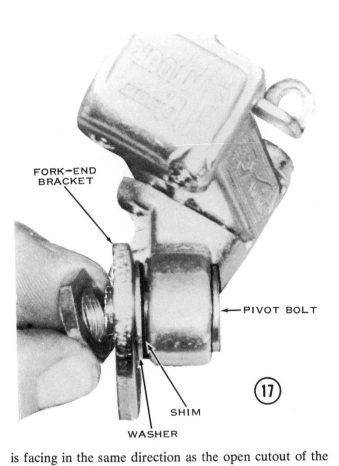

FORK-END BRACKET

PIVOT BOLT

SHIM

WASHER

(17)

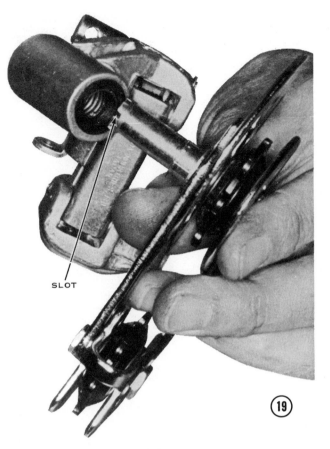

SLOT

(19)

is facing in the same direction as the open cutout of the fork-end bracket.

⑳ Thread the pulley cage spindle cap into the spindle with an Allen wrench until the outer surface is flush with the edge of the traversing arm body. If you cannot tighten the cap until it is flush, back it out and position the short leg of the spring into the nearest slot

in the end of the spindle. The cap will not seat properly unless the spring leg is correctly seated in one of the spindle slots.

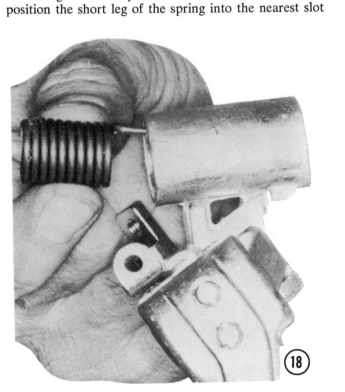

(18)

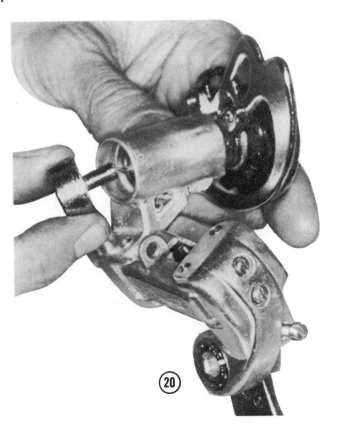

(20)

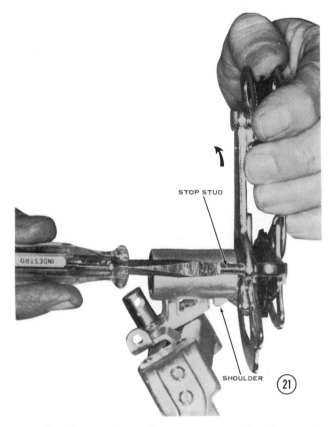

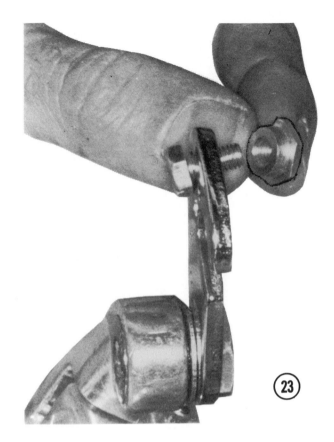

㉑ Rotate the pulley cage assembly ½ turn in the direction indicated. Hold the cage in this position, and then thread the stop stud into the cage until the shoulder of the stud "bottoms out" against the inside face of the cage. Allow the cage to move back until the stop stud contacts the shoulder on the traversing arm body.

㉒ Install the cable adjusting barrel and the fork-end bracket stop screw.

㉓ Slide the mounting bolt through the fork-end bracket, and then start the locknut onto the bolt, with the shoulder facing the bracket, as shown.

INSTALLING

Refer to the first section of this chapter for complete instructions to install and adjust the derailleur.

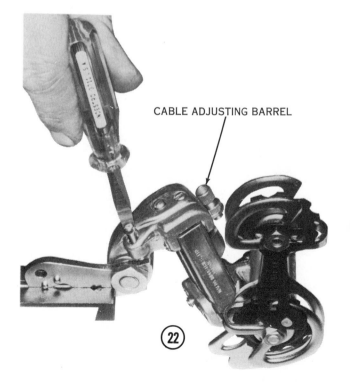

A properly adjusted and lubricated rear derailleur unit performs a vital function on cross-country tours. Torsvphoto

8
OVERHAULING
FRONT DERAILLEURS

The purpose of the front derailleur is to shift the drive chain from one chain wheel to another in order to change the gearing ratio. There are two such chain wheels mounted at the hanger set on a 10-speed bike, or three chain wheels on a 15-speed bike.

Two types of front derailleurs are used. One utilizes the parallelogram principle similar to the rear derailleur, and the other, a push-rod type, utilizes a spring-loaded mechanism.

The parallelogram-type front derailleur contains two pivot arms, which form and maintain a parallelogram. The sides of the chain guide can, therefore, be kept in alignment with the edges of the chain wheels as the guide shifts the chain from one chain wheel to the other. Pulling on the control lever moves the derailleur away from the bicycle frame and shifts the chain from the smaller chain wheel to the larger. Spring tension returns the chain guide toward the bike frame and this shifts the chain onto the smaller wheel when the control lever is pushed back. The pivot arms on many parallelogram-type front derailleurs are riveted together and, therefore, cannot be disassembled for overhauling.

The push-rod type front derailleur contains a spring-loaded rod connected to the chain guide. The control cable forces the rod to the extended position, placing the chain on the largest sprocket; the spring retracts the rod and moves the chain to the smaller sprocket. The internal mechanism of most models, including the traversing spring, is contained in a sealed housing and cannot be opened for service. Many, however, do have a removable cap for lubrication.

OVERHAULING A SPRINT, HURET, SHIMANO, AND SCHWINN-APPROVED FRONT DERAILLEUR

The following step-by-step illustrated instructions cover disassembling, assembling, and adjusting a Sprint, Huret, Shimano, and Schwinn-Approved front derailleur unit. The illustrations were made of a Schwinn-Approved unit, which is similar to the others. An exploded drawing of this series of derailleurs follows the Cleaning and Inspecting section. An exploded view of a Campagnolo Record, Campagnolo Gran Sport, and

Simplex Prestige front derailleur is also included.

Each derailleur unit can be identified by the manufacturer's name embossed on the exposed surface of the chain guide and on the face of the mounting clamp.

DISASSEMBLING

① Loosen the acorn nut on the cable anchor bolt, and then free the control cable from the derailleur. Remove the clamp bolt, acorn nut, washer, and clamp. Remove the locknut, lockwasher, bushing, and bolt from the rear of the derailleur guide, and then remove the derailleur from the bicycle.

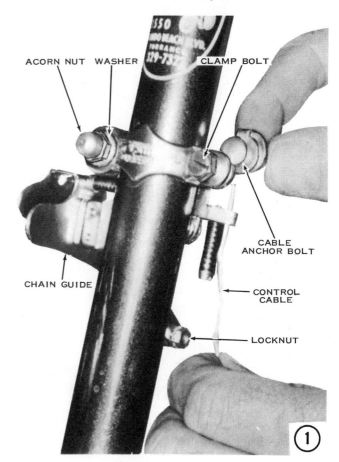

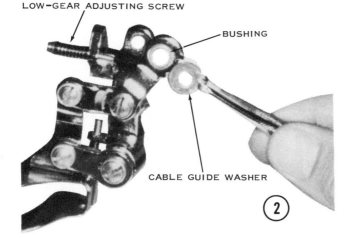

LOW-GEAR ADJUSTING SCREW
BUSHING
CABLE GUIDE WASHER

②

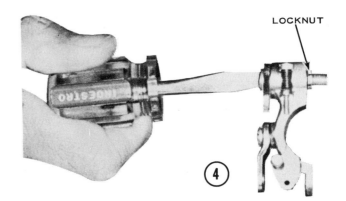

LOCKNUT

④

② Turn the low-gear adjusting screw into the main body as far as possible. Remove the acorn nut, and then the cable anchor bolt. Pull the cable-guide washer free, and then remove the bushing. *NOTE: Some models of derailleurs use two washers instead of the single guide washer shown.*

③ Remove the two bolts from the chain-guide bracket, and then remove the chain guide. Be careful not to lose the small bushing on the bolt that passes through the bracket and the end of the pivot arm.

NOTE: The pivot arm cannot be removed because the end of the bolt securing it is flared during manufacture.

④ Hold the main pivot bolt with a screwdriver, and then remove the locknut.

⑤ Back out the main pivot bolt. Remove the link and the traversing spring. Take out the low-gear and high-gear limit screws and their springs.

CLEANING AND INSPECTING

Inspect all parts for stripped threads.

Check the springs for a crack or loss of tension.

Inspect the inside surfaces of the chain guide for damage caused by the chain.

Inspect the linkage for being bent, twisted, or damaged.

ASSEMBLING

⑥ Slide the shorter limit screw spring onto the low-gear limit screw (the screw with the larger head), and then thread it into the body as far as it will go. Insert the high-gear limit screw through the other limit spring, and then thread it into the body about five turns. Apply a thin coating of multipurpose lubricant onto the traversing spring.

⑦ Insert the traversing spring into the main body, with one leg of the spring indexed through the hole in the body. *NOTE: The spring may be installed either way.* Slide the link onto the main pivot bolt, with the flat side facing the threaded end of the bolt. Thread the pivot bolt into the body, with the exposed leg of the spring indexed in the hole of the link. Check to be

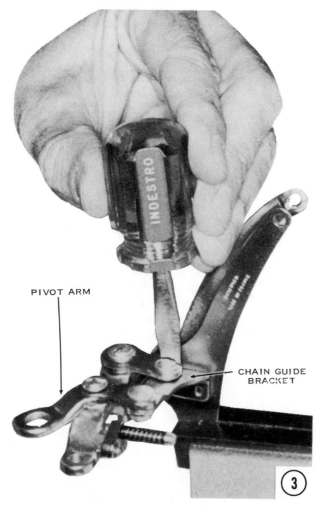

PIVOT ARM
CHAIN GUIDE BRACKET

③

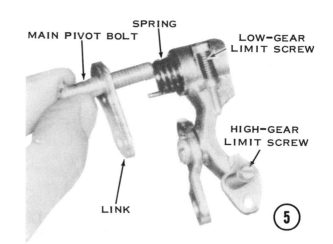

SPRING
MAIN PIVOT BOLT
LOW-GEAR LIMIT SCREW
HIGH-GEAR LIMIT SCREW
LINK

⑤

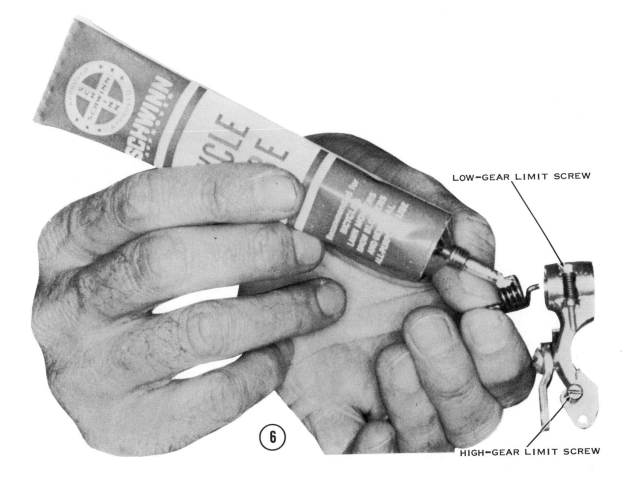

LOW-GEAR LIMIT SCREW

6

HIGH-GEAR LIMIT SCREW

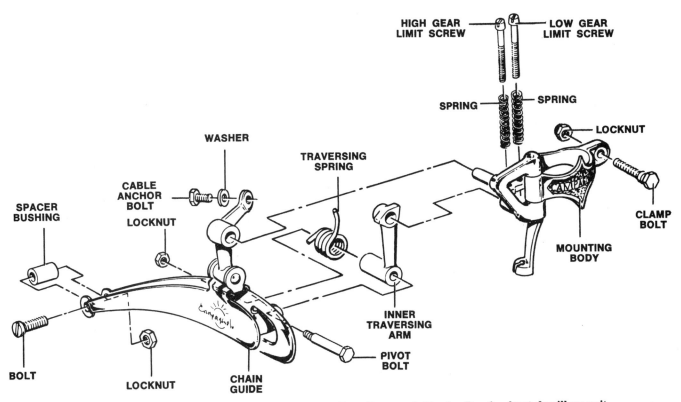

HIGH GEAR
LIMIT SCREW   LOW GEAR
LIMIT SCREW

SPRING   SPRING

LOCKNUT

WASHER

CABLE
ANCHOR
BOLT

TRAVERSING
SPRING

CLAMP
BOLT

SPACER
BUSHING

LOCKNUT

MOUNTING
BODY

BOLT

INNER
TRAVERSING
ARM

LOCKNUT   CHAIN
GUIDE   PIVOT
BOLT

Exploded view of a Campagnolo Record, Campagnolo Gran Sport, and Simplex Prestige front derailleur unit.

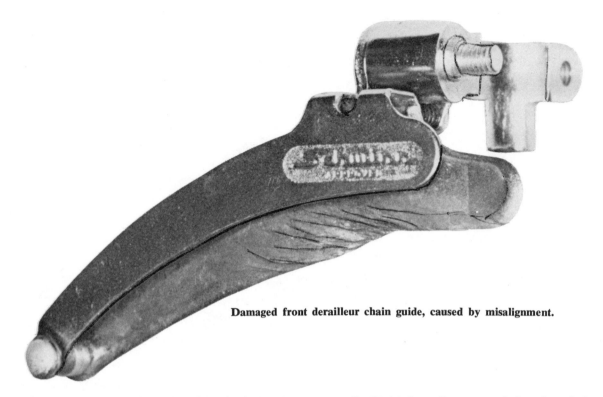

Damaged front derailleur chain guide, caused by misalignment.

sure the other spring leg is still indexed in the hole of the body. Tighten the bolt securely, and then back it off approximately ¼ turn as a preliminary adjustment.

⑧ Hold the adjustment of the pivot bolt with a screwdriver; thread the locknut onto the bolt and tighten it securely. Check the link adjustment; it should rotate

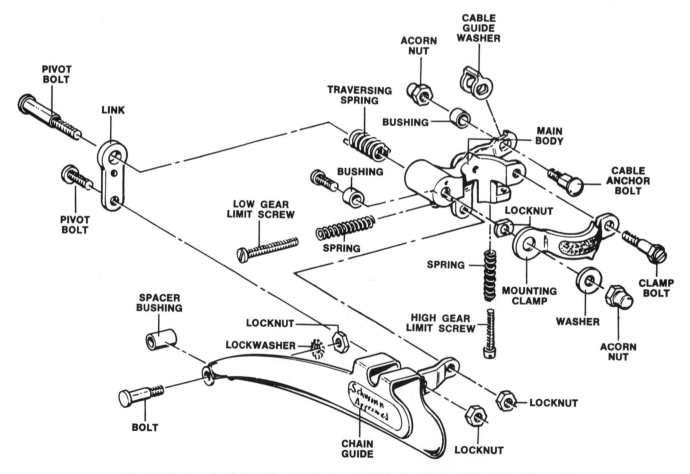

Exploded view of a Sprint, Huret, Shimano, and Schwinn-Approved front derailleur unit.

freely (under tension of the spring) with no end play. If an adjustment is required, loosen the locknut slightly, rotate the pivot bolt in the desired direction to tighten or loosen it, and then retighten the locknut.

⑨ Observe the position of the traversing pivot bolt slot because it is now necessary to tighten the bolt in order to hold the link for further assembly. Loosen the locknut slightly, swing the link against the tension of the spring until it is positioned approximately as shown, and then tighten the pivot bolt securely to hold the link in position.

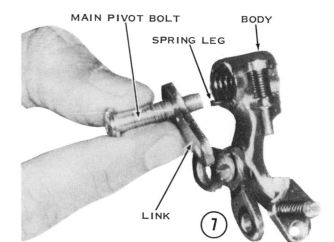

MAIN PIVOT BOLT   BODY

SPRING LEG

LINK

⑦

⑧

⑨

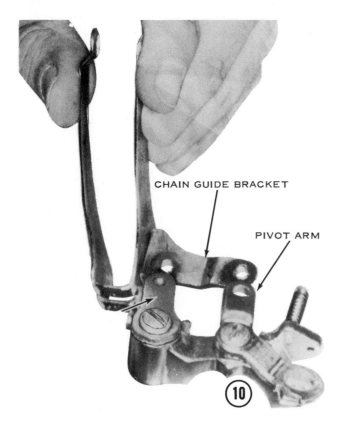

CHAIN GUIDE BRACKET

PIVOT ARM

⑩

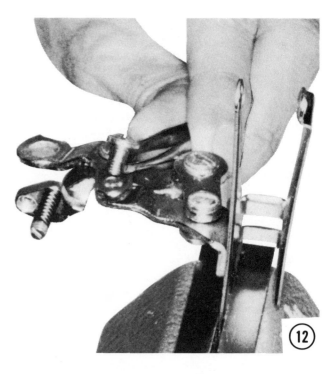

⑫

⑩ Slide the chain-guide bracket into place under the link and pivot arm.

⑪ Slide the bushing onto the smaller pivot bolt; thread the bolt tightly into the chain-guide bracket, with the bushing fully indexed in the pivot arm hole; and

then back it off approximately ¼ turn as an adjustment. Hold this adjustment with a screwdriver while you install and then fully tighten the locknut.

⑫ Thread the larger pivot bolt through the link and into the chain guide. Tighten it firmly, and then back it off approximately ¼ turn as an adjustment. Hold this adjustment with a screwdriver, and then install and securely tighten the locknut.

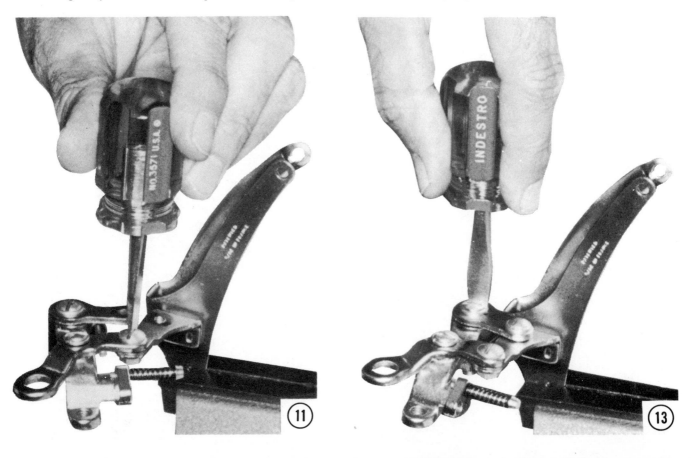

⑪

⑬

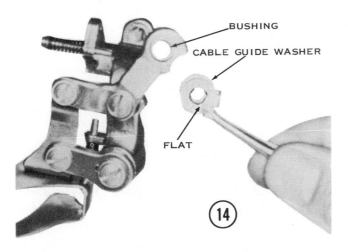

BUSHING

CABLE GUIDE WASHER

FLAT

(14)

⑬ Loosen the traversing pivot bolt to the same position you noted in Step ⑨ before you tightened it to hold the link in position. Hold this adjustment with a screwdriver while you firmly tighten the locknut.

⑭ Insert the bushing in the hole of the traversing arm. Slide the cable-guide washer onto the arm, as shown, with the hole having the flats facing the rear of the derailleur. If the derailleur you are working on uses two washers instead of the cable-guide washer shown, proceed as follows: Slide the cable anchor bolt through the arm, with the head of the bolt facing away from the body. Install a thin washer, a thick washer, and then the acorn nut. Some derailleurs have a stud riveted to the arm with the same arrangement of washers. Back out the low-gear adjusting screw approximately halfway, for a preliminary setting.

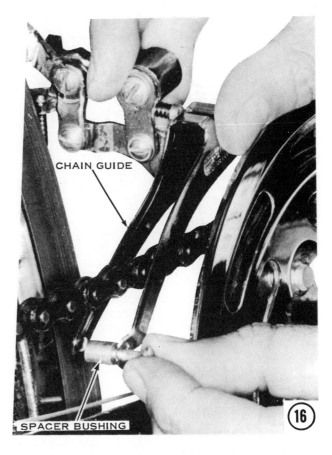

CHAIN GUIDE

SPACER BUSHING

(16)

⑮ Install the anchor bolt from the back side of the pivot arm, with the flats on the bolt indexed with the flats of the washer. Thread the acorn nut onto the anchor bolt.

⑯ Place the derailleur in position on the bicycle, with the chain between the sides of the chain guide. Insert the bolt from the outer side of the guide, as shown. Slide the bolt through the spacer bushing. Rotate the bolt until the small ear at the head indexes with the slot in the chain-guide hole. Push the bolt on through the other side of the chain guide, and then install the lockwasher and locknut.

⑰ Position the derailleur on the frame. Place the clamp over the forward side with the manufacturer's identification upright and the large hole in one end of

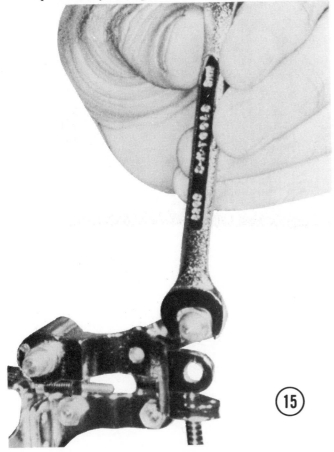

(15)

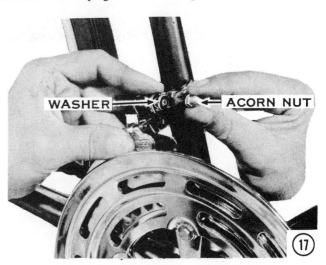

WASHER   ACORN NUT

(17)

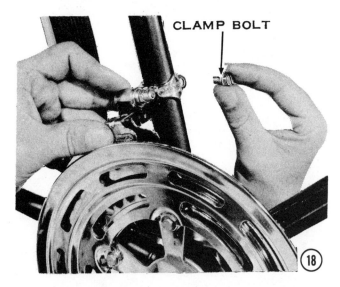

CLAMP BOLT

⑱

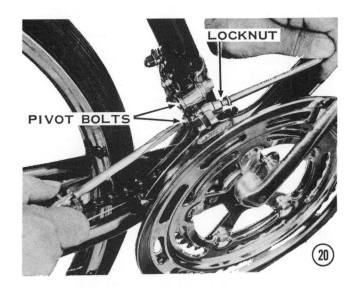

LOCKNUT

PIVOT BOLTS

⑳

the clamp indexed over the locknut on the pivot bolt. Install the washer, and then the acorn nut finger-tight.

⑱ Thread the clamp bolt into the body finger-tight. Feed the control cable through the hole in the body and the anchor bolt. Place the control lever in the full-forward position, pull the cable taut, and then tighten the locknut.

MAKING A MAJOR ADJUSTMENT

⑲ Shift the derailleur unit on the frame until the lower edge of the outer chain guide is not over ⅛ inch above the tip of the teeth of the largest chain wheel. Rotate the derailleur until the chain guide is parallel with the flat surface of the chain wheel. Securely tighten the mounting plate acorn nut and bolt.

⑳ Check the movement of the traversing arms to be sure they pivot freely and that the spring returns the derailleur to the non-extended position (largest chain wheel to the smaller one). If the pivot arms seem to bind or the derailleur remains in the extended position, loosen the pivot bolt locknut. Turn the pivot bolt clockwise until it is snug, and then back it off approximately

¼ turn. Hold this adjustment with a screwdriver while you securely tighten the locknut. Repeat this procedure for the other pivot bolts by first loosening the locknut, firmly tightening the pivot bolt, holding the adjustment with a screwdriver, and then firmly tightening the lock-nut. *NOTE: On some front derailleurs, the traversing arm linkages are riveted and cannot be adjusted.*

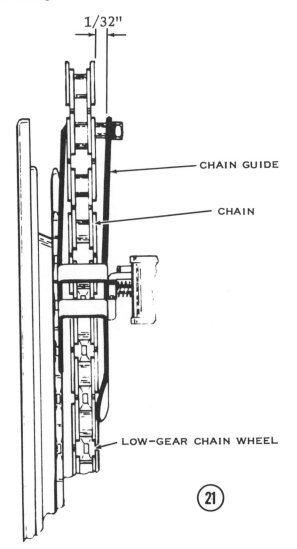

1/32"

CHAIN GUIDE

CHAIN

LOW-GEAR CHAIN WHEEL

㉑

CHAIN GUIDE

1/8"

⑲

MAKING A MINOR ADJUSTMENT

Setting the Low-Gear Limit Screw

㉑ Position the chain onto the low-gear (largest) rear sprocket and the low-gear (smaller) chain wheel. Loosen the cable anchor locknut. Place the control lever in the low-gear (full-forward) position. Turn the low-gear limit screw until the inner side of the chain guide just clears the inner side of the chain (by approximately $\frac{1}{32}$ inch), as shown. *NOTE: The illustration exaggerates the clearance for clarity.* If the front derailleur does not have a low-gear limit screw, loosen the chain-guide mounting bolt and position the chain guide until the inner side of the chain guide just clears the inner side of the chain and the guide follows the contour of the chain wheel. Tighten the mounting bolt.

㉒ Pull the cable taut with a pair of pliers, and then tighten the locknut. Force the control lever down several times to prestress the cable and casing.

Setting the High-Gear Limit Screw

㉓ Place the chain onto the high-gear (smallest) rear sprocket. *NOTE: The crank must be rotated in the forward direction while making this adjustment.* Turn out the high-gear limit screw until the derailleur shifts the chain onto the high-gear (larger) chain wheel. Move the front control lever very slightly until the outer side of the chain guide just clears the outer side of the chain (by approximately $\frac{1}{32}$ inch). Leave the front derailleur in this position, and then turn in the high-gear limit screw until it just contacts the traversing arm.

Adjusting the Chain Guide

㉔ Rotate the crank in the forward direction and, at the same time, shift the chain back and forth from one chain wheel to the other. If movement of the chain onto the large chain wheel is sluggish, use a pair of pliers to bend the front end of the inner side of the chain guide toward the chain. If the chain rubs or makes

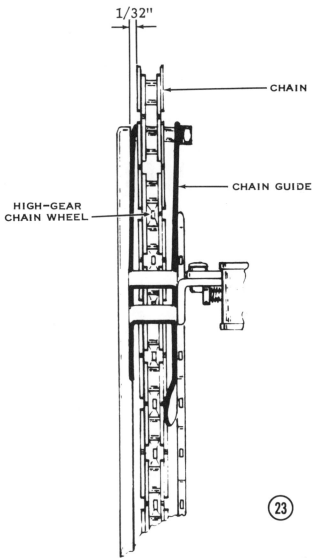

1/32"

CHAIN

CHAIN GUIDE

HIGH-GEAR CHAIN WHEEL

㉓

noise when it is positioned on the largest rear sprocket and the largest chain wheel, or vice versa, adjust the position of the control lever until the chain runs clear of the guide. **CAUTION: Do not turn the limit screws, which have already been adjusted.**

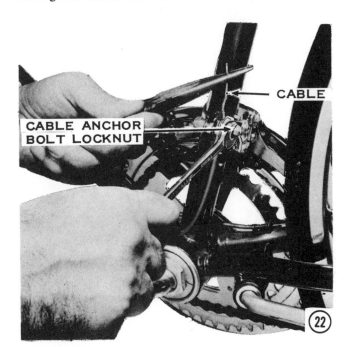

CABLE

CABLE ANCHOR BOLT LOCKNUT

㉒

CHAIN GUIDE

㉔

9
HANGER SETS AND PEDALS

A complete hanger set consists of an axle passing through the bottom bracket of the bicycle frame, chain wheels and cranks attached to the axle, pedals threaded into the ends of the cranks, and the necessary bearings, bearing cups, washers, and locknuts or lock rings to hold it all together for efficient operation.

HANGER SETS

Three types of hanger sets are used on modern bicycles: (1) *A one-piece unit* with the axle and both cranks made from a single steel forging. This type of hanger set is commonly referred to as an American one-piece crank and is found on less expensive bicycles. Overhaul procedures for the one-piece hanger set begin on page 283.

(2) *A cottered crank assembly,* usually made of steel in three pieces with the cranks attached to the axle by large cotters (tapered pins), are used on precision-built bicycles. These sets are known as European cottered cranks although they may be manufactured in many parts of the world. Procedures for overhauling a cottered crank hanger set begin on page 288.

(3) *A cotterless crank hanger set* is similar to the cottered crank type, except for materials used in its construction and the method of attaching the cranks to the axle. This assembly is used on the best touring and racing machines. The axle is made of steel and the cranks and chain wheels are made of lightweight, tough aluminum alloy. This type of hanger set is the more difficult to overhaul because the cranks are secured to the axle with crank bolts and a special tool set is required for each make and model in order to "pull" the cranks free of the axle. Procedures for overhaul of the cotterless crank begin on page 293.

PEDALS

Pedals are classified as either the *American* or *Continental type*. Several variations in style and construction of each are on the market. Some years ago the terms American and Continental had definite meanings—referring to the location of the manufacturer and use. Today almost all pedals are made outside the United States, but the terminology still differentiates the two types.

American-type pedals have two rubber pads secured to the pedal frame by bolts or studs; the frame rotates about a spindle which is attached to the crank. Bearings and cones are used at each end of the spindle. One of the cones is adjustable to provide minimum friction and efficient operation. This type of pedal must be removed from the bicycle and partly disassembled in order to make an adjustment. It is used on almost all juvenile, coaster brake, two-speed and three-speed bicycles. Overhaul procedures for an American-type pedal begin on page 298.

HEAVY DUTY   BOWED   DIAMOND TREAD

Examples of American-type pedals.

Continental-type pedals are constructed quite differently from their American counterparts. A complete metal frame is used for the cyclist's foot instead of the rubber pads. Such a surface provides an excellent grip and minimizes shoe slippage in wet weather or while pedaling under strained conditions. A wide variety of frame designs is available to suit the individual's preference for touring or racing. This type of pedal is used on almost all better 5- and 10-speed bicycles. One of the greatest advantages of the Continental pedal over the American-type, from a maintenance standpoint, is that a cone adjustment can be made by removing a dust cap from the outer end of the spindle. Overhaul procedures for Continental pedals begin on page 302.

SERVICE NOTE

For optimum service, the hanger set should be overhauled, thoroughly lubricated, and adjusted every six months or once a year, depending on the extent of touring, type of terrain, or racing for which the bicycle is used.

OVERHAULING AN AMERICAN-TYPE ONE-PIECE CRANK

The step-by-step illustrated instructions in this section cover disassembling, assembling, and adjusting American-type, one-piece cranks. A detailed exploded drawing of this crank is included with the Cleaning and Inspecting portion.

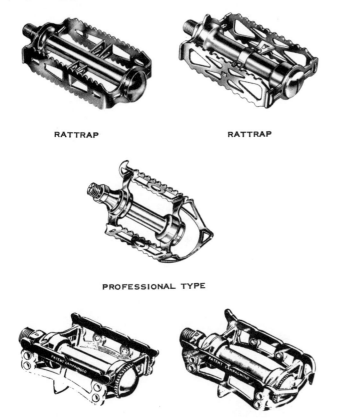

RATTRAP   RATTRAP

PROFESSIONAL TYPE

CAMPAGNOLO TRACK   CAMPAGNOLO ROAD

Examples of Continental-type pedals.

REMOVING AND DISASSEMBLING

① Remove the nuts and bolts securing the chain guard, and then slide off the guard.

② Remove the left-side pedal by turning the spindle clockwise. **CAUTION: Threads on the left-side spindle have left-hand threads.**

③ Remove the left-side locknut by turning it clockwise until it is clear of the ball cup and then sliding it off the crank. **CAUTION: The locknut has a left-hand thread.** Remove the keyed lockwasher.

④ Turn the lock ring clockwise with a screwdriver indexed in one of the slots until it is clear of the frame housing, and then slide the lock ring off the crank.

BALL BEARING RETAINER ASSEMBLY

⑤ Remove the chain from the sprocket. Pull out the ball bearing and retainer assembly from the housing.

⑥ Slide the crank assembly out of the frame housing from the sprocket side. Remove the sprocket-side ball bearing and retainer assembly. Take off the right-side pedal by turning the spindle counterclockwise.

CLEANING AND INSPECTING

Clean all parts with solvent and blow them dry with compressed air or wipe them dry with a lintless cloth. Clean out the inside of the frame housing with solvent and wipe it dry.

Inspect the ball bearing retainer assemblies for cracks or visible signs of damage. If any of the ball bearings come out of the retainer, are pitted (pencil-point dots), show signs of excessive wear (dull spots), or are cracked, the complete assembly must be replaced.

Check the threads on the crank arms to be sure they are not stripped or damaged. Check the teeth on the chain wheel. If any of them are not in line with the wheel, carefully bend them back using a wrench and a steady, even pressure. Try not to bend them back and forth too much as this causes metal fatigue and the teeth may snap off under strain while the bike is in use.

Check the frame housing for stripped or damaged threads and for pits or scores (scratchlike marks) on the internal bearing races.

Check the lock ring and locknut for stripped or damaged threads.

ASSEMBLING

⑦ Pack both ball bearing retainer assemblies with a generous amount of multipurpose lubricant. Work

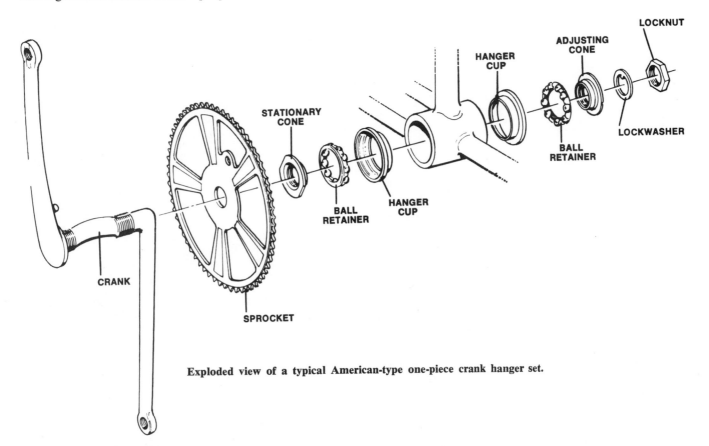

Exploded view of a typical American-type one-piece crank hanger set.

8

10

the lubricant throughout the bearings and retainer with your fingers. Slide one of the lubricated retainers over the crank and onto the chain wheel, with the flat side of the retainer against the wheel. Insert the crank through the frame housing, and then install the other lubricated retainer assembly, with the flat side facing out, as shown.

9

11

⑧ Engage the chain over the chain wheel with the links fitting properly onto the wheel teeth. Thread the lock ring counterclockwise into the frame housing.

⑨ Tighten the lock ring counterclockwise with a screwdriver indexed in one of the slots. Adjust the lock ring until the crank turns freely with just a discernible amount of end play when you attempt to move the crank in and out of the frame housing.

⑩ Install the keyed lockwasher, with the key indexed to the keyway of the crank. *NOTE: This lockwasher keeps the lock ring in place so that the bearing adjustment does not change during assembly.*

⑪ Thread the locknut onto the crank in a counterclockwise direction. **CAUTION: The locknut has left-hand threads.** Tighten the locknut firmly against the lockwasher.

⑫ Turn the left-side pedal counterclockwise onto the crank. Turn the right-side pedal clockwise onto the crank. *NOTE: The pedals have an L or R stamped on the flat of the inside cone for identification.*

⑬ Tighten each pedal using a thin wrench on the flats of the spindle to turn them in the proper direction.

⑭ Install the chain guard. Tighten the attaching bolts and nuts securely.

ADJUSTING

Check the adjustment of the crank by lifting the rear wheel clear of the floor and turning the crank, which should turn freely without drag and have only

a discernible amount of end play. If there is drag or excessive end play, back off the locknut, and then tighten or loosen the lock ring with a screwdriver. Retighten the locknut.

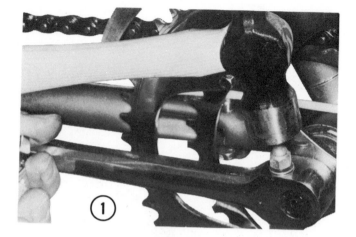

OVERHAULING A EUROPEAN-TYPE COTTER CRANK

The following step-by-step illustrated instructions cover disassembling, assembling, and adjusting a European-type crank with a cotter. *NOTE: A cotter is a tapered steel pin that holds the crank onto the pedal spindle.* A detailed exploded drawing of this type crank is included with the Cleaning and Inspecting portion of this section.

REMOVING AND DISASSEMBLING

① Loosen the acorn nut on the cotter of the right-side crank until it is approximately ⅛ inch above

the washer. If a standard nut is used instead of an acorn nut, loosen the nut until the upper surface is even with the end of the cotter. Support the underside of the crank with a block of wood with a hole in it large enough to receive the head of the cotter. **CAUTION: The crank must be solidly supported to prevent damage to the bearings or the pedal spindle while driving out the cotter.** Strike the nut squarely with a single, sharp blow in order to loosen the cotter. **CAUTION: If the nut is not hit squarely and firmly, the cotter may bend and be very difficult to remove.** An alternate method would be to remove the cotter nut, place a piece of very hard wood on the threaded end of the cotter, and then hit the wood a solid rap.

② Remove the cotter nut, and then drive the cotter out with a drift punch. Place the punch in the center of the cotter and strike it a sharp blow. Slide the right-side crank-and-chain wheel off the spindle.

③ Remove the left-side crank in a similar manner.

④ Loosen the lock ring on the left side using a drift punch and hammer to turn the lock ring in a counterclockwise direction.

⑤ Turn the adjustable cup on the left side counterclockwise until it is free of the frame. **CAUTION: Most bearing cups contain loose ball bearings. Be prepared to catch them.**

⑥ Pull the pedal spindle straight out of the frame. Catch and count the loose ball bearings from

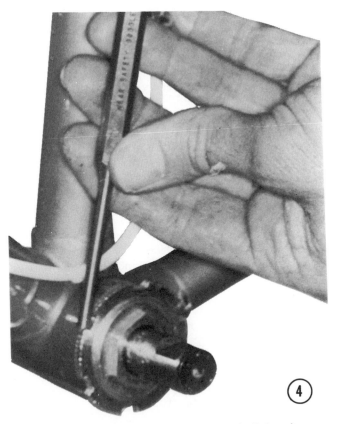

(4)

inside the adjustable cup. Remove the ball bearing retainer assembly, if used, instead of loose bearings.

⑦ Remove the right-hand stationary cup by turning it clockwise. Catch and count the loose ball

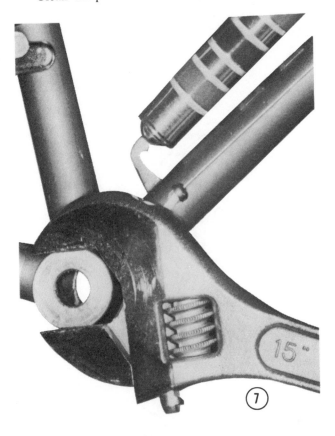

(6)

bearings, or remove the ball bearing retainer assembly, if one is used. The chain wheel(s) can be removed through their attaching bolts to the right-hand crank.

CLEANING AND INSPECTING

Clean all parts with solvent, and blow them dry

(5)

(7)

with compressed air or wipe them dry with a lintless cloth. Clean the inside of the frame housing with solvent and wipe it dry.

Check the bearing surfaces of the adjustable and stationary cups for pits, pencil-point dots, or scoring (scratchlike marks). Inspect both cups for stripped threads.

Carefully inspect the loose ball bearings for signs of excessive wear (dull spots, pits, or cracks). Replace the complete set if any of them is damaged. Replacing the complete set will ensure even distribution of the bearing load on all the ball bearings.

Check the ball bearing retainers for cracks or visible signs of damage. If any of the ball bearings come out of the retainer, are pitted, show signs of excessive wear (dull spots), or are cracked, the bearing and retainer assembly must be replaced.

Inspect the lock ring for stripped threads.

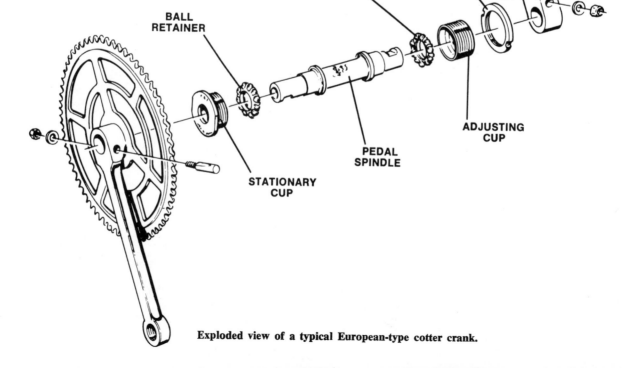

Exploded view of a typical European-type cotter crank.

Check the pedal spindle for worn cotter keyways (rounded edges), pitted or scored bearing races, and for other visible signs of damage. Check to be sure the spindle is not bent.

Inspect both cotters for stripped or damaged threads. Check them for rounded edges indicating the cotter has been loose in the crank.

Check the chain wheel for bent teeth. If any of the teeth are out of line with the chain wheel, carefully bend them back using a wrench with steady, even pressure. Try not to bend them back and forth too much as this could cause metal fatigue and the teeth may snap off under strain while the bike is in use.

Check the cotter keyway of the cranks for excessive wear (rounded edges). Check the cranks to be sure they are not bent.

ASSEMBLING

⑧ The pedal spindle has a long end and a short end, which is the distance measured from the bearing race to the spindle end. Place the spindle in a vise (equipped with soft jaws) with the longest end facing up, as shown. Apply a generous coating of multipurpose lubricant to the race, and then imbed the same number of loose ball bearings as you counted during disassembly. If you lost count, the number of bearings should fill the circumference of the bearing race, with just a small amount of clearance between each bearing. If you are working on a bicycle equipped with ball bearing retainer assemblies, pack the assemblies with a generous amount of multipurpose lubricant. Work the lubricant throughout the bearings and retainers with your fingers, and then set them to one side on a clean paper towel.

⑨ Install the right-hand ball cup snugly by turning it into the frame housing counterclockwise. **CAUTION: The right-hand ball cup has left-hand threads. Be careful to start the cup evenly to prevent stripping the threads of the cup or the frame housing.**

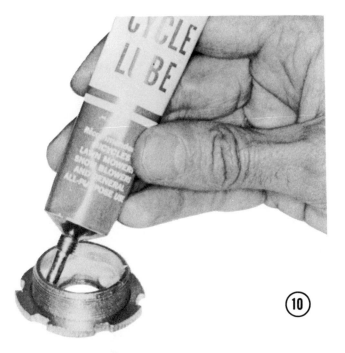

⑩

Slowly and carefully insert the spindle through the housing and right-hand cup to keep from jarring the bearings off the spindle. If the bicycle is held firmly as shown, and the spindle is centered, it will help to keep the bearings from being jarred or knocked loose. If you are working on a bicycle with ball bearing retainer assemblies, slide one of the lubricated retainer assemblies onto the spindle, with the flat side against the spindle race.

⑩ Apply a generous coating of multipurpose lubricant to the inside of the left-hand adjustable ball cup.

⑪ Imbed the same number of loose ball bearings in the cup as you counted during disassembly. If you lost count, fill the inside circumference of the cup with just a small amount of clearance between each bearing but not enough to enable another bearing to be inserted. If ball bearing retainer assemblies are used, insert the retainer assembly into the cup, with the flat side of the retainer facing up.

⑨

⑪

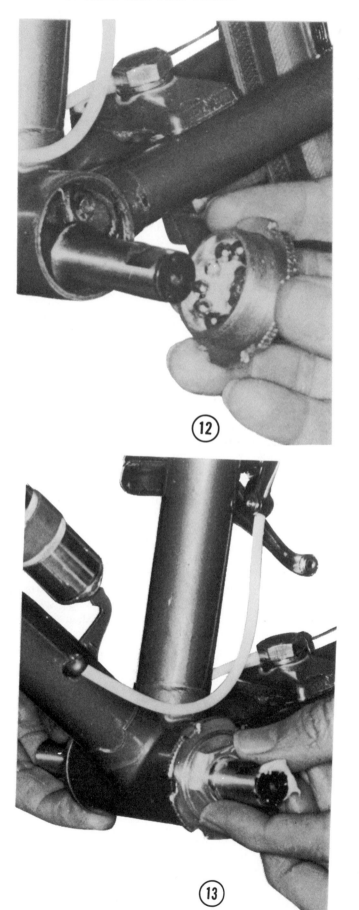

⑫

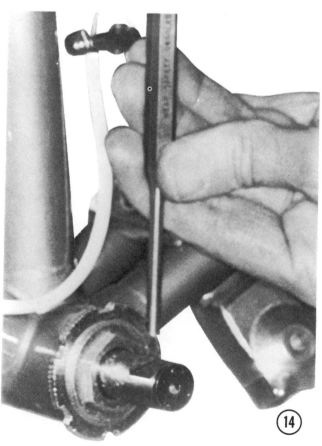

⑬

⑭

⑫ Carefully slide the adjustable cup onto the spindle and thread it clockwise into the housing.

⑬ Hold the spindle on the right side of the frame, and then tighten the adjustable cup finger-tight. Adjust the cup until the spindle turns freely and there is just a trace of end play when you attempt to move the spindle in and out of the frame housing.

⑭ Turn the lock ring clockwise, using a drift punch and hammer to tighten it securely. Check the spindle for free rotation with just a discernible amount of end play.

⑮ Install the chain wheel(s) on the crank assembly with the small wheel facing away from the crank. Lay the chain over the frame housing, and then slide the right-side crank and chain wheel(s) onto the spindle, with the hole in the crank aligned with the flat of the spindle. Hold the crank in position while you slide the cotter through the crank, with the flat on the cotter indexing with the flat of the spindle. When the crank is held forward and horizontal, the flat of the spindle must face forward.

⑯ Set the block of wood you used during disassembly under the crank with the end of the cotter over the hole in the block. **CAUTION: The crank must be solidly supported to prevent damage to the bearings or the pedal spindle when you drive the cotter home.** Strike the cotter a solid blow to seat it, and then check to be sure at least ¼ inch of thread is exposed. Install the washer, and tighten the nut to pull the cotter firmly into position. Strike the cotter once again, with the block

(15)

OVERHAULING A EUROPEAN-TYPE COTTERLESS CRANK

The following procedures provide step-by-step illustrated instructions for disassembling, assembling, and adjusting a European-type cotterless crank. A special tool is required for removing and installing a cotterless crank assembly; it consists of a socket for removing the crank bolt from the axle and an extractor for pulling the crank free of the axle. Most first-rate bicycle shops carry a complete line of cotterless-crank tool sets. Always specify the manufacturer of your crank when making a tool purchase and double check to be sure you have the correct set before leaving the store. Attempting to work on a cotterless crank assembly with the wrong tool can cause serious damage and result in a needless and expensive replacement of parts.

REMOVING AND DISASSEMBLING

① Remove the dust cap from the right and left cranks using the correct size Allen wrench. *NOTE: The dust caps on many makes of cotterless cranks have a slot and must be removed with a wide-bladed screwdriver.*

② Remove the crank bolt using a thin-walled socket or the socket from the cotterless-crank tool set. Remove the washer. Disengage the chain from the chain wheel and let it rest on the frame.

③ Thread the extractor part of the tool set into the crank, and then slowly rotate the extractor clockwise with the socket part of the tool to pull the crank free of the axle. **CAUTION: Exercise care when pulling the**

of wood under the crank, and then retighten the nut securely. Install the left-hand crank in a similar manner. Again, when the crank is held forward and horizontal, the flat of the spindle must face forward. Install the chain over the small chain wheel.

(16)

(1)

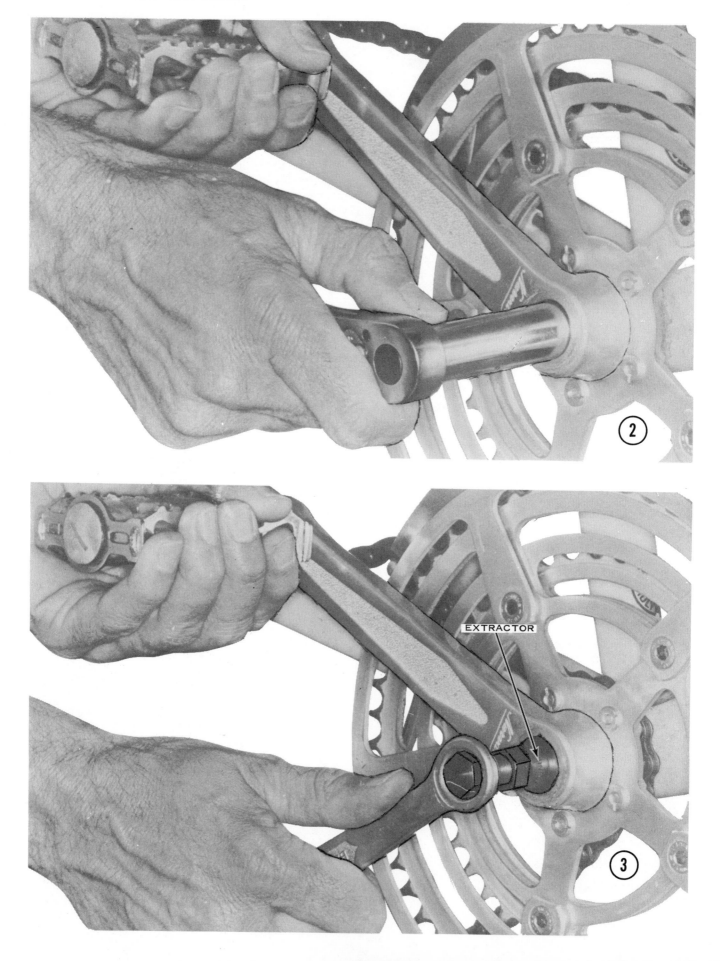

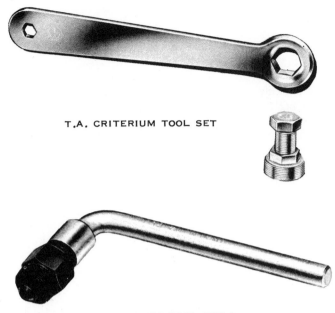

T.A. CRITERIUM TOOL SET

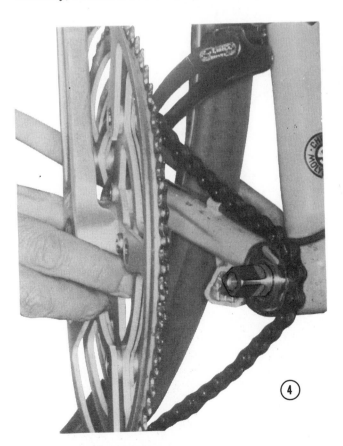

NURVAR TOOL SET

Examples of cotterless crank tool sets. Be sure to use only the set for the crank you are working on to prevent damaging the parts.

crank. The extractor works similar to a wheel puller for an automobile. As the extractor is moved in against the end of the axle, the crank will be forced off. The crank is made of aluminum alloy and it is softer than the extractor or the axle. Therefore, if you are having difficulty, remove the socket, tap the end of the extractor

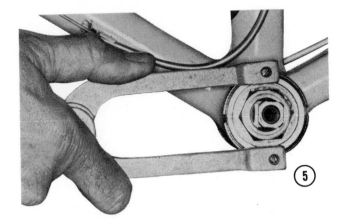

lightly with a ball-peen hammer, and then rotate the extractor about ⅛ turn. Repeat striking the extractor and turning it until the crank is loose. Remove the extractor from the crank.

④ Slide the crank and wheel free of the axle. Remove the crank bolt, washer, and left-side crank in a similar manner.

⑤ Remove the lock ring or locknut from the left-side adjustable bearing cup with a pin spanner wrench or drift punch and hammer. **CAUTION: Lay a clean cloth under the bicycle and be prepared to catch loose ball bearings when performing the next two steps.**

⑥ Back out the left-side bearing cup until it is free of the frame. Catch and count the loose ball bearings, or remove the ball bearing and retainer assembly, which may be used on some models of cotterless cranks.

⑦ Withdraw the axle from the frame. If ball bearing retainer assemblies are used, the retainers will come out with the axle. If loose bearings are used, as on most cotterless cranks, tilt the bicycle to the left and allow the bearings to roll out. An alternate method is to have the bicycle tilted to the right when you withdraw the axle. The bearings on that side will then remain in the right-side stationary bearing cup. With the bike still leaning to the right, remove the right-side ball cup and the loose bearings will probably stay in the cup.

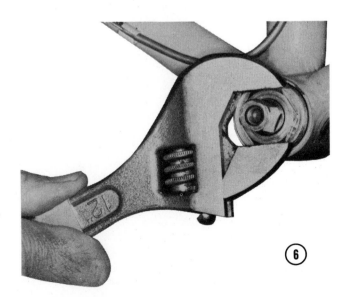

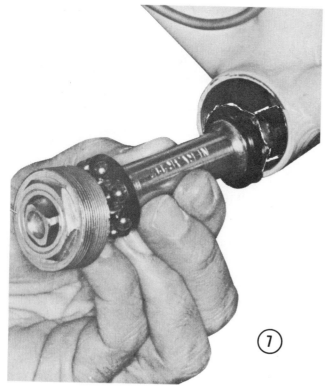

(7)

CLEANING AND INSPECTING

Clean all parts with solvent and blow them dry with compressed air or wipe them dry with a lintless cloth. Keep the cleaned parts on paper towels to avoid contamination. Cover them with a clean towel to keep grit from sticking to the internal parts and the bearings.

Carefully inspect the loose ball bearings or ball bearing and retainer assemblies. If any of the loose bearings are pitted, show signs of excessive wear (dull spots), or are cracked, the complete set must be replaced. Replacing the entire set will ensure even distribution of the bearing load. Check the retainers for cracks or visible signs of damage; replace the bearing assembly if any of the ball bearings fall out.

Check the bearing races of both bearing cups and the axle for scores, pits, or corrosion. Inspect the threads of the cups, lock ring, dust caps, ends of the axle, and the crank bolts for being stripped.

ASSEMBLING

⑧ Apply a generous coating of multipurpose lubricant to the inside race of the stationary bearing cup. Thread the lubricated cup into the frame and tighten it securely. Apply a generous coating of multipurpose lubricant to both bearing races of the axle.

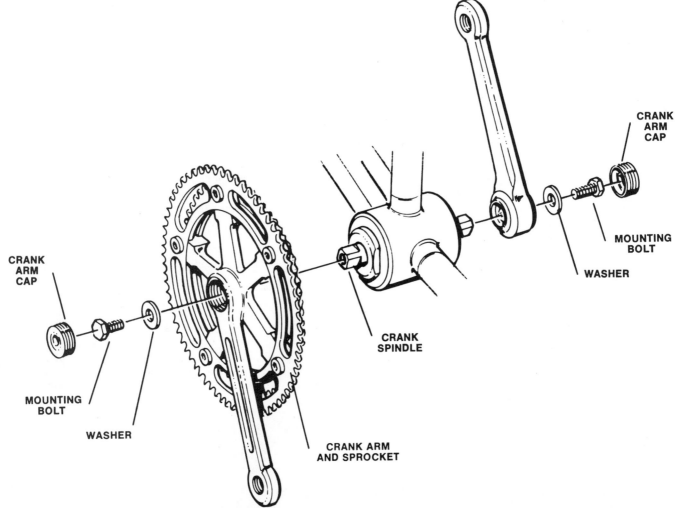

Exploded view of a typical European-type cotterless crank.

Carefully imbed the same number of loose ball bearings in each lubricated race as you counted during removal. If the count was lost, imbed enough bearings until they fit snugly around the outer edge of the race and then remove one for the proper clearance. If the crank assembly you are working on has ball bearing retainer assemblies, pack the retainers with a generous amount of multipurpose lubricant. Work the lubricant throughout the bearings and retainer with your fingers, and then slide a retainer assembly onto each end of the axle, with the flat side of the retainer facing toward the center of the axle. Coat the inside of the adjustable bearing cup with multipurpose lubricant. Notice that the distance from the bearing race to the end of the axle is greater on one end. Hold the adjustable bearing cup in place on the short end of the axle, and then slowly slide the axle through the frame and stationary bearing cup on the right-side of the frame. The lubricant will hold the bearings in place provided you do not jar or bump the axle during installation.

⑨ Thread the adjustable bearing cup into the frame, and then check the axle rotation. It should turn freely, with only a discernible amount of end play when you attempt to move the axle in and out of the frame.

⑩ Turn the lock ring onto the adjustable bearing cup and tighten it using a pin spanner wrench or a drift punch and hammer. Check the bearing adjustment. If the axle does not rotate freely with only a discernible amount of end play, loosen the lock ring by turning it counterclockwise, and then rotate the adjustable bearing cup either clockwise to tighten and remove excessive end play, or counterclockwise to allow the axle to turn freely; tighten the lock ring.

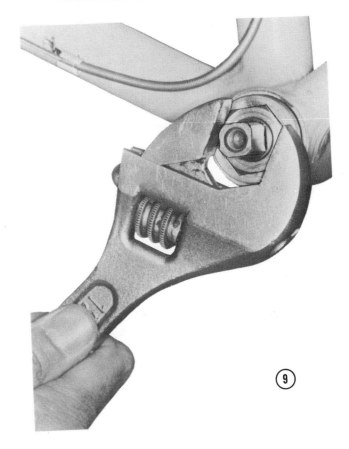

⑨

⑪ Slide the chain wheels and right-side crank assembly onto the axle, with the flats inside the wheels indexed with the flats on the axle; simultaneously engage the chain on the teeth of the small sprocket.

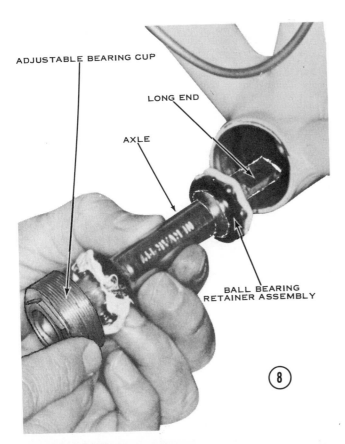

ADJUSTABLE BEARING CUP

LONG END

AXLE

BALL BEARING RETAINER ASSEMBLY

⑧

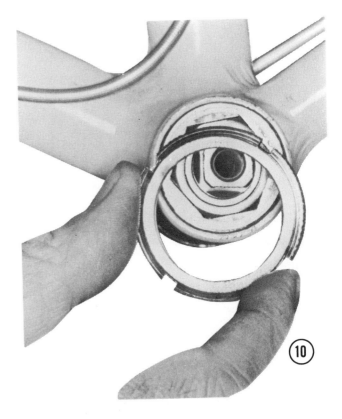

⑩

AXLE FLATS

⑪

⑫ Slip the washer onto the crank bolt, and then thread it into the end of the axle; tighten it securely using a thin-walled socket or the socket part of the cotterless tool set. Install the left-side crank in a similar manner, with the crank facing 180° in the opposite direction from the right-side crank. **CAUTION: The crank bolt of each crank must be retightened every 50 miles for the first 150 miles following an overhaul.** The axle is made of steel and the crank of an aluminum alloy; therefore, if the crank is allowed to move on the axle during pedaling, the machined fit of the crank will be ruined.

⑬ Thread a dust cap into each crank. Tighten it securely, using a correct size Allen wrench, or a screwdriver if the cap has a slot.

OVERHAULING AMERICAN-TYPE PEDALS

The following step-by-step illustrated instructions cover disassembling, assembling, and adjusting American-type pedals.

REMOVING AND DISASSEMBLING

① Remove the pedal from the crank using a wrench to grip the flats of the spindle. *NOTE: The left-side pedal spindle has left-hand threads and must be*

①

⑫

⑬

turned clockwise to remove it. *The right-side pedal spindle has conventional threads and must be turned counterclockwise to remove it.* Clamp the pedal in a vise with the jaws gripping the pads. Remove the nuts from the ends of each pad stud.

② Separate the spindle barrel from the dust cap and end plate, as shown.

③ Clamp the barrel and spindle assembly in a vise, with the jaws gripping the flats of the spindle collar. Remove the locknut and lockwasher from the spindle.

④ Back off the adjusting cone, using a narrow-bladed screwdriver indexed in one of the cone slots. Remove the bearing cup. Catch and count the loose ball bearings. Remove the spindle from the vise, but hold the spindle in the barrel until you have it over a piece of cloth to catch the loose bearings. Withdraw the spindle.

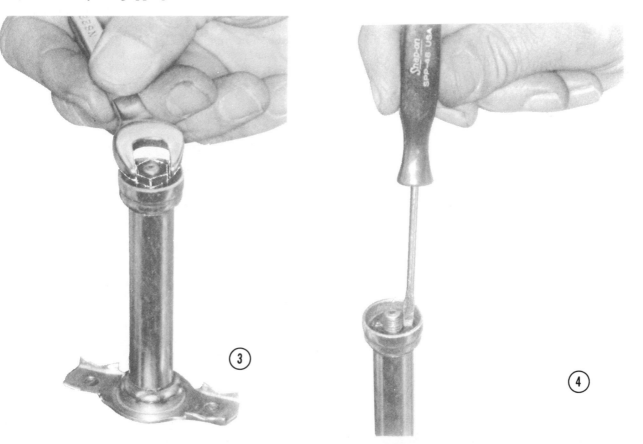

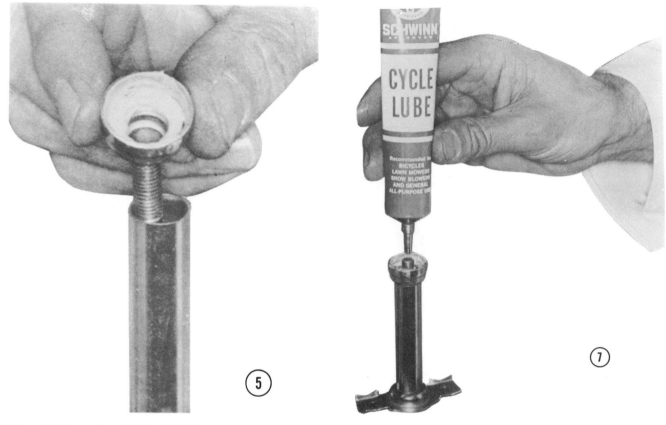

5

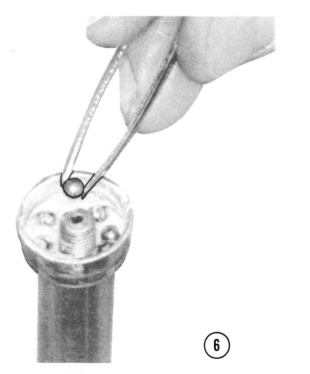

6

7

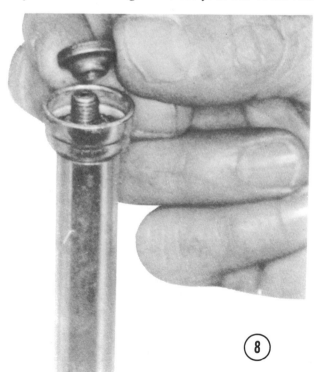

8

CLEANING AND INSPECTING

Clean all parts with solvent and blow them dry with compressed air or wipe them dry with a lintless cloth.

Carefully inspect the loose ball bearings for pits, scores, or dull spots, indicating excessive wear. If any of the bearings are damaged, the entire set must be replaced to ensure even distribution of the load on all of them.

Check the spindle for stripped or damaged threads. Inspect the bearing cups and the adjusting cones for scores, pits, or corrosion.

ASSEMBLING

⑤ Apply a generous amount of multipurpose lubricant to the nonremovable bearing cup, and then insert the same number of loose ball bearings in the cup that you counted during disassembly. If the count was lost, insert half the total number you have or enough bearings until they fit snugly around the cone of the cup, and then remove one for the proper clearance. Slide the spindle through the barrel, and then clamp it in a vise, with the jaws gripping the flats of the spindle collar. Apply a generous coating of multipurpose lubricant to the other bearing cup and insert it into the barrel over the spindle.

⑥ Imbed the remaining ball bearings in the lubricated bearing cup or enough to fill the cone of the cup, and then remove one for proper clearance.

⑦ Apply a thin coating of multipurpose lubricant over the bearings.

⑧ Thread the adjusting cone onto the spindle snugly against the bearings, and then back it off approximately ⅛ turn for a preliminary adjustment.

⑨ Adjust the cone with a narrow-bladed screwdriver until the pedal turns freely with only a discernible amount of end play when you attempt to move it up and down on the spindle.

⑩ Slide the keyed lockwasher onto the spindle, with the key indexed in the keyway of the spindle.

⑪ Turn the locknut onto the spindle firmly against the lockwasher.

⑫ Slide the assembled spindle and barrel into position between the pedal pads, with the outer bearing cup seated in the dust cap and the holes in the inner plate indexed over the pad studs. Thread both nuts onto the pad studs and tighten them securely. Thread the spindles into the crank. *NOTE: The left-side pedal has left-hand threads and must be turned on counterclockwise while the right-side pedal has conventional right-hand threads and should be turned on clockwise. Each pedal can be identified by an L or R stamped on the flat of the spindle collar or on the threaded end of the spindle. Tighten the spindles securely.*

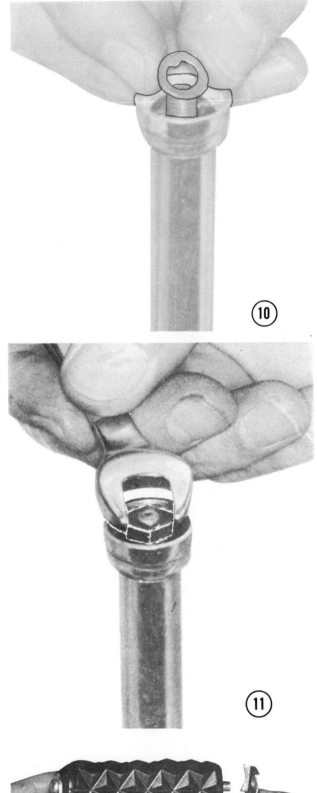

⑨

⑩

⑪

⑫

OVERHAULING CONTINENTAL-TYPE PEDALS

The following step-by-step illustrated instructions cover disassembling, assembling, and adjusting Continental-type pedals. An exploded drawing of this type of pedal is included with the Cleaning and Inspecting portion of this section.

REMOVING AND DISASSEMBLING

① Remove the pedals from the cranks using a wrench to grip the flats of the spindles. Turn the left pedal spindle clockwise and the right one counterclockwise.

② Clamp the pedal in a vise, with the closed end of the spindle facing up. Use a wrench to remove the dust cap.

③ Remove the locknut and keyed washer.

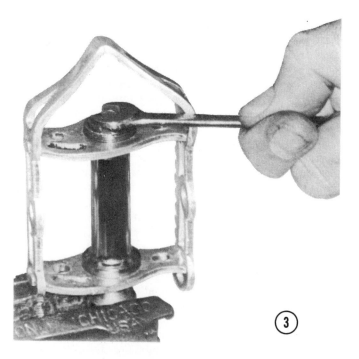

④ Remove the cone by turning it counterclockwise with a thin-bladed screwdriver, as shown. Remove and count the loose ball bearings.

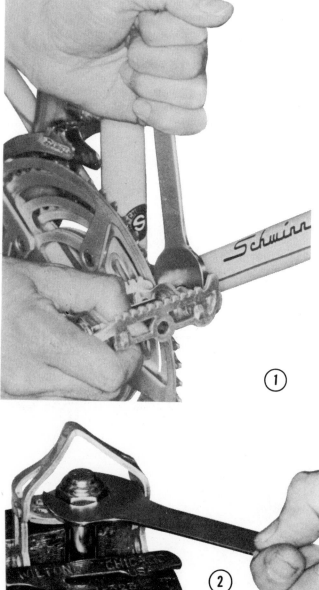

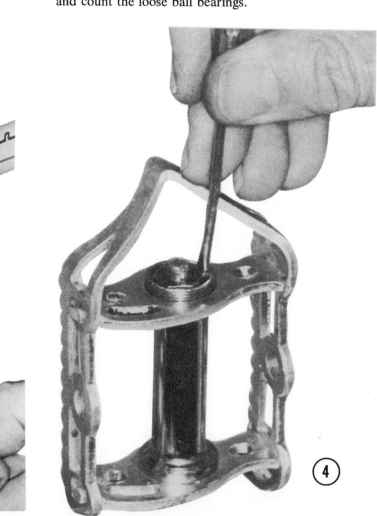

⑤ Hold the pedal over a piece of cloth and withdraw the spindle. Catch and count the loose ball bearings. You should have the same number of bearings as you counted from the other end of the pedal.

CLEANING AND INSPECTING

Clean all parts with solvent and blow them dry with compressed air or wipe them dry with a lintless cloth.

Carefully inspect the loose ball bearings for pits (pencil-point dots) and excessive wear (dull spots). If any of the bearings are damaged, the entire set must be replaced to ensure even distribution of the load on all the bearings.

Check the spindle for stripped or damaged threads.

Check the bearing surface of the cone for scores (scratchlike marks) or pits.

Inspect the cone and locknut for stripped or damaged threads.

Inspect the bearing cups of the pedal for scores, pits, or corrosion.

ASSEMBLING

⑥ Apply a generous coating of multipurpose lubricant to the bearing cup at the open end of the pedal.

⑤

PEDAL
BODY

LOOSE
BALLS

CONE
LOCKNUT

PEDAL
SPINDLE
CAP

CONE

CONE
LOCKWASHER

LOOSE
BALLS

PEDAL
SPINDLE

Exploded view of a typical Continental-type pedal.

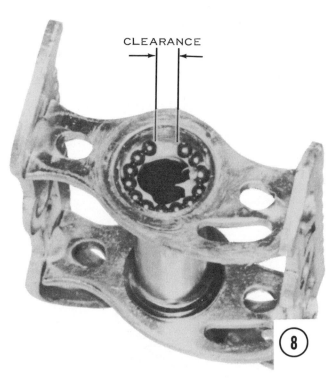

⑦ Imbed the same number of loose ball bearings in the lubricant as you counted during disassembly.

⑧ If the count was lost, imbed half the number you have, or enough to fill the circumference of the cup, and then remove one ball bearing for the proper clearance, as shown in the illustration. Cover the ball bearings with a thin coating of the lubricant. Carefully turn

the pedal end for end, apply lubricant to the bearing cup on the other side, and then imbed the same number of loose ball bearings as you did at the open end of the pedal.

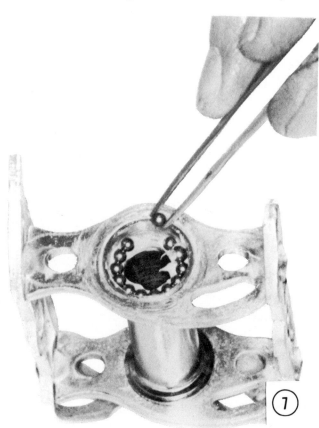

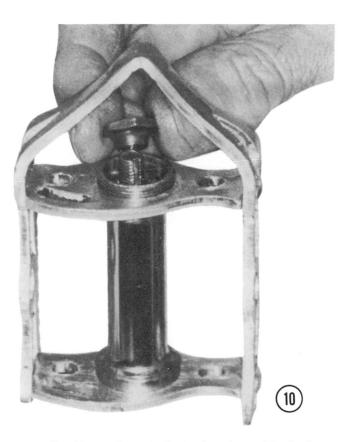

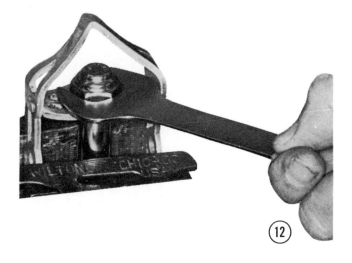

⑨ Clamp the spindle in the vise, with the jaws gripping the flats of the stationary cone. Carefully and slowly slide the pedal down the spindle into place with the closed end of the pedal facing up. **CAUTION: Don't bump the pedal or the bearings will be jarred out of place.**

⑩ Thread the adjustable cone onto the spindle finger-tight, then back it off approximately ¼ turn as a preliminary adjustment. Slide the lockwasher onto the spindle with the key indexing in the keyway of the spindle.

⑪ Thread the locknut onto the spindle. Hold the cone with the flat of a thin-bladed screwdriver, and then tighten the locknut. Rotate the pedal about the spindle and check to be sure it turns freely with just a discernible amount of end play. If the pedal does not turn freely, loosen the locknut, and then back off the cone approximately ⅛ turn. Hold the cone in place, and then retighten the locknut. If the pedal has too much end play, loosen the locknut and tighten the cone about ⅛ turn and then retighten the locknut while holding the cone with a screwdriver.

⑫ Turn the dust cap onto the pedal and tighten it securely with a wrench.

⑬ Thread the spindle onto the crank. The left-side pedal has left-hand threads and, therefore, must be turned on counterclockwise. The right-side pedal has right-hand threads and turns on clockwise. The spindles are stamped L and R on the flat of the stationary cone or on the end of the spindle for identification. Tighten the spindles in the crank securely.

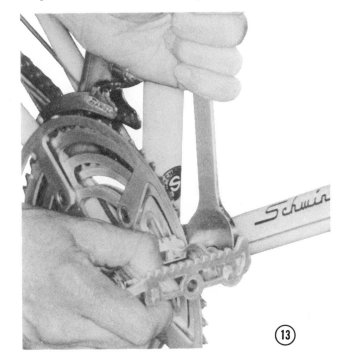

10
OVERHAULING BRAKES

Four types of brakes are used on modern bicycles and they are classified according to their method of operation as follows: (1) caliper-type brakes; (2) the disk brake, which is mounted only on the rear wheel; (3) coaster brakes used with single- or multiple-speed rear-wheel hubs; and (4) the internal-expanding, double-shoe, drum-type brake.

This chapter contains complete overhaul procedures for the *side-pull* and *center-pull caliper brakes,* and the *disk brake.*

The *coaster brake* mechanism is an integral part of the rear hub equipped with this type of braking arrangement. Therefore, complete instructions for most makes and types of coaster brakes are given in Chapter 5. Refer to the introductory section and its pictorial table of contents of that chapter for your particular coaster brake and rear-wheel hub.

Detailed procedures for overhaul of the *internal-expanding, drum-type brake* are given in the third section of Chapter 4, Overhauling Front-Wheel Hubs. Procedures for work on rear-wheel hubs equipped with drum-type brakes are similar to those outlined for the front hub after the rear wheel is removed.

CALIPER BRAKES

All caliper brakes are mounted over the bicycle wheel and are activated by operating a hand lever that is connected to the braking mechanism by a cable. The wheel is slowed or stopped by the brake shoes being pressed against the wheel rim. These shoes are mounted on the ends of caliper-type arms. Regardless of manufacturer, all caliper brakes are either a side-pull or center-pull type.

SIDE-PULL CALIPER BRAKES

Both brake arms of side-pull caliper brakes have a common pivot point, which also serves as the mounting bolt for the assembly. Both arms extend to one side of the bicycle, usually the left side, as shown in the accompanying illustration. The actuating cable is attached to the arms to move one of them slightly upward and the other downward when the brake lever on the handlebar is squeezed. This movement forces the two shoes against the wheel rim for the braking action.

Overhaul procedures for Schwinn-Approved, Weinmann, and Altenburger side-pull caliper brakes, including an exploded view of the Phillips and Raleigh assemblies, begin on page 308.

Internal-expanding, drum-type brake assembly.

Coaster brake and rear hub assembly.

CENTER-PULL CALIPER BRAKES

The arms of center-pull-type caliper brakes have separate pivot points at the ends of a brake-arm bridge. A short cable connecting the ends of the arms passes through an anchor plate. The actuating cable is attached to this plate. When the brake lever on the handlebar is squeezed, the anchor plate rises slightly, both brake arms pivot, and the shoes are pressed against the wheel rim simultaneously, as indicated in the illustration.

This arrangement allows the tension on the cable to be directed to the center, instead of to one side of the caliper assembly, thus equalizing the force on the two brake arms. The arms of the center-pull caliper unit are more rigid than those of the side-pull type. This rigidity minimizes the amount of forward movement on the arms when the brakes are applied. Center-pull assemblies are easier to adjust, hold their adjustment longer, and give more efficient braking service.

Overhaul procedures for Schwinn-Approved and Weinmann Vainquer 999 center-pull caliper brakes, including an exploded view of the G. B. Coureur 66 unit, begin on page 315.

CALIPER BRAKE SIZE

The size of caliper brakes is determined by the distance from the center of the mounting bolt to the center of the brake-arm slot. To obtain the proper size when purchasing a new set of caliper brakes, measure the distance from the center of the mounting-bolt hole to the center of the wheel rim, then choose the assembly closest in size. The correct caliper-brake assembly is essential for proper service, in case you have to change the size of the wheel for any reason.

Since 1969, the Schwinn Bicycle Company has used a coding system stamped on the face of the outer brake arm to indicate the type of wheel on which the caliper brake assembly is to be used, the type of caliper brake, and the size of the brake unit. The coding consists of two letters followed by two numbers, and their meaning is as follows:

Center-pull caliper brake assembly.

First Letter:

L—caliper brake to be used with lightweight wheels
M—caliper brake to be used with middleweight wheels
B—caliper brake to be used with balloon-tired wheels

Second Letter:

S—indicates the caliper brake is a side-pull type
C—indicates the caliper brake is a center-pull type

Numbers:

The two numbers indicate (in inches) the distance from the center of the mounting bolt to the center of the brake-arm slot, as depicted in the accompanying illustration, with the tenths equaling $\frac{3}{32}$ inch.

From the illustration, the distance of 2.3 indicates $2\frac{9}{32}$ inches from the center of the mounting bolt to the center of the brake-arm slot or the center of the wheel rim.

Side-pull caliper brake assembly.

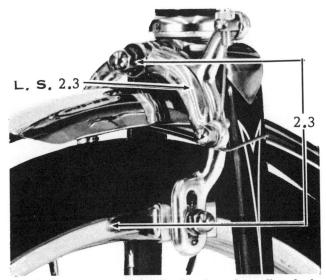

Coding system used for identification of a caliper brake assembly to ensure use of the proper-sized unit.

Rear-wheel disc brake assembly.

DISK BRAKES

The disk brake arrangement, installed on bicycles as shown in the accompanying illustration, is similar to that used on automobiles. The assembly consists of a disk attached to the rear-wheel hub, a caliper assembly with brake pads that can bear on both sides of the disk, and the necessary actuating and releasing mechanism required for efficient operation.

The disk brake is installed only on the rear wheel and is actuated by squeezing a lever mounted on the handlebar. This lever is connected with cable linkage to a brake lever bracket at the rear wheel.

Overhaul procedures for a Schwinn disk brake begin on page 322.

OVERHAULING SIDE-PULL CALIPER BRAKES

This section provides step-by-step illustrated instructions for disassembling, assembling, and adjusting a typical set of side-pull caliper brakes. Procedures for front and rear brakes are essentially the same, except as noted in the specific step.

The illustrations in this section were made of a Schwinn-Approved set of side-pull caliper brakes, which is similar to the Weinmann and Altenburger units, and is typical for this type of assembly. An exploded view showing all parts of these three sets of brakes follows the Cleaning and Inspecting section.

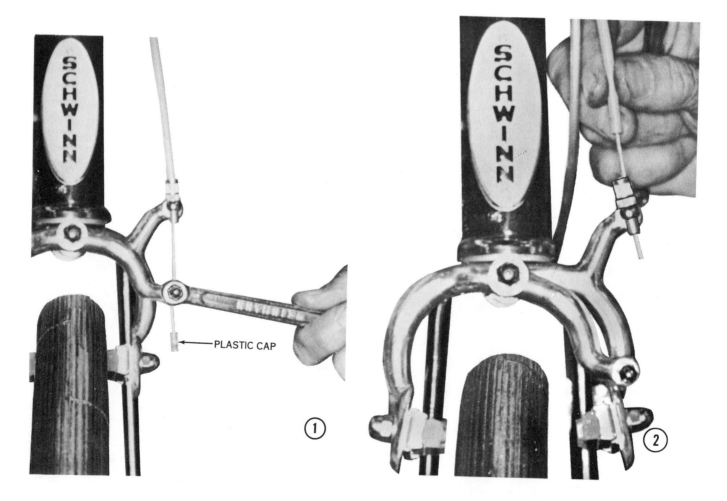

PLASTIC CAP

①

②

Side-pull caliper brakes of other manufacturers may vary slightly due to the shape of the spring, the type of pivot bolt, the arrangement of bushings and washers, and the knob design on the brake shoes. An exploded view showing all parts of the Phillips and Raleigh side-pull caliper brakes also follows the Cleaning and Inspecting instructions.

REMOVING THE CALIPER ASSEMBLY

① Loosen the cable adjusting nut. Remove the plastic cap from the end of the cable.

② Back off the knurled collar on the cable guide until the cable and guide can be pulled free of the brake-arm eyebolt.

③ Remove the locknut, lockwasher, and washer from the pivot bolt on the back side of the forks for the front caliper brakes or from the front side of the frame for the rear brakes.

④ Withdraw the pivot bolt and complete brake assembly from the front fork or rear frame.

⑤ Pry the spring ends up over the spring posts on each brake arm.

⑥ Clamp the long end of the pivot bolt in a vise, using soft jaws to protect the threads. Remove the locknut, adjusting nut, and washers. Lift off the outer brake arm and washer from the pivot bolt. Remove the anchor nut and bolt.

⑦ Lift off the inner brake arm, washer, and spring. Remove the cable guide and eyebolt from the inner brake arm.

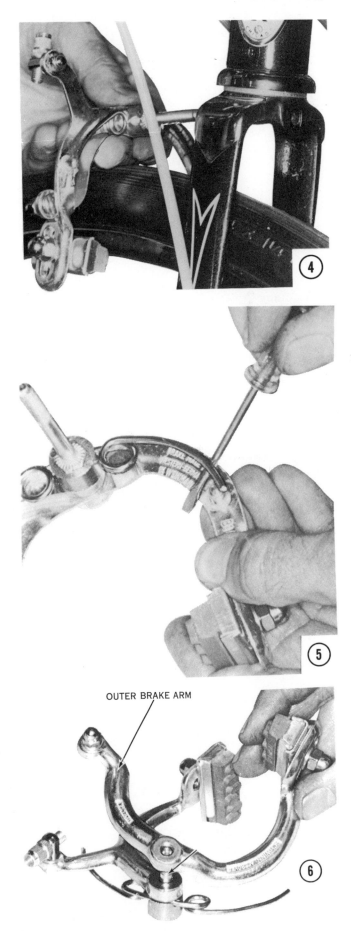

OUTER BRAKE ARM

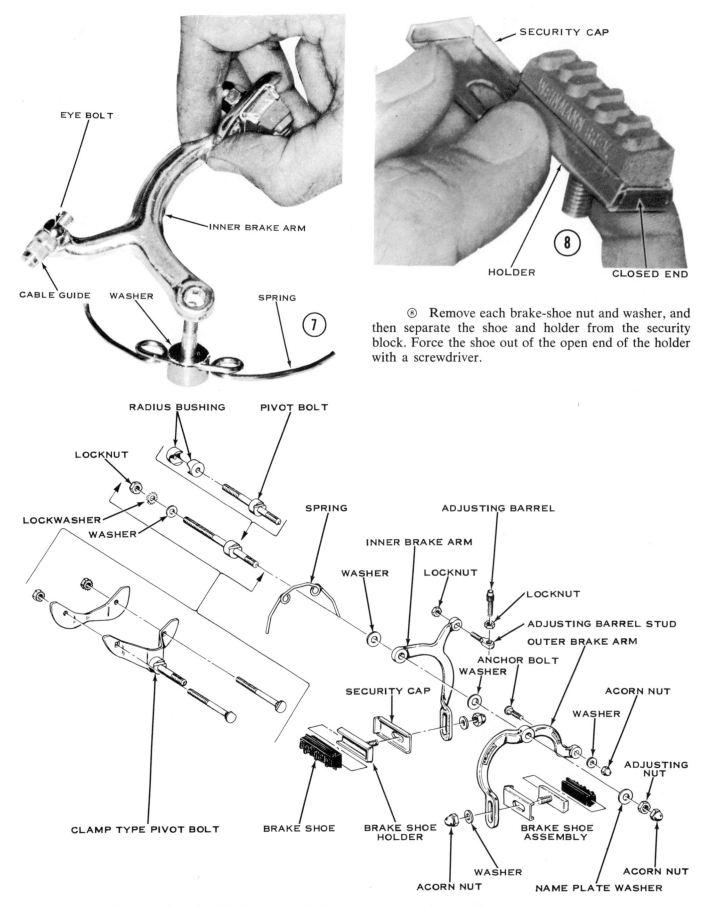

EYE BOLT

INNER BRAKE ARM

CABLE GUIDE   WASHER   SPRING

⑦

SECURITY CAP

HOLDER   CLOSED END

⑧

⑧ Remove each brake-shoe nut and washer, and then separate the shoe and holder from the security block. Force the shoe out of the open end of the holder with a screwdriver.

RADIUS BUSHING   PIVOT BOLT

LOCKNUT

LOCKWASHER

WASHER

SPRING   ADJUSTING BARREL

INNER BRAKE ARM

WASHER   LOCKNUT

LOCKNUT

ADJUSTING BARREL STUD

OUTER BRAKE ARM

ANCHOR BOLT

WASHER

ACORN NUT

WASHER

SECURITY CAP

ADJUSTING NUT

CLAMP TYPE PIVOT BOLT   BRAKE SHOE   BRAKE SHOE HOLDER   BRAKE SHOE ASSEMBLY   ACORN NUT

WASHER

ACORN NUT   NAME PLATE WASHER

Exploded view of a Schwinn-Approved, Weinmann, and Altenburger side-pull caliper brake assembly.

CLEANING AND INSPECTING

Clean all parts, except the brake shoes, with solvent and then blow them dry with compressed air or wipe them dry with a lintless cloth.

Inspect the mounting bolt, anchor bolt, and cable-guide pieces for stripped threads. Check the threads of all nuts to be sure they are not stripped or damaged.

Check the brake arms to be sure they are not bent or twisted.

Check the spring for a crack or lost tension.

ASSEMBLING

⑨ Clamp the long end of the mounting bolt in a vise with soft jaws to protect the threads. Lay the center of the spring in the mounting bolt groove, with the ends of the spring arched back toward the opposite side of the bolt from the groove and on the lower side of the coil, as shown.

⑩ Slide a new brake shoe into each of the brake-shoe holders. Install the holders into the security caps, with the open end of the holder facing the closed end of the security cap. Install the assembled brake-shoe

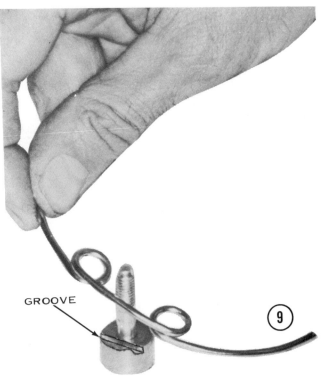

GROOVE

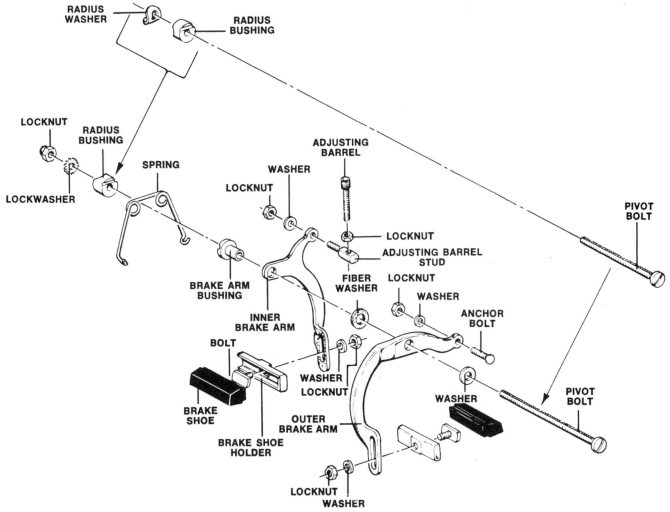

Exploded view of a Phillips and Raleigh side-pull caliper brake assembly.

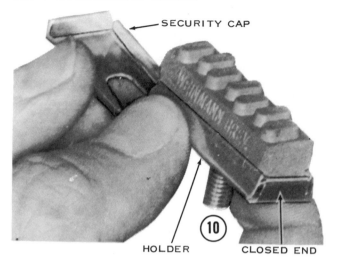

SECURITY CAP

⑩

HOLDER   CLOSED END

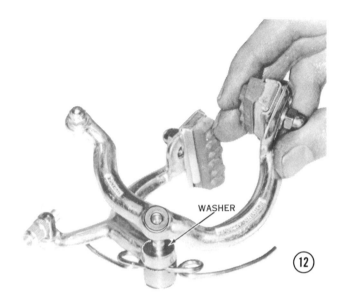

WASHER

⑫

units on each brake arm so the closed end of the holder faces forward and the beveled surface of the shoe matches the angle of the wheel rim when installed on the bicycle. **CAUTION: The brake-shoe assembly must be installed with the closed end of the holder facing forward to prevent the shoe from working out when the brakes are applied.**

⑪ Thread the cable-guide eyebolt onto the forward side of the brake arm, and then thread the cable guide into the eyebolt, with the locking collar on the same side as the knurled end, as shown. Insert the anchor bolt through the front side of the outer brake arm, and then install the nut finger-tight. Position the washer over the spring on the pivot bolt. Place the inner

(left-side) brake arm on the pivot bolt, with the spring knob facing down and the arm arched in the same direction as the spring on that side.

⑫ Position the washer on top of the inner brake arm, and then install the outer brake arm, with the spring knob facing down.

⑬ Place the nameplate washer or plain washer on top of the outer brake arm. Thread the adjusting nut onto the pivot bolt finger-tight, and then back it off approximately ¼ turn for operating clearance. Check movement of the brake arms, which should rotate freely without any end play (movement back and forth on the pivot bolt). Hold the adjusting nut in position, and then turn the locknut tight against the adjusting nut.

⑭ Remove the assembly from the vise, turn it over, and then snap the ends of the spring over the spring knobs with a screwdriver.

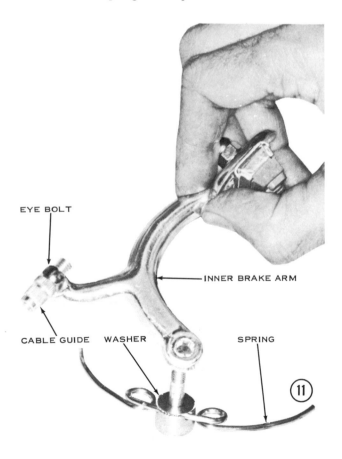

EYE BOLT

INNER BRAKE ARM

CABLE GUIDE   WASHER   SPRING

⑪

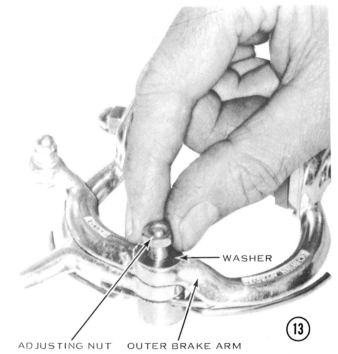

WASHER

⑬

ADJUSTING NUT   OUTER BRAKE ARM

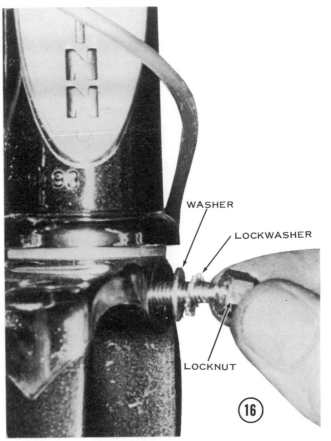

⑮ Install a radius bushing onto the pivot bolt, with the flat side of the bushing against the brake arm. Slide the pivot bolt through the mounting hole in the front fork or rear frame.

⑯ At the front-wheel position, slide a radius bushing onto the pivot bolt, with the flat side facing out. Slide a washer and then a lockwasher onto the mounting bolt. Tighten the locknut securely.

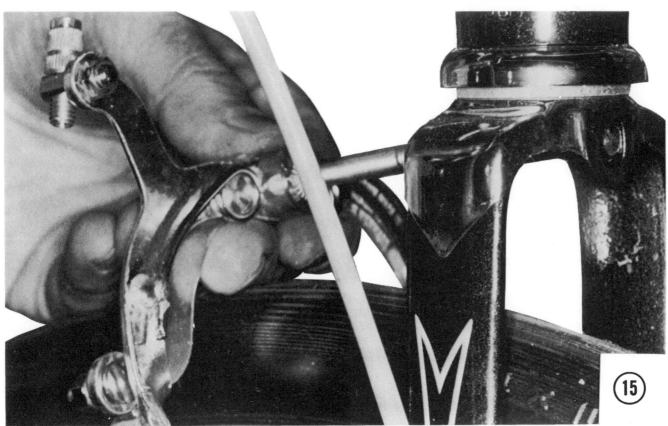

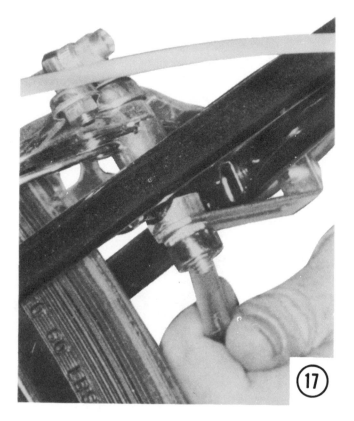

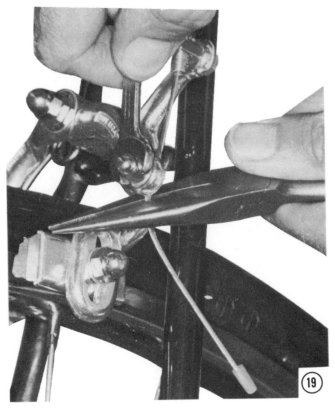

⑰ Position the reflector bracket on top of the radius bushing at the rear-wheel position, and then install the washer, lockwasher, and locknut.

⑱ Check the brake arms for free movement. If they do not rotate easily, loosen the locknut slightly,

and then turn the adjusting nut approximately ¼ turn. Hold the adjusting nut, and then retighten the locknut. The arms should move freely but must have no end play when moved in and out on the pivot bolt.

⑲ Squeeze the brake shoes against the rim, using

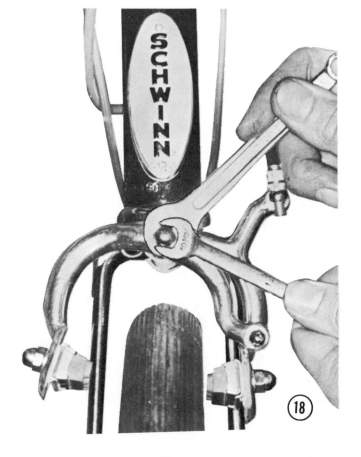

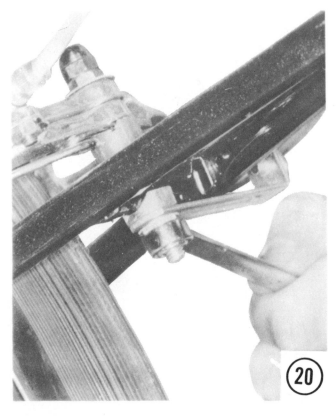

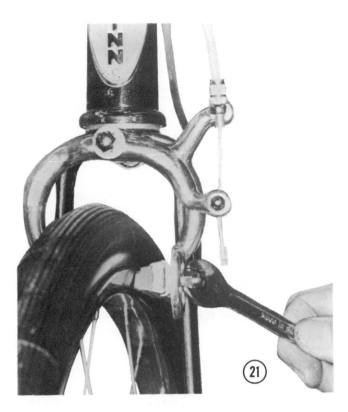

a "third hand" tool or tighten a piece of cord around both arms and through the wheel. Feed the cable through the cable guide and anchor bolt. Slide the plastic cap over the end of the cable. Pull the cable taut with a pair of pliers and simultaneously tighten the anchor nut. Remove the "third hand" tool or piece of cord. The brake shoes should release to about ⅛ inch from the rim. If they release more than ⅛ inch or do not move clear of the rim, loosen the anchor nut, tighten or loosen the cable as required, and then retighten the anchor nut.

⑳ Center the assembled brake unit over the wheel rim, by loosening the mounting locknut slightly and then turning the brake arms and pivot bolt until the brake shoes are approximately equally distant from the wheel rim. Tighten the pivot bolt locknut securely.

㉑ Loosen the acorn nut of each brake shoe slightly, and then move the shoe assembly in the brake-arm slot until the top edge of the shoe is approximately

$\frac{1}{32}$ inch below the top of the wheel rim. Tilt the shoe to the approximate angle of the wheel rim, and then tighten the acorn nut securely.

㉒ Check to be sure the front end of the brake shoe is approximately $\frac{1}{32}$ inch closer to the wheel rim than the rear end. If it is not, grip the brake arm with a wrench directly below the brake-shoe assembly, and then twist the arm slightly until the front end of the shoe contacts the wheel rim first when the brake lever is actuated. This position will keep the brake from squeaking.

OVERHAULING CENTER-PULL CALIPER BRAKES

The following step-by-step illustrated procedures cover disassembling, assembling, and adjusting a typical set of center-pull caliper brakes. Procedures for front and rear caliper brakes are essentially the same, except as noted in the specific step.

The illustrations in this section were made of a Schwinn-Approved set of center-pull caliper brakes, which is identical to the Weinmann Vainquer 999 and is typical for this type of assembly. An exploded view showing all parts of these two sets of brakes follows the Cleaning and Inspecting section.

Center-pull caliper brakes of other manufacturers may vary slightly due to the springs used, the arrangement of bushings and washers, the type of pivot stud or bolt for securing the brake arms to the bridge, and the knob design on the brake shoes. An exploded view showing all parts of the G. B. Coureur 66 center-pull caliper brakes also follows the Cleaning and Inspecting instructions. One unique feature of this brake set is that you must first pry the nameplate dust caps out of the brake arms with a screwdriver in order to separate the brake arm from the bridge. Then you can drive the pivot studs out with a drift punch and hammer.

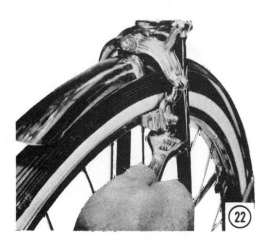

Adjust the brake shoe so that the top edge of the shoe is $\frac{1}{32}$ inch below the top of the wheel rim, as shown.

REMOVING THE CALIPER ASSEMBLY

① Remove the acorn nut and washer from one of the brake arms. Pull the brake arm away from the tire enough to slide the stud of the brake-shoe assembly out of the slot in the brake arm.

② Remove the brake shoe and holder from the security cap. If the brake shoe needs to be replaced because the knobs are worn smooth, slide the shoe out of the open end of the holder with a screwdriver.

③ Compress the brake arms against the wheel rim and, simultaneously, turn the cable end of the opposite arm from which the brake shoe was removed, until the cable is aligned with the slot in the brake arm. Slide the cable free of the arm. Remove the cable from the other brake arm in a similar manner.

④ Remove the nut, lockwasher, reflector bracket, and radius bushing from the mounting bolt at the rear-wheel position. Remove the nut, lockwasher, and spacers from the front-wheel position.

⑤ Withdraw the complete brake unit, including the mounting bolt and the other radius bushing, from the frame. Slide the radius bushing off the mounting bolt.

⑥ Lay the brake unit on the bench, with the mounting bolt facing up. Pry the spring end from each of the brake-arm anchor posts with a screwdriver. Remove the nuts from the pivot bolts.

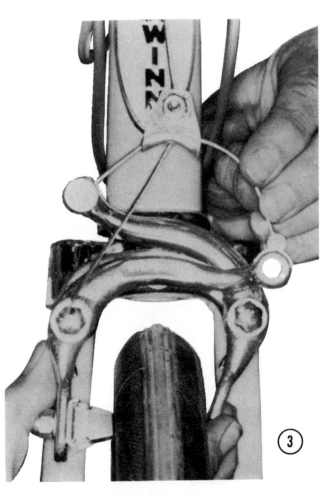

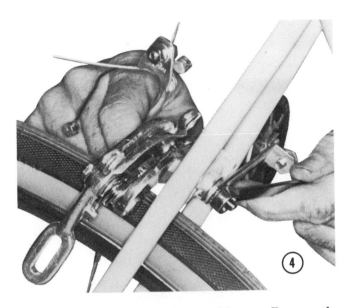

⑦ Turn the complete assembly over. Remove the outer brake arm and pivot bolt from the bridge. Lift off the spring. Withdraw the pivot bolt and note the arrangement of the steel bushing in the center of the brake arm and the nylon bushing on each side. Remove the inner brake arm from the bridge, and then lift the bolt and bushings from the arm. Withdraw the mounting bolt from the bridge.

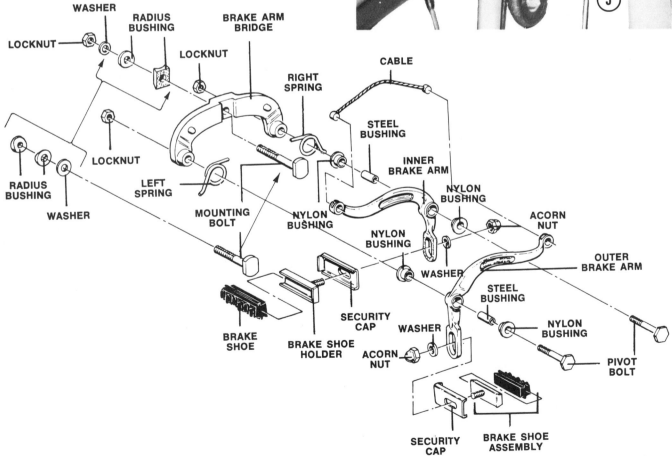

Exploded view of a Schwinn-Approved and Weinmann Vainqueur Model 999 center-pull caliper brake assembly.

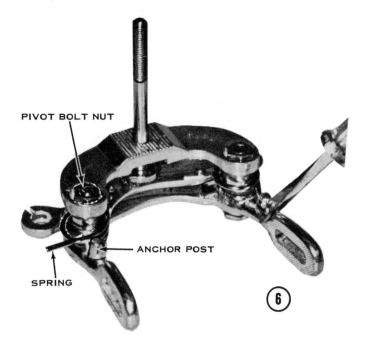

PIVOT BOLT NUT

ANCHOR POST

SPRING

⑥

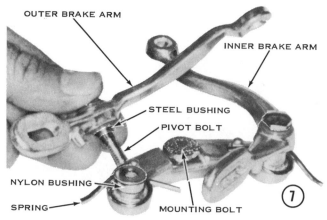

OUTER BRAKE ARM

INNER BRAKE ARM

STEEL BUSHING

PIVOT BOLT

NYLON BUSHING

SPRING

MOUNTING BOLT

⑦

CLEANING AND INSPECTING

Clean all parts except the brake shoes with solvent and blow them dry with compressed air or wipe them dry with a lintless cloth.

Inspect the mounting bolt and pivot bolts for stripped threads. Check the threads of all the nuts to be sure they are not stripped or damaged.

Check the brake arms to be sure they are not bent or twisted.

Check the springs for cracks or lost tension.

ASSEMBLING

⑧ Insert the mounting bolt through the bridge, with the flats of the bolt head indexing with the recesses in the bridge.

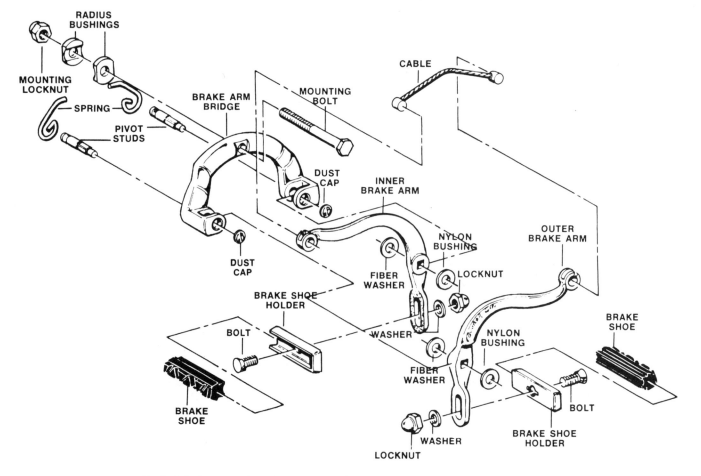

RADIUS BUSHINGS

MOUNTING LOCKNUT

SPRING

PIVOT STUDS

BRAKE ARM BRIDGE

MOUNTING BOLT

CABLE

DUST CAP

INNER BRAKE ARM

NYLON BUSHING

OUTER BRAKE ARM

DUST CAP

FIBER WASHER

LOCKNUT

BRAKE SHOE

BRAKE SHOE HOLDER

BOLT

WASHER

NYLON BUSHING

BRAKE SHOE

FIBER WASHER

BOLT

LOCKNUT

WASHER

BRAKE SHOE HOLDER

Exploded view of a G.B. Coureur Model 66 center-pull caliper brake assembly.

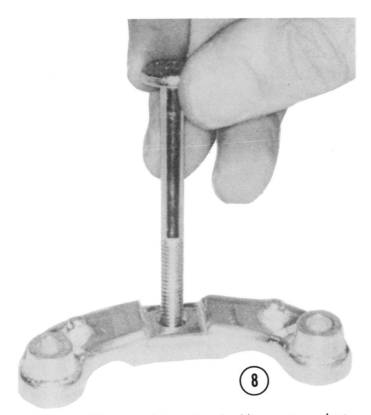

⑧

NYLON BUSHING

STEEL BUSHING

⑨

⑨ Slide one of the nylon bushings onto a pivot bolt, with the flat side of the bushing against the bolt head. Slide the steel bushing onto the bolt, and then insert the assembled bolt through the inner brake arm from the side opposite the spring anchor post.

⑩ Place the right-side spring on the bridge, with the hooked end of the spring on top of the coil facing away from the bridge; and then place the straight end of the spring on the lower side of the post, as shown. *NOTE: The right and left springs are identified by the*

hook end being on top of the coil and facing outward when placed on the spring post. Hold the inner brake arm and assembled pivot bolt in place, and then insert the bolt through the bridge. Slide another nylon bushing onto the bolt, with the flat side facing out, and then thread the locknut onto the bolt and into the slot in the bridge. Hold the nut in place, and then tighten the pivot bolt. Install the outside brake arm in a similar manner.

⑪ Turn the assembled unit over, and then snap

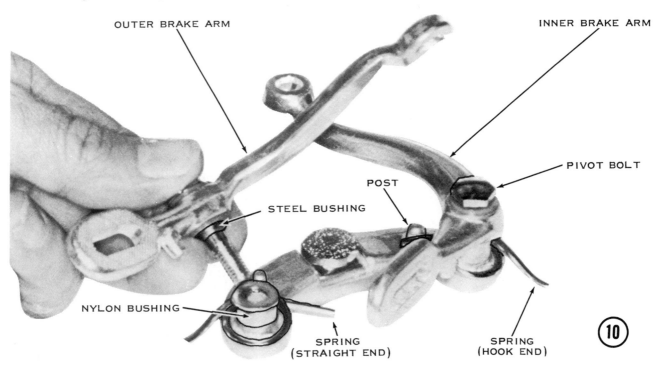

OUTER BRAKE ARM

INNER BRAKE ARM

PIVOT BOLT

POST

STEEL BUSHING

NYLON BUSHING

SPRING (STRAIGHT END)

SPRING (HOOK END)

⑩

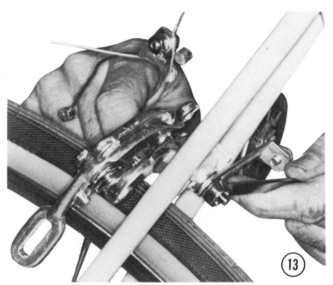

PIVOT BOLT NUT

ANCHOR POST

SPRING

(11)

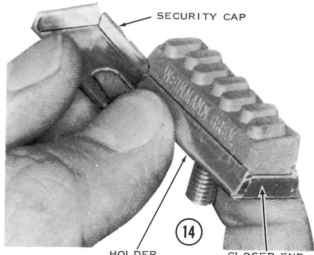

(13)

the hook end of the springs over the anchor posts on the brake arms.

⑫ Slide the spacer and radius bushing onto the mounting bolt, with the concave side of the bushing facing up, and then install the bolt through the hole in the front forks or rear frame.

⑬ Install the radius bushing on the mounting bolt, with the concave side against the frame. At the rear-wheel position, slide the reflector bracket onto

the bolt, with the reflector extending to the left side of the bicycle. Install the lockwasher on the bolt, thread the locknut on, and then tighten it securely.

⑭ Push a new brake shoe into each of the brake shoe holders until the shoe contacts the closed end of the holder. Insert the brake-shoe-holder bolt through the slot of the security cap, with the open end of the holder toward the closed end of the cap, as shown. Install an assembled brake shoe into one of the brake arms, with the closed end of the holder facing forward and the beveled surface of the shoe matching the angle of the wheel rim. The closed end of the security cap will then be facing toward the rear of the bicycle. **CAUTION: The brake-shoe assembly must be installed with the closed end of the holder facing forward to prevent the shoe from working out when the brakes are applied and subsequent complete loss of braking ability at that wheel.** Install a washer, and then thread an acorn nut onto the brake-shoe bolt finger-tight.

⑮ Insert one end of the brake cable loop into the hole and slot of the brake arm without the brake shoe assembly being installed. Squeeze the brake arms together against the wheel rim, and then insert the other end of the brake cable loop into its hole and slot.

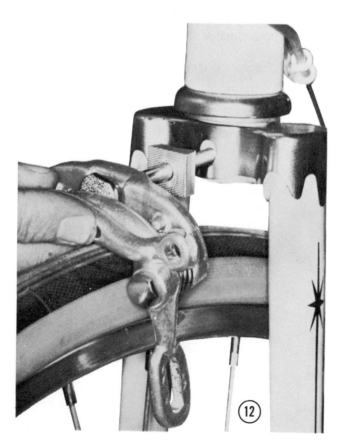

(12)

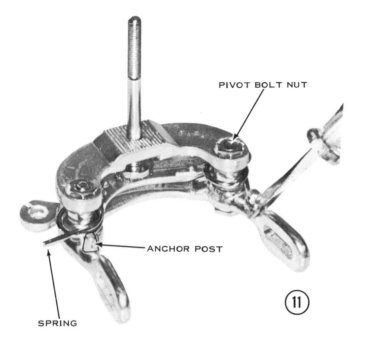

SECURITY CAP

(14)

HOLDER

CLOSED END

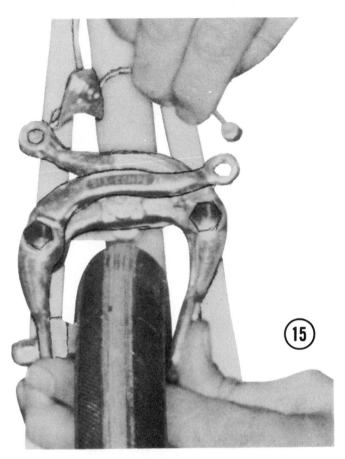

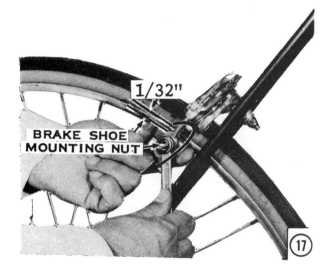

ADJUSTING

⑰ Loosen the acorn nut of each brake shoe slightly, and then slide the shoe assembly in the brake-arm slot until the top edge of the shoe is approximately $\frac{1}{32}$ inch below the top of the wheel rim. Tilt the shoe to the approximate angle of the wheel rim, and then tighten the acorn nut securely.

⑱ Center the assembled brake unit over the wheel rim, by loosening the mounting locknut slightly and then turning the brake-arm bridge and mounting bolt until the brake shoes are approximately equally distant from the wheel rim. Tighten the locknut securely.

⑯ Install the other brake shoe assembly on the brake arm, with the closed end of the brake-shoe holder facing forward. Install a washer, and then thread an acorn nut onto the brake-shoe bolt; tighten it securely.

BRAKE ARM

⑲ Check to be sure the front end of the brake shoe is approximately $\frac{1}{32}$ inch closer to the wheel rim than the rear end. If it is not, grip the brake arm with a wrench directly below the brake-shoe assembly, and then twist the arm slightly until the front end of the shoe contacts the wheel rim first when the brake lever is actuated. This will keep the brake from squeaking.

OVERHAULING A DISK BRAKE

This section provides step-by-step illustrated instructions for disassembling, assembling, and adjusting a disk brake. The illustrations were made of a Schwinn unit and an exploded view showing all parts of this assembly follows the Cleaning and Inspecting section.

If the spokes of a wheel equipped with a disk

brake need replacing, Steps ① through ④ must be performed to gain access to the spokes, and Steps ⑪ through ⑯ must be accomplished following installation of the new spokes.

REMOVING THE WHEEL

① Shift the chain onto the smallest sprocket. Turn the bicycle upside down, resting it on the seat and handlebars. Loosen the cable anchor bolt, and then remove the cable from the anchor bolt and the cable-adjusting barrel. Remove the screw from the brake

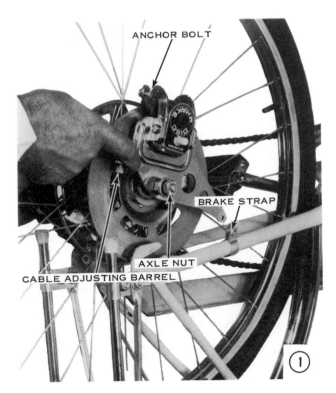

ANCHOR BOLT

BRAKE STRAP

AXLE NUT

CABLE ADJUSTING BARREL

strap. Loosen both axle nuts. Move the kickstand to the down position. Pivot the derailleur arm toward the rear of the bicycle to obtain slack in the chain and, at the same time, move the wheel forward out of the rear-fork dropouts. Release the derailleur unit, remove the chain from the sprocket, and then guide the wheel free of the frame.

DISASSEMBLING

② Clamp the wheel assembly in a vise, with the jaws gripping the axle and the brake unit facing up. **CAUTION: Use soft vise jaws to protect the axle threads.** Remove the mounting nut and bolt from the caliper assembly, and then slide the assembly free of the disk and mounting bracket.

③ Remove the axle nut and washer, and then take off the nut securing the mounting bracket. Lift the mounting bracket off the axle.

④ Rotate the outer disk lock ring clockwise using a pin spanner wrench or a drift punch and hammer until it is clear of the hub. **CAUTION: The outer lock ring has left-hand threads and must be turned clockwise to be removed.** Rotate the inner disk lock ring counterclockwise until it is clear of the hub. Lift the disk off the hub.

⑤ Pull the plastic cap off the pivot assembly shaft, and then remove the cable-mounting bracket. Push out the nylon bushing with a screwdriver. Remove the cable-adjusting barrel.

⑥ Press the spring retaining pin inward with a screwdriver, turn the pin ¼ turn, release pressure, and then remove the pin and the spring.

⑦ Rotate the pivot-pin assembly 180° out of the caliper assembly, and then slide the shaft out of the bushing. Withdraw the tilt pin from the pad-adjusting barrel. Remove the cable anchor nut and bolt. Remove

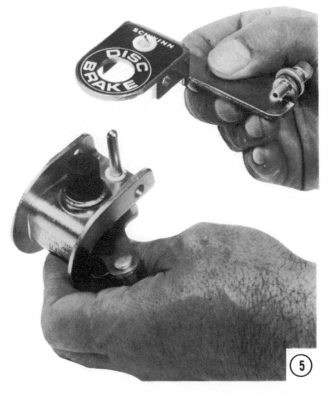

the nylon bushing, and then turn out the pad-adjusting barrel from the caliper housing. **CAUTION: The pad-adjusting barrel has a nylon lock. Do not turn or remove the pad barrel unless necessary. This would weaken the lock.**

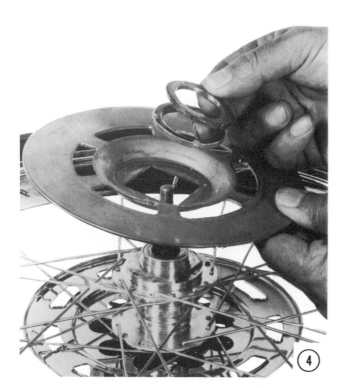

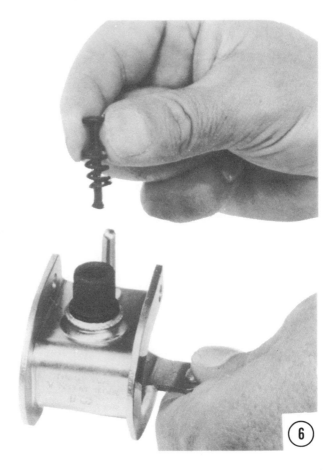

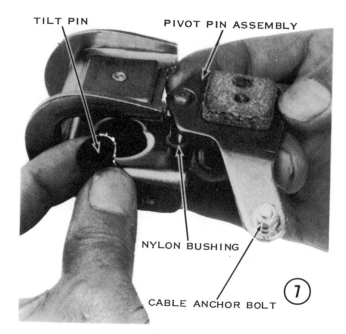

CLEANING AND INSPECTING

Clean all parts, except the brake pads, with solvent, and then blow them dry with compressed air or wipe them dry with a lintless cloth. Be sure to remove any grease or oil from the pads and the disk.

Check the threads of all nuts, bolts, both lock rings, the pad-adjusting barrel, and the caliper assembly for stripped threads.

Inspect both mounting brackets and the disk for cracks or bends. Check the surface of the disk for scores indicating worn pads.

Carefully check the thickness of the brake pads. If either of the pads is worn to within $\frac{1}{16}$ inch of the studs, both pads must be replaced as a set to ensure proper service and to prevent scoring of the disk.

Inspect the spring for cracks or lost tension.

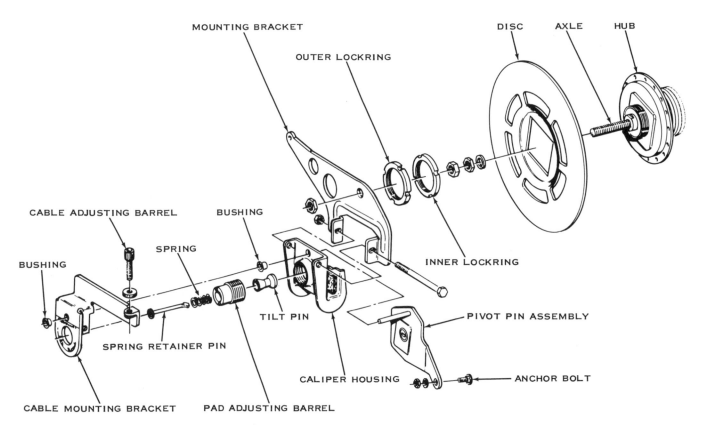

Exploded view of a rear-wheel disk-brake assembly.

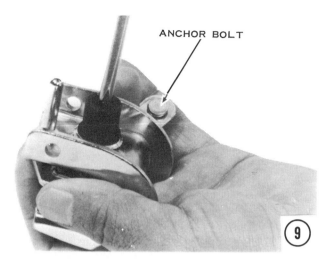

ANCHOR BOLT

⑨

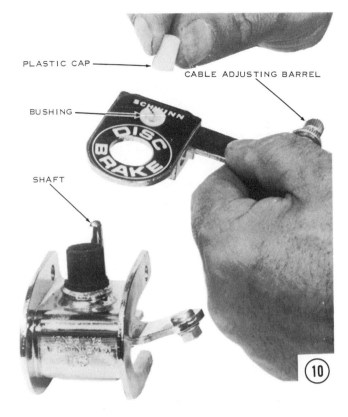

PLASTIC CAP

CABLE ADJUSTING BARREL

BUSHING

SHAFT

⑩

ASSEMBLING

⑧ Clamp the wheel in a vise, with the jaws gripping the axle. **CAUTION: Use soft vise jaws to protect the axle threads.** Push the nylon bushing for the shaft of the pivot-pin assembly through the hole in the caliper assembly from the outside surface. Turn the pad-adjusting barrel into the caliper assembly until the end of the barrel is flush with the inside surface of the housing. Insert the tilt pin into the pad-adjusting barrel. Guide the shaft of the pivot-pin assembly into the bushing, and then rotate it 180° until the assembly is seated over the tilt pin.

⑨ Install the anchor bolt, washer, and nut in the end of the pivot pin assembly, as shown. Slide the spring onto the spring pin, and then insert the pin into the pad-adjusting barrel. Hold the pivot assembly and press the spring and pin inward, then rotate the pin approximately ¼ turn until it is locked in the keyway.

⑩ Thread the knurled lockwasher onto the cable-adjusting barrel, and then thread the adjusting barrel into the cable-mounting bracket as far as it will go. Place the mounting bracket onto the shaft of the caliper assembly, with the manufacturer's identification facing up and the hole in the bracket fitting over the pad-adjusting barrel. Press the plastic cap onto the end of the pivot assembly shaft.

⑪ Place the disk onto the hub, with the dished

PIN SPANNER WRENCH

OUTER LOCKRING

INNER LOCKRING

DISC

⑪

side facing up and the square hole in the center indexed over the flats on the end of the hub. Thread the inner lock ring onto the hub by turning it clockwise, and then tightening it securely against the disk by using a pin

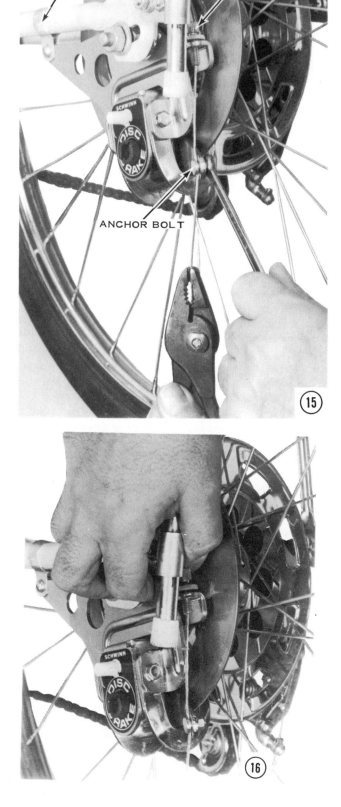

BRAKE STRAP   CABLE ADJUSTING BARREL

ANCHOR BOLT

spanner wrench or drift punch and hammer. **CAUTION: The outer lock ring has left-hand threads.** Thread the outer lock ring counterclockwise onto the hub and secure it against the inner lock ring with a pin spanner wrench or a drift punch and hammer.

⑫ Slide the mounting bracket onto the axle and secure it with the axle nut.

⑬ Place the caliper assembly in position between the arms of the bracket and secure it with the bolt and locknut.

⑭ Turn the pad-adjusting barrel clockwise until the brake pads are fully seated against the disk, and then back the barrel out ½ turn for a preliminary adjustment.

INSTALLING THE WHEEL

⑮ Start the axle nuts onto the ends of the axle. Guide the wheel into position between the frame members, place the chain onto the smallest sprocket, pull the derailleur unit toward the rear of the bicycle, and then move the wheel back into the rear-fork dropouts. Slip the brake arm into the strap on the frame, and then secure it with the mounting screw and nut. If the brake strap has several mounting holes, bend the strap around the frame so the brake arm will be as close to the frame as possible. Center the wheel between the frame members, and then tighten the axle nuts securely.

⑯ Insert the control cable through the adjusting barrel and anchor bolt. Check that the adjusting barrel is turned down as far as it will go. Pull the cable taut through the anchor bolt, and then secure it with the anchor nut. Work the brake lever on the handlebar several times to stretch the cable, and then readjust the cable until it is taut. Back out the cable-adjusting barrel until you feel the brake pads drag on the disk, and then turn the barrel in approximately ½ turn, or until the wheel turns freely.

Members of the American Youth Hostels on tour through the California countryside. Properly adjusted and maintained brakes are an essential part of their safety program. Courtesy American Youth Hostels, Inc.

11
OVERHAULING HEADSETS

The headset consists of the following parts: the handle-bar stem; the upper portion of the front fork above the crown, which is called the fork stem; the head portion of the frame; and the necessary bearings, bearing cups, cones, and a locking device to hold the handlebar stem firmly in the fork stem and still allow the complete fork assembly to rotate freely inside the frame head for steering purposes.

Headsets are grouped into two broad classifications: *American-type* and *European-type*. Today the name has no reference to geographical location or national origin because, like so many other parts of the bicycle, both are manufactured in various parts of the world. The terms are used merely for identification purposes.

American-type headsets have the handlebar stem and fork assembly made of forged steel, with an external-type wedge in the lower end of the handlebar stem. The ball bearings are held in place by retainer assemblies.

European-type headsets are made of aluminum alloy and, therefore, are much lighter than American units. These headsets have an internal-wedge arrangement in the handlebar stem for locking it in position. They use loose ball bearings, but lately some manufacturers have started to use plastic retainers to hold the bearings in place.

This chapter contains complete overhaul procedures for both types of headsets. To obtain maximum service, the headset should be overhauled, thoroughly lubricated, and adjusted at least once a year.

OVERHAULING AN AMERICAN-TYPE HEADSET

This section provides step-by-step illustrated instructions for disassembling, assembling, and adjusting a typical American-type headset. The illustrations were made of a headset on a Schwinn bicycle, but they apply to many makes of bikes. An exploded drawing of a typical assembly is included in the Cleaning and Inspecting section.

DISASSEMBLING

① Loosen the stem bolt on top of the handlebar stem approximately two turns. **CAUTION: The wedge**

will fall down into the head of the frame if you back the bolt out too far. Strike the head of the bolt squarely with a single, sharp blow of a mallet to jar the wedge loose.

② Lift up on the handlebars to remove the stem from the frame head. If the stem is rusted in place, apply some penetrating oil or liquid wrench around

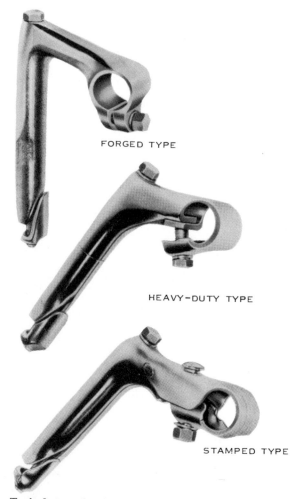

FORGED TYPE

HEAVY-DUTY TYPE

STAMPED TYPE

Typical stems for American-type headsets, with an external wedge (bottom) for securing the headset in the front fork stem.

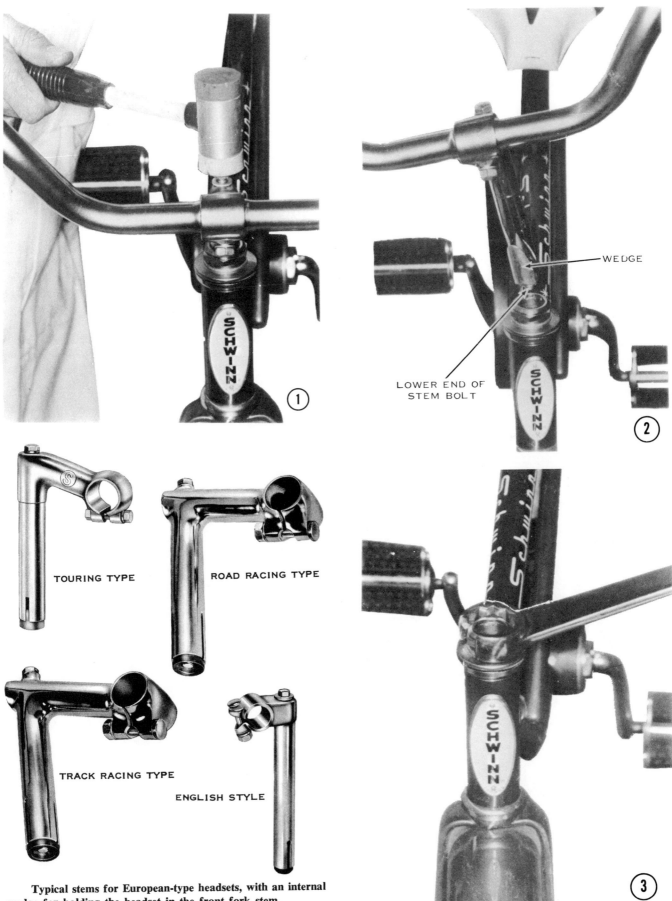

WEDGE

LOWER END OF
STEM BOLT

①

②

③

Typical stems for European-type headsets, with an internal
wedge for holding the headset in the front fork stem.

TOURING TYPE

ROAD RACING TYPE

TRACK RACING TYPE

ENGLISH STYLE

④

the bicycle upside down and shake it out after you have removed the handlebar stem.

③ Remove the locknut and keyed lockwasher from the fork stem.

④ Grasp the adjustable cup firmly with a pair of water-pump-type pliers and turn it counterclockwise off the fork stem.

⑤ Lower the fork stem from the bottom of the frame head, and then remove the upper and lower ball bearing retainer assemblies.

CLEANING AND INSPECTING

Clean all parts in solvent and blow dry with compressed air, or wipe them dry with a lintless cloth. Keep the cleaned parts on paper towels to avoid contamination.

Carefully inspect the ball bearing retainer assemblies. If any of the ball bearings fall out of the retainer, are pitted, cracked, or show other signs of damage, replace the assembly. Check the retainer for cracks or pits.

Inspect the race of the upper and lower bearing cups for scores (scratchlike marks), pits (pencil-point dots), or excessive wear (dull spots). If one of the bearing cups in the head of the frame is damaged and needs to be replaced, remove it with a drift punch and hammer from the opposite end of the head. Insert a new one by gently tapping it into position with a mallet.

the stem and bolt, let it set for a few minutes, and then tap the stem from side to side with a mallet while attempting to pull it out. If the wedge has fallen off, turn

BALL BEARING RETAINER ASSEMBLY

BALL BEARING RETAINER ASSEMBLY

⑤

⑥

Be careful not to distort or damage the cup by striking it too hard.

Check all threaded parts for stripped threads.

ASSEMBLING

⑥ Pack the ball bearing retainer assemblies with a generous amount of multipurpose lubricant. Work the lubricant throughout the bearings and retainer with your fingers. Coat the inside of the bearing cups with lubrication.

⑦ Insert the larger lubricated bearing assembly into the upper bearing cup, with the flat side of the retainer facing down. Slide the smaller lubricated bearing assembly onto the fork stem, with the flat side of the retainer facing up.

⑧ Thread the adjustable cup onto the fork stem, with the bearing race side facing down.

⑨ Tighten the adjustable cup until the fork stem is just snug in the head of the frame, but is still free enough to rotate with no discernible end play.

⑩ Place the keyed lockwasher over the end of the fork stem, with the key indexed in the keyway of the stem.

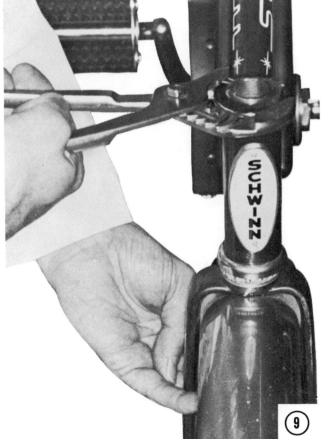

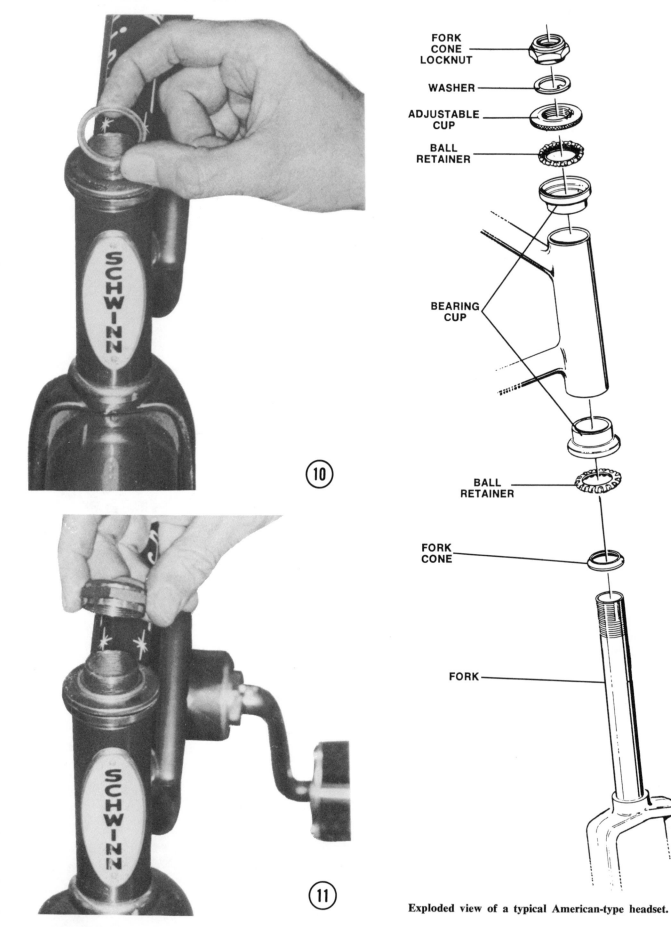

⑩

⑪

FORK
CONE
LOCKNUT

WASHER

ADJUSTABLE
CUP

BALL
RETAINER

BEARING
CUP

BALL
RETAINER

FORK
CONE

FORK

Exploded view of a typical American-type headset.

⑪ Thread the locknut onto the stem, with the crowned side facing up. Firmly tighten the locknut against the lockwasher.

⑫ Check the cone adjustment. The fork should rotate freely with no end play. If an adjustment is required, first loosen the locknut, tighten or loosen the adjustable cup, and then securely tighten the locknut. Recheck the adjustment after tightening the locknut.

⑬ Lubricate the stem bolt and wedge threads with high-quality cycle oil to prevent thread seizure and to ensure proper tightening. Slide the handlebar stem into the fork stem until the handlebars are at the desired height, and then hand-tighten the stem bolt. On some makes of bicycles, the handlebar stem has a mark to indicate the maximum height the stem can be raised. **CAUTION: Do not raise the stem above this mark, because the grip of the contact surfaces between the two stems would be insufficient for safe cycling.** If the handlebar stem does not have a maximum height mark, measure 2½ inches from the lower end of the stem, make your own mark, and then raise the stem to the desired height, but not so high that the mark shows above the locknut.

⑭ Swing the handlebars right or left until the upper portion of the handlebar stem is aligned with the wheel. Hold the wheel between your legs for a firm grip and securely tighten the stem bolt.

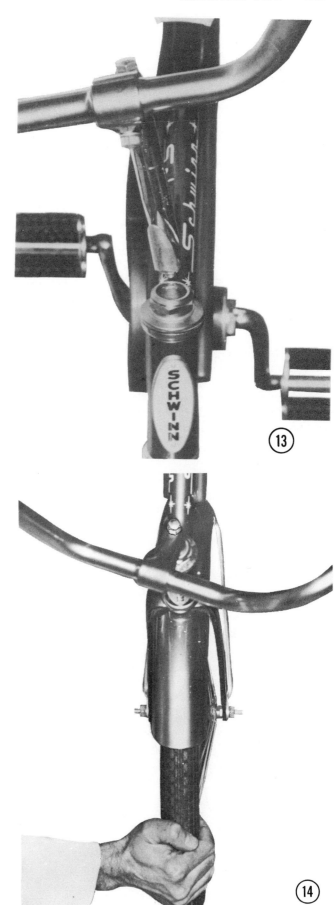

OVERHAULING A EUROPEAN-TYPE HEADSET

This section provides step-by-step illustrated instructions for disassembling, assembling, and adjusting a typical European-type headset. The illustrations were made of a headset on a Peugeot bicycle, but they apply to many makes of bicycles.

DISCONNECTING THE CONTROL CABLES

NOTE: It is not necessary to disconnect the brake cables or shifting cables in order to overhaul the headset, because the slack in the cables is usually sufficient to allow the handlebar stem to be raised clear of the frame head. However, on bicycles equipped with cables to the front wheel it will be necessary to disconnect them as follows: On bicycles with center-pull type caliper brakes, squeeze the front-brake handle slightly, push in on the quick-release button, and then release the brake handle. If you are working on a bicycle without a quick-release button, there may be a quick-release lever just above the brake on the cable hanger. If neither of these quick-release mechanisms is used, remove the mounting nut from one of the brake-shoe holders and then take off the complete brake-shoe assembly. Squeeze the caliper arms against the wheel and simultaneously unhook the cable from the bridge.

For bikes with side-pull caliper brakes or internal-expanding brake shoes, disconnect the cable from the anchor bolt, and then feed it back through the cable adjusting barrel.

DISASSEMBLING

① Loosen the stem bolt on top of the handlebar stem approximately two turns. **CAUTION: The wedge will fall down into the head of the frame if you back the bolt out too far.** Strike the head of the bolt squarely with a single, sharp blow of a mallet to jar loose the wedge at the bottom of the stem.

② Lift up on the handlebars to remove the stem from the frame head. If the stem is rusted in place, apply some penetrating oil or liquid wrench around the stem and the bolt, let it set for a few minutes, and then tap the stem from side to side with a mallet while attempting to pull it out. If the wedge has fallen into the head of the frame, turn the bicycle upside down and shake the wedge out after you have removed the handlebar stem.

③ Remove the collar locknut by turning it counterclockwise.

④ Unhook the brake cable collar guide from the slot in the fork stem, and then remove it.

⑤ Lift the lock ring off the adjustable cup.

⑥ Grasp the adjustable cup firmly with a pair of locknut pliers or a pair of expandable water-pump-type pliers. **CAUTION: Be sure the teeth of the pliers are covered with plastic, rubber, or tape to prevent damage to the knurled surface of the cup.**

⑦ Remove and count the loose ball bearings from the upper bearing cup. Hold the fork tightly against the head of the frame and, at the same time, carefully turn the bicycle upside down. Pull the fork out

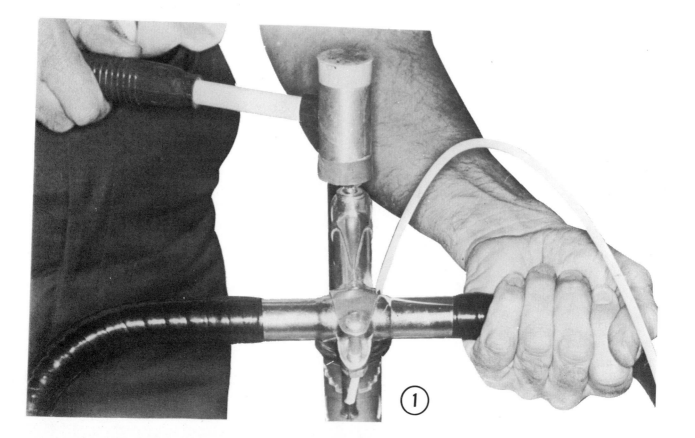

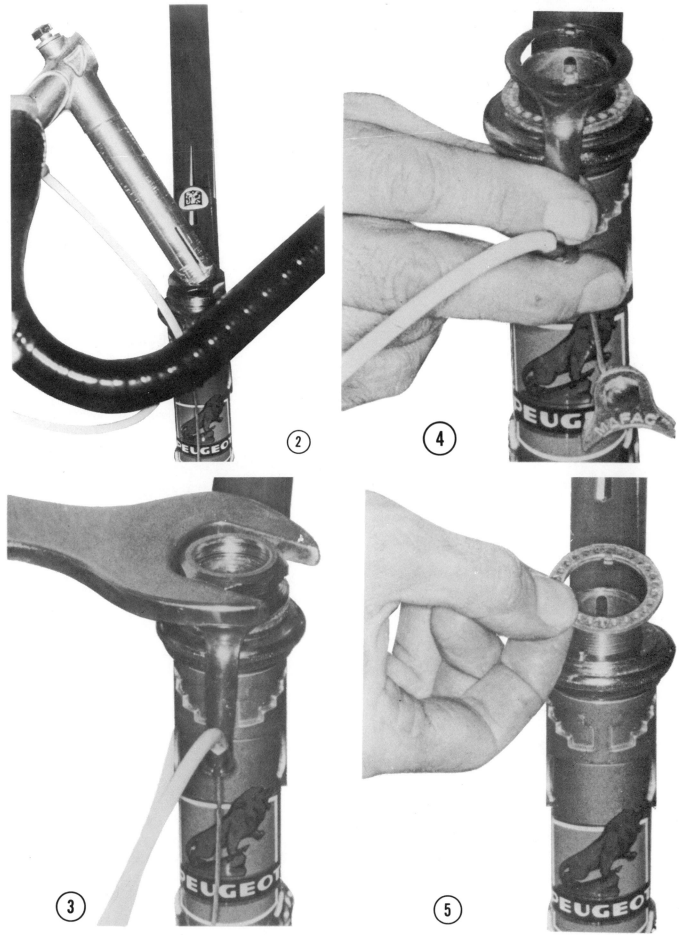

② ③ ④ ⑤

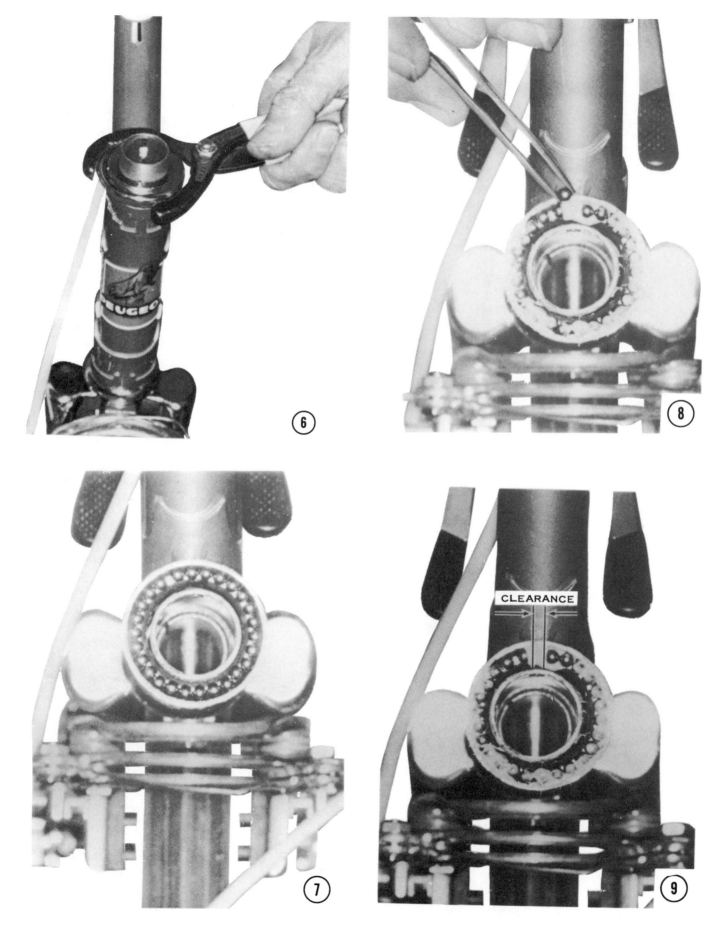

CLEARANCE

of the frame head, and then remove and count the loose ball bearings in the lower bearing cup. *NOTE: On some late-model European-type headsets the ball bearings may be held in a plastic retainer.*

CLEANING AND INSPECTING

Clean all parts in solvent and blow dry with compressed air, or wipe them dry with a lintless cloth. Keep all cleaned parts on paper towels to avoid contamination, especially the bearings.

Carefully inspect the ball bearings for pits, cracks, or dull spots indicating excessive wear. If any of the bearings are worn, replace the complete set, to ensure even distribution of the bearing load on all the bearings.

Inspect the races of the upper and lower bearing cups for scores, pits, or excessive wear (dull spots). If one of the bearing cups is damaged, remove it from the head of the frame, using a drift punch and hammer from the opposite end of the head. Insert a new one by placing it on the head and then gently tapping it into position with a mallet. Be careful not to distort or damage the cup by striking it too hard.

Check all parts for stripped threads.

ASSEMBLING

⑧ Turn the bicycle upside down and coat the inside of the lower bearing cup with a liberal amount of multipurpose lubricant. Imbed the same number of loose ball bearings that you counted during disassembly. If the count was lost, insert enough bearings until they fit snugly around the edge of the cup, and then remove one for the proper clearance. If the bearings are held in a retainer, pack both assemblies with a generous amount of multipurpose lubricant. Work the lubricant throughout the bearings and retainer with your fingers. Insert one of the retainers in the lower ball cup, with the flat side facing down (with the bicycle upside down) into the cup. Cover the bearings with a thin coating of lubricant, and then slide the fork stem through the frame head. Hold the fork tight against the frame to hold the bearings in place, and then turn the bicycle right side up. Apply a generous amount of multipurpose lubricant to the upper bearing cup. Imbed the same number of bearings you counted during disassembly, or fill the cup and then remove one bearing for the proper clearance. If retainers are used, insert the other assembly into the bearing cup, with the flat side facing down (with the bicycle right side up).

⑨ Check to be sure the bearings fit snugly and evenly, with just enough room for one more (for proper running clearance), as indicated in the illustration.

⑩ Cover the bearings with a thin layer of lubricant.

⑪ Thread the adjustable cup onto the fork stem with the small pin facing up. Adjust the cup with a pair of locknut pliers or expandable water-pump-type pliers until the fork turns freely in the frame head, with no up and down or side play. **CAUTION: Be sure the teeth of the pliers are covered with plastic, rubber, or tape to prevent damage to the knurled surface of the**

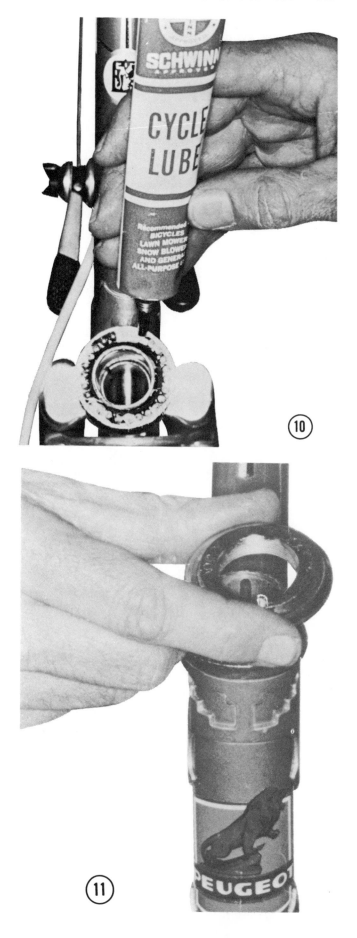

cup. If you have any difficulty in making the adjustment, you may have too many bearings in either the upper or lower bearing cup, or you may have lost one bearing and are, therefore, short in one of the cups. In this case it will be necessary to disassemble the headset, check the cups for the correct number of bearings, and then reassemble it properly before making the adjustment.

⑫ Install the lock ring, with the ear of the ring indexed in the slot of the fork stem and one of the holes indexed over the pin of the adjustable cup. If necessary, you may have to rotate the adjustable cone slightly in order for one of the holes to fit over the pin.

⑬ Place the cable collar guide on top of the lock ring, with the ear of the collar indexed in the slot of the fork stem.

⑪ Thread the locknut onto the stem, and then tighten it securely.

⑮ Lubricate the stem bolt and wedge threads with high-quality cycle oil to prevent thread seizure and to ensure proper tightening. Slide the handlebar stem into the fork stem until it is at the desired height, and then hand-tighten the stem bolt. On some makes of bicycles, the handlebar stem has a mark to indicate the maximum height the stem can be raised. **CAUTION: Do not raise the stem above this mark,** because the

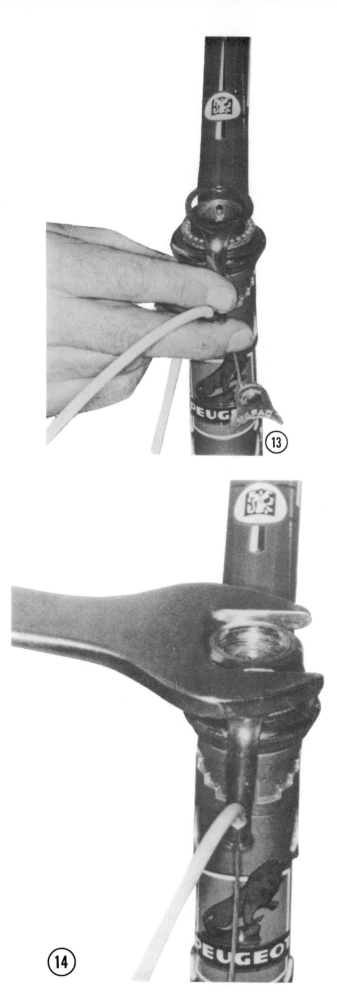

contact surfaces of the two stems would be insufficient for safe cycling. If the handlebar stem does not have a maximum height mark, measure 2½ inches from the lower end of the stem, make your own mark, and then raise the stem to the desired height but not so high that the mark shows above the locknut. Swing the handlebars right or left until the upper portion of the handlebar stem is aligned with the wheel. Hold the wheel between

your legs for a firm grip, and then securely tighten the stem bolt.

⑯ Return the caliper brakes to the operating position. If you removed the cable from the bridge of the center-pull type, replace the cable. If you removed the cable from the adjusting barrel of the side-pull-type caliper brakes, feed the cable through the barrel and the anchor bolt, and then tighten the bolt. If you removed one of the brake-shoe assemblies, install the holder, with the closed end facing forward and with the beveled surface of the shoe matching the angle of the wheel rim. **CAUTION: Be sure the closed end of the holder is facing forward to prevent the shoe from being forced out when the brakes are applied with subsequent complete loss of braking ability at the front wheel.** Adjust the brake-shoe holder in the brake-arm slot until the upper edge of the shoe makes contact just below the edge of the wheel rim, when the brake lever on the handlebar is squeezed. Tighten the mounting nut securely.

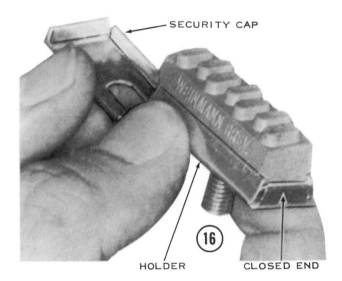

SECURITY CAP

⑯

HOLDER   CLOSED END